PRAISE FOR *THE GERALDO SHOW*

"Let me begin with an incontrovertible truth: It is simply impossible to know Geraldo personally and not love him as the true American original that he is. In my case, he is my adopted brother. The older brother I always wanted in life, and the older brother I am so proud of. His love of life is simply infectious. His fearlessness, and his courage are inspiring to everyone he comes into contact with. You have not lived a full and complete life unless and until you have the opportunity to listen to Geraldo tell the stories of each chapter in his life. To listen, to each and every detail, you marvel at the life Geraldo has lived. He has lived 500 full lives in one, and he loves every second of it, and he's building new chapters every single day. *The Geraldo Show* gives you insight into the man I know and love. The life lessons in this book will help all of us to grow and will inspire us to take more chances and 'go where the action is.' While some people recoil from danger, Geraldo dives in head first.

The passion and love he has for this country, our military, his work ethic, now almost 50 years on television, makes him The Godfather of tough hard-hitting, know-no-fear, go-anywhere reporting. *The Geraldo Show* takes us on a journey. A journey that few people in life will ever get to go on. A journey to some of the most remote places in the world. To me, Geraldo's greatest and most courageous journeys were those he took as a FNC war correspondent. I'll never forget the moment Geraldo pointed to the mountains of Tora Bora, emphatically telling the world 'Bin Laden is hidden right now in those mountains.' And Geraldo was correct.

This page-turning roller coaster ride Geraldo takes us on will truly inspire every reader to want to dive even deeper into themselves, to find that part of our souls that wish to be more courageous and bold in the lives we live. *The Geraldo Show* will also tell you the true story of how Geraldo and I first met, my initial skepticism when I first heard he was hired, and the evolution of one of the dearest friendships in my life."

—SEAN HANNITY, FOX News anchor, host of Hannity on Radio, bestselling author, motivational speaker, and producer

"With unrelenting pursuit, few were more dedicated to understanding the War on Terror than Geraldo Rivera. A must-read to understand the complexities of the battle overseas and the war over public opinion here at home."

—BILL HEMMER, FOX News anchor

"The Geraldo Show is a poignant account of combat as seen from the one person who has been there with our soldiers every step of the way. He captures war as it was fought; in all its ugliness, all its sacrifices, and all its heroism. As a war correspondent in Iraq and Afghanistan, there is no one who spent more time sharing in the hardships that our men and women endured than Geraldo; he also told their stories so that the true heroes . . . those selfless men and women that served our nation would not go uncelebrated. Geraldo's passion and love for GIs is unquestionable. I am proud to call Geraldo a true patriot and friend."

—JOHN F. CAMPBELL, General, US Army (Retired)

"Geraldo and I have been best buds since before I can remember smoking weed . . . which we never did together . . . even when no one was looking. I would go on an adventure with him anytime. *The Geraldo Show* is just the ticket."

—RICHARD "CHEECH" MARIN, author, comedian, and art collector

THE
GERALDO SHOW

THE
GERALDO SHOW

A Memoir

Geraldo Rivera

BenBella Books, Inc.
Dallas, TX

Copyright © 2018 by Geraldo Rivera
Interior photos © Craig Rivera

BenBella

10440 N. Central Expressway, Suite 800
Dallas, TX 75231
www.benbellabooks.com
Send feedback to feedback@benbellabooks.com

Printed in the United States of America
10 9 8 7 6 5 4 3 2 1

Library of Congress Cataloging-in-Publication Data is available upon request.
ISBN: 9781944648909
e-ISBN: 9781946885203

Editing by Glenn Yeffeth and Brian Nicol
Copyediting by Brian Buchanan
Proofreading by Michael Fedison and Cape Cod Compositors, Inc.
Text design and composition by Aaron Edmiston
Cover design by Marc Whitaker/MTWdesign.net
Jacket design by Sarah Avinger
Front cover photography by Craig Rivera
Back cover photography courtesy of Fox News Channel
Printed by Lake Book Manufacturing

Distributed to the trade by Two Rivers Distribution, an Ingram brand
www.tworiversdistribution.com

Special discounts for bulk sales (minimum of 25 copies) are available.
Please contact Aida Herrera at aida@benbellabooks.com.

To wife Erica, and daughters Isabella, Simone, and Sol, the dauntless women in my life

CONTENTS

GERALDO CHRONOLOGY

Born, Manhattan, July 1943
Move to Long Island, 1951
Graduate from West Babylon High School, 1961
Maritime College, the Bronx, 1961–1963
Move to Los Angeles, 1963
University of Arizona, 1963–1965
Marry Linda Coblenz, Scottsdale, Arizona, August 1965
Reside Lower East Side, Manhattan, January 1966
Brooklyn Law School, 1966–1969
Intern, New York County District Attorney, summer 1967
Divorce Linda, 1968
Intern Harlem Assertion of Rights, summer 1968
Graduate from BLS, June 1969
Fellowship, Poverty Law, University of Pennsylvania, 1969–1970
Represent the Young Lords, 1969–1970
Fellowship, Fred Friendly, Columbia University Graduate School of
    Journalism, 1970
Hired, WABC *Eyewitness News*, September 1970
Marry Edith Vonnegut, Barnstable, Massachusetts, December 1971
Expose Willowbrook, January 1972
Win Peabody, 1973
Host ABC's *Goodnight America*, 1973–1977
Report Chile coup, September 1973
Report Yom Kippur War, October 1973

Divorce Edith, 1975
Debut, *Good Morning America*, November 1975
Meet Donald J. Trump, 1976
Establish Malibu residence, summer 1976
Marry Sheri Raymond, Malibu, December 1976
ABC Evening News, Barbara Walters, "Summer of Sam," Fidel Castro
    Debut, ABC's *20/20*, August 1977–1978
First child, Gabriel, born, Manhattan, July 1979
Divorce Sheri, 1981
Fired by ABC News, December 1985
Host *Al Capone's Vault*, Chicago, April 1986
Reporter, *Entertainment Tonight*, 1986–1987
Marry C.C. Dyer, Marion, Massachusetts, August 1987
Geraldo! syndicated talk show, 1987–1998
Brawl skinheads, 1987
Second child, Cruz, born, Dallas, Texas, November 1987
Interview Charles Manson, 1988
Third child, Isabella, born, Manhattan, November 1992
Fourth child, Simone, born, Manhattan, September 1994
CNBC's *Rivera Live*, April 1994–November 2001
O.J. Simpson murder trials, June 1994–1997
Clinton impeachment, 1997–1999
Begin sail around the world, July 1997
Kosovo War, 1999
Separate from C.C., 2000
Complete circumnavigation, 2000
Quit NBC, hired by Fox News, November 2001
Afghanistan, eleven assignments, December 2001–2012
Fox News, *Geraldo-at-Large*, 2002–2015
Tour of terror, January–April, 2002
Engaged to Erica Levy, August 2002
Iraq War, eleven assignments, 2003–2011
Marry Erica, Manhattan, August 2003
Mosul, Iraq, ambush, 2004
Hurricane Katrina, 2005
Fifth child, Sol Liliana, born, Manhattan, August 2005
Firefight, Libya, April 2011

Celebrity Apprentice, New York (Trump Tower), February 2015
Baltimore riots, 2015
Dancing with the Stars, Los Angeles, 2016
Roger Ailes fired, July 2016
Donald Trump elected, November 2016
Trump inaugurated, January 2017
Bill O'Reilly fired, April 2017
Move to Cleveland, Ohio, August 2017
Hurricane Maria with President Trump, Puerto Rico, October 2017

PROLOGUE

In public life for half a century, my image and reputation have had more ups and downs than the Cyclone roller coaster at Coney Island. I have been called savior and sinner, fool and wise man, crusader and exploiter, hothead and dope. I am routinely scorned, admired, beloved, and belittled. Those passing judgment usually base it on when they tuned in. Were you around for my early days as a crusading local newsman? Did you waste an evening inside Al Capone's empty vault? Were you watching when the bombs dropped in Afghanistan or Iraq, or did you tune in to the raucous talk show when my nose got broken in the best television studio brawl ever caught on tape?

I am hard to nail down because of a shifting self-image. A moving target, even to myself, I have been intent variously on doing good or doing well, being taken seriously or just being successful. In the beginning it was easy. Money was a byproduct. The media was the message, and I used its power to fix what ails us. I made a historic start. In 1972, at age twenty-eight and with only two years in the news business, I changed the world for families touched by developmental disabilities. With a crusade targeting Willowbrook, a notorious institution that was America's largest and worst, I wrote and reported a searing exposé, "The Last Great Disgrace."

The blockbuster launched a movement that eventually closed all of the nation's major institutions for the population once described as mentally retarded. That was forty-five years ago, but in many ways it was my professional peak. I have never been more popular or highly regarded. The rest of my life since Willowbrook has been a postscript, a long and winding follow-up, never matching that period of renown and acceptance. Respected by peers and public, I had it all. I was famous. Coming from a mediocre background—a skinny, asthmatic, pimply-faced mutt—to have wealth and fame was enormously appealing. It drew me into the quandary that tormented much of my professional life. Am I a journalist or a celebrity? Juggling those sometimes-competing goals is a challenge I have not always won.

Since the attacks of September 11, 2001, and my employment by the conservative rabble-rousers of Fox News, and more recently with the coming of the Age of Trump, my professional life has been even more difficult to define. How could a sincerely progressive native-born Jew-Rican New Yorker like me ever work for an outfit better suited to the vibes of Orange County, Dixie, Appalachia, or the Mountain West? How could I not condemn and obstruct a wrecking ball like Donald Trump, who so many of my progressive friends abhor?

Don't get me wrong. I am not complaining about the choices I made. Sometimes seduced by the dark side of show business, I have been on a hell of a ride. Despite macho posturing and more serious lapses, I have also kicked some major journalistic butt. What makes me grind my teeth is that because of my tabloid history I am not taken as seriously as my work often deserves.

This narrative will reassure friends, infuriate enemies, and settle some grudges, especially surrounding my obsessive pursuit of Osama bin Laden, which is the real core of this book. It will also explain where my head and heart are late in a life lived in plain sight. Not as self-assured or certain as I once was, for better and worse, I have followed the traditional cliché that if you are not liberal as a young person, you have no heart, but if you are not more conservative deeper in life, you have no brain. I still support Roe v Wade, gun control, civil and immigrants' rights, and the need for universal health care, but detest liberals who shun responsibility and blame cops, rich white people, and corporations for everything that ails us. I call it pragmatic idealism.

Over five decades, I have met most of the era's good guys and bad, from Ronald Reagan to Charles Manson, Fidel Castro to Yasser Arafat, Muhammad Ali to Elvis, John Lennon, and Michael Jackson. Two from that larger-than-life crowd figure heavily in this book, both longtime friends. Donald J. Trump, who I met as an up-and-coming real estate

Erica and me with Roger and Beth Ailes. Chelsea Piers, New York, August 2003.

developer and playboy from Queens, New York, is our President. Despite the fact that I disagree with many of his policies, and despite the peer pressure from my old downtown crowd, our friendship endures.

The late Roger Ailes was a mentor and founding chief of Fox News. Once ruler of the media universe, and brilliant creator of the most important conservative news outlet ever, Roger was forced to resign in July 2016 after being accused of serial sexual harassment of young female staffers. The scandal that destroyed his career also ended his life. With his already deteriorating health, compromised by the stress and shame of his dismissal, he died less than a year after being outed by a ground-breaking lawsuit filed by former Fox News anchor Gretchen Carlson. His scandal was the fuse that helped ignite a firestorm of harassment allegations that burns to this day from New York newsrooms to Congress and the White House, to the casting couches of Hollywood, scorching scores of powerful old men including sixty-eight year-old Bill O'Reilly, another former colleague from my unfashionable era whose ratings long dominated cable news.

Ironically, many of those targeted in the purge had until recently been hailed as champions of progressive life. Celebrated actors Bill Cosby and Kevin Spacey and Democratic Party stalwart Harvey Weinstein apparently hid disgusting secrets behind masks of political correctness. Former

Saturday Night Live comedian Al Franken was forced to resign from the Senate when photos surfaced of him pretending to grope the breasts of a bulletproof vest-wearing female radio host as she slept. Civil rights icon, eighty-eight year old Congressman John Conyers left public life in tottering disgrace as did three more friends, CBS' Charlie Rose, PBS' Tavis Smiley and, stunningly, NBC *Today*'s long-reigning host Matt Lauer.

I tweeted in sympathy for the wreck of Lauer's career that "News is a flirty business & it seems like the current epidemic of #SexHarassmentAllegations may be criminalizing courtship & conflating it with predation." An explosion of anger and ridicule followed. In attempting to be compassionate to someone who always treated my family and me with respect, I was insensitive to his alleged victims. I survived the cacophony of outrage, but have much in common with those who did not. Our generation are dinosaurs, creatures of a bygone era struggling despite our success to remain relevant. Because our lives crisscrossed during this pivotal time in America's history and mine, some of my contemporaries are necessarily part of this narrative, especially Roger Ailes and President Trump. I am not here to tell their stories, only how they intersected and impacted my own.

Several months after I completed the first draft of this manuscript in 2016, all hell broke loose at Fox News. With Beth and Roger Ailes at Erica's fortieth birthday party at the Monkey Bar, New York, January 2015.

Chapter 1

ROGER & ME

"Now is when you'll need all your courage," Roger Ailes said with his usual blend of bravado and brutal honesty. "You're getting near the end of the line and it's only going to get tougher."

"Getting near the end of the line?" Not me. Not Geraldo. It was a slap in the face for ageless Mr. Macho. In that twilight of Roger's glory days, two years before he was laid low by the toxic sexual harassment scandal that rocked my network and upended his world, my shrewd, blunt boss was still on top of the media world.

Before he became a pariah, scorned by friend and foe alike, he was the blustering genius who invented our mighty Fox News Channel. A kingmaker who made stars of O'Reilly, Hannity, and Kelly, he almost single-handedly invented the Tea Party, shaped the modern Republican Party, and enabled its eventual 2016 embrace of Donald Trump.

A short yet towering figure, Roger inspired respect and affection from hundreds of loyal staffers, including me. To be a F.O.R. at Fox News, a Friend of Roger, meant you were essentially untouchable, immune from management comings and goings. He was king and if you were a useful and, most important, loyal subject, then the old lion would make sure you were kept safe and secure. He demanded fealty, which he repaid with kindness, generosity, and, more practically, extended contracts.

Conversely, in his court, no crime was more infamous than disloyalty. If anyone chose publicly to challenge Roger on his decisions, he would savage them with an explosive, barely controlled temper that could rattle a stone sculpture. Even conservative idols who strayed from the boss in public felt his wrath.

Sean Hannity, my hangout buddy and the hardest of conservative hardliners, tells the story of how displeased he was personally when a liberal scoundrel like me came to Fox News from CNBC in 2001. The move was fraught with controversy within the Fox News family and Sean complained bitterly about my hire, both on his radio show and on his cable program, which was then called *Hannity and Colmes.*

Sean tells how he was summoned into Roger's office to be dressed down as if he were Benedict Arnold caught red-handed committing treason. At the time, before he was hobbled by age, infirmity, and scandal, Roger was a pear-shaped, pulsing human bomb, which could go nuclear if angered. His face could become a contorted mask that was terrible to behold.

"How dare you question my decision!" Sean quotes Roger at the time of my controversial hire. When Sean tried to explain to Roger that he did not have anything personal against me, that what he objected to were my liberal leanings, Roger went off on him again. Jabbing his pointed index finger, red-faced and spitting, he told Sean, "Don't you ever question me again!"

His occasional rages were not gender-specific. Most often wise, wisecracking, insightful, and jocular, Roger sometimes exploded with no specific incident triggering his rage, at least none that we knew about. At a birthday dinner for my wife, Erica, I seated Roger across from Laurie Dhue, one of his star correspondents in the formative years of the Fox News Channel. A tall, blonde, self-described "Carolina Girl," Laurie was a terrific reporter/anchor with the charm and effervescence of a thirty-something cheerleader.

In a private dining room in a hip restaurant in SoHo, Roger out of the blue attacked her verbally. To the dismay of Roger's wife, Beth, and to the embarrassment of Erica and everyone at the long table, in his booming voice, he savaged Laurie's looks, specifically her big necklace that seemed made of brass marbles. "Didn't I tell you never to wear big necklaces?" he spat, unprovoked.

Laurie Dhue and Erica at our Edgewater, New Jersey, home. June 2015.

To break the ice, I made a lame joke about fashion. Laurie did her best to ride out the acute embarrassment with her usual grace, gently removing the offending jewelry. The moment passed, and the evening resumed course.

Still a family friend, Laurie for years afterward publicly attributed her downfall at Fox to her alcoholism, becoming a spokesperson for the anti-addiction cause. A decade later it was revealed that whatever else had been going on, she was one of at least five women who accused our star anchor Bill O'Reilly of sexual misconduct, and, according to the *New York Times*, "received payouts from either Mr. O'Reilly or the company in exchange for agreeing to not pursue litigation or speak about their accusations against him."

That initial report was followed six months later by the shocking news that O'Reilly paid another dear friend of ours, legal analyst Lis Wiehl, an extraordinary $32 million settlement for allegations including non-consensual sex. In accepting their settlements, both Lis and Laurie signed confidentiality agreements, and neither ever spoke of any misbehavior by anyone at Fox, either to Erica or me.

During Hurricane Roger's all-powerful reign, his wrath and rage were awesome in their ability to intimidate. With his friends scared quiet, the fear he instilled in his media enemies was even more daunting. To take on Roger Ailes was to risk humiliation and insult, much like those seeking to probe or criticize President Trump today. Roger buried any reporter digging for dirt in a ferocious campaign of opposition research. For years, his intimidating rage kept the world at bay, despite his closet filled with skeletons. In retrospect, maybe his roar was meant to scare away hunters of secrets.

At the time of our private meeting in his office on the second floor at Fox News in February 2014 he was still the Bully of Big Media, but not to me.

He had a heart of gold to those he let into his inner circle, a kindness and generosity that belies his sullied legacy. If he loved you, he was enormously supportive. At that meeting that February day, he delivered bad news about my career as a gentle older brother might. Eye-to-eye, he told me to buck up and get ready for my career's last dance. In fact, physically speaking we had both seen better days. He was heading to hip replacement surgery and just starting to walk with a cane. I was and am increasingly hobbled by the disastrous aftermath of back surgery that killed my right foot and gave me an increasingly pronounced limp.

Still, I was on a different page, personally and professionally, than he was that day, when he told me the end was in sight for my career in television news. I saw myself then as battle-scarred but still near the top of the news game. Old and busted up for sure, but not broken down.

A four-time-divorced, five-time-married, doting father of five more-or-less dependent children, including one then still in second grade, loving grandfather, and devoted husband of Erica, a stunning woman thirty-two years younger, I felt the last thing I needed to hear from the boss was essentially, "The end is near, so get over it."

For one thing, I need the dough. It's easy to spend money, not so easy to make or preserve it. Don't get me wrong, I am well enough off, just not compared to how things were during the fat days of my syndicated talk show, which I owned, produced, and starred in. Regardless of how flush a career you have had, as the legions of retiring Boomers are rapidly discovering, your nest egg cracks in a hurry once there is no salary to support it. That is especially true when the cost of maintaining multiple dwellings, alimonies, and the press of philanthropy is piled on top of prep-school and private-college tuitions, and the always-alarming price of an otherwise full life.

I am resigned now to never being rich. Gone is my benchmark dream of being flush enough to own a private jet one day like my pal Hannity, who started out nearly as humbly as I did. These days my financial goal is more down to earth. Mainly, I want enough to be comfortable and generous, helping the less fortunate, without outliving my stash or term life insurance policies, or worse, being forced to spend my wife's and kids' inheritance.

To prove my physical prowess and convince her friends that I was up to the role of Erica's husband, on the occasion of her twenty-sixth birthday in January 2001 we invited a bunch, and flew them all out to celebrate with us at our home in Malibu.

It was a great party with a guest list that included several of the supporting characters in the then-still-fresh O.J. Simpson saga, which had been one of my career preoccupations. Faye Resnick, a friend of O.J.'s murdered ex-wife, Nicole, and later a *Real Housewife* hanger-on, was there at the Malibu party with a posse of blonde, big-breasted, made-for-tabloid girlfriends, and so were Hollywood glitterati like Arianna Huffington, in those days before *The Huffington Post*.

What I remember most vividly about that day was playing touch football on the beach with Erica's girlfriends' boyfriends and husbands and outrunning them all. "Man, you've still got some wheels," I remember one of them exclaiming. Nowadays, they would use my carcass for second base.

When I went with Erica to Cleveland during that introductory period to spend some quality time with her parents, Howard and Nancy Levy, her dad and I went off alone to bond. We went to the Rock & Roll Hall of Fame, the city's gem. Howard offered to pay. I swaggered up to the booth alongside him only to be deflated when my future father-in-law asked the clerk, "Can I have two senior citizen tickets, please?"

Erica and me with baby Jace, my first grandchild, and his
parents, Cruz and Lauren. November 2012.

SHE WAS TWENTY-EIGHT WHEN
WE MARRIED; I WAS SIXTY

Here is the rough domestic chronology of this phase of my life before the
attacks of 9/11 unraveled everyone's plans for the future. After twenty
years together, and several attempts at reconciliation, which lasted into
the opening months of the new millennium, C.C. Dyer, my fourth wife
and mother of our dear daughters, Isabella and Simone, and I separated
forever. It was February 2000, and I wanted to be single.

The life lesson is to be careful what you wish for. After months of
extraordinary indulgence I got sick of myself. At my age and position
at the time, as many of my contemporaries today are discovering, there
was no such thing as a casual date. It is fun playing the field, until you
realize it is laden with land mines and opportunities for self-inflicted
wounds.

This is one of the core reasons I was not as hard on President Trump
during the 2015–2016 campaign as his noxious statements about people
with disabilities, Muslims, Mexicans, and former Fox News and current NBC anchor Megyn Kelly probably required. I knew him when.
Regardless of our ups and downs, and the obvious disparities in wealth,
power, and notoriety, we were products of our time and circumstance.
We grew to manhood in the chauvinistic promiscuity and nativist, clumsy
closed-mindedness of the locker rooms of metro New York in the late
1950s and early 1960s, before JFK was killed and before civil rights, the
Vietnam War, and the women's movement changed the rules, obviously
for the better.

As a loyal and loving husband and father of five, including three
daughters, I find it impossible not to be impressed by the progress women
have made since Baby Boomers were teenagers. When Trump and I came
of age, it was a much different time. Marilyn Monroe, Kim Novak, Jayne
Mansfield, and Jane Russell were our cool cat's meow, and *Playboy* and
Esquire magazines were the sexy style bibles. Women were to be admired,
protected, and enjoyed. No one I knew spoke of gender equality in sports,
academia, or professional life back in those dark ages before, say, the Summer of Love in 1967. As primitive and dumb as it seems today, our ethos
was real-life *Mad Men* meets *Father Knows Best*. Cheerleaders and volup-
tuous centerfolds were the ideal, and trading in your partner when her

warranty expired was routine. Divorce was not as common as infidelity, unless the protagonist was wealthy and irreligious, which for key decades the President and I both were. He and I navigated some hard social storms of our own making and figured out the grossness of that piggy approach at around the same phase in life.

Looking back at who I was back in the day, I feel uncomfortable with my old self, but I stopped being that person long before it became open season on horny old men. My bad was so last century, and even then, unlike the long and growing list of fallen contemporaries, I never took advantage of anyone. I joke that I married every woman I ever harassed. Why five marriages? It is because I am so old school, I believed my whole life that if you love and respect a woman, you (in the words of Beyoncé) "put a ring on it." Everybody was treated with generosity of spirit, and is doing well. They returned the favor with friendship and loyalty. None ever said anything negative about me, at least not out loud.

In Donald Trump's life, the tabloid lifestyle was also shed, and all's well that ends well, in his case very well, although by his own admission, the presidency is proving a bigger challenge than he ever imagined. Trump found Melania around 1998, and eighteen years later the two of them together forged an extraordinary path to the highest office in the land. Hate him if you must, but you cannot deny the guy has a great wife and family. I found Erica deep in life, along with humility and respect for family and fidelity.

Everything changed with Erica and our improbable match-up. We met and fell in love at first sight in December 2000. Both of us were working for CNBC in Fort Lee, New Jersey. We actually had met a bit earlier in the year at an office outing at ever-hip Tao restaurant on West Fifty-Eighth Street, but did not really notice each other until that winter day when she walked into my office wearing a black tube skirt and a white dress shirt, her arms filled with papers for me to review. I knew Erica was going to be my wife that first time I really looked at her.

With my bride celebrating her fortieth. January 2015.

Stunning inside and out, razor sharp, and straightforward, she happened also to be an excellent producer, with an adventurer's heart. Once our affair was exposed, she was urged by NBC News management and human resources to give up her staff job. Given appearances and my reputation, they were beyond freaked that I might be what I certainly seemed, an aging super predator and she, my helpless young victim.

The lawyers for the network made sure that even her parents were made aware of the situation; the resolution of the fraught issue required a signed contract between Erica and NBC. In return for giving up her staff job, she was simultaneously hired as my freelance field producer. As such, she was allowed to travel with me to the West Coast or wherever the story took us, and it took us most often to our lovely home on the sandy beach near Paradise Cove in Malibu, where our immediate neighbors included impresario Dick Clark, my former agent Jerry Weintraub, and queen diva Barbra Streisand and her husband, actor James Brolin. In addition to the perks, Erica was given a year to change her mind and return to her staff job if our relationship didn't work out. As with many of our friends and associates, the network was betting we would not last.

In our eighteenth year together, she is my deeply connected partner for life and a wonderful mother to Sol, our twelve-year-old daughter. More than that, Erica is the glue that keeps my wild bunch of children together as a family. She handles with patience and intelligence the idio-syncrasies of our spreading herd, which ranges from Sol to Simone, age twenty-three and an honors graduate of Northwestern University; Isabella, twenty-five, a graduate of NYU and an associate producer at CNN; Cruz, who graduated with a degree in engineering from Texas A&M after a rough skid through two other schools, who at thirty already has three kids of his own, and who, happily, has a job as a union engi-neer installing elevators in New York City high-rises; and first-born, but not least, Gabriel, thirty-nine, who lives in Holland with his wife, Deb, a brilliant scientist, and their three-year-old son, Desmond.

With four kids at the time, from three different mothers, and then getting married for the fifth time to a woman half my age, I realize what a long shot Erica and I were to succeed, how funky my personal life must seem to outsiders. Yet we have succeeded and thrived as a family. Despite the kids' religious, ethnic, and genetic potpourri, we are a func-tioning, caring unit. Like our daughter Sol, my older children love Erica and rely on her as a mom, although one much closer to their age than mine.

Spiritually, I feel forever young in Erica's presence, even though at the time we married she was twenty-eight and I was sixty. Our wedding at New York Central Synagogue in August 2003 was a party for the ageless. Before four hundred far-flung guests from the four corners of our lives, we lavishly celebrated our improbable pairing. I came down the aisle leading thirty groomsmen, including my two sons, two brothers, and best man: blood brother, stoner comic, art collector, *Celebrity Jeopardy!* champion, and all around Renaissance man, Cheech Marin. My wedding march was Tito Puente's "Oye Como Va," which I am reasonably certain had never been heard in Central Synagogue's ornate grand chamber.

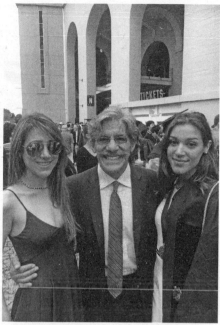

Left: "She is my deeply connected partner for life." Mother's Day, May 2017.
Right: Isabella and Dad at Simone's graduation from Northwestern University, June 2017.

At Erica's extravagant fortieth birthday party, January 2015.

Erica and I are wed at New York's Central Synagogue, August 2003.

Best man, blood brother, stoner comic, art collector, *Celebrity Jeopardy* champion, and all-around Renaissance man, Cheech Marin.

We capped it off with a blowout party at the now defunct Four Seasons Restaurant on Park Avenue and a honeymoon in the South of France, staying at the fabled Hotel du Cap-Eden-Roc in Cap Antibes, then to Monte Carlo, where we stayed in Winston Churchill's suite, St. Tropez, Nikki Beach. Exhausting, but Erica loved it all, saying at one point, "Can't we go to one more place? I have such a cute outfit on."

As I wrote during this wildly romantic interlude, "I am resolved that I will die married to this splendid, warm, loving, daring, beautiful, stylish, exhilarating, fun, Jewish temptress!!! And I will streamline my life for the big push ahead."

But back to Roger and me. My stunning, sobering 2014 meeting with him happened eleven years after Erica and I married. Until then, my career ambition had been relatively modest, given my notoriety and longevity. Mainly I was seeking to preserve a measure of success and swagger in the news business, while socially not looking ridiculous or mismatched out on the town with my stylish wife, who had blossomed into a sophisticated partner—glamorous, but not haughty, a lover of the arts, a fabulous mom, and a concerned citizen.

The only wrinkle to the honeymoon story is that, at the end, Erica had to fly home alone from Europe. I went the other direction, back to Iraq, where battles raged. Begun that past March, the fighting was already careening out of control. For the eleven years between 2001 and 2012, war was the setting and context for my life, preoccupying and defining all planning and perspective.

Our daughter, Sol Liliana, born in August 2005, is our unadulterated joy. Like her siblings, adorable and smart beyond her years, Sol is the antidote to the morbid melancholy that afflicts men my age when we realize our lives are best measured in days. That, by the way, is another of Roger's deep thoughts. "You realize that you've got about three thousand days left before someone's wheeling you around or throwing dirt on your dead body," he shared with me about a thousand days ago.

Like her big sisters, Sol is gifted with shocking wisdom. On the edge of a grown-up conversation and seemingly immersed in her book or video, she often pops her head up with a question or deep thought that is right on point. She wakes up happy and starts each day with an eager optimism that rubs off on her sometimes gloomy or melancholy dad. More than any other catalyst, she keeps me energized and positive about life.

"For the eleven years between 2001 and 2012, war was the
setting and context for my life." Afghanistan, 2003.

Through fifth grade, and until our move to the Midwest, Sol attended
Spence, the same private school on the Upper East Side of Manhattan as
older sisters Isabella and Simone graduated from a decade earlier. The
biggest difference from Sol's time in the school and theirs is that I was
that much older than most of the other fathers. The A-list superdads were
mostly around Erica's age, thirty or so years younger than I am. My only
comfort is that I had better hair than most of them, although since most
are either in big-time finance or the scions of big real estate families, they
already had more money.

During the several years I spent getting around to finally writing this
book, Erica, Sol, and I lived on the top floor of a Madison Avenue apartment opposite the Jackie Kennedy Reservoir in Central Park. From our
fortieth-floor windows we actually looked down on Sol's school about a
block away, which is why we lived there.

There is nothing pleasant about urban slipping and sliding when it
comes to getting your kid to school in a grueling New York City winter.
We sold the apartment in the summer of 2017. About the same time, we
also sold our most fanciful possession, a mile-square private island off
Playa Salinas on the southeast coast of Puerto Rico. Immodestly dubbed
Cayo Geraldo, our personal paradise island was the scene of raucous pig

roasts and countless clan reunions, but became expendable as we downsized in anticipation of my running into the deep woods of old age, but it was a great fourteen years of rum-drenched fun while it lasted.

We still have a small but charming home alongside the Hudson River in Edgewater, New Jersey. Opposite Washington Heights in Manhattan, it is only eight miles from Fox News headquarters in Midtown. The "Edge" is our base when we are in the New York area, but unless or until I get drafted in a late-season career comeback, our principal residence is now a gracious old home in a perhaps surprisingly lovely neighborhood in suburban Cleveland, Ohio. I have a television and radio studio inside the modestly rambling manor with an indoor swimming pool, which would have cost far more than we paid for it were this a more favored location. Remember, after only Chicago, Boston, and Alaska, Cleveland has the worst winters in America.

Erica loves her hometown, which in recent years has shaken off its reputation as the "Mistake on the Lake." The lake would be Lake Erie, one of the Great Lakes, which together hold more freshwater than any other body in the world. The "mistake" was the awful industrial pollution that in the 1960s and 1970s mucked up the Cuyahoga River, which cuts through downtown, bearing the ships that bring the ore to the steel mills upriver. Randy Newman forever shamed the city with his epic satirical song "Burn On," which goes in part, "Cleveland, city of light, city of music . . . Even now I can remember. 'Cause the Cuyahoga River goes smokin' in my dreams. Burn on, big river, burn on . . ."

The idea of my moving to the Midwest, where I have never lived, may shock those who have followed my big-city public life, but aside from being about half as expensive as New York or Los Angeles, Cleveland has a lot going for it. A major article in the *Los Angeles Times* in July 2017 said the town was "on the cusp of cool." Aside from the Rock & Roll Hall of Fame, there is pretty good theater, a new casino, microbreweries, trendy bars and restaurants, the 2016 NBA Champion Cleveland Cavaliers, and the 2016 MLB American League Champion Cleveland Indians. Nowadays, thanks to LeBron James, who we hope sticks around, and the Indians relief pitchers, folks call it Believeland. In any case, the family and I were ready for a change. After three-quarters of a century in the city at the center of the universe, I think the slower pace of semi-suburban life will either extend my life or kill me, leaving me buried under one of Cleveland's notorious lake-effect snowstorms.

During the years spent writing this book, we lived behind
the Guggenheim Museum near Central Park.

Cayo Geraldo, the island off the south coast of Puerto Rico
we owned from 2004 to 2017. May 2016.

OLD DADS

Like Mick Jagger, who had his eighth child at age seventy-three, having baby Sol at my age was even more controversial than my marriage to her mother. Sol was conceived just as all those reports were breaking about the dangers of birth defects or complications due to old sperm. Some of the people closest to me lobbied against it. "What's going to happen when she's in Little League and you're using a walker?" was a typical query. I told whoever doubted the decision that I had made up my mind, and that the main reason was that I could not marry a woman of childbearing age and not give her a child to bear.

Happily, Sol has ten fingers and toes, is healthy emotionally and physically, and loves math, swimming, piano, and theater. If any of my kids follow in my footsteps as an oversized media personality, it will probably be she. Sol is also her mom's hangout buddy. I joke that they should do a show like the *Gilmore Girls* where best-friend mom and daughter live, work, and play together in a quirky Connecticut town.

Less than 10 percent of men my age, seventy at the time of the 2014 Roger meeting, are still working. Even so, his mention at that meeting of my exit being imminent was stunning. My goal was and still is to stay in the game as long as I can compete with the endless flow of ambitious reporters and commentators, many of them less than a third my age, who continually swell the ranks of media.

In fire, flood, tornado, hurricane, eruption, earthquake, urban upheaval, dope-fiend confrontation, anarchy, and war, I managed to stay true to the No Guts, No Glory ethos in lands near and far. Even now, a beat-up old man, I am the reporter you do not want to compete against. Gimp or not, I will die before I let you beat me. Except for the bad foot and its accompanying, ever-growing limp, I am trim and relatively fit, with a solid exercise regimen and an undiminished competitive spirit. I might have trouble dodging bullets or blows these days, but I managed to rouse myself to go to the aid of Puerto Rico in distress from historic Hurricane Maria in September 2017, and I can still do hard interviews as well as any reporter in the business, although it feels pathetic and defensive to say so.

On our beloved Cayo in 2017 before Puerto Rico was ravaged by hurricanes Irma and Maria.

"DIDN'T YOU USED TO BE GERALDO RIVERA?" FEBRUARY 2014

In 2014 we thought our new millennium shooting wars were over or ending. At the time Roger told me to stiffen my upper lip and prepare for the end of my active career, the world was a different place from what it was when he hired me in the wake of the September 11, 2001, attacks. Our combat forces were already out of Iraq, and the war in Afghanistan, the longest in American history, was also ending, or at least downsizing. By the end of 2014, no US ground forces were supposed to remain in that hardscrabble country except trainers and security.

As we deflated our out-sized military presence everywhere, President Barack Obama dismissed upstart ISIS as the "JV team." The extremists were just beginning to cut off heads and burn people alive. Syria was screwed, but only a trickle of refugees had yet been set loose on Europe. Battlefield reports no longer interested our television audience, and demand for threescore-and-ten-year-old war correspondents was particularly low.

Roger called the meeting in his second-floor office at the Fox News World Headquarters on Avenue of the Americas, across from Radio City in Manhattan. It was a specific response to something I had said in an interview with commentator Will Cain. It was on *The Blaze*, that cable news and internet outfit owned and operated by Glenn Beck, a strange and powerful man, who is a whole other story.

Asked by Cain to comment on the recent death of a journalist in combat, I told him I envied the fallen reporter and wanted nothing less for myself. "I want to die with my boots on. That's half the reason why I go to these places—Libya, Afghanistan, Iraq, getting shot at—I'd rather die. I've been looking to get killed in action for years. That's one of the reasons I'm so bold, because I don't give a shit."

Cain asked, was I "addicted to fame"?

"I'm addicted to paying the bills," I quipped, but added straight from the heart, "I don't want people coming up to me and saying, 'Didn't you used to be Geraldo Rivera?'"

After I repeated the remarks on our own morning show *Fox and Friends*, Roger must have thought I was about to become a suicide bomber. His customarily gruff, direct, and strangely kind advice was to get a grip, take care of my family, and prepare for the ravages of old age. How could I not love the guy, and not recognize the monster he was later accused of becoming?

Chapter 2

WILLOWBROOK, O.J., AND THE

SEMEN-STAINED DRESS

In rough strokes, I was a twenty-six-year-old, long-haired, radical street lawyer from a big, blue-collar New York Puerto Rican Catholic Jewish family when the media discovered me in 1970. Representing an East Harlem–based activist group called the Young Lords, I was thrust into the limelight as the group's spokesman when my clients refused to give interviews to the press. Their attitude toward the media was similar to President Trump's disdain for "fake news."

The first US-based Puerto Rican activist group not concerned primarily with the political status of the island, but rather with the social conditions of the Puerto Rican community in the States, the Lords had occupied a church complex in Spanish Harlem. They set up a free breakfast program for neighborhood children and were advocating testing for lead paint poisoning and addressing other health issues.

Even though the church congregation did not use the facility during the week, the Lords' occupation was illegal. The cops were surrounding the complex, and city officials under progressive Republican mayor John V. Lindsay were frantically trying to negotiate a peaceful end to the standoff.

For a week, it was a front-page story in the *New York Times* and even attracted national attention from the *Today* show and elsewhere. This was 1969–1970, during a period of urban rioting and widespread unrest. Harlem had burned before in 1964, followed by Watts in L.A., Newark, Baltimore, Detroit, and other battered cities. New York was a racial tinderbox that officials feared would be ignited by the church standoff.

After participating in the intense negotiations to resolve the crisis, I was singled out by pioneering news director Al Primo as a potential recruit for a new program at Columbia University's Graduate School of Journalism. I could not refuse the chance to attend that prestigious educational institution and learn how to be a television reporter, under Columbia's professor Fred Friendly.

The legendary producer for venerated CBS newsman Edward R. Murrow, Professor Friendly was running a program to train young black and brown professionals as reporters. It was designed to integrate the TV news business, which was overwhelmingly white and male. Mostly African Americans, with a sprinkling of Latinos, my class at Columbia was mostly lawyers, teachers, and law enforcement personnel. I turned twenty-seven on the Columbia campus and I was raring to go.

Funded by the Ford Foundation, the idea was to have a news team that reflected the racially diverse audience the particular channels were seeking to serve. It was a crash course during a tumultuous summer that saw the collision of the civil rights and anti-war movements and roughly spanned from the tragic Kent State massacre in May 1970 to the ruinous Asbury Park, New Jersey, race riots that July, which was my first assignment.

Each student was sponsored by a local TV station and had a promised job waiting upon graduation. None of the recruits had as high-octane a sponsor as mine. Al Primo had just come to the Big Apple bearing his potent invention, the *Eyewitness News* format, to WABC-TV, the huge ABC-owned and -operated station that was soon to begin a ratings dominance that has lasted almost a half-century in the nation's largest, most diverse market, the 23.7 million potential viewers in the New York metropolitan area.

Many years later, in December 2016, I was honored to introduce Al as he was inducted into the Golden Circle of the National Academy of Television Arts and Sciences, better known as the Emmys, for his more than fifty years in the business. Reaching that half-century milestone is a goal

I also covet. Only a handful of colleagues have managed to stick around that long. It's tough for lots of reasons, including the difficulty of staying relevant through five decades, a dozen wars, nine presidencies, countless fashion and style trends, and high-definition television. My fiftieth anniversary hits on Labor Day, 2020. Inshallah, which means "God willing," I will be around to celebrate.

Essentially I was hired in 1970 because of affirmative action, and I went on to my first fame as the Puerto Rican cog in the trailblazing news team's multiethnic wheel. During those action-packed early years, I covered gritty New York, a nightmarish city broke, broken, and reeling from racial tension, rampant crime, slashing graffiti, civic disengagement, filthy transit, and a heroin epidemic that was visible on virtually every stoop and alleyway. Those omnipresent junkie zombies could have been prototypes for *The Walking Dead*.

In 1971, I reported a special called "Drug Crisis in East Harlem," shot entirely on East 100th Street, which I said at the time was the worst street in America. It featured confrontational interviews with junkies shooting up, throwing up, and overdosing, and was the first time they were shown full-face on camera. It won my first major journalism acknowledgement, the Columbia DuPont Silver Baton. The city's response was to seize the entire street through eminent domain and bulldoze it. Now the block features attractive and hard-to-get public housing.

Reporting my Emmy-winning story, "Migrants, Dirt Cheap," 1974.

"THE LAST GREAT DISGRACE," JANUARY 1972

My life-altering crusade during that early period was a searing exposé targeting the nation's institutions for the developmentally disabled. There were several in the New York metropolitan area. On a bleak January morning, I broke into the Willowbrook State School on Staten Island. It was a chamber of horrors for more than five thousand so-called "residents," who were actually intellectually disabled inmates.

Two activist doctors, Mike Wilkins and Bill Bronston, whom I had met months before when they were volunteering at the Young Lords' health-care clinic in the occupied church in Spanish Harlem, were now working at Willowbrook. Both were planning to leave because of the abuse and neglect all around them. They told me they had a stolen key to the B Ward of Building 6, and that I could sneak in with my cameras rolling. It housed perhaps sixty severely and profoundly disabled children.

In exposing the wretched conditions at Willowbrook, I broadcast our searing footage (which you can still see on Geraldo.com) of naked children unattended and smeared with their own feces. They were making a pitiful sound, a kind of mournful wail that I will never forget.

As I reported in the plain, brutal language of the time:

When Dr. Wilkins slid back the heavy metal door of B Ward, building No. 6, the horrible smell of the place staggered me. It was so wretched that my first thought was that the air was poisonous and would kill me. I looked down to steady myself and I saw a freak: a grotesque caricature of a person, lying under the sink on an incredibly filthy floor in an incredibly filthy bathroom. It was wearing trousers, but they were pulled down around its ankles. It was skinny. It was twisted. It was lying in its own feces. And it wasn't alone. Sitting next to this thing was another freak. In a parody of human emotion they were holding hands. They were making a noise. It was a wailing sound that I still hear and that I will never forget. I said out loud, but to nobody in particular, "My God, they're children." Wilkins looked at me and said, "Welcome to Willowbrook."

If I am remembered for anything, it will be these lines I wrote at the time: "This is what it looked like. This is what it sounded like. But how can I tell you about the way it smelled? It smelled of filth. It smelled of disease. It smelled of death."

Deeply shaken and enraged by what I had just seen, I hustled the fifteen miles' driving distance between Staten Island and the West Side studios of *Eyewitness News*. En route I interviewed Bernard Carabello, the Willowbrook resident whose story would come to represent those of many thousands of others forced to live in these horrible institutions. Bernard had just turned twenty-one and, under the sponsorship of the rebel doctors, had signed out of Willowbrook on his birthday to live on his own. His tragedy is that he was not retarded, and again I apologize for using that outdated "R" word. He was born with cerebral palsy. His intelligence is otherwise normal, but at age three his impoverished Puerto Rican immigrant mom had been persuaded by public health doctors to admit him to Willowbrook for his own good.

That is what parents did in those days, institutionalized their disabled youngsters. Even JFK and Robert F. Kennedy's sister Rosemary was institutionalized by her parents, Rose and Joseph Kennedy. So, for eighteen years, Bernard had been trapped in Willowbrook, physically handicapped but intellectually fully aware of the horrors all around him, which he charitably described as "a disgrace."

Leaving Bernard and calling ahead, I alerted management that my footage was earth-shaking: kids being treated worse than dogs at the worst kennel imaginable, and not in some distant land, but in a borough of New York City. The blockbuster reports did shake the world. I do not think there has ever been a bigger reaction to any investigative story, not even Edward R. Murrow's seminal "Harvest of Shame." The phones at the station rang off the hook. Politicians jumped all over themselves to deny responsibility and profess outrage and demand change. The station's ratings soared. In Bernard's honor, our half hour special was titled "The Last Great Disgrace."

A crusade to close Willowbrook and similar institutions began, including countless follow-ups, legislative lobbying, class action lawsuits, and, over the years, grand fund-raising events, including benefit boxing matches, golf outings, and concerts starring the likes of John Lennon and Yoko Ono, John Denver, the Allman Brothers, Stevie Wonder, and others, all of it helping change the way modern societies care for the developmentally disabled.

After Willowbrook, with friend-for-life Bernard Carabello. We joke that
the older we get, the more we look alike. September 1997.

With the funds raised and the high-profile promotions on programs
such as Donald Trump's last season of *Celebrity Apprentice*, of which I'll
have a lot more to say later, we have helped get the word out that this is
a population too long neglected and abused. More practically, we have
helped open scores of small, humane, community-based residences, and
have provided job training and educational facilities for a population once
condemned to short brutish lives, while also providing respite and support
for their often stressed-out parents.

When asked to speak about the Willowbrook experience, I am
unavoidably drawn to tears. There is hardly a day that I do not remember
those afflicted children in the B Ward of Building 6. In social situations
with relatives of intellectually and emotionally disabled folk, especially
kids, I am treated with the love and honor usually afforded a close friend
or family member. They know I get their special circumstance.

Advocating and fundraising for the disabled remains my principal charity, one especially necessary now that we are beset by the deeply troubling and mysterious epidemic of a developmental disability once known as mild retardation but now known as autism.

The crusade to humanize the care and treatment of the disabled is my best work and lasting legacy. The saga is the stuff of my pride and nightmares, and is still the main thing random strangers bring up, particularly in New York. They tell me how they remember the exposés, how the reports changed their lives and led them into social work or medicine, or how the stories saved the life of their brother or auntie or cousin, and how grateful they are that I am still involved in the cause.

In September 1987, Willowbrook was finally closed, along with virtually all similar large facilities for the disabled across the country and, eventually, around the civilized world. Community-based care—small, personal housing featuring remedial and vocational training—is now standard. At an emotional ceremony on the grounds, attended by families and activists, including Bernard, Governor Mario Cuomo presented me a commemorative award, the B Ward key I had used to gain entry. It is mounted on a small wooden plaque, with the inscription, "A Promise Fulfilled," and is my most treasured memento.

The lovely twenty-six acres of prime real estate on which the grim institution stood are now occupied by the College of Staten Island, which boasts a new Department of Sociology, with which Bernard and I remain involved.

Forty-five years after that January 1972 day we met in the Staten Island diner, Bernard and I are still best friends, joking that the older we get the more we look alike, although my mustache is sexier. He went on to a full career as a client advocate and is still employed by the New York State Developmental Disabilities Services Office, although he keeps talking about his "imminent" retirement. We did a series of interviews together to commemorate the 30th anniversary of Willowbrook's closure, and he was honored at a gala dinner benefiting the College of Staten Island in December 2017 that brought together Willowbrook survivors, advocates, friends, and families who helped triumph over its bitter legacy, and who fight the never-ending battle to provide care and attention to the disabled.

YOM KIPPUR WAR, OCTOBER 1973

My first international assignment was the September 1973 coup in Chile, in which a military junta headed by armed forces chief Augusto Pinochet, and supported by our CIA, overthrew the democratically elected socialist government of Salvador Allende. Although I was still formally a WABC *Eyewitness* newsman, this was my first assignment for the big network, ABC News. Aside from tearing General Pinochet's throat out in a very aggressive interview, my most vivid memory from the trip was surviving the 8.3-magnitude earthquake that rocked our downtown Santiago high-rise hotel.

During my time in the Chilean capital, a full-blown war broke out halfway around the world in the Mideast. After a quick trip back to New York, during which I was the principal speaker at a fundraiser for Israeli charities, held at the home of Senator and Mrs. Jacob Javits, I flew in a chartered El Al flight to Tel Aviv. Everyone else onboard was a member of the Israeli Defense Forces.

I was reporting from the Golan Heights during the Yom Kippur War, when my team and I were bracketed by Syrian artillery, rounds exploding on both sides of our vehicle. At the time, this incident was the subject of intense scrutiny by critics alleging that it had been staged or misrepresented. Nothing is more damaging to a correspondent than to have his or her professional honor impugned.

The source of the false accusation was my *Eyewitness News* colleague, the late anchorman Roger Grimsby. In October 1973 he contacted a reporter from *Rolling Stone* to point out how miraculous it was for me to have survived a precisely targeted artillery strike just as the camera rolled.

When, given the gravity of the charge of staging, the magazine reporter ratted out Grimsby, telling me the details of his allegation, I was in a rage. I lured Grimsby to my office between his 6 PM and 11 PM newscasts. I told him we urgently had to talk about a matter of mutual importance. We were alone in the basement when I asked him face-to-face if he had indeed told the *Rolling Stone* reporter that I staged the barrage. He confessed. I started punching him, saying over and over that I was going to kill him, until he fell to the floor defenseless.

I stopped myself as my rage dissipated, leaving him seemingly unconscious on the newsroom basement floor. Worried that I had killed him, I went to my old friend producer Marty Berman's apartment on the Upper East Side of Manhattan. After I told Marty what had happened, we waited the hour or so until the 11 PM *Eyewitness News* came on. Needless to say, I was enormously relieved to see Roger give his signature line, "I'm Roger Grimsby, hear now the news." Or maybe it was "*here* now the news."

To his credit, the badly bruised Grimsby never told anyone what happened, as far as I know. The *Eyewitness* anchor unblinkingly went on the air and did the newscast flawlessly, even while sporting a badly made-over black eye.

My point is that war memories are cherished above all others. A glass top covers the wooden desk at which I write this; under the glass lies a field of service coins given me by hundreds of US combat units, mostly from Iraq and Afghanistan. Known as challenge coins, they are displayed with old press passes and a special service medal from an Iraqi general. All were personally handed to me by commanders of units large and small, here and abroad. Like the key to Willowbrook, the coins are cherished possessions, and each has a story attached.

Of course, we remember weddings and funerals, and especially children being born. But no memory is as vivid as a genuine war story, especially one caught on tape in a good cause. Those who have actually been in combat as warrior or reporter are ferocious defenders against "stolen valor" poseurs who claim peril they never experienced.

That is why NBC anchor Brian Williams got into such hot water in 2015 when caught embellishing his reporting during the Iraq War. He told a tallish tale of flying in a chopper in combat that got hit by an RPG, an enemy rocket. It turns out that although he did fly in a chopper at the time and place described, it was actually a different chopper in the unit that got hit by the rocket—a braggart's mistake that really was untrue, but at least the guy was there, unlike his critics. More about Brian's troubles later.

When Fox News and others began vigorously reporting Brian's scandal, liberal media wolves started hunting for similar misreporting by the right. That is when *Mother Jones*, the hard left-wing magazine, wrongfully attacked Bill O'Reilly. It was obviously a case of ideological tit-for-tat. A minor thirty-three-year-old discrepancy in O'Reilly's reporting over whether he was covering a "demonstration" or a "riot" in Buenos Aires, Argentina, during the 1982 Falklands War was being puffed to make it seem similar to Brian's fabrication, which it was not.

O'Reilly fought back with furious indignation. Fox News stuck by our star, which the network ultimately did not do when he was later forced out in the post–Roger Ailes frenzy over sexual harassment, but this time, his critics slunk away. By relentlessly revealing the left-wing agenda of the magazine and the paucity of facts in its reporting, O'Reilly defanged the critics of his war coverage. I should have done the same when my own scandal broke out in Afghanistan in 2001, but much more about that later.

HE'S NOT HEAVY, HE'S MY BROTHER, OCTOBER 1954–PRESENT

When Roger offered me the job at Fox in the fall of 2001, he promised substantial raises over time, if I lasted at the network, and agreed to hire my brother, Craig, as my field producer. Craig was middle-aged and desperate for a job after having a fight with his boss and quitting after thirteen years as a roving reporter at the syndicated show *Inside Edition*.

I remember the day Craig sheepishly told me he was taking that job at *Inside* for the chance to move from the role of sidekick field producer to on-air correspondent on his own. I was delighted for him, although miffed that he had kept the process secret from me. Until he made the jump, he had worked for me from the age of seventeen. He was tough and brave; in our time together before he went off on his own, Craig and I traveled near and far reporting for ABC News and later syndicated specials covering the KKK, devil worship, urban gangbangers, war, rebellion, the mob, militias, and mass murderers, including Charles Manson in an exclusive 1988 interview at San Quentin prison.

When Manson died in November 2017, I wrote, "It couldn't happen to a nicer guy." He was responsible for nine of the bloodiest murders ever committed, including that of the lovely actress Sharon Tate, who was eight-and-a-half months pregnant when Manson's devoted acolytes chopped her up and hung her upside down. The other victims were similarly savaged.

Devoid of remorse, his head filled with notions of grandeur, for decades, Manson enjoyed infamy among successive generations of young people seduced by the fact this murdering scum couched his crimes in environmental and antiracist babble. I hate the fact that, despite the brutality of his crimes, or perhaps because of them, his face adorned what were America's biggest-selling T-shirts. Thus, more popular than Che Guevara or Chairman Mao, Charlie was a charismatic snake charmer, an articulate, eco-friendly homicidal maniac who was part Jim Jones and part Adolf Hitler. His twisted soul shone through that hateful swastika tattoo carved on his forehead between those glaring, piercing, beady eyes.

He told me in our epic televised 1988 face-to-face confrontation inside San Quentin that he could save our overpopulated planet if he could just "kill 50 million" of us. I told him he was "a mass-murdering dog." He told me that if he didn't like the way our interview was presented he would have my head handed to my family in a basket. I told him that if anything happened to me his roomies in the joint would set him on fire again, as they did in 1984. As testament to his curious appeal, the hugely rated interview has been downloaded many millions of times.

Manson had been living on borrowed time anyway. He was originally sentenced to die in the gas chamber, but was spared in 1972 when the California Supreme Court ruled that the statute under which he was condemned was unconstitutional. His sentence commuted to life, he was denied parole twelve times. Most of his so-called family is either dead or still in prison. Only one of the largely well-educated, middle-class kids he convinced to kill for him has been granted parole. Just nineteen when she admittedly devolved into barbarism to please Charlie, now sixty-nine-year-old Leslie Van Houten remains behind bars as I write this, awaiting Governor Jerry Brown's decision to accept or reject the California parole board's recommendation that she be set free.

Manson was a lowlife whose enduringly perverse popularity was testimony to something dark in America's psyche. Don't rest in peace, Charlie. Go instead to be with your friend the devil. Go to hell.

Mass murders aside, in the decades before Fox News and the talk-show era, our real specialty was dope. Hands down, I am the Edward R. Murrow of dope reporters, which made Craig my *High Times* Fred Friendly. If there was a new stoner scourge, whether shooting, snorting, or smoking anything from heroin to crack to meth, we were on it. Often with brother Craig and/or Greg Hart, another fearless producer and cameraman by my side, I chronicled countless battles in the drug wars, from Bogota, Colombia, to Karachi, Pakistan, from Harlem to Hollywood. A wiry perpetual-motion machine, Greg came to work with me right out of Fordham University.

Together we patrolled the bloody hills of Guerrero State with the Mexican Army, the high seas with the United States Coast Guard, and across five continents with the Drug Enforcement Administration. We busted into countless homes and businesses with scores of SWAT teams, eager to put on a show, sometimes live, like *American Vice*, a revolutionary program that in 1988 used multiple, simultaneous satellite remotes to show how deeply the nation had fallen into dope's embrace.

The danger with doing all those live remotes is that you never know exactly what you are going to get. In the case of the recklessly innovative *American Vice*, we snared a relatively innocent Texas woman, who happened to be at one of the locations when the cops busted in on live television, announcing that everybody there was under arrest. She was so transparently not a dope dealer that many audience members were outraged that she was caught on camera. Actor Bruce Willis, a great guy who for years dated my third ex-wife, Gabriel's mother, Sheri, wrote me to say how unfair it was to expose her. When the cops cut her loose, she sued me for millions, but settled for about $200,000. She was subsequently busted on separate drug charges, a few months down the road.

CHASING DRAGONS, 1970–PRESENT

Chasing dope stories is a crazy, scary job. Peril is routine. Flying with bad pilots in overloaded airplanes or driving on heart-stopping roads, barely steering clear of the precipice, and dealing with scumbag drug killers and overly macho cops—it is a miracle we were not killed by bad guys or good intentions.

I have mixed feelings about narcotics enforcement. Pot should be universally legalized. Despite the best efforts of our retro Attorney General Jeff Sessions, it already is, effectively, in about half the country. The harder stuff is a tougher call. As a believer in personal responsibility and as a libertarian, I think grown-ups should be allowed to get high as long as they are done working or studying and are not hurting others or infringing on their right to be sober and safe. Despite being open-minded and

Despite being open-minded and sometimes surrounded by forests of dewy pot plants, we almost never succumbed to the obvious temptations. March 2003.

sometimes surrounded by everything from wheelbarrows full of coke to forests of dewy pot plants, we never succumbed to the obvious temptations. Well, almost never. In Afghanistan and especially in South America, it is hard not to light up occasionally since it grows along the roads like crabgrass. But I have never been stoned or drunk on the air. We never bought any drugs for personal use on the job or brought anything home from the front. It just was not worth the career-destroying risk.

We were *Vice News* before cable. No story was too dangerous. I know that sounds like pretentious babble, but it is true. The criteria for doing a story were intrinsic worth and potential audience appeal, regardless of risk. Craig was experienced on both sides of the camera, correspondent and producer, and Roger's agreeing to hire both him and Greg Hart was a big reason I took the leap from NBC to Fox News after 9/11.

We knew the ground we were about to cover for Fox News in Afghanistan, because we had been there years before, on an assignment for ABC's *20/20*. In 1980, we traveled through the frontier town of Peshawar, the fabled Khyber Pass, and the lawless Tribal Territories, posing as opium buyers, shooting a gritty hour-long *20/20* special called "Chasing the Dragon," which is what junkies call smoking heroin.

Using a crude hidden camera in a gym bag, Craig managed to film me negotiating with representatives of local opium growers to buy a thousand kilos of opium paste neatly stuffed into a water-tank truck that was going to be delivered to our boat waiting in the dense, chaotic harbor of Karachi, Pakistan. Of course, we never consummated the deal, or took possession of the dope. Once we caught the sellers on hidden camera, we told them we would return soon with the cash . . . never to return. A correspondent for *Newsday* covering the area several years later reported that there was a price on my head, put there by the dope dealers whom our dramatic broadcast had acutely embarrassed.

That was 1980. Twenty-one years later, in 2001, as Craig and I started our careers at Fox News, the mastermind of the 9/11 attacks, Osama bin Laden, was thought to be in that same area along the Pakistan-Afghanistan border. He was said to be literally underground in a cave, certainly uncaught. I dreamed night and day of killing him with my own hands and was mocked for saying so publicly. I did not care. My main worry was that he would be caught or killed before I got there, and that there would be no war by the time we returned to the Khyber Pass, in November 2001.

ZAPRUDER, MARCH 1975

Eyewitness News propelled me to local celebrity, helping create a new one-name wonder to follow Elvis, Ringo, Dylan, Dion, and Lassie in those days before Oprah and Madonna. Because I was the most important New York media commentator of the period, TV critic John J. O'Connor of the *New York Times* predicted in 1973, "New York has a way of nationalizing its local celebrities." It is another way of phrasing Liza Minnelli's famous "New York, New York" lyrics, "If you can make it here, you can make it anywhere."

I went national soon after Willowbrook with a show called *Goodnight America*. It was a late-night, news-oriented variety show we called a "Second Generation TV Newsmagazine," a counterpoint to *60 Minutes*, which was so first generation. The bi-monthly show ran from 1973–1977. That show's theme song from Ringo Starr still applies. It features the lyrics, "You gotta pay your dues if you want to sing the blues. And you know, It Don't Come Easy."

GNA is best remembered for its pre–*Saturday Night Live*, late-night hipster sensibility and included interviews with all the Beatles and Rolling Stones, the Grateful Dead, and the Hell's Angels. I hung with Jerry Garcia before he was a flavor at Ben & Jerry's. The more notable *GNA* achievement was the first network airing of the Abraham Zapruder home movie of the 1963 Kennedy assassination.

In the grainy film, you see in the backseat of the open limousine driving through Dealey Plaza, the president's head jerk backward as he is shot. He instantly grabs his throat as his battered and bloodied head then snaps forward. The inevitable question became how could his head initially jerk backward if a lone assassin, Lee Harvey Oswald, shot from behind from his sniper's perch on the sixth floor of the Texas School Book Depository?

The enormous response to that airing on March 6, 1975, gave birth to generations of conspiracy theories claiming that dark forces within the US government or the Chicago mob or Cuba or extraterrestrials from a galaxy far, far away killed the young and gracious thirty-fifth president, who did not really live in Camelot and had lots of secrets in real life.

For the next several years, I investigated every facet of the disturbing mystery before concluding that the Warren Commission was probably right about Lee Harvey Oswald's being the lone assassin, and that JFK's apparently anomalous head movement was the result of a measurable involuntary reflex.

During those years, I was a hybrid reporter/celebrity, a role I describe as being the first "rock 'n' roll newsman." Until I decided life was too tempting to stay married, I was an accepted member of the jet set, or at least a tolerated presence. During that flashy period I was with Edith Vonnegut, the beautiful, skilled, spiritual artist and daughter of one of the twentieth century's literary lions, Kurt Vonnegut Jr., author of *Slaughterhouse Five* and other now-iconic novels. We married in the Vonnegut family home in Barnstable, Massachusetts, in December 1971.

THE HIGH LIFE, 1972–1991

It is no excuse, but in the early 1970s, in my late twenties and early thirties, I was a young man from nowhere, fresh to fame following the Willowbrook exposés and for the first time relatively flush with money. I ran in gauche and glittering circles and I am not blaming anyone but myself.

This was the time in New York before AIDS changed mores and Ronald and Nancy "Just Say No" Reagan became the social scene setters. It was the ten years from 1970 to 1980 when the drug- and sex-fueled arts crowd flourished in the midst of a horde of larger-than-life characters. Part of the scene centered on the mustachioed and flamboyantly erratic Salvador Dali, whom I met through billionaire Huntington Hartford, the A & P heir, who had the best bacchanals in his expansive crash pad inside his modern art museum, an entire building overlooking Columbus Circle.

The unparalleled Andy Warhol was out everywhere, his dead eyes and droll humor counterpoints to his vivacious talent. He was usually the quiet, unblinking center of attention, along with his Pop Art rivals Robert Rauschenberg and Jasper Johns, whose American flag paintings also became iconic. Warhol once complained how late one night I was the most famous person in Studio 54. When he published a book of his art, I asked him to autograph one for me. "I'll do more than that," he said with his perpetual smirk. Flourishing his magic marker, he started drawing random lines on a book's cover. "I'll make you priceless art." I have moved so many times since then and have no idea where that book is, although I am reasonably certain it will turn up when my estate does an inventory.

Thomas Hoving was often around. His family owned Tiffany, and he was the larger-than-life president of the Metropolitan Museum of Art. A connoisseur of art and existentialism, he later ran the NYC parks. Tom once told me how as parks commissioner he sometimes instructed his police officers on how to cut the skyrocketing crime wave sweeping the parks in the crime-riddled Manhattan of Mayors John Lindsay and later Abe Beame. "I told my cops to throw the bodies over the wall onto Central Park West, so the homicide would be recorded as having happened in the Nineteenth Precinct, not in Central Park," he told me, perhaps jokingly.

My first real home, a rehabilitated triplex apartment, over a cuchifritos (deep-fried Puerto Rican food) joint, on Avenue C in Manhattan's then predominantly poor and Puerto Rican Lower East Side, became party hearty central. If a street is ever named after me, it should be Avenue C, say between Third and Tenth Streets. Mayor Lindsay, Mick Jagger, ballet superstar Rudolph Nureyev, and many more luminaries frequented my soirees there. The wild night that Jagger and Nureyev put me in a grinding men sandwich convinced me that I could not be gay, because if I were, that would have been the night.

I especially enjoyed my late-night hangout royals, who unintentionally taught me the lesson never, ever to envy anyone, however high-born or hereditarily noble. Classically handsome Prince Egon Von Furstenberg made his wife, Diane, royalty. She went on to become one of the most successful designers in history. He basically drank himself to death. After not seeing him for several years, I ran into him by chance in 1983, drinking alone in a random bar in Rome. Having been undeniably blood royalty, he went from being baptized by the pope, to dying of hepatitis C in 2004 from an infection left over from years of self-indulgence and melancholia. He was fifty-seven.

I met my other royal hangout buddy taping a notable segment on the glitzy extravagant opening of a new resort called Las Hadas (the Fairies) near Manzanillo, Mexico. Three passenger jets were chartered for the gala, one coming in from Los Angeles, one from New York, and another from Europe. My main interview was with actor and perennially tanned playboy George Hamilton. What made the segment unusual is that it was done on the beach with each of us wearing a skin-tight Speedo. Much later, in an appearance on *Fox and Friends* in April 2016, George and I joked about the old "daze."

Baron Arnot des Rosnay, a French nobleman, arranged the event at Las Hadas. His wife's, Isabel Goldsmith's, enormously wealthy family owned the resort. When they divorced, Arnot became a daredevil who set long-distance surf-sailing records that to his rivals seemed too good to be true. In 1984, after other windsurfers had questioned his record surf sailing his thirteen-foot board the almost nine hundred miles from the Marquesas to Tahiti, he decided to sail solo on his tiny board through shark-infested waters from Mainland China to Taiwan, never to be heard from again. He was thirty-eight.

Through Kurt Vonnegut, I met and spent time with many of the macho, literary, and show business luminaries of the era, often at Elaine's extraordinary pub on Second Avenue. They included swaggering, confident, over-the-top role models such as novelist Norman (*The Naked and the Dead*) Mailer; filmmaker Sidney Lumet, who thought I should be an actor, which I took as high praise coming from the man who directed *12 Angry Men*, *Equus*, *Dog Day Afternoon*, and *Serpico*; elegant Gay Talese;

bitchy but brilliant Gore Vidal before his Italian sojourn; classy and cool, deep Harry Belafonte; Tom "White Suit" Wolfe; Joseph (*Catch 22*) Heller; Peter (*Valachi Papers*) Maas; tiny, chatty Truman (*In Cold Blood*) Capote; William F. Buckley, the inventor of modern smart conservatism, and his imperial wife, Patricia; unfailingly pleasant poet Allen Ginsberg; and occasionally, Chicago's blue-collar oracle Studs Terkel; among many others. There were also plenty of tough guy reporters around, including three I admired, Jimmy Breslin and Mike McAlary of the *New York Daily News* and Pete Hamill of the *New York Post*. The inventor of participatory journalism, George Plimpton, was also a regular. I learned from the *Paper Lion* author to be physically and emotionally involved with my stories, to live them and be them, not merely to report them. George and Kurt were both guests on the first edition of my show, along with the hero of the farmworkers' struggle, Cesar Chavez, who became a friend I idolized.

Vonnegut taught me another eye-opening lesson. He told me how witnessing the carnage and horror of World War II had convinced him that he was an atheist. He reasoned that if there was a God, then why did the heavens not open up and consume the Nazis, those ultimate doers of evil, or even our GIs, who in destroying cities and killing enemies were also taking lives?

I embraced that dark reflection. After sixty, seventy, or eighty years that fly by way too fast, you die. There is no moral cost for sins on this Earth. There might be a reckoning eventually, but unless you get caught, not here and now. When I succumbed to infidelity, I knew God was not going to punish me, at least not in this world. If God existed, he, she, or it did not care. Yet now that I'm an old man, my certainty that no judgment awaits has wavered, as it often does when showoffs face the end of their time onstage.

As the disco years faded, Edie and I divorced. Keeping to what became my sorry pattern of middle life, my philandering caused our breakup. For that, I am filled with regret and embarrassment, half a century later. I skipped around for a while, never staying put for too long. The party continued even as cadres of friends began dying of the mystery disease we thought was a "gay plague," including a dear friend, the incredible fashion designer and bon vivant Giorgio di Sant' Angelo. Still, I remained a glutton for the easy attention semi-stardom brings.

GOOD MORNING AMERICA, NOVEMBER 1975

My career moved forward in fits and starts. In November 1975, I was assigned to the inaugural cast of ABC's *Good Morning America,* roving the country for the team for the next several years until the network's *20/20* debuted in June 1978. In that year I investigated and exposed the drug-overdose death of Elvis Presley, setting a ratings record for the show that stood for twenty-one years, until Barbara Walters interviewed Monica Lewinsky in 1999.

Personal upheavals aside, those were fifteen great years with the ABC network, before I was ignominiously fired in 1985 by yet another legend, my boss Roone Arledge. The creator of modern sports and news programming, who coined the phrase "up close and personal," Roone fired me because I complained publicly when he killed a colleague's story about dark rumors concerning the Kennedy family.

Reported by Sylvia Chase, the story included allegations of an inappropriate relationship between Marilyn Monroe, the sex goddess of her time, and both President Kennedy and his brother, Attorney General Robert F. Kennedy. There were more whispers of Chicago mobster involvement—those criminals must have stayed busy nefariously plotting big stuff—and also malignant rumors that Monroe's accidental drug-overdose death was actually murder.

Roone claimed he canceled the story only because it was badly reported and poorly sourced, both of which were true. The salacious allegation of presidential infidelity at its core has since been widely published, but never proven. After decades pondering every major investigation on the subject, I have come to the conclusion that Marilyn, the aging and lonely sex symbol of my teens, just gave up on life. Like so many others, she took more of the drugs she was then taking than she should have and slipped into last, deepest sleep.

Anyway, I was furious that the story was spiked, and without proof foolishly alleged to *People* magazine and other media that Roone killed the report out of loyalty to his dear friend Ethel Kennedy, Bobby's widow.

Perhaps ironically, Ethel and Bobby Kennedy's second youngest of eleven children, Douglas Kennedy, is a friend and colleague of mine at Fox. He is a straight-arrow news correspondent, only assigned non-political stories, and he is never put professionally close to his legendary family's politics, which are antithetical to big Fox. He has no shortage of strong, smart political opinions, however, and if unleashed in private, he will set your clock right with intensity.

My career at *20/20* ended when two other friends, Hugh Downs and Barbara Walters, assured the staff that they were just as outraged as I was that the Kennedy story was being killed. They said they stood shoulder-to-shoulder with me, but in the end, I was the only one to speak out. Roone saw my accusatory rant as a personal betrayal. It was my stupidest career move because, at forty-two years old, I was soon the most famous unemployed person in the nation.

NATION'S MOST FAMOUS UNEMPLOYED PERSON, JANUARY 1986

Unable to move to another major network-news division because of that aggressive personal style so many news pros still consider too flamboyant, in desperation, and for $50,000 paid up front, I agreed in 1986 to solve *The Mystery of Al Capone's Vault* on live television. The vault was empty and I was a humiliated laughingstock—until the live telecast proved to be the highest-rated syndicated show in television history, which it still is. I like to say it was my greatest failure and most noteworthy commercial triumph; the only thing in the vault was ratings.

In April 2016, just about every news and entertainment outlet in the country made note of the thirtieth anniversary of the special. The *Chicago Tribune* commented how the show out-rated Super Bowl XX that year despite the fact that the big football game featured a 46-10 victory by the hometown Chicago Bears, *Da Bears*, over the New England Patriots. I was proud to have a thirtieth anniversary of anything to celebrate.

As a result of the Capone show's colossal commercial success, I was deluged with job offers from programs like *Entertainment Tonight*, where I worked long enough to interview the one Beatle I never spent any quality time with, the great "While My Guitar Gently Weeps" George Harrison. He had some of the same humility I saw in Elvis, too much for the occasion, but probably born of shyness. I stayed at *ET* only until I got my own syndicated show up and running the following year. Initially called *Geraldo!*, the shockingly successful program ran from 1987 to 1998, and along with some related business deals, earned my fortune, such as remains.

Opinion makers and critics soon forgot my hard work as an ABC News crusading reporter. During much of the talk-show period, I was best known for getting my nose broken in that genuinely violent on-air rumble with racist skinheads, for multiple interviews with the playboy of the era, Donald J. Trump, and for talk-show segments like "Men in Lace Panties and the Women Who Love Them."

TIES THAT BIND

My ghosts, and ultimate career redemption, help explain my mixed response to the alleged misdeeds of my late boss and friend Roger Ailes. Before he was exposed as an alleged misogynist, we had known each other for decades, introduced by another powerful media maestro, the late, great Jerry Weintraub.

One of Hollywood's most important producers, Jerry first met Roger when Roger was executive producer of *The Mike Douglas Show* in the late 1960s. Both men orbited the world of Kennebunkport's favorite son, George H.W. Bush, before, during, and after his presidency, the forty-first, from 1988 to 1992. Jerry was my first agent. He and I remained friends long after our professional relationship ended, until his death in July 2015. There is no mystery as to why so many big stars, from Elvis to Frank Sinatra, George Clooney to Matt Damon, adored the man.

He was a creative powerhouse, loving and loyal, and a terrific movie producer, with films such as *Karate Kid* and *Ocean's 11* to his credit. He played a big role in my life, helping to craft *Goodnight America*, my first network show. He negotiated my first, huge-for-those-days ABC News deal, which made me the first million-dollar street reporter. In the early 1970s especially, that was a ton of money, even for anchors like Barbara Walters.

Erica and I reminisced about the great man with Jerry's son Michael in March 2016 when we were staying out in L.A. during my improbable stint on *Dancing with the Stars*. At The Lobster, a Santa Monica restaurant overlooking the famous pier, we laughed remembering how I had brought two hookers to Michael's bar mitzvah at his family mansion on Doheny Road in Beverly Hills in 1975.

It was not as bad as it sounds. I was up in San Francisco with Jane Fonda doing a story about her speech on empowerment at an international hookers' convention. Jane wanted the world's oldest profession decriminalized and prostitutes given all the employment protections of any other profession.

A two-time Academy Award winner, Jane has been one of America's most underrated public personalities for the last couple of decades. The star of *Barbarella*, *Klute*, and *Coming Home* went from stunning ingénue to America's antiwar conscience. She did take her activism a step too far in making the pilgrimage to North Vietnam at the time that nation was killing American GIs. Showing obscene sympathy to our enemies, she became a pariah during the 1970s, cursed by everyone who ever wore the uniform of the United States. For that Jane was never forgiven. Indeed, host Megyn Kelly brought up the incident in 2018 when the two argued on the air about something totally unrelated, plastic surgery.

Typically, I saw Jane's notorious history differently. "Hanoi Jane's" visit to North Vietnam, even as hundreds of brave Americans were POWs in its prison camps, was a serious mistake, for which she apologized and deserved forgiveness. She is too smart, talented, and sincere to be written off for that lapse in judgment. Viewed by the prism of today, her actions seem treasonous, particularly to Vietnam vets. In the context of 1972, however, when tens of thousands were protesting the wildly unpopular war every day, what she did was not that egregious. Her biggest mistake was being photographed in a North Vietnamese antiaircraft gun emplacement wearing a commie helmet.

Vietnam was a long way from San Francisco, where, after interviewing two of Jane's ladies of the night at the hookers' convention, I invited them to Michael Weintraub's grand Beverly Hills bar mitzvah. Both were immediately eager to attend. Even more eager were the ABC television executives who were guests at the bar mitzvah, and the teenagers, all of them buzzing around my special guests. What can I say, other than it was a different era, the ethos of which seemed cool, but feels boorish in the retelling decades later?

Michael brought pictures of the girls to our dinner at The Lobster. Erica said how classy they looked: "They look like college girls, not at all trampy." Michael, who is now in his fifties, told me how thankful he was at the time. In a town where these Jewish rites of passage can be outrageously excessive, I helped make his celebration special. We also laughed about how his fabulous father managed to balance wife and mistress so well that the women lived together after Jerry passed. Isn't that the best evidence that Jerry was a remarkable negotiator and a terrific agent?

My second agent was Jon Peters, a dramatic-looking, long-haired, part-Native American, mostly-Italian former hairstylist to the stars. I call him Cochise of Beverly Hills. He was the real-life *Shampoo*; the Warren Beatty character in the movie was obviously modeled after Jon. Through pure chutzpah and charisma, he courted Hollywood's biggest prize, wooing and landing Barbra Streisand, the ultimate show-business icon. The power couple enjoyed a long-time passionate, tumultuous love and business relationship.

Our friendship started when Jon and Barbra watched some of my Willowbrook exposés. As with John Lennon and Yoko before them, that story was our introduction. Jon and I have been best buds for four decades, during which I watched his evolution from hairdresser to one of Hollywood's most powerful tycoons. His movies include the Oscar-winning *The Color Purple*, Barbra's hugely successful remake of *A Star Is Born*, *Footloose*, *Batman*, *Superman*, and about a hundred others.

A couple of years after we met, in 1976, Sheri, my third wife and mother of my firstborn child, Gabriel, and I moved next door to Jon and Barbra in Malibu. Our modest Ramirez Canyon home abutted their vast and lovely seven-mansion complex, which Barbra has since donated as a park to Los Angeles County. Sheri and Barbra were close friends. Jon and I became

In Malibu, CA, with Jon Peters, Cochise of Beverly Hills. January 2001.

inseparable, getting loaded, street fighting, and riding our powerful motorcycles recklessly through the canyons of the Santa Monica Mountains and along Pacific Coast Highway. We joked about how we had the same trick gene that forced us to push the limits and routinely risk everything.

One unforgettable near-death incident on the bikes happened when both of us were barefoot and wearing nothing but Speedos. We went too fast on a curve on Ramirez Canyon Drive on the way home and almost went off the road, skidding and braking just shy of the cliff and catastrophe. That was the last time Jon rode his bike. My riding lasted longer, until 2014 when I dumped my old Harley while making an illegal left turn in New Jersey. I was pinned under the heavy bike, but four guys came running to my assistance. When they saw who it was, three of them stopped their rescue efforts and whipped out their cell phone cameras.

Jon made my 1977 ABC *20/20* deal with Roone Arledge, and we fancied ourselves standing back-to-back in the barroom brawl of life, often literally. We were constantly punching and jabbing each other, testing who was more macho. He was fiercely protective of Barbra and had a hair-trigger temper, which I saw him unleash several times on intrusive, aggressive, stalker fans trespassing on their Malibu and Aspen properties. Twice I was called on to swear to cops investigating allegations of assault that the other guy had started it.

I was an amateur boxer for about twenty-five years, beginning in the early 1970s. For six of those years, I owned a gym called Broadcast Boxing on West Fifty-Seventh Street, a block from Carnegie Hall. To raise money for my Willowbrook-related charities during that period, aside from concerts and golf tournaments, I would fight whichever Wall Street broker bid the most money. Jon was in my corner when I won one particularly violent three-round brawl before a packed house in Madison Square Garden, and we have stayed friends to this day. If he is the last man standing, Jon Peters will be among my pallbearers when the time comes. I won some and lost some of the charity bouts, including one unforgettable, Howard Stern–sponsored (instigated) three-rounder against Sylvester Stallone's brother Frank. I was game, but Frank was better, bigger, and younger. You can still find that near-death match on the internet.

When you think of the men who mentored me—Fred Friendly, Jerry Weintraub, Roone Arledge, Jon Peters, and until the summer of 2016, Roger Ailes—it is clear that whatever you think of the student, his teachers were all legends in their own right. In Roger's case there was apparently something else going on that I did not know about until his world dissolved in scandal and shame, but his travails aside, he was also a historic innovator.

Before I get into Roger's personal Armageddon, as I recognize those responsible for giving me the skills and opportunity to stay on television for so long, let me thank the deeply impressive ex-chairmen of the Tribune Co., Dennis FitzSimons, and his predecessor, the late Jim Dowdle. They ran the vast Chicago-based media conglomerate, which during its 1980s and 1990s glory days owned dozens of big-city newspapers, major market television stations, and the Chicago Cubs. They not only produced my long-running daytime talk show, but also cut me and several other prominent minorities in as partners on a deal to buy local television stations in Atlanta and New Orleans. Our partnership, which included Quincy Jones, the eminent songwriter and philanthropist, and the late Don Cornelius, the charismatic host of *Soul Train*, sold the two stations a few years later. The sale came at the top of the market, and to this day the money made is, as I said, a hefty portion of retirement stash.

Like almost every executive at Fox News, from Rupert Murdoch on down to Ailes's protégé Bill Shine and his co-president, Jack Abernethy, my partners at Tribune were also self-made Irishmen. For that matter, so was their sometime rival, sometime ally, the gregarious Roger King, founder of King World. He was another roaring, larger-than-life media giant who was the boisterous syndicator of my talk show late in its run, and more consequentially Oprah's. I want to give props, too, to Jack Welsh, another Irishman and the legendary GE chairman, who gave me the sweet 1997 NBC News deal that I will soon describe. And, love those Irish, their ranks include the leading prime-time host at Fox, my amigo Sean Hannity. Megyn Kelly is also a notable member of the tribe, but now she belongs to another network. Bill O'Reilly, as emerald green as they come, has joined the ranks of Irish exiles, now ignominiously banned from the network he led to prosperity for two decades, until running afoul of sexual politics, exacerbated by bad judgment and lavish settlements.

A last note on the Irish thing: For the twenty-plus years Fox News has been on the air, but especially following the Trump triumph in the 2016 presidential election, observers and critics of Big Media, including former President Obama, have pointed to the difference between Fox and the

With my improbable dear friend Sean Hannity, June 2016.

other networks as being basically ideological. Essentially, they say, there is
the conservative network, Fox, standing alone against an array of liberal
news networks, principally MSNBC and CNN.

Which is true, but there is something much more basic going on.
Those Irishmen are mostly Catholic. Hannity was an altar boy, and like
O'Reilly went to parochial school. Many of their beliefs and attitudes
are forged from that identity, which helps explain their feelings about
hot-button issues like abortion, racial and sexual politics, immigration,
and gay marriage. They are just as sharp and smart as any high-flying
liberal. They have an opposing worldview, not reactionary or dumber, just
different. They are what they were raised, people who believe, for example, that all life is sacred and begins with conception. Their sincerity and
intellect aside, I do think O'Reilly's obsession with the imaginary "War
on Christmas" was excessive, but better than, say, War on North Korea.

Many mainstream, Big Media pundits who are generally more liberal,
Blue State and New York/Los Angeles–centric than Fox, shudder to talk

about the fact that a disproportionate percentage of editorial management is, like me, Jewish. Still, as ABC News titan Roone Arledge, a WASP, once suggested to me, in crude, broad strokes, the allegation is true. If you want a list of all of us Jews in news and entertainment, listen to Adam Sandler's Hanukkah song or Google it. What makes the age-old complaints about Jewish people "controlling" the media anti-Semitic is the implication that religion skews our presentation and professionalism, which is not true.

The truth is subtler. Although we come in all ideologies, the bottom-line truth is that Jewish people, like the Fox Irish, are partly what we were raised. How could that not be true? Jewish folk are more progressive than not, urban or at least suburban, seldom rural or gun-toting, relatively cosmopolitan, usually college-educated, and slightly superior, or even smug, regarding folks from the great red working-class heart of Middle America—you know, the "Deplorables." That is why so many of us missed the 2015–16 Trump phenomena happening from Michigan to Miami to Maine.

What changed with the coming of age of Fox News, is that there is now a major news network that reflects a bundle of personal, educational, professional, and religious experiences different from what many were used to seeing in charge of a news network. Despite its recent agonies, and the loss of both Ailes and chief anchor O'Reilly, the network's basic identity remains intact, a testament to Roger's enduring vision.

He made a network in his self-image. Whatever else he was, or became, he was also a born-again Irish Catholic who passionately believed in the basic tenets of his church. He saw in its underrepresentation on television news and in the disdain with which age-old Catholic traditions and teachings were viewed by the mainstream the vast opening for his often embattled but undeniably successful creation, Fox News.

EXPOSING MYSELF, 1990

My personal controversies predate my move to Fox. In 1990 I wrote the vastly controversial memoir the Vonnegut family hated. It combined a gritty recounting of my early career as an investigative reporter uncovering injustice, with a steamy, sexploitation tell-all of the wild and crazy 1970s. A minor best seller, *Exposing Myself* named names, condemning me to both the literary junk pile and the Tackiness Hall of Fame. It came back to bite me badly in 2017. Truth is no defense for bad manners, and I continue to apologize for writing it.

Exposing Myself described the devastating chink in my character that had plagued me from the beginning of my fame: ego-gratifying lust. The inability to remain monogamous became the central fact of my serial divorces. I am speaking about promiscuity, not predation; romance, not rape. Any man who uses his power, position, or prestige to force himself on a woman deserves punishment ranging from shame to castration. Weinstein and his ilk are loser sadists. I'm just a retired Romeo who has seen the light. In the happiest of coincidences, I met Erica and went straight just before public life became a harsh place for aging playboys. Finally I have personal values that match my professional ethics; I have been clean and sober in that regard since my marriage to Erica in 2003. I have never cheated on my wife. Monogamy is now the central tenet of my secular religion.

About five years ago, at a black tie event at the Manhattan Club on Fifth Avenue, one of the prominent older women exposed in the book, one with whom I had a ten-year illicit relationship, confronted me as we stood in line waiting to enter the formal dining hall. Nineteen years older, she was then deep in her eighties, her noble husband long gone. We had not seen each other for at least a quarter century. After a double take, I recognized her and gasped her name out loud. She approached until we were almost nose-to-nose. "Yes, it's me," she replied in a strong, pained voice.

Having drawn the attention of everyone around us, including her current partner, a dignified older gentleman, she said sharply with a measure of hurt, "You ruined my life." It is a condemnation I shall take to the grave. "And he hates you too," she added indicating her courtly friend, who nodded. "Indeed." The grande dame passed away in February 2017. She was ninety-two.

ELAINE'S

For four years, 1994 to 1998, I taped the syndicated *Geraldo!* show, later re-branded *The Geraldo Rivera Show*, during the afternoons at CBS Studios on West Fifty-Seventh Street. Then, I would drive up the West Side

Highway and take the George Washington Bridge to CNBC headquarters across the Hudson River in Fort Lee, New Jersey, to do *Rivera Live*, at 9 PM. The pair of programs represented the two sides of my personality: tabloid ringmaster by day, sharp-tongued, progressive lawyer-advocate by night. The grueling schedule was mitigated by the money and posh lifestyle. With the family happily ensconced at our lovely home in Monmouth County, New Jersey, about fifty miles south, I was a weekday bachelor living in a suite at the Parker Meridian Hotel. Aside from an ample show staff, I had a tough ex-Marine driver and bodyguard I called Tommy Guns, and a personal assistant, Tommy Roles, a dedicated Deadhead who took care of everything else.

We had a post-show ritual, going out every night after I got off the air at 10 PM. If I felt like keeping it low key, we would go to Ms. Elle's, a dive bar on the West Side, which plays a bigger part in this story later. Usually, I would have one or more of my studio guests with me. Ms. Elle's never saw so many celebrities and public officials, including New York's great three-term governor, Mario Cuomo. If I wanted something higher profile, we would head to Elaine's, the celebrity haunt in uptown Manhattan on Second Avenue, where I had been a fixture since my Vonnegut period.

As Woody Allen once said, Elaine's was perfect for someone with a disorganized social life. I had dinner with the reclusive and increasingly embattled Woody and spouse Soon-Yi in June 2017 and reminded him of that sage assessment of Elaine's. If you were welcome there—a big if—there was a ready-made party waiting. From the Beatles and Rolling Stones to Willie Nelson, Jackie Kennedy, Joan Rivers, Frank Sinatra and Mia Farrow to Clint Eastwood and Truman Capote, every star of stage, screen, literature, politics, and public life on the New York scene during that forty-five-year era eventually went to the relatively dumpy bar, with its barely edible menu, presided over by its gregarious, backslapping, sharply judgmental and opinionated owner, the late Elaine Kaufman. She loved her smoky, throwback joint. She even loved the fact that I had two late-night, tequila-fueled brawls there, one of which ended with a broken window. Dragging my entourage of that night's guests and favored staffers, we would also make a stop every week or so at China Club near Times Square, a late-night spot also favored by Donald J. Trump.

Rivera Live on CNBC was not an instant success, but was close enough. The show went on the air in April 1994. After two months of middling performance, which did not move the ratings needle, and my growing regret that it was not worth the effort of working two jobs, lightning struck when something really bad happened to a pretty celebrity mom, Nicole Brown Simpson. Her famous ex-husband slaughtered her and a friend, and then tried to escape to Mexico on live television.

On monitors throughout the network on the day of his bizarre attempted escape, every station was broadcasting the slow-speed Bronco chase involving former football great O.J. Simpson riding in a white Bronco on California's 405 Freeway with a phalanx of cop cars in slow pursuit. "That's our show," I exclaimed to my staff, excitedly pointing at the incredible scene unfolding before the eyes of uncounted millions around the globe. "Stick with it. Drop everything else."

O.J. SIMPSON AND ME, JUNE 1994

Evolving on the spot from a straight-up public affairs program into television's first show devoted to intense legal analysis of a single case, *Rivera Live* pioneered wall-to-wall trial coverage of the subsequent Simpson double-murder trials, criminal and civil. Much later, watching the excellent 2016 ten-part FX series re-creating the murders and the trial was like a rewind of my 1990s life. As a function of my insistence that O.J. did it, some in the black community complained that I acted more like an advocate for the white victims' families than an objective reporter.

Working the case nightly, I also got to know Simpson's attorneys, his Dream Team. As high-profile lawyers typically do, they were attracted like moths to O.J.'s peculiar flame, basking in the extraordinary attention. The brilliant Johnnie Cochran became leader of the pack that included the social butterfly Robert Kardashian, who fathered the infamous clan and through them posthumously invented reality television. As Simpson's private attorney, and maybe the only person in L.A. who thought the Juice was innocent, Kardashian brought smooth local ace Robert Shapiro into the case, and then gnarly veteran F. Lee Bailey. The eminent, peripatetic Harvard Law professor Alan Dershowitz came too, armed with the brilliance of his army of students, and also the potent Barry Scheck, who pioneered the use of DNA and invented the *Innocence Project*, which works to free the incarcerated innocent.

The sincere but otherwise pedestrian prosecutors Marcia Clarke and Chris Darden never had a chance against those titans. They were not only outgunned, but also on the wrong side of the racial divide. I openly sided with the prosecution, and their de facto clients the Browns and the Goldmans. It wasn't just sympathy, but anger at the defense for playing the race card from the bottom of the deck. They cracked our country in half to beat an easy conviction for a barbaric double-murder.

There was no question that the affable, universally known former football great, actor, and pitchman slaughtered, slashed, and butchered his ex-wife, Nicole, the mother of his children, in an insane jealous rage. Simpson killed her friend Ronald Goldman, a waiter, because he was in the wrong place at the wrong time. Ron was returning Nicole's sunglasses that she had left behind in his restaurant, Mezza Luna, at a dinner earlier that evening. Maybe Ron also wanted to hook up with Nicole, but that is not a crime punishable by double decapitation.

When the downtown jury later acquitted the former football great, I led the way in blaming their obviously distorted judgment on the fact most of the jurors were urban and black. To me it was clear that the nation had fractured along racial lines, and that Johnnie Cochran, the clever and dynamic African American lead defense attorney, had correctly perceived that divide and driven a train through it.

Again, timing is everything in life. The Simpson trial took place in the wake of the savage 1991 videotaped police beating of Rodney King, a black man, and the April 1992 L.A. riots, which I covered following the acquittal of the four white cops captured on tape doing the beating. Two years later, there was no way a predominantly black L.A. jury was going to convict a famous black man of killing two white people. They certainly were not going to convict him on the testimony of white cops, especially not cops like Detective Mark Fuhrman, who had been caught on tape detestably referring to African American suspects as "n*ggers."

Among the celebrity guests I brought on the daytime talk show to comment during the Simpson saga were Donald Trump and his then-wife, Marla Maples. Aside from about an interview a year, Trump and I sometimes hung out. In June 1995, I had joined the couple ringside at the Atlantic City Convention Center to watch local boy Vinny Pazienza overcome a broken neck to beat up a worn-out Roberto Duran to retain his super-middleweight boxing title. The Trumps were the

Kanye/Kim, Jay Z/Beyoncé of that era, marrying after first wife Ivana caught him seducing the younger woman with what Marla described as "the best sex I ever had."

Marla and Donald married in 1993 in New York's grand Plaza Hotel, which he owned at the time, along with dozens of other trophy properties, including the Empire State Building and Mar-a-Lago in Palm Beach, Florida, which he described to me with typical immodesty as, "Maybe the greatest house in America. It's been rated and ranked the greatest house in America, beyond San Simeon, which is in California, and the Breakers, which is in Newport, Rhode Island." Among the guests at his wedding was O.J. Simpson, who attended the lavish affair with bombshell girlfriend Tawny Kitaen. His ex-wife Nicole, whom O.J. was still dating when he allegedly killed her the next year, in June 1994, was at her home in Brentwood, California, with their two children.

It turned out that Trump's take on the case was much more in sync with the jurors' than my own. In an episode of my daytime show that featured Donald and Marla, and aired in February 1995 after Simpson's murder trial had begun, I asked Donald to explain how he could describe O.J. Simpson as "a nice guy," given all the testimony about O.J.'s domestic brutality before the murder of Nicole.

Donald Trump: Well, now, I can only say O.J. as I know O.J. I'm not saying O.J. is guilty, innocent, or anything. What I see is appalling, and what I see certainly doesn't lead to . . . from my viewpoint, if I were a juror, I'd have a real, real hard time with this one. I can only tell you from a personal standpoint, as somebody that knows O.J. well, I found it really incredibly hard to believe that he could do an act, a violent act like this. He's just a very different guy.

Geraldo Rivera: May I ask Marla?

Marla Trump: Hi.

Geraldo Rivera: Was he always pleasant to you?

Marla Trump: I only met O.J. on a couple of occasions in passing, and he was very pleasant on those occasions. But you know, in life you never know what really happens on the other side of things, in any personal relationship.

I always thought Marla wise beyond her stereotype, and that impression was reinforced during the weeks we spent together doing *Dancing with the Stars*. She was calm and dignified in the midst of the tumult of her ex-husband's improbable run for the White House. Her marriage to Mr. Trump ended in 1997. *Rivera Live* lasted longer, successfully anchoring CNBC's prime-time schedule for a total of seven years, 1994 to 2001, spanning the Clinton impeachment and the investigation into the disappearance of Democratic congressman Gary Condit's intern/girlfriend, Chandra Levy. (When the intern's skeletal remains were found in a DC park and her murder was pinned on an undocumented Latino immigrant, the congressman was cleared. By then, however, after his harsh exposure on programs like mine, his political life was ruined. A decade later, on a live edition of my weekend Fox News show *At Large*, his adult son angrily confronted me. I let him slide, understanding that his family had suffered, though not nearly as much as Chandra's.)

To give you an idea of the powerhouse *Rivera Live* became, remember there were two Simpson trials, the murder case in which he was acquitted in October 1995, and the civil case, decided on February 11, 1997. The night of the civil court verdict, which found Simpson civilly liable for the wrongful deaths of his ex-wife Nicole and her friend Ron Goldman, the once-tiny cable channel CNBC outperformed the mighty CBS broadcast network, achieving a 6.4 rating. That was more than thirty times higher than the 0.2 rating the network averaged when I took over the time slot; it was a ratings record for the network that lasted eighteen years, until CNBC hosted a Republican presidential primary debate starring Donald Trump in October 2015.

SEMEN-STAINED DRESS, 1997–1998

After the Simpson saga had run its extraordinary course, I inserted myself into the heart of President Clinton's lurid impeachment and defended him as if he were a member of my own family. At a time when it seemed every other reporter and commentator in the country saw him as guilty of perjury and on the verge of inevitable resignation, I took the opposite view, telling skeptical commentators such as his former press secretary Dee Dee Meyers, a frequent guest, "I like his chances." A sharp, smart, battle-hardened Washington insider, she answered, "I'm eager to hear why you think that."

Clearly, like Dee Dee, almost everyone in and around government thought Clinton was toast. Coming from outside the Beltway, I saw it differently. My angle was that President Clinton would soon be forgiven by most Americans because all spouses lie when caught getting blowjobs from secretaries, flight attendants, trainers, pool boys, family friends, or neighbors. Such matters are best left to the aggrieved spouse or significant other to settle. At least that was the prevailing thought back in 1998. Times have changed. It is no longer the conventional wisdom. We are much more judgmental and politically correct now than we were before the turn of the century. Thanks to men like Bill Cosby and Harvey Weinstein, Bill Clinton's sins feel much sleazier today than they did back in the old millennium.

Representing the hawkish House Republicans in the Clinton impeachment proceedings, Kenneth Starr, the prudish lead prosecutor, became the target of my nightly wrath. I scolded him mercilessly for hunting down the president for lies prominent Republicans were routinely caught telling. The GOP Hypocrites Hall of Fame then included Congressman Buz Lukens, Republican of Ohio, who was caught having sex with a 16-year-old; Dan Crane, Republican of Illinois, who did the dirty deed with a congressional aide; frisky senator Bob Packwood, Republican of Oregon, who kept a diary he denied having, which listed twenty-nine conquests. Representative Helen Chenoweth-Hage, Republican of Idaho, was one of the first to call for Clinton's resignation. She was later embarrassed by the revelation of an affair with a married rancher.

As bad as President Clinton's behavior was, it was reflected also in the seedy lives of cheaters like fiery representative Bob Barr of Georgia; Speaker of the House Dennis Hastert of Illinois, who later got caught paying a hunk of hush money to a boy he'd abused; Dan Burton of Indiana; Bob Livingston of Louisiana; Mark Foley, who specialized in House interns; Newt Gingrich of Georgia, who was also House speaker; Henry "No Abortion" Hyde of Illinois; Senator Pete Domenici of New Mexico; and Representative and later Senator David Vitter, who before being revealed as a hooker connoisseur said, "President Clinton having had a workplace affair with an intern in the Oval Office complex . . . some meaningful action must be taken against the president."

It was on *Rivera Live* that the world learned that Monica's semen-stained cocktail dress had tested positive for Bill Clinton's DNA. Here is how I found that out. A close friend of the Machiavellian President Clinton leaked that information to me exclusively, as he did other less liquid details on an almost nightly basis. This unimpeachable source stood shoulder-to-shoulder with the embattled president every day, and every day I would get a message from the White House guiding and advising my coverage with a specificity that invariably turned out to be true. For that period, Bill Clinton was my news director.

The revelation that an ejaculating president deposited the semen stain on Monica's pretty blue dress was received skeptically. The White House knew it would be. Coming from anyone at the *New York Times* or the *Washington Post*, the scoop would have been explosive. Coming from me, a non-Washington insider with a limited following inside the Beltway, the news made only a slight bump.

In leaking the story to me, the White House made the following calculation: Geraldo puts it out there, where it is received with high skepticism. But because it is out there, it blunts the impact of the shocking news when it will be ultimately confessed to and confirmed by more reputable, reliable sources. That confirmation did not happen for three interminable weeks. With my neck stuck way out because I was the only reporter making the positive-DNA results claim, that three weeks was the longest of my professional life.

President Clinton modestly rewarded my unfailing loyalty with a couple of phone interviews following his February 12, 1999, acquittal by the Senate. He later invited Erica and me to the VIP celebration of the opening of the Clinton Library in Little Rock, Arkansas, on a rainy day in November 2004.

That occasion was memorable because we sat between Barbra Streisand, the idol of every Jewish woman on the planet, especially my wife, and the late Robin Williams, who was hilarious, making fun of everything and everyone. Barbra could not have been nicer, inquisitive about how George W. Bush's recent reelection would affect the country and how our lives had changed since the days when we were neighbors in Malibu. Having dumped Jon Peters and married actor James Brolin, she was already much more politically engaged than she was back in the Diva Days. Twelve years after the library opening, she remained a prominent and loyal friend to the Clintons throughout Hillary's disastrous 2016 campaign.

I also had a chat at the opening with a wan-looking Senator John Kerry, who had just lost the 2004 election to Bush 43. In the connected world, Kerry went to Yale with my lawyer, Leo Kayser III, and the senator's family was active in the charity I founded to deinstitutionalize the care and treatment of the emotionally and intellectually disabled like the kids in Willowbrook.

Until mid-campaign, Kerry had been favored to beat Bush, already an unpopular incumbent, having started the disastrous war in Iraq. But Bush chopped him up and the senator was smarting from the vicious "Swift Boat" attacks that denigrated his heroic service in Vietnam. He still could not believe he "lost to a loser" like Bush 43. In a quiet, somber, and sincere conversation off to the side at the VIP reception, Kerry confided that the reason he thought he lost was an unfortunately timed terrorist attack in Europe that happened the final weekend before the vote. His pollsters had just explained to him how many voters decided only in that final weekend to stick with the incumbent, as Americans often do in war, deciding not to change horses in midstream.

President Clinton has also been exceedingly gracious when we run into each other in public. The problem is that his people never acceded to my many requests for a sit-down interview. His wife, the former first lady, senator, secretary of state, and two-time failed presidential aspirant Hillary Clinton, has never really given me the time of day, at least not professionally. In fact, she has often given me the brush-off.

One snub I remember clearly was when I tried to grab a quick interview on the airport tarmac in Port au Prince, Haiti, in the aftermath of the ruinous 2010 earthquake; she physically turned her back on me in a reporter scrum. I got the interview anyway, but only by elbowing my way around her favored reporters and the gaggle of aides and security guards that surrounded her.

More to the editorial point, Secretary Clinton was asking the outside world for governmental and private aid to the stricken island nation. I wanted to know how she could be confident Haiti's notoriously corrupt ruling class would not hijack that generosity. Most of the aid was indeed stolen by phony charities like Wyclef Jean's *Yéle Haiti*, and the poor people victimized by the earthquake received precious little of it. The Clinton Foundation foundered in Haiti as the greedy sponge of corruption sucked up much of the money raised, as I knew it would.

Her failure to embrace me is one reason I did not mourn her loss to Donald Trump, who, as I mentioned, is unfailingly cordial. I know that sounds petty, especially since her politics are much more in sync with mine than President Trump's are, but at my age little things mean a lot. Besides, I am stubbornly hopeful that President Trump will not be as inflexible as his first year in office is leading the world to believe. Focus on what he has actually done, as opposed to what he tweets. He is thin-skinned and impetuous, but he is not the right-wing rabble rouser he seems.

Incidentally, when Erica heard me on television making that charge of Secretary Clinton's alleged disrespect, my wife reminded me how nice Hillary has been to us on the several occasions we have met socially in recent years, including running into the Clintons at Barbetta, the elegant northern Italian Theater District restaurant on West Forty-Sixth Street. And in fairness, by the time of the Haitian encounter, I was working for Fox News, Hillary's archenemy. That Fox affiliation also soured President Obama, despite my record of having been generally supportive. He was cordial when we saw each other at the White House correspondents' dinner, but never once agreed to be interviewed. I used to joke on my old radio show that Obama would grant an interview to the Dog Food Channel before he said yes to me.

Despite the lack of a personal relationship, I came to Hillary's defense time and again during what I considered the phony-baloney Benghazi scandal and its toxic cousin, the utterly stupid email scandal. However illegitimately, those hyped-up nonissues, fueled by well-placed Russian hacks, put a nail in the coffin of her presidential aspirations. She hastened her political demise by lazy-scolding campaigning and lecturing coal miners on their imminent irrelevance.

$30 MILLION MAN, 1997

Although my daytime talk show was never as bad as its reputation, it made me a punch line, draining whatever was left of my reputation as an investigative crusader. Following the on-camera studio brawl with the skinheads, *Newsweek* ran a cover picture of me with my nose bleeding and the caption, "Trash TV." The footage of the brawl, definitely the wildest and most violent in the colorful history of daytime television, is available on the internet. Its notoriety has outlasted the print edition of *Newsweek*.

As the owner and producer of the show, as well as its host, I reaped crazy money, which did soothe the cruelty of critics and my occasional hurt feelings. Besides, there is something culturally significant in being mocked, mimicked, and imitated in five different decades on *Saturday Night Live*.

By 1997 I had been doing both the syndicated afternoon talk show and the CNBC evening show *Rivera Live* for four years, and the NBC show had become so important to the network they offered a six-year, multimillion-dollar deal if I would give up daytime and work just for them. That made it lucrative enough to walk away from the money tree growing in the backyard. I wanted out anyway. Eleven years was enough, both financially and spiritually. I had no debt and there was enough in the bank to live comfortably, get the kids through college, and still be reasonably endowed. At least it was until I got divorced for the fourth and final time a few years later.

Chapter 3

9/11 CHANGED EVERYTHING

My decision to leave daytime TV was cemented by a 1997 incident during the taping of a show involving DNA testing. The easy, inexpensive test to identify a baby's daddy was about to change the genre and breathe new life into the careers of long-running hosts Jerry Springer and Maury Povich. But I was the first to use the technology to create dramatic moments of raw revelation. There are few canned dramas as fundamental as solving the mystery of fatherhood on live television.

As we crafted the DNA segments, the show had a redeeming social value in that we provided a safe space for abused spouses to confront their abusers under the cover of getting them counseling. During one episode, after confronting an insanely jealous husband with his battered wife's allegations of abuse, I took great satisfaction in telling the arrogant slug, "By the way, you're not the baby's father."

The shocked young man looked at me with contempt. "Thanks, Geraldo," he spat out as he punched a hole in the set and stormed off, as the audience gasped. I looked at my longtime stage manager, Mike Jacobs, and told him I had to get out of the business or go straight to hell.

My first instinct was to go back to Roger Ailes, who had made an informal pitch for my services in 1996, when he was creating Fox News. This time, he honored me with a formal multimillion-dollar offer. I initially accepted, but NBC had the right to match any outside offer, which it did. When I inked that pact, the *New York Times* ran an oversized picture of me on the first page of the business section with the caption "$30 Million Man." Said the story: "NBC moved aggressively to keep Mr. Rivera after he accepted an offer from the Fox News Channel last week. NBC had a right to match the Fox offer and did so rather than lose his *Rivera Live* program, which has been the most successful show on CNBC, an increasingly important corporate asset to NBC."

"This is something I need for my honor, for my family, for my own self-image," I told Bill Carter, the new media writer for the *Times*. Referring to some of my most criticized moments in the years since leaving ABC, I continued, "A lot of the problems people have had with me have been of my own creation. But I want to go down as doing something to open up TV news to being more human, not as someone who opened up Al Capone's vault or had his nose broken on TV by some skinhead."

Being embraced by a major network news organization appealed to my ego. It signaled respect. "Andy Lack [once again the president of NBC News, and the man who negotiated Megyn Kelly's big deal when she left Fox in January 2017 and survived the Lauer dismissal in November 2017] sat down with me and said, 'I want you to be an NBC News correspondent,'" I told the *Times*. "That was the most important thing to me." I was a rare media creature, a former news correspondent allowed back into the rarefied ranks of the network-news profession after leaving thirteen years earlier to go into show business.

Also included in the deal was a monthly appearance on the then-dominant *Today* show, at the time hosted by Katie Couric and Matt Lauer. Katie was an ebullient star and a rival to Barbara Walters for preeminence among women in broadcasting. She and I had an emotional bond because of my relationship with her husband, John Paul (Jay) Monahan III, a lawyer and NBC News legal analyst. Dashing and handsome, Jay at the time was battling the cancer that would kill him less than two months later at age forty-two. To show him my love and support, I insisted that my new contract contain a clause in writing naming Jay as my permanent substitute host on *Rivera Live*.

It was an important role because beginning earlier that year, in July 1997, I was taking big chunks of time away from the show to skipper my sailboat, *Voyager*, around the world, on an odyssey I will describe shortly. Jay hosted the show every Friday night during that important time when

With friends Marianne Bertuna and her future husband Arthur Aidala on board *Voyager* off Martha's Vineyard. Summer 2014.

the O.J. Simpson civil trial still commanded enormous attention, also covering the Unabomber and Timothy McVeigh trials.

Jay was so touched by the gesture of being written into my contract that for a time he carried the letter around with him to show people how highly he was valued by CNBC and me. A couple of weeks after I signed the deal, he asked to see me about a personal matter, which I figured was bad news about his health. We dreaded the possibility that his heroic treatments at New York-Presbyterian Hospital had come too late to save him from the ravages of the disease. He and Katie had been very public about his battle with cancer and were already crusading for men to get colonoscopies as soon as they hit age forty. The couple had two little girls who later attended school in New York with my daughters Isabella and Simone.

After playing phone tag, Jay and I caught up outside a car dealership in the Chelsea neighborhood, where I had come to buy a Bentley to celebrate the signing of the NBC deal. "What's up?" I asked, fearing the answer. "I almost died last week," he told me. "Things don't look good. I wanted you to know."

Katie asked me to deliver one of the eulogies at his grand funeral service in January 1998 at a packed Park Avenue church, St. Ignatius Loyola.

Everyone in the news business attended. He was beloved. A Civil War reen-
actor, Jay always assumed the role of a heroic Confederate cavalryman.
In my corny and overwrought eulogy I put him in character from those
long-ago days and spoke of how he and Katie were soul mates through
the ages. Thanks to Katie's generosity and fundraising there is now a Jay
Monahan Center for Gastrointestinal Health at New York-Presbyterian
Hospital.

The last part of the NBC deal was for four prime-time, network-news
specials a year, one of which, "Women in Prison," won the 2000 Robert
F. Kennedy Award for Journalism, my third. In those days before *Orange Is
the New Black*, it was a stark and revealing exposé on the exploitation and
abuse that was endemic to the privately owned women's prisons throughout the South.

"HE DOES WHAT HE DOES," JUNE 1999

There was no love lost between me and anchor Tom Brokaw. He was a
news snob and I was an outlier. Knowing that bad blood simmered, David
Corvo, the excellent NBC News executive who supervised my work,
arranged to make my office two feet wider than that of the network's
principal star. Of course, as befitting the anchor and managing editor of
NBC Nightly News, Brokaw's office overlooked the skating rink and elegant
Rockefeller Plaza in Midtown Manhattan, while mine in Fort Lee, New
Jersey, looked out at the extensive King's Plaza parking lot, a gas station,
and a Korean market.

While I enjoyed regular appearances on the *Today* show and *Dateline
NBC*, the only NBC News program I could not get on was *Nightly News*,
helmed by Brokaw. In those days before humbled by father time, he was
still the NBC News god and had strict say over which correspondents
could appear on his broadcast. I was not one of them.

In spring 1999, I volunteered to cover the Balkan Wars for the *Today*
show and CNBC's *Rivera Live*. That conflict resulted from the breakup of
Yugoslavia in the post-Soviet era. Serbia, an Orthodox Christian country,
was vying to become dominant, but had just lost Bosnia, a Muslim region,
after a bitter war marked by Serbian genocide of Bosnians, who were buried by the thousands in mass graves.

In 1999, Christian Serbia was still fighting to hold onto another majority-Muslim region, Kosovo. Kosovo was supported in its independence bid by neighboring Albania and much of Europe and the United States. Ethnically, Muslim Kosovars and Muslim Albanians are virtually indistinguishable, a people divided by an invisible line on a map.

I had great contacts within the Kosovo Liberation Army (KLA) in New York. Some worked at Elaine's. Little-known fact of Big Apple life: Many of the suave Italian waiters at the best restaurants are actually Muslims from Albania who learned their Italian by listening to RAI, Radiotelevisione Italiana S.p.A., Italy's national public broadcasting company. Italy is separated from Albania by just forty-five miles of water across the Strait of Otranto, which connects the Adriatic to the Ionian Sea.

This Italianization of Albania happened from 1945 to 1992, when the country was a repressed, cloistered communist dictatorship run by the Soviet Union. Now it is a free country and like Kosovo, its little brother republic, sends its children to America where they also control New York City's roofing jobs, and make up most of Manhattan's porters and doormen.

The KLA had a rough reputation for mobsterism in the United States, which I thought was not relevant to their countrymen's struggle for nationhood and independence in Europe. I chose to trust them, and they trusted me. To this day, they are among my favorite folks, along with the Lebanese. In May 2012, Albanian president Bamir Topi awarded me the "Medal of Gratitude," Albania's highest honor accorded a foreigner, for my work during the war and since in support of Kosovo and Albania.

During the bloody conflict in the Balkans, in June 1999, like true friends, the Albanians rolled out the red carpet for me when I flew into Tirana, the Albanian capital. They also provided transportation and armed support to the front lines across the border into Kosovo. We got behind Serbian lines, had some close-up, on-camera encounters with Serbian artillery, snipers, and mortars, and gained exclusive access to a Serbian position that had been overrun by the KLA.

Aside from the drama of nearby explosions, our foray was newsworthy because we discovered Russian Army identification on the dead, which proved that Russia, led by Vladimir Putin, its pugnacious prime minister and once and future president, was assisting its Orthodox cousins the Serbs in the fight against Muslim Albania.

The problem was with NBC News. Though Jeff Zucker, the wunder-kind executive producer of the *Today* show (and now president of CNN), made extensive use of my reporting from the front lines, Tom Brokaw's *Nightly News* ignored the dramatic reports.

Syndicated television columnist David Bauder wrote in the *Philadel-phia Inquirer* on June 18, 1999, that "It's not hard to find NBC's $5 million man, Geraldo Rivera, on television. You just have to know where to look.

"Try the *Today* show, where Rivera's action-packed reports on the Kosovo Liberation Army first aired this month. But don't try the NBC *Nightly News*, where a Rivera report has never been shown. Better yet, try cable, where MSNBC repeatedly ran the Kosovo reports.

"A year and a half into his lucrative new contract with NBC, the for-mer syndicated talk-show host still doesn't feel completely accepted at the Peacock Network. He may get more camera time than anyone else in the company, but he yearns for the time he doesn't get. It's a strange dynamic.

"Since signing his NBC deal in November 1997, Rivera has been ran-kled at not having any reports aired on NBC *Nightly News*, the network's flagship show anchored by Tom Brokaw. In December 1997, Brokaw said of Rivera: 'He does what he does, and I do what I do. There's very little common ground between us. That doesn't mean he doesn't have the right to do what he does.' Brokaw hasn't talked much about his colleague since then.

"Yet Rivera's feelings were hurt anew by the treatment of his Kosovo reports. He hoped they were good enough for *Nightly* to seek them out. 'The writing is on the wall, the sky, and the ground,' Rivera said. 'It's just not going to happen. I don't think it will ever happen. If that piece didn't get on, I don't think they'd use anything. I know that *Dateline* and *Nightly* are like the country club in my neighborhood. I'm not allowed in.' The network's only comment was that 'each NBC News program makes its own editorial decisions,' said spokeswoman Alex Constantinople."

SAIL TO THE CENTURY, 1997–2000

My marriage to C.C. was already on the rocks by the time of my NBC News disenchantment in 1999. We were estranged but not yet formally separated as the world approached the new millennium, anticipated around the globe with a mixture of superstitious awe and more-grounded fears of computer malfunctions and systemic technology breakdowns. We were commemorating that historic New Year in January 2000 with a monumental sailboat journey around the world. It was an awesome experience that checked a key item on my existential bucket list.

With the permission of NBC, through my personal company, Maravilla Productions, I sold the Travel Channel a four-hour series documenting the once-in-a-lifetime journey on board *Voyager*, my classic, vintage ketch. Designed by Sparkman & Stephens Naval Architects, she was built in 1972 in Lemwerder, Germany by famed shipbuilders Abeking & Rasmussen. Seventy feet long, with two soaring masts, *Voyager* is a graceful beauty. She is also rugged, with a hull made of half-inch-thick aluminum, and four watertight compartments. She was purpose-built for Tom Watson Jr., who was retiring as CEO of IBM. A world-class sailor, Watson wanted to take her farther north than any cruising sailboat had ever gone. He achieved that goal, taking the sturdy vessel through the ice-bound seas north of Greenland.

I bought her third- or fourth-hand in 1995, in bad shape, but her peerless lines and sailing soul remained intact. I rebuilt her in Howdy Bailey's Boatyard in Norfolk, Virginia. Together, *Voyager* and I sailed tens of thousands of miles, around the world, and up the mighty Amazon River. When my age and lifestyle no longer favored grand sailing adventures, I still could not bear to sell her, so I gave her away. In 2014, nineteen years after setting foot on board, Erica and I donated the beautiful boat to the Maine Maritime Academy in Castine, appropriately close to the Watson family compound in North Haven, Maine.

The grand journey around the world started at Rough Point, my home on the Navesink River in New Jersey, through New York Harbor to Marion, Massachusetts, on Buzzards Bay, down east off New England, into the great circle route across the Atlantic Ocean to the mid-ocean Azores archipelago, and on to Lisbon, Portugal, on the European mainland. Then it was through the Strait of Gibraltar, gateway to the Mediterranean Sea. We stopped in Tangier, Morocco; Malaga and Palmas, Spain; the South of France; Corsica to Sardinia; Italy to Sicily; Malta to Santorini, Greece; Crete, Turkey, and Cyprus; and then across to Tel Aviv, Israel. From there, it was through the Suez Canal, up the Gulf of Aqaba, dreaming of Lawrence of Arabia, to Eilat, Israel,

At the helm of *Voyager*, which I sailed around the world and
1,400 miles up the Amazon River. January 2000.

then after an unpleasant encounter with an Egyptian Navy frigate, it
was down the Red Sea, around the pirate-infested Horn of Africa to the
Seychelles Islands, and Kenya. From Africa, we headed to the island
nation of the Maldives, across the Indian Ocean to Saba, Indonesia;
Singapore, Bali, Australia, and New Zealand; and into the vast Pacific to
the island nation of Tonga, which is located directly on the International
Date Line.

There, after doing a live shot for NBC, which was broadcasting
around the clock as the various time zones hit the historic Y2K marker, we
held our collective breaths hoping that our computer-driven navigational
systems would not crash along with every other computer in the world.
When that did not happen, we celebrated the Once-in-a-Millennium
New Year at a party at the rotund and gregarious Tongan Crown Prince's
lavish home. From those long-dreamed-of festivities, it was on to Tahiti,
and the other islands of French Polynesia, including Bora Bora, across
the broad Pacific to the miraculous Galapagos. We dry-docked *Voyager* in
Guayaquil, Ecuador, to repair a broken propeller shaft, then headed up
the northwest coast of South America, through the Panama Canal, passing the east coast of Central America and Mexico, through the Florida

Straits, riding the swift, strong Gulf Stream current up the Atlantic coast of the US, past Cape Hatteras, and home to North Cove Marina in Lower Manhattan. There, in the shadow of the World Trade Center's Twin Towers, which still had a year of life left, we jumped overboard to celebrate our circumnavigation.

Called *Sail to the Century*, the 30,000-mile journey took several years, from 1997–2000. I managed to do it and my job by taking six weeks off every six months. As I mentioned earlier, Jay Monahan was my semi-permanent substitute host, and after he passed, Dan Abrams, now the skilled legal analyst for ABC News and a dapper internet entrepreneur, filled my chair.

Typically as we sailed east through the Mediterranean, I would leave New York after *Rivera Live* on a Thursday evening, catching an overnight flight to either London or Paris. Then I would fly from that European or Asian airport on Friday morning to wherever *Voyager* was waiting, arriving on board by Friday afternoon.

We would spend the weekend on the move, always sailing easterly. Then on Monday morning I would take an early-morning flight back to London or Paris from wherever we had docked, in time to catch the noon flight on the supersonic Concorde back to New York.

With a cruising speed of Mach 2 (1,354 mph), Concorde got me home in less than three hours. Since there was a five- or six-hour time difference, the ride outraced the sun, getting me back to New York two or three hours earlier than when I'd left Europe. Sadly, months later in July 2000, Concorde stopped flying after an awful Paris crash, which killed all one hundred passengers and nine crewmembers aboard.

In grand style, we achieved the Travel Channel series' big idea to be astride the International Date Line at midnight, January 1, 2000, but along the way I lost my marriage. Chastened and abashed by decades of self-indulgence, I swear I am transformed, faithful during my entire marriage to Erica, and as proud of that as I am ashamed of the earlier philandering that diminishes me. But that is now. Back in 2000, I was getting that fourth and final divorce. I kept the boat and to escape dealing with my shortcomings, kept sailing.

FROM ROOTS TO RAIN FOREST, 2000–2002

Upon returning from Tonga and the Date Line, I was asked by the Travel Channel for another *Voyager*-based, four-part series. We called it *From Roots to Rain Forest*. It documented a second grand journey onboard the old sailboat, this time from Puerto Rico (my "roots") across the Caribbean Sea and down the Atlantic Ocean off the bulge of South America, across the equator, entering the gigantic delta of the enormous Amazon River, then heading 1,400 miles up the big river, across the entire nation of Brazil (hence the "rain forest"), touching Amazonian Colombia, all the way to Peru, farther up the river than any ocean-faring foreign sailboat had yet gone.

This journey began in February 2001 when I brought Erica to a huge family reunion in San Juan Harbor attended by scores of local relatives, who despite the impressive number of guests, still represented a mere fraction of the Rivera clan. My dad, Cruz Rivera, was one of seventeen children. We partied with my cousins and uncles and aunties and reminisced for the cameras. Then we set sail on the tough upwind journey a couple of hundred miles to the Windward and Leeward Caribbean Islands en route to South America's great river.

From the special: "Our short and easy first leg of our journey hasn't turned out that way. We have been battered for the last hour by the wet and driving wind. And now this squall; when it hit, packing rain blown as if by fire hose at forty-plus knots, *Voyager* was soaked and pummeled. Nothing, certainly no synthetic amusement park thrill ride, can match the terror and the satisfaction of riding the wrath of elemental fury. We don't sail the oceans looking for trouble. But we're reasonably competent to deal with it, and relish the glow of flamboyant survival."

A Travel Channel executive who wanted to be hands-on joined us, but he was puking so badly after the first few hours we had to drop him off on Vieques Island, a mere forty choppy miles from our starting point in San Juan Harbor.

As I did for the original 1997–2000 around-the-world voyage, I flew back and forth during this Amazon River odyssey, balancing my day job at CNBC with long weekends and scattered vacations in the jungle. From that February 2001 through the late summer, usually with Erica, I would join the big boat as her crew steamed and sailed her up the legendary river, reporting from the special: "Having sailed *Voyager* over six of the Seven

Seas, in the spring of 2001, we began our exploration of one of the world's most mighty rivers. So vast is the Amazon that its fresh water can be found two hundred miles out in the ocean.

"Home to three thousand species of fish, including the piranha, one of the world's most terrifying; three hundred species of mammals, including these magnificent cats (jaguars, leopards, and mountain lions); and a billion acres of rain forest, there is peace here—and war. Harmony and conflict, and the lure of the jungle and its river, proved irresistible.

"Welcome to the Amazon. Of all the world's exotic destinations, few rival the Amazon in mystery and allure. It is the world's mightiest, largest, and at 4,200 miles, the longest river on the planet. It is a watery highway through an adventure land that stretches the distance from New York to Los Angeles and halfway back again. The journey up the incredible waterway will pass through the immense jungles of Brazil, touch the corner of Colombia, and travel up into the Andes Mountains of Peru."

We met indigenous people, saw boundless rain forest and abundant critters, from monkeys to piranha to pink river dolphin. We wondered at the bizarrely ornate opera house in the jungle capital of Manaus and often ran into stern-faced police and local military forces on and around the river. During our jungle adventure, the vast expanse of the Amazon through Brazil, especially where it gets close to neighboring Colombia, was heavily patrolled to curtail rain-forest and wildlife poachers, battle the endemic ordinary crime, and most urgently, to deter or catch the dope smugglers who were running rampant.

Aside from the four-hour Travel Channel documentary, I also sold my real employer, NBC News, on an hour-long network *Dateline* special using the river journey to probe the huge extent of drug production and distribution surrounding the Amazon River basin. In those days before the Mexican drug lords took control, we were sailing right through the dark heart of the most important cocaine and heroin production and transport artery in the New World, and the adventure made for compelling television.

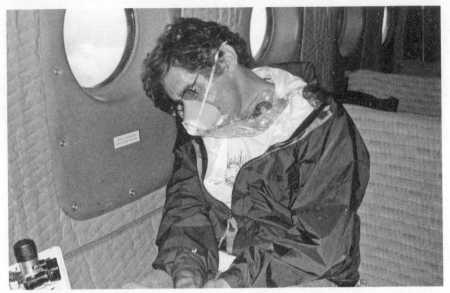

An oxygen-deprived nap on small plane flying over the Andes Mountains. July 2003.

PLAN COLOMBIA, MAY 2001

Voyager docked for the duration of the NBC News shoot in hot, humid, seedy, scary Leticia, Colombia's southernmost city and principal Amazon River port. It was a scene torn from a *Casablanca*-style movie. The shady riverfront was filled with nefarious characters, the majority of whom were ne'er-do-wells engaged in aspects of the drug trade. From Leticia, I chartered small planes to various locations in the region to document the extensive coca and poppy fields and accompany authorities in their raids on production laboratories.

We taped an interview with US Marine General (and later Chairman of the Joint Chiefs of Staff) Peter Pace at the splendidly exotic, semi-secret US jungle base where hundreds of our GIs were deployed. They were there for the now largely forgotten military effort called Plan Colombia. The goal was to counter narcotics production and transport, as well as direct the fight against leftist guerrillas who were facilitating the drug trade and destabilizing regional governments.

As extraordinary as it sounds today, the terrorists had their own mini-country within a country, and in our own hemisphere. In one hairy

With US-trained paramilitary, Plan Colombia. July 2003.

Covering Plan Colombia. July 2003.

sequence, we made contact with and gained access to FARC-landia, the quasi-official chunk of Colombian territory that had been ceded to the Revolutionary Armed Forces of Colombia, known by their Spanish initials FARC. Frantic to get to our rendezvous before the nighttime curfew, the violation of which was death, we drove our borrowed vehicle hard into that rebel-held territory, past numerous checkpoints manned by edgy boy soldiers bearing big weapons.

FARC's leadership was made up of vicious, extreme-leftist revolutionary drug barons responsible for decades of kidnapping and murders that presaged ISIS, only without the artifice of religion. We reached our predetermined jungle clearing just as night fell. The next morning, we were thoroughly searched before being introduced to the boss, Raúl Reyes. Wearing jungle camo, short, bespectacled, and bearded in the Che Guevara mode, he was known as El Comandante and was wanted around the world, including in the United States. I questioned him hard about FARC's dope-dealing ways. He answered calmly. Denying the allegations of drug dealing, he claimed his group only collected taxes on those who were the actual cocaine producers. Seven years later, after peace talks with the government failed, Reyes was killed in a massive US-Colombian assault on his camp. When my brother, Craig, and Greg Hart told me the news, there were high fives all around.

Called "Drug Bust: The Longest War," our NBC special aired in June 2001. I thought it would be a big award magnet, like "Women in Prison." By awards season, though, I was gone from NBC News, and the world's attention was focused on another menace, Osama bin Laden.

PICKING UP THE PIECES, FEBRUARY– SEPTEMBER 2001

The rest of that summer of 2001 was taken up sailing the old boat back down the Amazon toward home. The awesome power of the river flow is fascinating. While we struggled on the way in as if going up a steep hill, averaging just two knots against the mighty current, we virtually flew on the way out, sometimes hitting fifteen or even twenty knots (twenty-three mph) as we were swept downriver toward the Atlantic Ocean and the two hundred-mile-wide delta of this incredible stream.

Out of the river, our most notable stop on the way up north was Devil's Island, France's remote and notorious former prison colony off the northeast coast of South America. It once held Capt. Alfred Dreyfus, the Jewish artillery officer whose trial and conviction came to define institutional anti-Semitism. The brutality and inhumanity of the penal colony are brilliantly described in Henri Charrière's classic memoir *Papillon,* which became a great 1973 movie starring Steve McQueen and Dustin Hoffman.

By staying on the move, I was also postponing dealing with the upheavals in my personal life, especially the divorce from C.C. Our estate was large and complicated, so the process was drawn out, and Isabella and Simone were whipsawed as a result. Born during the flush times, they spent their early childhood helicoptering between our two homes. Rough Point, a 105-year-old Victorian home on eight acres on the Navesink River in leafy Monmouth County, New Jersey, was our principal residence. When we sold it to a newly minted hedge-fund millionaire, he knocked down the old but meticulously maintained landmark the same day in an act of civic vandalism, replacing it with a McMansion.

Our second home was Sea Gate, which C.C. still owns in her sweet hometown, Marion, Massachusetts. It is another lovely landmark, which I try to visit by boat each summer. Built in 1926 on a bluff on Buzzards Bay, it is bordered on the landward side by the seventeenth hole of the world-famous Kittansett Club. Incidentally, neither the Navesink Country Club in New Jersey nor Kittansett in Massachusetts allowed me to become a member. A Jewish Puerto Rican (who is 10% Native American, according to Ancestry.com) was more than either club could abide. These rejections just fueled my drive to succeed.

In late summer 2001, C.C. and the girls moved to Manhattan, into a homey brownstone near their new school. They were there on 9/11 when the planes crashed into the World Trade Center towers downtown. It was a Tuesday and their first day of school. When the authorities sealed the island of Manhattan, even closing the bridges and tunnels, it was temporarily impossible for some of their fellow students from the outer boroughs to get home. Two girls stayed with Simone and Isabella in their brand-new home. Five miles from Ground Zero, the terror of the attacks still reached them. The brownstone has an elevator, but when Simone heard on the news that people were trapped in elevators in the Twin Towers when they collapsed, she refused from then on to use hers.

Reunited in Paris with daughter Simone after a close call in terror attacks, November 2015.

Fourteen years later, Simone had a closer, more personal encounter with terror. She was studying abroad in Paris in November 2015 and attending a high-profile soccer match, Germany vs. France, in the *Stade de France*, when three suicide bombers blew themselves up outside. French president Francoise Hollande was also at the game. Like all the spectators, he was unhurt by the blasts. Some of Simone's school friends were trampled and injured in the stampede that followed the evacuation of the stadium. Other Parisian venues suffered far worse. There were scores of casualties in coordinated attacks that stunned the world.

It is ironic that Simone's near miss from terrorist violence happened in Paris. There was a standing joke in our family. I traveled to and from desolate, violent Afghanistan so often that a flamboyant friend of ours, real estate broker to the stars Robby Brown, once told C.C., "Geraldo must like it there," (in Afghanistan). "I prefer Paris," was C.C.'s punch line, always getting a laugh when she repeated the story. "But Geraldo doesn't because there's no war there."

Then Islamic extremism reached even the City of Light, twice in one year, 2015. In January, seventeen were killed in and around Paris during an attack on the offices of the satirical magazine *Charlie Hebdo* and the three-day murder spree that followed. Then, in November, it happened again, when our own daughter was nearly touched by the horror.

Despite various close calls over the years as a war correspondent, nothing rattled me as much as the uncertainty and helpless feeling of having a child in distress. Simone and three of her friends were marooned outside the stadium, located in a shady part of Paris, after the bomb blasts. The stadium doors were locked once the frantic crowds were emptied out. The Metro subway was shut down, and all the hotels and restaurants in the area locked their doors. The bodies of 132 innocent civilians lay in street cafés and in the landmark Bataclan Theater.

Paris was reeling and it took us an hour of frantic calling around before we got in touch with a savvy Parisian friend of friends who managed to extricate my darling girl and her companions. I was on the air live with my friend and colleague Shepard Smith during the ordeal, and millions watched as my terrified family dealt with the crisis of uncertainty in the midst of the panic and chaos of the massive attack. Few stories generated more statements of concern from viewers than Simone's plight

My three daughters on holiday in London after Simone's close call in Paris, November 2015.

in Paris; total strangers taking time to email or otherwise let us know they were relieved she was safe and unharmed.

CHASING THE FOX, SEPTEMBER 2001

Roger Ailes created Fox News in 1996, asking me early on to come over to see what he was doing, which I did as a courtesy. It did not look like much. In a huge empty basement space that used to be a discount drug store, he used his arms to describe what would be where in his world news headquarters. There were disconnected wires, unassembled desks, and eager, bleary-eyed kids running around, and I told him maybe later. I was in the middle of reporting the O.J. Simpson murders, the crime story of the century, and ratings at CNBC were soaring.

Despite that success, by 2001, a broad range of issues from patriotism to nepotism, pride and hubris, and the periodic need for chaos in my life fueled the decision to leave NBC News and join Roger at Fox News. By then, his headquarters had been built, and he was in the process of making the conservative news channel a competitive force. CNN was clinging to its status as the number-one-rated cable news channel, but barely. Fox was in second place, coming on strong.

Smoldering from the refusal of NBC News in that pre-9/11 era to count me among its top correspondents, I felt that the big money the network was paying me did not seem enough. The stage set, the immediate catalyst to leave came on the day al Qaeda attacked the United States, crashing hijacked airliners into the Twin Towers in New York, the Pentagon in Arlington, Virginia, and into a field near Shanksville, Pennsylvania.

The events of that day were shocking and traumatic for every American in different ways for different reasons. My trauma was nothing compared to so many others'. Still, it left a scar. Erica and I were in Malibu. Longtime sidekick Greg Hart called shortly after 6 AM Pacific Time and told me to put on the *Today* show. As soon as I saw the horrifying sight of the towers burning, I tried frantically to arrange travel back to New York to the girls, but nearby airports were all closed and would remain so for days.

Commentators were speculating on the probability of further attacks, and the world was coming to grips with the fact that everything had just changed. Usually paradise, Malibu was hell on this wrenching day.

Initially unable to reach my daughters on the phone or to get back, I felt as if God was punishing me for every sin I'd ever committed, including leaving our family behind. Frustrated, I was desperate to hear from Isabella, then age eight, and Simone, almost seven, both stuck in stricken Manhattan. I tried repeatedly to get through, but the phones were either disabled or overloaded.

I called the NBC News desk, suggesting that since I was stuck on the West Coast I should go to LAX to report on the situation there. The airport was the intended destination of the four doomed planes, and it made sense to report on the grieving families of passengers and crews. They noted my volunteering ("Thanks, Geraldo, we'll keep it in mind"), but told me lead anchor Tom Brokaw was personally managing all NBC coverage.

Riddled with guilt, I was fuming and about to blow. It got horrifyingly worse when I heard from my sister Sharon, who told me what had befallen our New Jersey neighbors. She was head of ad sales for the local weekly newspaper I published there, the *Two River Times*, based in Red Bank. Sharon told me that when the towers went down, the calamity took many of our friends with them. Our Middletown, New Jersey, area was devastated. Many of the dead were executives from Cantor Fitzgerald, the big financial firm headquartered on the top floors of the North Tower of the Trade Center. Cantor Fitzgerald lost 658 of its 960 New York employees. Some had kids in Rumson Country Day School, the New Jersey school the girls had left before their move to Manhattan. At least six school dads were missing and presumed dead.

When the smoke and rubble cleared and the bodies at the Trade Center were counted, the area had the highest per capita toll of any community outside Lower Manhattan; 135 of our friends and neighbors lost their lives in the attacks. Later I was proud to join two other dads from the school, Bruce Springsteen and Jon Bon Jovi, in helping host a benefit concert at Red Bank's Count Basie Theatre.

Aside from their boundless talent, these two men were stalwarts of the community, often performing for surprised fans and worthy causes, usually unannounced. That night at Count Basie and in many subsequent events, they helped steady the community and build its resolve to help one another. Bruce's song "The Rising" became America's anthem of recovery and resolve to right this terrible wrong.

"DADDY, I KNOW KIDS WHOSE DADDIES ARE DEAD!" SEPTEMBER 2001

I wrote in the next week in the *Two River Times* about how the attacks destroyed everyone's peace of mind, including little Simone's:

"'Daddy, I know kids whose daddies are dead!' she told me when I finally got through on the phone. How do you respond when a statement so fraught with anxiety and alarm bursts from the lips of your kid? What do you say to comfort your child under these circumstances?" Feeling that I had deserted my children in their time of need, I felt guilt wash over me.

I do not mention my two sons in this context because they were spectators to this particular chapter of our tumultuous family life. Cruz, who was born in Dallas and educated at St. Mark's School of Texas there until tenth grade, was with his mom and stepdad living in Portland, Oregon, when 9/11 happened. Gabriel, then twenty-two years old, was commuting between his mom's home in Los Angeles and mine in New Jersey, trying to decide on a career path involving computers. He was with his friends in Brooklyn when the world changed, watching the tortured Lower Manhattan skyline from across the East River in Williamsburg, as shocked and disoriented as the rest of us.

As I wrote at the time: "Now the Two River community and Americans everywhere will have to deal with the awful reality that people we knew and loved and laughed with and attended parents' day with and went to cocktail parties with and stood on the sidelines watching soccer games with are gone.

"They are gone before their time. They are gone despite all the sit-ups and jogging and annual check-ups and careful estate planning and the kids' college funds and the clear career paths and the retirement dreams. Our hearts cannot bear the thought of the pain and loss of those children. Their fathers or mothers are gone with the wind of terror and dismay."

My anger, anxiety, and frustration got worse because there was to be no *Rivera Live* from L.A. or anywhere else on September 11. Shortly after my conversation with the assignment desk offering to go to LAX, I got a call from my Fort Lee staff telling me Tom Brokaw's newscast would be airing simultaneously on all three NBC channels, preempting all programming on both MSNBC and CNBC, including mine.

It was clear the network's coverage of the war on these terrorists was not going to include me in any significant way. I was cut out of the biggest story of our time. Over the next few weeks, as other enterprising war correspondents were already making their way to the battle zones, I paced, filling with impatient rage.

A message I wrote during that week to my dear friend Kevin Overmeyer, then captain of *Voyager*, sums up my emotions. The boat was in dry dock being refitted in Trinidad, West Indies, for its journey back to her Hudson River mooring off my new home in Edgewater, New Jersey.

I wrote Captain Kevin: "The losses are wicked bad for NYC. 343 firemen alone! It's fucking awful. So many funerals and memorials, it's like the Blitz during WWII. I hate the mother fuckers who did this and so does the whole country. Everybody's also scared things will never be the same again. The view from the dock here in Edgewater feels amputated now. Remember, the towers used to be framed by the kitchen window. Now it feels like a gravestone."

MS. ELLE'S, NOVEMBER 2001

To its credit, the Peacock Network agreed reluctantly to let me leave. I told NBC I was leaving one way or the other, but the network was reasonably gracious. Because the show was so important to CNBC's prime-time lineup, they asked for more time to produce a substitute. I resisted, but Roger insisted that I leave NBC on good terms and with a signed release, so I stayed two more months, deep into November. It was a long goodbye that ended on the day of my farewell party at Ms. Elle's.

The city was shaken and smoldering in the wake of the 9/11 attacks. The mass grave of nearly three thousand friends and neighbors was still being exhumed a couple of miles downtown. And I was heading off to Afghanistan to cover the just and popular war to punish the perpetrators and impose restorative justice.

On the social scale of hipster New York, my November 2001 going-away party at Ms. Elle's Restaurant on West Seventy-Ninth Street was a career high point. In a life that was no stranger to parties, this was a milestone. It had a seriousness of purpose that made it more important than other rowdier but less-focused celebrations.

The ambience at the party was somewhere between kamikaze fatalism and Irish wake. I vowed to bathe in glory or die trying. I conflated various clichés, invented others, and came up with my own epitaph:

Evil Heart's Bane
Wild Song Sustained
No Pain, No Gain
No Guts, No Glory.

I told Erica, brother Craig, and all my confidants that I wanted it inscribed on my tombstone. Still do, although at this last stage of an increasingly enfeebled life it seems silly and pretentious. Erica joked that it sounds like a stoner's epitaph, more Stan Lee than Joseph Conrad. Back then, a grim, dramatic time, the whole country was in my corner. It felt like everyone I had ever known from ABC, NBC, and the talk-show days packed my favorite joint that night, that dim, usually gloomy dive on West Seventy-Ninth Street off Broadway.

The place has since closed, but at the time, three lesbians, who took turns cooking and tending bar, owned it. What their joint lacked in flash or décor, it made up for in vibe that night. It was exactly the place, and exactly the emotion-laden moment, I craved and envisioned when giving up the CNBC job. Professional respectability beckoned, and even the possibility of a martyr's death covering righteous combat was a small price to pay for immortality.

As in the Willowbrook days of my youth, everyone was cheering. In this normally cynical, skeptical town, for ten minutes New Yorkers suspended disbelief. Mocking chatter about my tabloid excesses was replaced by reluctant acceptance that I was leaving a safe, lucrative job to risk life and limb for God and country. The *New Yorker* magazine ran a cartoon showing two mujahideen fighters ducking bullets in an Afghan foxhole, one saying to the other, "I hear Geraldo Rivera is coming."

Not everyone was applauding. Speaking for the snots on *SNL*, Tina Fey said, "I hope nothing bad happens to Geraldo in Afghanistan or I'll have to pretend to be sad." I hated it, but it was a funny line, and she is in the business of making fun of people. Her impression of Sarah Palin during the 2008 presidential campaign is among the best ever of anybody. Still, in 2016, when her Afghan-set war movie *Whiskey Tango Foxtrot* bombed, laying a rotten egg at the box office, I experienced a few seconds of gloating, thinking that what goes around comes around.

Roger hired me as a war correspondent for $2 million a year, plus the nice Fort Lee office. I also got to take my two long-time, skeptical, eyebrows raised, take-no-prisoner secretary/assistants: JoAnn Torres Conte, a loyal, street-smart Bronx Puerto Rican who was married to a Bronx Italian cop, and Sharon Campbell, a competent, confident, don't-mess-with-me-either African American. Plus, I got first-class travel. I know that's a sweet deal in real life, but it was just 40 percent of the money I was making at NBC and a fraction of the fat talk-show years. I told Roger that the opportunity to go to war against the 9/11 terrorists was worth the sacrifice, but asked if he couldn't sweeten the pot a bit to ease the pain. He said he could not give me any more cash because in the time since he had first offered me a job several years before, he had "given all the money to O'Reilly."

Chapter 4

AFGHANISTAN AND THE
DEVIL'S WORKSHOP

In the two months following the September 11th attacks, allied air forces were pounding al Qaeda and the Taliban government of Afghanistan, pushing them everywhere in retreat. The pro-American Northern Alliance was advancing under the cover of those withering coalition air strikes, and Kabul, the capital, was about to fall. A Taliban commander was quoted as saying the American planes were "destroying everything metal."

My highly anticipated, widely hyped Fox News job finally began on Friday, November 16, 2001, but modestly and close to home. It required just a trip over the George Washington Bridge to the big Sunni mosque in Paterson, New Jersey. The story focused on something that had irked my old/new boss, Roger Ailes, since the attacks: what he saw as the disturbing lack of mainstream US Muslim outrage at al Qaeda and 9/11.

Many conservative Americans especially could not shake the suspicion that in millions of Muslim living rooms around the world, including a handful in the United States, viewers cheered as the towers fell. Later, as a presidential candidate, Donald Trump alleged that "thousands" of American Muslims had done exactly that, cheered as the towers fell. No videotape ever surfaced to prove it happened, because it never did. Candidate Trump was widely disparaged for insisting he saw it on TV, but if you were inclined to believe it happened regardless of the lack of videotape, then Trump was just telling it like it was.

That is the real point. Whether it is factually accurate to say there is relatively little mainstream Muslim outrage at acts of terror committed against American and other Western, Judeo-Christian targets by Muslim extremists, there is no doubt that is the perception held by many, and not just nut-job racists. Truth or fiction, race loyalty continues to be a gnawing, if distasteful and generally avoided, issue leading to the vilification of millions of innocent Muslims who just want productive, peaceful lives. Every attack committed by a Muslim who seemed an otherwise integrated member of society in the United States or Europe drags the issue back to center stage. In the US it is most often brought up in conservative Christian or Jewish circles, and by iconoclastic, button-pushing TV hosts like Bill Maher or Sean Hannity, although it is fair to say that the underlying sentiment probably helped fuel the Trump rebellion and led him to the White House, and his attempts to ban Muslim immigrants

Have Arabic-speaking, American-based Muslim leaders been sufficiently critical of extremism in their Arab-language sermons? I have not seen any deep study that revealed divided loyalties, neither do I recall intense public Muslim-American outrage and condemnation. Privately, it is much different. Many Muslim friends from all walks of life expressed acute distress to me at how the World Trade Center attacks, the mass murders committed in the name of Allah by Muslim maniacs at Fort Hood, San Bernardino, Orlando, Paris, Nice, Berlin, Istanbul, and much more recently in Manhattan itself are negatively impacting their lives. It is not fair to question all Muslims for the acts of the few, yet that is our new reality.

Several friends fret and fear reprisal by jerk-offs who blame the entire religion for every Islamist attack. The fear and loathing is so widespread, some relatively secular friends tell me they want to convert, just to avoid the communal blame. One mom wants her twelve-year-old, blond, blue-eyed son to convert at least nominally to Christianity because "it is just too much of a burden for a child to carry," which is disturbingly reminiscent of other waves of religion-blaming in the previous century. President Trump's executive orders sixteen years later, which, after court challenges, were ultimately allowed to ban some refugees from seven majority-Muslim countries, renewed their 2001 angst. It reminds me of how my father, Cruz Rivera of Bayamón, Puerto Rico, worried that we would be sullied and blamed every time a Puerto Rican committed a notorious crime.

A prominent Muslim-American businessman named Mansoor Ijaz accompanied us on that first Fox News assignment to the Paterson mosque. Hardly typical of the mosque's congregants, Mansoor is a highly connected, politically conservative, bon vivant, hedge-fund entrepreneur with a natty mustache and snappy suit, and he is not ambivalent about extremism, which he vigorously condemns. Erica and I later attended his lavish wedding at a seaside villa in Monaco.

We entered the New Jersey mosque in time for the religious service. It was filled for Friday prayers by a kneeling, shoeless sea of obviously devout parishioners. There are more than four million Muslims in America, many of whom are African-American, either converts or families belonging to sects like the Nation of Islam. The crowd in this mosque was pure South Asian, mostly young Pakistanis, many of them cab/limo driver/working class.

After commenting on camera about the lack of communal outrage, Mansour began his ritual prayers as Craig and I taped the service. We were being watched and were cordially but cautiously welcomed with the combination of warmth and hesitancy that has characterized my relationship with scores of Muslims overseas, east of Suez in the years since the clash of civilizations began. The congregants seemed wary and worried about what I was thinking. Was I painting them with the broad brush of collective guilt? In any case, I did not find anyone at that New Jersey mosque who cheered the 9/11 attacks. Instead, it was their discomfort and fear of guilt by association that was the angle of my unremarkable premiere report.

KILLING REPORTERS, NOVEMBER 2001

We flew out the next day, Saturday, November 17, flying United Airlines to London, where we rendezvoused with more Fox personnel heading to the war. Staying at the old Conrad Hotel near the Thames River, we ate fish and chips at a neighborhood pub and got drunk on endless pints of beer, figuring it was for the last time in a long time. Pakistan Airways, my least favorite, is dry all the way to Islamabad.

We arrived in the Pakistani capital Monday morning, greeted by the news that several Western reporters had just been killed in Afghanistan. It was the subject of my first report from the field for my new network, from a satellite set up on the roof of the relatively upscale Marriott Hotel near the US Embassy in what is called the Blue Zone of the capital. It is a super-secure neighborhood that was nevertheless eventually penetrated by suicide bombers later in the war.

The appearance was live at 4 PM local time, 6 AM in New York, for *Fox & Friends*, the long-running number-one-rated cable morning show, which later became President Trump's favorite. I have been on every Friday of every working week since that November 2001. In that first appearance, I followed a report from the White House quoting President Bush as saying, "The noose is beginning to narrow" around our enemies.

After being welcomed to the network via satellite by hosts Steve Doocy, Brian Kilmeade, and E.D. Hill in New York, I told them the shocking news. "We are receiving confirmed but sketchy reports that a convoy of journalists has been attacked on the road between Kabul and Jalalabad, Afghanistan. We believe four are dead." We had learned that the four slain reporters were taken out of their vehicles, robbed, beaten, and murdered.

I reported:

Here's what we know about the journalists' murders. A roving band of brigands, [who were] probably defeated local Taliban soldiers desperate for money and filled with rage, have added homicide to their existing long list of war crimes.

A gunman boasted to a survivor, "You think the Taliban are finished. We are still in power and we will have our revenge."

The murders of the reporters early in the Afghan War are a forgotten precursor of better-known atrocities involving journalists later. They set the stage for the videotaped butchering of Daniel Pearl, Steve Sotloff, James Foley, and the other reporters tortured and beheaded by al Qaeda, ISIS, and other Sunni Muslim extremists.

The World Association of Newspapers condemned the Taliban attacks as "outrageous and barbaric," as Reuters confirmed that two of the dead and defiled were their own, Harry Burton and Azizullah

Afghanistan, November 2001.

We traveled in a caravan of journalists and security
guards into Afghanistan. November 2001.

Haidari. The others were Julio Fuentes of Spain's *El Mundo* newspaper and a woman, Maria Grazia Cutuli, who was reporting for Italy's *Corriere della Sera*.

Coming as they did a week after five other Western journalists were attacked by the Taliban while riding a tank up in Bamyan Province, leaving three killed, it looked like an all-out war had been declared on journalists.

Those three dead were Pierre Billard of Radio Luxembourg; Volker Handloik, a German freelancer; and another intrepid woman, Johanne Sutton of Radio France International. Female war reporters in my experience are gutsy and skilled, and Islamist extremists cut them no slack. The two journalists to survive that earlier attack were Australian Paul McGeough and another woman, Véronique Rebeyrotte of France.

Because none of those killed was American, these war crimes gained little attention in the States. But their deaths weighed heavily on our minds, heading up that same bad road. After months of anticipation, horror and glory were finally close at hand.

Craig Rivera in our first Afghan hotel, where the talk
was of slain journalists. November 2001.

WAR-ZONE HOTELS, A RISKY BUSINESS, NOVEMBER 2001 TO 2012

Since there were no flights landing in war-ravaged Kabul in those early days, the Islamabad Marriott was the staging place for correspondents heading by land convoy through the Khyber Pass into Afghanistan.

What I remember most about the hotel from my various stays over the years was that, like Pakistan Airways, it was dry except for infidels like us who were allowed to drink in a small, windowless hotel lounge that felt like an asylum. On the lone lounge TV, a satellite channel from India continuously ran an R-rated version of Fashion TV, featuring scantily clad lingerie models, heightening the feeling that our hosts considered us perverts.

Any Muslim attempting to use the wet room was reported to the police. This strict prohibition gave me an outsized bad feeling that this was a brave new incarnation of Islam that was further from Western civilization than ever. I cannot say the anti-modern drinking ban foreshadowed everything bad about the Islamic world, from improvised explosive devices to beheadings, but it was quick proof they play by different rules out east.

Craig and I on the banks of the Kabul River, scene of historic massacres. December 2001.

With Manny, keeper of the Fox News safe house. Kabul, Afghanistan, September 2002.

Even the hotel's professed sobriety for Muslim guests was not protection enough. A truck bomb blew it up in 2008. Fifty-four died and 266 were wounded in that attack when the façade was torn off in a tremendous explosion that left a crater where the front entrance had been.

In fact, many of my favorite hotels have been blown up or shot up over the years, some multiple times. I have considered doing a guidebook of high-end places to stay in wartime, such as the Commodore or Phoenicia Inter-Continental, both savaged in fierce fighting in Beirut 1975–76, and the five-star-rated Serena in Kabul, which was attacked in 2008 and again in 2014. The Inter-Continental in Kabul got savagely hit in January 2018. Americans, including Glenn Selig, a former investigative reporter for Tampa's Fox 13, were among the twenty-two slaughtered when five gunmen dressed as Afghan government soldiers gained access. Security was so shaky in some of our hotels that I often slept with a chair wedged against the room door. Ultimately, we gave up on hotels altogether, preferring our own network safe house.

Fortunately, none of our accommodations was ever attacked with me in it. Still, I have a recurring dream of being caught in bed by a nighttime attack. The only hotel invasion dreams that end happily are those when I am packing a weapon, which is prohibited by the one ethical rule of journalism that I consider dopey and out-of-date.

KHYBER PASS, NOVEMBER 2001

We joined a caravan of journalists and security guards from various media outlets, heading first to Peshawar, the last outpost of relative civilization in Pakistan, before entering the lawless Tribal Territories and then the Khyber Pass, doing satellite reports along the way. I say relative civilization because Peshawar to this day exists on the edge of anarchy. In 2014, terrorists killed 145 people in an attack on a school there. Most of the dead were children.

My urgent worry that Tuesday, November 20, 2001, was the same as at my farewell party at Ms. Elle's earlier in the month: Would the war be over before I got there?

Organized Taliban resistance was collapsing all across Afghanistan. In a phenomenon unique to warfare, Afghan forces were allowing most Taliban fighters to just go home if they promised informally to stop fighting. It was one reason we failed then to catch Osama bin Laden or his closest allies in the senior Taliban leadership.

As I reported: "Mullah Omar, the Taliban supreme leader thought about to yield power in return for immunity, now says he had a prophetic dream in which he's been told he'll remain in power for as long as he lives. Of course that could be five years or five days." (It turned out to be twelve years. Omar outlived his pal Osama bin Laden, dying in hiding in Pakistan in April 2013 of tuberculosis, according to various Afghan and Pakistani sources. The $10 million bounty the U.S. State Department had placed on his head in 2001 went uncollected. Because Omar had become so central to the Taliban resistance to the American occupation, his death was kept secret until 2015.)

I continued that report from the field in 2001: "Elsewhere in Afghanistan it is painfully clear now that our military successes have left a huge and dangerous power vacuum. Chaos rules the countryside. Roving bands of defeated Taliban troops are reportedly turning to freelance murder and robbery," as evidenced by the killings of the four journalists the day before.

"Anti-Taliban fighters from the Northern Alliance are reportedly pursuing the perpetrators of that hideous crime."

On the road from Peshawar to the Khyber Pass we got word from Nancy Harmeyer, then coordinating producer, via satellite phone from Islamabad that in response to President Bush's announcement of a $25 million dollar reward for the capture "dead or alive" of Osama bin Laden, the Taliban had placed a $100,000 cash bounty "on the head of each journalist."

The news we were being targeted stirred fear and impatience. I urged our team to hurry toward the pass. Like caviar or champagne, Khyber is one of those realities that lives up to our imagining. It inspires anxiety and awe no matter how many times I have driven through. Part of the Silk Road, one of the ancient world's most important trade routes, the pass itself is a steep cut in the Spin Ghar Mountains, foothills of the mighty Hindu Kush. It consists of a narrow, curving, mostly dirt road with often deadly drop-offs into the abyss.

Aside from invaders, smugglers, refugees, and drug dealers, "jangle trucks" crowd the narrow roadway. They are usually battered but gaily decorated cargo and tanker vehicles festooned with bells and jingle-jangles. Pashtun tribesmen drive them hard and fast, seemingly oblivious to the impossibly dangerous cliffs and curves.

But getting through the pass did not mean we were out of Pakistan. We drove uneventfully through Landi Kotal, the town at the summit, but at the bustling border town of Torkham, a substantial Pakistani military presence prevailed. Heavy Soviet-era tanks, armored personnel carriers (APCs), and combat troops were everywhere arrayed. All was vigilance and bureaucracy.

To schmooze us through, we hired a Pashtun tribesman, a member of the Shinwari clan, which holds sway along much of the ordinarily porous border. Akbar Shinwari, who became my friend for life, was then twenty-two years old. He guided me in negotiations with local border authorities, an ordinarily easy task he had done dozens of times before the war. But even his efforts on our behalf were in vain this first time. We were informed that the road was too dangerous, and that since the deaths of the journalists, Pakistan was no longer permitting foreigners to cross.

We were further informed that the decision to close the border had been made at the highest levels of the Pakistani government. I was frantic. After all the hype and buildup, to be turned away from Afghanistan now would be a crushing blow. We spent hours in panicked communications with our base in Islamabad, trying to finesse ourselves across. It took thirteen hours of cajoling and about $4,000 in payments to various authorities to buy our way in. Buying our way to the scene of the slaughter, how sick is that? The money was officially a "fee"; still, in the far reaches of the civilized world, cash and muscle often talk louder than legitimate process. When the reach of order and government fades into chaos and savagery, you sometimes have to pay for protection and access.

We were relieved to be finally on the Afghan side. Once we got there, everybody else was leaving. A miles-long line of refugees was waiting, desperate to escape from Afghanistan into Pakistan. In disasters natural and man-made, this is a common occurrence. Journalists are a kind of first-responders, going in when everyone else is trying to get out.

I reported: "Once through the border area, the pass widens into parched plains that show the ravages of years of drought and war. The two have conspired to create a nation of refugees scratching out a meager life on the side of the road."

Later, "Closer to our first destination, the recently liberated Afghan city of Jalalabad, we saw something even more melancholy than the refugees fleeing the war. It was the Red Cross convoy carrying the bodies of three of the four journalists killed by Taliban thugs on Monday morning." New York told us we were the first to confirm the atrocity on the air; our first sad scoop, such as it was.

Driving the dusty road from the Khyber Pass to Jalalabad, Afghanistan, November 2001.

SPINGHAR HOTEL, NOVEMBER 2001

We arrived at Jalalabad on Wednesday morning, November 21. Working for Fox News for just five days, I was already at the end of the earth, a swaggering, mustachioed Walter Mitty. Walking through the main bazaar, I found it surprising how little time it had taken for the city to return to market bustle. Just a week before, the Taliban held sway here.

I also reported triumphantly how their collapse appeared nearly complete. "We made a monkey of their promise to fight to the last man," I gloated in mixed metaphorical splendor. Their military camps "must have looked like a big fat cherry pie from our satellites in space."

Heavy weapons were still as common on the streets of Jalalabad as Citi Bikes in New York. But something else was going on. While higher-ranking Taliban officials had disappeared into the parched and unforgiving Afghan landscape, many of their ordinary soldiers were simply switching sides, shifting allegiance with breathtaking suddenness. Sorting the good guys from the bad in that place is problematic to this day, as the bloody January 2018 attack by extremists wearing Afghan Army uniforms on the Inter-Continental attests..

We checked into the rundown Spinghar Hotel, a rambling, ramshackle building set in a dusty garden in the middle of a town where Osama bin Laden just weeks before had lived in comfort and relatively out in the open. Feeling like a movie set in the World War II era, the place was filled with gloomy, agitated war correspondents waiting to convoy up to Kabul. Ashleigh Banfield and Mike Taibbi of NBC News, both solid reporters, were the only ones I recognized in the group.

There was great urgency to get to Kabul because of the general feeling that the deadline was coming for the ultimate fight that would end the war. At this point it was thought to be just days away. But no team wanted to go it alone on that blood-soaked road.

The fact that four of the slain journalists were caught and killed just three days before, and on the exact same route we were about to travel from Jalalabad to Kabul, was deeply unsettling. Mullah Omar's bounty payable to any gunman who killed a Western journalist also weighed heavily. So did survivors' accounts that vividly recounted how the four killed were dragged from their vehicles and marched into the surrounding hills, where entire AK-47 magazines were emptied in each of their bodies.

The hotel was buzzing with dark tales of how the bodies had been defiled, some of them skinned, a horror that made me again wish I carried a gun. There was a makeshift memorial plaque mounted on the hotel wall nearest the garden, acknowledging the seven line-of-duty deaths. The murder of Maria Grazia Cutuli felt especially barbarous. The thought of the lovely Italian newswoman being dragged from her vehicle by fanatic brutes was enraging. It was another reason I wanted the Taliban and their terror masters to pay.

THANKSGIVING, NOVEMBER 2001

This was just the first of two dozen or so War on Terror–era holidays spent overseas in Afghanistan, Iraq, or some other desperate corner of the world during my eleven years as Fox News Senior War Correspondent. On another Thanksgiving two years later in 2003, I interviewed Senator Hillary Clinton at the Bagram Air Base in Afghanistan. When Hillary later got into a jam for allegedly exaggerating the danger she experienced visiting our troops in war-torn Bosnia, talking about snipers shooting at her and so forth, I came to her defense, saying that at least she had the guts to put herself in harm's way, unlike the vast majority of her safely desk-bound critics.

As much as I missed my family, especially the little girls, who, as I later wrote in my diary, "always hugged me so sincerely and sweetly when I went away," I did not mind missing holidays in the early years. From 2001 to 2012, contrary to my critics' assessment that I was borrowing reflected glory from our GIs, I considered myself a quasi-service member, representing another branch of the Armed Forces of the United States of America: war correspondent. There were deep personal reasons I sought this calling. Having dodged the draft during the Vietnam era, first getting married, then enrolling in law school, I had a gnawing guilty conscience that others went to war in my stead. I only assuaged that guilt in later life by getting as close to combat as possible. Beginning in Chile and Israel in 1973, then across battlefields in Asia, Africa, the Balkans, and Central and South America, I became what Ernest Hemingway in covering the Spanish Civil War called a "whore de combat," or war tourist. Actually, there was more to it than either guilt or glory. When the real warriors are on your side and need your editorial and emotional support, running into battle with war fighters is a virtuous undertaking. I used to revel in presenting live shows from forward-operating bases featuring scores of happy GIs beaming and sending messages home to loved ones watching. I just wish we had had some of our own GIs around at this crucial early time in Afghanistan, November and December 2001.

On this first Thanksgiving on this first assignment in Afghanistan, everyone staying at the Spinghar Hotel chipped in on a communal dinner featuring two winged creatures that were not turkeys. Whatever they were, the Fox News crew got screwed out of our share of the scrawny birds because we got back late from working our contacts in town.

Our first stop was to pay respects at the provincial palace to the recently installed Governor Haji Abdul Qadir, a courtly middle-aged gentleman dressed in traditional Afghan tribal garb.

Newly designated as my right-hand man, Akbar Shinwari advised me that Governor Qadir was an important man to know. After watching Akbar negotiate our way through Pakistan's impossible bureaucratic maze to get us across the border and into Afghanistan, I was learning to trust the young Pashtun implicitly, even with my life. But at the time, I had no idea how important Governor Qadir would be to getting me as close to Osama bin Laden as any American got until ten years later when the Navy SEALs killed the son of a bitch.

The governor was the brother of a renowned anti-Taliban fighter, Abdul Haq. Captured and executed by the Taliban during their desperate retreat in late 2001, Haq had been a border bandit and drug runner. Like most Afghan warlords fighting against the Taliban, Haq had done so for commercial rather than ideological reasons.

Tumultuous Afghanistan's what's-in-it-for-me nationalism even extended to the family that would soon rule the country, the Karzais. Hamid Karzai was little known outside his native city of Kandahar, but this scion of the most important Pashtun clan had the personal good fortune of being from a family opposed to the Taliban, probably for the same reason as Abdul Haq: The religious fanatics were bad for the drug business.

Karzai always struck me as an almost folkloric, though slippery, character. The one question I never asked him was who came up with the brilliant idea of wearing the green robe, which made him look like a Marvel superhero and gave him instant ethnic credibility. That personal style harkened back to the glory days of Afghan royalty. He was our golden boy at the moment, authentic and yet modern, symbolic of our evolving ambition regarding Afghanistan.

I have seen no proof directly linking him to drug trafficking. But after serving two terms, he is said to have left office in 2014 the richest man in the country, worth tens of millions. His brother Ahmed Wali Karzai was notorious, more American than Afghan, a hustler from Chicago with a stable of children and ex-wives left behind in the United States when the American-funded gold rush began in his native country. By the time a trusted bodyguard finally killed him in Afghanistan in July 2011, Wali had survived eight assassination attempts and was worth millions from drug dealing, bank looting, and CIA payoffs.

Before America declared them our enemy for harboring al Qaeda, the Taliban were the good guys. In early 2001 their religiously conservative, rigidly Islamic government won a United Nations citation for suppressing the opium trade, having reduced production from 4,500 tons before they took over in 1996 to just fifty tons in 2000. Six months before America began bombing the Taliban government of Afghanistan back to the Stone Age, our State Department awarded them $43 million as a reward for their anti-drug efforts.

The Taliban are nastier today than they were back when they were merely a savage and regressive government. They continue to host violent extremists, have totally embraced global Jihad and domestic barbarism, and have also abandoned that once-admirable abhorrence of drug trafficking. These days, it is how they fund their insurgency. The Taliban ranks now among the planet's most prolific dope dealers.

It is also true that our forces have been put in the painful and embarrassing position of effectively defending the opium crop. As I reported doing a "show-and-tell" years later in April 2010, from a gigantic poppy field in Helmand Province:

> So the deadly harvest has begun. The idea is they scrape these poppy bulbs, then the sap starts coming out and the sap that they collect, that is the opium paste. Then they package it in larger clumps. It looks like cow manure. But obviously it's much more deadly than that. It will soon be made into heroin for the junkies of Europe and the United States.

It is the most unintended and awkward consequence of our military offensive here in Afghanistan: The rout by our Marines of the Taliban from their former stronghold here in Helmand Province, has put us in the position of being protectors of the largest crop of opium in the world.

Geraldo Rivera: And how much is this field worth in Afghani money?

Afghan man (speaking in native language): Like a hundred thousand Afghanis.

Akbar Shinwari (translating): So about two thousand dollars.

Geraldo Rivera: So this field, when harvested, will reap for these farmers two thousand dollars?

Obviously there is no way on earth that this amount of wheat or cotton in a patch this small would reap that kind of money. That's the obvious economic incentive. That's why they plant the opium poppies, because of the value.

Ninety percent of the world's supply comes from this one Afghan province, enough poison easily to supply America's half a million junkies, and the almost three times that many in Europe.

Our Marine and allied bases have been located literally in the middle of poppy fields. When the plants bud prior to harvest, the deceptively pretty flowers carpet entire valleys. No beauty on earth is more evil.

Our commanders are ordered not to mess with the growing season for fear of further alienating the local populace by interrupting or interfering with their principal cash crop. It is depressing to see our young GIs camped in fields of opium that will soon be harvested and on its way to junkies everywhere.

ENEMY ON THE RUN, NOVEMBER 2001

In 2017, sixteen years after 9/11 and seven years after my exposé of the tragic and ridiculous proliferation of the poppy fields, the Marines would be dragged back into Helmand Province to suppress a resurgent Taliban, but in November 2001, the fresh, optimistic, early days of the war in Afghanistan, the enemy was everywhere on the run. Then acting governor Abdul Qadir granted us an immediate audience in his large, darkened office, which when the wall rugs were removed, overlooked the surprisingly resilient and orderly city of Jalalabad. Like the Karzais, the governor was just returned from five years' living in exile across the border in Pakistan.

He expressed misgivings about the prospects for long-term peace. What concerned him was that Taliban forces still loyal to their fugitive leader, Mullah Omar, were going underground and becoming either guerilla fighters or anarchist bandits motivated by greed or rage. This concern turned out to be prophetic.

The governor assigned two of his top military aides to show us around al Qaeda's abandoned facilities in Jalalabad. Both men could easily have been mistaken for enemy combatants. One was a rough-hewn veteran fighter named Misrullah, the other a tough-guy commander named Sohrab Qadir, who may have been related to the boss.

One apparent al Qaeda safe house was littered with personal items such as clothing and Jordanian passports. We also saw an abandoned grade school for the children of the terrorists. One of the most interesting extracurricular activities for the little tots was practice firing on their AK-47 target range, which I reported via satellite to the horrified Fox News audience.

The commanders and governor were of the opinion that bin Laden and his most hard-core Arab fighters were hiding out near the Afghan town of Asadabad, about forty-five miles from our current location and only eight miles from the Pakistani border. They told us his fighters were hard-pressed because winter weather was closing in on that mountainous region in Kunar Province, and they lacked warm clothing and appropriate footwear.

The commanders also mentioned reports claiming that on or around November 13, about ten days before we got to Jalalabad, Osama bin Laden hosted a dinner for his Pakistani, Arab, and other foreign volunteers in a

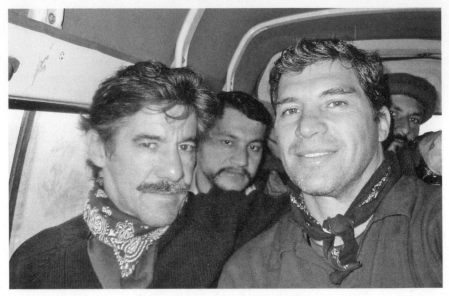

En route to Tora Bora, December 2001.

place not far from Asadabad, nestled in the White Mountains, a place called Tora Bora.

TORA BORA, I wrote the name in caps in my reporter's notebook, not realizing how much it would affect the rest of my life. Tora Bora, my recurring nightmare.

THE DEVIL'S WORKSHOP, NOVEMBER 2001

Back at the Spinghar Hotel, just after midnight on Thanksgiving night, we were all jarred awake by several huge explosions nearby. Every reporter in the building rushed outside to see the action. I reported via satellite that Friday, November 23:

> Just after midnight this morning, we were all jarred awake by a couple of nearby explosions. One of our guides [Akbar] who was awake at the time of the blasts reports seeing flashes of what seemed American fighter bombers firing two missiles each at bases bin Laden operated about three or four miles from here. The other strike was about twice that far away.

The story behind those attacks got really interesting when the Pentagon announced later that morning that they had targeted a chemical and biological weapons factory in our area the night before. As America tightened the grips on al Qaeda, finding their weapons of mass destruction (WMD) was our obsession—and this was way before Saddam Hussein stole their spotlight two years later. In the case of Afghanistan, the WMD were real. I know because we found them.

I noted, "Earlier the Associated Press reported that at an agricultural ministry lab they had found concentrated anthrax spores. Well, we found the rest of the Devil's Workshop."

Continuing: "The big fear with bin Laden has always been his pursuit of weapons of mass destruction: chemical, biological, even nuclear. So when the Pentagon announced that those nearby air strikes on Thanksgiving night were against a chemical and biological weapons factory, we decided to try to find the target ourselves."

With Akbar and several locals leading us toward the sounds of the explosions the night before, we found the area hit. Close to a vital dam being guarded by a lone anti-Taliban fighter, bomb craters showed the way to a medium-size al Qaeda safe house. Abandoned but undisturbed, it was filled with boxes of documents, including what could only be described as how-to-commit-terror manuals. Everything was intact, and aside from the doors being forced open, it was truly a complete Devil's Workshop.

Because it contained so many manuals for using the components to make weapons, we also called the place "Bomb U." Aside from the incriminating documents, I made a list of what we found jammed in vials, bottles, and cans inside the small wooden-framed building:

- potassium iodate, a treatment for radiation poisoning
- cyanide
- sodium hydrochloride, used to treat exposure to nerve gas
- highly concentrated hydrogen peroxide and lime, used for basic bomb making
- pure potassium, which explodes when it touches water
- hydrazine hydrate, also known as rocket fuel
- concentrated sulfuric acid, useful for poison gas, plus nitric acid, hydrogen, charcoal acetone, calcium carbonate, menthol, talc, dimenthylaniline, urea, dichloromethane, and ammonium nitrate

The find was significant for several reasons. First, and most obviously, it proved that al Qaeda was working actively to procure, manufacture, and deploy weapons of mass destruction for use in the region or abroad. The attacks of September 11, three months before, were obviously not intended as a onetime event, and the terrorists were working hard to get more bangs for their buck.

Second, the aerial assault intended to destroy the facility missed its target by a hundred meters or more. Worse, there was no follow-up on the ground. During the hours we spent there, no allied personnel came by to see if the target had been hit or even what it contained. It was shocking negligence on our part, bordering on incompetence. How could the Pentagon target a suspected chemical- and biological-weapons facility and then not send someone to see if they'd hit it?

Third, clearly by choosing not to commit ground forces to the fight, the Pentagon was missing a lot. Fighter-bombers zooming at 400–500 mph don't make the best collectors of data. Remember, this was before today's drone-centric warfare allowing remote pilots to read the color of a target's eyes.

This specific lapse, vaguely correct intelligence followed by a near miss on an announced target, was my first clear example of why the minimal boots-on-the-ground strategy devised by Defense Secretary Donald Rumsfeld and Commanding General Tommy Franks for the tediously named Operation Enduring Freedom was flawed. The worst example came later in Tora Bora with bin Laden's great escape, but there were miles to go between then and that.

It was hard for a reporter to be critical of or even less than enthusiastic about the way the Bush administration was waging this wildly popular war of revenge. In the super-heated, righteously patriotic, pro-war environment in the days following the Trade Center attacks, any correspondent, but especially a high-profile celebrity Fox News correspondent like me, quickly learned to stifle doubts about the war effort.

For example, I told the anchors debriefing me during the safe-house scoop that I just wished the Pentagon would send someone to my location to investigate the treasure trove of terror we had discovered. I wished out loud that we could take a duffel bag of the stuff we found here to someone who knew the score, who could define and describe the havoc that could be wreaked on America with these toxins and poisons. The only audience feedback I got were angry calls demanding to know why after just a week with Fox News I thought I could criticize the war effort or tell the Pentagon its business.

Because the story seemed so important, I was shocked when no other media picked up on it. This leads to my familiar refrain: If a *New York Times* reporter had found exactly the same stuff in the same place at the same time, it would have ignited a national discussion, and a special mention at a Foreign Correspondents Association award dinner.

The AP reporter mentioned it in passing to the others at dinner that night at the Spinghar Hotel, but that was it. Except for our video, the incident went unremarked, at least until other journalists found what was left of the safe house a day later. By then it had already been ransacked by the local people, debris strewn everywhere.

I am convinced that prejudice against the network and me personally played a role in that story being ignored. The barely contained hatred and jealousy directed at Fox News for years was laid bare much later, when the mainstream media machine led by CNN, MSNBC, and the *New York Times* unleashed their crusade to destroy the network, after the 2016 Ailes scandal. It angers me now, and it angered me then. Damn it, this discovery of the weapons factory was pure journalism, and it should have attracted positive attention and respect.

BLOOD ROAD, NOVEMBER 2001

The ride out of Jalalabad was tense as we drove the chewed-up main road as it follows the storied Kabul River, snaking through the harsh, drought-riddled landscape of high desert desolation. I am a history aficionado, so it was hard not to think of the countless ambushes and monstrous butchery that has happened along this narrow stretch over the ages.

In this land, Alexander the Great in 330 BC watched his veteran army be destroyed and scattered piece by piece by guerilla warfare, which the chronicler Plutarch described centuries later as a hydra-headed monster. Much like with the Taliban today, as soon as Alexander's formidable veterans cut off one arm of the beast, three more grew in its place. Aside from the ruins of many fortified communities all named Alexandria and strategically located throughout the region, the only lasting monument to the otherwise most successful military commander in history is a scattering of blue- and green-eyed Afghans.

Genghis Khan and his horde came conquering down from the northeast reaches of the Asian continent in 1219, and though they engaged in widespread slaughter, the Mongols didn't stick either. Khan's acolyte, the fearless Tamerlane, invaded in 1383, but even his mighty empire could not suppress the ferocious local tribes over time.

In the golden age of Queen Victoria's empire, on this same road between Jalalabad and Kabul, a British army was massacred in 1842. Afghan tribesmen wiped out Major General Sir William Elphinstone's entire column of 16,000, leaving only one Brit alive and free to tell the tale of cruelty, murder, and enslavement of survivors. Here too, the Soviet Union committed suicide in a disastrous 1979 invasion, which cost so much in lives and treasure that the fifteen-nation communist empire split apart under the stress.

Like Empress Victoria in the nineteenth century and Soviet General Secretary Leonid Brezhnev in 1979, President George W. Bush in 2001 should have read more Plutarch. More to the point, the descendants of the hydra-headed beast the Greek philosopher had aptly described two thousand years before were alive and slaughtering Western journalists, among many others.

Following in the literal footsteps of those dead reporters, it was hard not to be preoccupied with the threat. Our ten-car convoy had several vehicles filled with armed guards, mostly Pashtun tribesmen, like the Taliban, but with a sprinkling of Tajiks, the minority ethnic group, who mostly sided with our friends, the anti-Taliban Northern Alliance.

We had one Tajik fixer, a schoolteacher we called "Teacher." He and Akbar, who is Pashtun, hated each other. They were constantly squabbling, Hatfield vs. McCoy. Teacher even tried to get us to fire Akbar for disloyalty or incompetence, I forget which.

I would not hear of firing Akbar, of course. He had morphed in my mind from Gunga Din to honorable peer, competent and totally trustworthy sidekick, translator, and editorial, historical, and geographical guide. And while you might think that Rudyard Kipling reference demeaning, or worse, racist, Akbar would not. He is my brother from another mother, good-luck charm and friend for life. I was not going anywhere

On the road in Afghanistan, November 2001.

without him. He is of that brutal land and its demanding religion and fierce tribal loyalties. But I worried at the time that if his and Teacher's mutual antagonism was representative of the nation writ large, then it was hard to see how their respective ethnic groups would ever be able to work together.

Naturally, we were fearful of a military attack during the drive from Jalalabad to Kabul, but we also worried about robbery. Cash was king in the early months of the Afghanistan war. We were carrying over a hundred grand US in small bills. There was so much cash that some of it literally blew away. It happened when Alistair, our mannered British coordinating producer, a brave and resilient but clumsy chap, opened his stuffed sack to pay off some locals selling produce. It was like the scene in Woody Allen's *Annie Hall* when he sneezes and blows away his host's precious cocaine. Money blew everywhere, swirling inside the car, some of it blowing out the windows to be lost in the dust.

We also carried a bag full of Afghan currency, which had been plummeting in value since Operation Enduring Freedom began. It took years to recover, but back then it was trading at even less than the official rate of 73,000 Afghanis to one US dollar. At various giddy times during this initial odyssey, I tossed huge handfuls of bills to children begging by the roadside.

FREE KABUL, NOVEMBER 2001

When we got there, Kabul was a dusty beat-up typical medium-size South Asian capital city with a sprinkling of recent high-rises towering over badly constructed two- and three-story adobe buildings. The shabby, hazy city is surrounded by sharp peaks, snow covered and breathtaking 15,000-foot giants that are mere half-sized foothills leading up to their awesome cousins, the Himalayas, a thousand miles east. The frightened town was barely stirring back to life after the Taliban retreat in the face of a short but withering aerial assault from the US-led coalition.

Actually, the enemy did not put up a fight for the capital. There was no heroic rearguard action, nor was there even an invading army. The bad guys just left one night, disappearing into the countryside. It gave the profoundly false illusion that this was going to be easy.

We were staying at the Intercontinental. Set on a small rise overlooking the city, it is far and away the biggest building in town. It had no electricity, but it did have running water. I met CNN's admired foreign correspondent Christiane Amanpour at the front entrance. At the time she was the news network's ace and a rarity. Now, as I mentioned, with Arwa Damon and Lara Logan and others, brave female foreign correspondents have near parity in the overseas news business, often proving more enterprising and gritty than their male counterparts.

Christiane was their role model, and she was sincere and elegant at our meeting, despite the attempts by media writers to stir up trouble between us. During the long wait for my announced move from CNBC to Fox News to take effect, some columnists had tried to instigate an anticipatory rivalry. I was intent on showing her respect. We had a nice conversation and went on to report the Afghan War our own ways, never crossing paths until Baghdad, Iraq, and another war two years later.

Checking into the disordered, barely functioning hotel, our crew met up with our Fox News colleagues, reporter Steve Harrigan and his intrepid cameraman, Joel Fagan, already on location.

Steve had been covering Afghanistan for CNN when his contract ran out that October. In his typically bold and clever fashion, Roger Ailes then out-hustled CNN, recruiting and signing Steve on the spot, thus giving us an instant, experienced presence at the heart of the story in these dramatic early days of the war.

Atlanta-based Joel, Steve's cameraman partner, incredibly had hiked in from the neighboring country of Tajikistan, in a heroic, grueling, dangerous five-day test that involved bumming rides on any available transport and literally walking much of the way through war-shattered countryside. He had been working nonstop since the first weeks of the war and welcomed us as necessary reinforcements. CNN, on the other hand, had a massive presence, with at least five crews in-country already.

The one meal I remember the battered hotel cafeteria staff preparing was an omelet. I was pleasantly surprised by the presence of eggs but was grossed out along with everyone at our table when I started eating my omelet, cooked in the filthy kitchen, and bit into something hard. I drew the thing out of my mouth the way you would draw out an offending but not particularly gross piece of pasta. Eyewitnesses report how I did not realize what it was until the bitter end when my mouth exploded, spitting frantically in disgust. It was a giant rat tail.

AL QAEDA POWs, NOVEMBER 2001

In Kabul, the most gut-wrenching story was the prisoner-of-war camp on the outskirts of town. In a cluster of perhaps a half dozen otherwise empty shipping containers, at least a hundred or more non-Afghan prisoners, mostly Arabs, were packed shoulder-to-shoulder inside. They were slowly baking. With no light, fresh air, or water, the foreign captives from Jordan, Chechnya, and elsewhere were bedraggled, beat up, hot, and thirsty. It was clear that the Afghans considered these foreign fighters dead already, grist for the savage mill. Their treatment was a mini-version of the 1915 Armenian Christian Death March; in a matter of days these prisoners would all be dead.

Rather than complain to someone in authority about the inhumane conditions under which the condemned prisoners were being kept, I instead yelled questions into their dirt-caked faces about why they killed our innocent civilians on 9/11.

A few defiant ones angrily tried to answer, which gave me a bad feeling about the war not ending anytime soon. The hatred inside these doomed fighters portended an enemy committed to a long struggle. Willing or not, the Afghan people were in for some major suffering, and so were our GIs and taxpayers.

That Saturday night, November 24, in Kabul, the interim government consisting of the Northern and Eastern Alliances and other regional and ethnic forces, and now calling itself the United Front, paraded out a former Taliban minister, a turban-wearing cleric named Mullah Khaksar, who was changing sides.

At a packed address to gathered tribesmen, the mullah announced that America's campaign against terror was "a good thing" and that he was throwing his support to the Front "to save" Afghanistan. As I noted at the time, "The news wasn't that the rat was deserting the sinking ship, but that the United Front was letting him."

Resistance was crumbling as the Front surged everywhere. The Taliban and its extremist allies were in total retreat. Sunday morning, November 25, we walked around dirty, exhausted Kabul. Much of its former bustle was back, "but street bustle aside, this is a ruined city in a wrecked country," I reported.

Winter was coming, food was scarce, shops and schools were closed. Highlighting the devastation, I reported, "Look what Osama bin Laden has wrought. To kill four thousand of us he has cost his allies the Taliban their country. He has led his thousands of loyalists to grotesque deaths or harrowing imprisonment, and he has made himself the world's most hunted man."

At this late stage, pockets of violence continued only around Kandahar in the west and Kunduz in the north, where the end of fighting seemed near. In addition, there were those persistent, unconfirmed reports of al Qaeda making a last stand back down near Jalalabad. With the option of heading anywhere, we chose Kunduz.

Joel and Steve bent over backward to help us prepare to chase whatever remained of the active fighting in the north. At my request, Joel hooked me up with a local guy who sold me a loaded Soviet-era Makarov 9mm semiautomatic pistol with a shoulder holster and bandolier filled with extra ammo. After all, my hero Ernest Hemingway carried a submachine gun during World War II's Battle of the Bulge. This fight was a fraction of that epic, existential struggle, but it was dangerous enough. We were just getting word of another murder earlier that day of another journalist, Swedish TV4 cameraman Ulf Strömberg, right where we were going in Kunduz. He was the eighth Western journalist killed in two weeks.

In that tense climate and heading north toward the scene of the crime, I mused on the air about wanting "to go down fighting" if someone tried

A local guy sold me a Russian-made Makarov 9mm, which I carried after eight reporters were killed. November 2001.

to jack us. "It's going to be a gunfight, not a murder," I half-jested during one live shot, thus beginning a controversy that would fester from Kunduz to Tora Bora.

HEADING NORTH, NOVEMBER 2001

From Kabul it was a haul to get to what was left of the active ground combat several hundred miles north of the capital. We left on a beat-up, 1970s-era, Soviet-built Mi-8 helicopter provided by the Tajik-dominated Northerners in the United Front. We were heading for the fighting just as it was reaching its climax around Kunduz.

If we had had GoPro or iPhones in those days, we could have been a Nat Geo reality show. Aside from courage, drive, equipment, connections, and sources, war reporting requires logistical enterprise. You need stamina and initiative. Sometimes the journey to get to the story is the most interesting part of the job. Over the years, brother Craig, Greg Hart, and I have come to the conclusion that we are far more likely to die at the hands of our own overenthusiastic pilots or drivers than from enemy fire. You have not lived until a buckaroo at the controls of a hot-rod Black Hawk helicopter does flips trying to impress or scare you.

But the rule is that you can never show fear to those pilots or drivers, or get sick. That just encourages the swashbucklers. What you do is whoop and holler joyfully at their maneuvers until they realize you are just as willing to go down with the ship for a thrill as they are. We all got to go sometime.

Our two-man chopper crew flying out of Kabul was not into aeronautical antics. Russian, maybe Chechen, I did not check, they had their hands full just making the drooping old bird fly. Their aged helicopter was so shabby and overloaded we thought our odyssey had an excellent chance of ending before it began.

In addition to the crew, the chopper was stuffed with eight of us, plus our massive pile of gear and a huge, leaky canvas bladder bursting at the seams with several hundred gallons of fuel, which dominated the cabin, sloshing back and forth in tandem with the chopper's maneuvers.

After taxiing past the remains of bombed-out, busted-up planes littering the city airfield, our old bird labored to take off, squeezing through narrow mountain passes because it did not have the power or oxygen to fly us over the surrounding peaks. I reported: "Flying from Kabul Airport on board one of the Northern Alliance's banged-up, bald-tired, patched-up old Soviet-era helicopters, we flew past the remnants of the Taliban Air Force, wiped out by our precision strikes. Then over the devastated Afghan capital and countryside up into the foothills of the Hindu Kush."

With villagers in Kunduz, Afghanistan, November 2001.

With the first team, Greg, Craig, me, Pat Muskopf, and Pat Buller,
boarding an old Soviet-era Mi-8 helicopter, November 2001.

In the Hindu Kush. If we had had GoPro or iPhones back then, we could
have been a *National Geographic* reality show. November 2001.

Piled into a Black Hawk helicopter: me, Craig, Greg, Carl
Glogg, Brian Donnelly. Iraq, March 2003.

Craig Rivera and I stand by a huge cache of rockets abandoned by
fleeing Taliban. Near Kunduz, Afghanistan, November 2001.

THE PANJSHIR, NOVEMBER 2001

Before getting to Kunduz, we stopped in the Panjshir Valley. "We have landed briefly near the home of America's greatest ally in the war, even though he was already dead by September 11," I reported as we landed at the mountainside hamlet that had been the home base of the late, great anti-Taliban leader Ahmed Shah Massoud. "This village is still the center of the revolt against the Taliban. This is their Lexington, Concord, or Bunker Hill," I reported as our helicopter set down on a snowy field.

Set in a part of the rugged Panjshir Valley that was green, lush, and partly snow-covered and could be the model for Shangri-La, the hamlet was lit by chilly, misty sunshine and was far from idyllic. Fierce, edgy Alliance fighters were everywhere. These ethnic Tajiks look much different from the desert Pashtun tribesman—sharper featured, more Macedonian than Mongol or South Asian.

"This lovely spot is the top of the Panjshir Valley. It is from here that Ahmed Shah Massoud, the legendary resistance fighter, held off first the Soviet Union in the 1980s, then the Taliban and its terrorist allies in the 1990s."

We stopped here for a couple of reasons. One was to pay homage to the fallen Massoud, the "Lion of Panjshir," who was killed in September 2001 by a Taliban suicide bombing that presaged the attacks on the United States.

"Massoud was assassinated by suicide bombers posing as journalists two days before the World Trade Center attacks," I reported. "Osama bin Laden knew the US would come looking for him so he killed Massoud to prevent him from helping us in the war on terror."

A pair of extremists had masqueraded as journalists to stalk the fearless but vain Massoud. He granted their request for an interview, disregarding pleas from advisers to keep a low profile. When he got close to them, the ersatz interviewers ignited the bomb hidden in their camera, killing Massoud as they gave praise to Allah and also died.

Happening just two days before the planes struck the Trade Center and Pentagon on the other side of the globe, the assassination of Sheik Massoud was the opening salvo in the war meant to cripple the fierce Northern Alliance. Indeed, without their charismatic leader, the Alliance was staggered, its future dark. But that near-mortal blow was undone just two days later when al Qaeda's attack on America dragged the mighty United States into the Alliance's war against the Taliban.

Far from being defeated by the death of Massoud, the reborn Alliance fighters were filled with rage. They were strengthened by American muscle and also sought revenge against our common enemy.

"The much-revered Massoud's Northern Alliance survived his assassination to provide us the ground troops, which now hold twenty-eight of Afghanistan's twenty-nine provinces," I reported.

Aside from respecting Massoud, we were in Panjshir more practically to meet and interview Dr. Abdullah Abdullah, at the time one of the most powerful men in Afghanistan. I had been corresponding with him for weeks before arriving in Afghanistan, knowing that we would need local contacts once we got there. And he proved the perfect source, reliable and totally connected.

With the shattering of the Taliban, he was running half the country as Alliance foreign minister. Later to be cheated out of the presidency twice by a process rigged by supporters of his rival, Hamid Karzai, Abdullah always put his country ahead of his personal ambitions. Part Pashtun, part Tajik, he was the perfect person to bring the nation's two dominant ethnic groups together.

Dr. Abdullah has a deceptively gentle manner, more doctor-like than warrior, but it masks tremendous courage and resolve. He is a fighter and more courageous than many combat veterans. He has stared down would-be assassins and despite his nation's patent dysfunction, he remains true to the probably unattainable ideal of a redeemed Afghanistan ready to play its part in the modern world.

In 2001 the war was new for the United States, but Dr. Abdullah had been fighting for decades, first with the mujahideen against the Soviets, then against the Taliban in his convulsed nation's twenty-five-year-long civil war. Filled with despair over the death of his hero Sheik Massoud less than three months before, Abdullah had feared all was lost.

I asked him, "You must have been relieved in a way when you heard two days after Massoud was killed that al Qaeda attacked New York, knowing America would come seeking revenge against the Taliban, against your enemy."

He shook his head no, giving me a small, sincere smile that is his trademark. "We had no idea who attacked New York. It could have been

My urgent worry was that the war would be over before
we got there. Afghanistan, November 2001.

some cowboy militia like Oklahoma City. Once we knew it was Osama
bin Laden, then everything changed."

KUNDUZ, NOVEMBER 2001

We left Panjshir heading north early on Tuesday, November 27, on our
belabored old Mi-8 helicopter, burdened by our satellite equipment, entourage, and a new load of fuel. "Once over the Hindu Kush we've arrived at
the Alliance's new prize, the city of Kunduz, the last Taliban stronghold in
Northern Afghanistan," I reported. "Kunduz fell Monday morning after
a siege that cost the Taliban and its terrorist allies well over a thousand
dead, most killed by our air strikes."

With live satellite reports filed every several hours, I was being propelled to the front rank of correspondents covering the war. Fox News was
surging in the ratings, and that rapidly expanding audience could not get
enough of our work in the field.

"You're looking at first pictures of the newly liberated town of Kunduz. As you know, this was the scene of a very bitter siege. The city is swarming with soldiers. Now remember, this was Taliban territory until yesterday and there's been this profound power change. Every vehicle commandeered by the army."

As often happened over the last four-and-a-half decades of high-profile reporting, my every step was being stalked, my reports igniting fierce controversy and smoldering resentment. The corps of mainstream journalists was just waiting for me to screw up, which I did, but that was later. Now I was flying high and certainly didn't care if my warrior-journalist style bugged my fellow reporters.

In Kunduz I broadcast from what was then a relatively rare live satellite hookup from on top of a moving armored vehicle. Just ten days on the job, I cut a dashing figure during that period, an Afghan scarf called a *shemagh* (or *keffiyeh* by the Palestinians) wrapped around my neck, gaining arrogant confidence that I alone among many reporters knew the score and how to tell it.

"As you can see, things are chaotic in Kunduz now. With fifteen thousand heavily armed troops in town, many of them young volunteers from the countryside, the local commander, General Atiquallah Baryalai Khan, told me they represent the biggest threat to public safety now and they've been ordered out of town and back to their homes. They'll be arrested if they don't comply by Wednesday [November 28]."

With General Baryalai Khan. Kunduz, Afghanistan, November 2001.

Thanks to General Khan we had a front-row seat for the action, such as it was. The problem from our point of view was there was not much of it. The most urgent development was the need to control those raucous volunteers. These were unsophisticated country kids who had rallied to the banner of the Alliance in the days following the start of the intensive American-led bombing campaign on October 7.

As I reported:

The twenty thousand Taliban fighters who once held this town are all gone, allowed to melt back into the countryside, granted an informal parole. The hard-core and the imported terrorists—Arab, Pakistani, Chechen, and other foreign fighters—have either been taken to the big prison in nearby Mazar-e Sharif or have escaped and are believed headed for Kandahar for a last stand.

I was right about their gathering for a last stand, but it was not to be in Kandahar, but in Tora Bora the following week.

Working the town and surrounding area after the retreat and disappearance of the once-fearsome enemy, we were introduced to a solitary US special operations soldier. Almost two months into Operation Enduring Freedom, he was our first glimpse of an American GI on the ground in combat in this war.

He was wearing undecorated camouflage and looked like every deer hunter in the Pennsylvania woods. Thin, bearded, dignified, and steely eyed, he told us to forget we'd met him. His commanders were not keen on our telling the world of the specific role special ops guys like him were playing in directing the war, although afterward some of them decided to write about their adventures.

There should have been a lot more of our fighters on the ground in more places a lot earlier in Afghanistan. It was certainly the fault of policymakers, not our troops, but a huge mistake nevertheless. While the 2003 invasion of Iraq two years later is recorded as the most serious failure of the Bush administration, the failure to deploy our army to take down the al Queda and Taliban militants in Afghanistan in 2001 is another historic strategic mistake. It gave Osama bin Laden ten more years to kill and maim us.

Because we came bearing Dr. Abdullah's endorsement, the swashbuckling General Khan guided us for the next several days through the territory under his control. Later military attaché to Afghanistan's embassy in Canada, the general was then a wiry, shaven-headed, total warrior committed to capturing or preferably killing Taliban.

One of those combat commanders who seem at ease, competent, and confident without being cocky, Khan had strong views on how to conduct the war against the Taliban. He was hard-core against trusting any turncoats, especially Pashtun Taliban. Scornful of his better-known Tajik commander General Daud Daud (Afghans often carry double surnames), Khan felt deserving of more credit for holding the northeast of Afghanistan in the early days of the fighting, and then leading the United Front, or more honestly the Tajiks of the Northern Alliance, on the offensive against the Taliban, once the American air strikes began.

Khan felt that he alone, or at least he primarily, had led the ground forces that pushed the assault on the enemy's strongholds, demonstrating the vulnerability of the once-feared Taliban foe and its inability to hold territory against a determined assault.

"Where is the genius?" General Khan fumed. "Daud masses artillery and kills everybody. How does that make him a military genius?"

My Fox News crew and I had the field pretty much to ourselves around Kunduz and the nearby city of Taloqan for this last week of November. With the fighting over, an uneasy peace, punctured by rampant criminality, prevailed.

The chaos was unnerving, even before word of Swedish cameraman Strömberg's Sunday-night murder. Troubled by thoughts of the three dead reporters in Bamyan Province and the four killed earlier, flayed by machine-gun fire on the road to Kabul, many news organizations pulled their reporters out of the unsettled and dangerous Kunduz area. In this gap between the Taliban's fleeing and the imposition of order by General Khan and the Alliance, gangsters and disorder were the real threats.

On Tuesday, November 27, I reported that:

Kunduz on its second day as a liberated city seems a town out of the old Wild West. Heavily armed men and boys, the army of the Northern Alliance, are everywhere. To the local commander, that is the most urgent problem. They sit around bored and intimidating, or drive through town, a dozen or more packed in their banged-up

Toyota pickups, all packing AK-47 machine guns or rocket-propelled grenade launchers.

Half these guys are volunteers from the surrounding countryside who've never been in a city. And their scary presence has caused most shops to stay shuttered. And one shudders to think how all these hungry mouths are going to be fed when winter comes.

The other big question in Kunduz is, where have all the Taliban gone? They're certainly not in the vast and empty prison. The town's airport is a busted and broken place littered with debris left by our precision strikes. In their desperation to hide their last working chopper, the Taliban nestled it alongside a small airliner. Our bombs incinerated both.

Kids with guns. Kunduz, northern Afghanistan, November 2001.

KUNDUZ, 2009 AND 2015

The Afghan War, the longest in our history, is largely an exercise in futility. The fate of Kunduz is a raw example. In 2009, eight years after its initial liberation from the Taliban, the United States had to re-bomb the city. Our pilots were trying to stop the next generation of Taliban from robbing two of our fuel trucks. Because of bad intelligence, we instead killed about ninety civilians.

It happened again in November 2015, when the Taliban reoccupied Kunduz. It was the first time since America had gone to war in Afghanistan that a major city fell back into the hands of our enemy. They were driven out only after fierce fighting and US air strikes that lasted two weeks. In the intense US military bombing, a civilian hospital being run by Doctors Without Borders was destroyed by one of our planes. It was the worst single incident of friendly fire in the entire war. Carried out by an AC-130 gunship, the attack caused a confirmed death toll of at least forty-two civilians, mostly doctors and patients.

Belatedly, President Obama personally apologized to the victims and to the head of Doctors Without Borders. It was a rare gesture that came only after our fine commander in Afghanistan in 2015, my friend for life, four-star general John F. Campbell, gave graphic testimony before Congress.

Rejecting the usual excuse that the responsibility for the attack lay with the enemy or with our Afghan allies who mistakenly identified the structure as an enemy facility, the brave general testified that the devastating attack by the AC-130 gunship was "a U.S. decision made within the U.S. chain of command."

His frankness was one reason he was not promoted to head up all-important Central Command (CentCom) or even be appointed Chairman of the Joint Chiefs of Staff, which he deserved. Instead, he chose to retire rather than accept a lesser command. Though friendly fire is the curse we brought the Afghan people, the United States is reluctant to acknowledge and apologize, citing the "fog of war" or inconclusive intelligence or theories that maybe it was the enemy's fault. For many reasons, including domestic politics, the USA does not like to say we are sorry.

It is tough politically. Former vice president Dick Cheney has been among the many hardliners critical of any appeasement-like apology that makes us look weak or inept. Former presidential contender Mitt Romney even wrote a book called *No Apology*, which the *New York Times* said was a "not so subtle dig at Mr. Obama." The forty-fourth president was at least somewhat open-minded about admitting error. Republicans particularly have an institutional reluctance to acknowledge that in the hell of war even the good guys sometimes inflict pain and suffering on innocents and allies. The almost-automatic denials of responsibility for friendly casualties are relevant to this story.

THE MAKAROV 9MM, NOVEMBER 2001

In the tense twenty-four hours between hearing about Strömberg's murder while still in Kabul and then heading up to Kunduz and the hot zone where he was killed, I vowed to go down fighting if someone tried to jack us the way they did the Swedish reporter. I carried the pistol I got in Kabul in the battered shoulder holster for the rest of the war. It led to the first of my Afghan War disputes, setting the stage for the bigger, more destructive controversy later.

Our friend Laurie Dhue, who later incurred the wrath of Roger Ailes, was, at this early stage of the war in 2001, the "Belle of Fox News," widely adored. She was anchoring from New York, while I reported via satellite from Kunduz. During one report, Strömberg's nearby murder was noted. The trouble for me started when Laurie brought up that offhand comment I had made on the air earlier in Kabul about "not going down without a fight." Laurie asked me straight out if I was "packing."

I answered, "If they're going to get us, it's going to be in a gunfight." When Laurie asked me again and specifically whether I meant I was carrying a gun, I did not answer, but finally half-nodded yes, enough to set me up as a giant target for competing reporters.

"If word gets out that a journalist is carrying a gun, it makes it difficult for everyone," Peter Arnett, the veteran NBC reporter, sourly told the Associated Press in a widely circulated interview.

Arnett got into big trouble of his own a couple of years later during the 2003 invasion of Iraq for seeming to give aid and comfort to the enemy, the regime of Saddam Hussein. But on this issue he was on firmer ground, voicing a rule that governed journalists.

The ethos at the time was that we reporters are noncombatants, neutral, impartial observers who deserve to be treated as civilians if snared in war's embrace. I knew I was in trouble when in its February 2002 magazine the NRA weighed in. Calling me a "so-called" reporter, the magazine posited that I was a hypocrite who once I arrived in Afghanistan had changed the pro-gun-control views I expressed after the mass murder of twelve students and a teacher in Columbine, Colorado, in April 1999.

The magazine called the article "The Two Faces of Geraldo Rivera" and said, "Rivera, who has made plenty of noise in the past by promoting various anti-gun proposals, revealed recently that while covering the war in Afghanistan, where he does not feel quite so safe, he's conveniently jumped to the other side of the fence . . . Hopefully, Rivera will remember that experience when he comes home to the United States, where law-abiding unarmed citizens in some neighborhoods are arguably in more danger than he ever was while traveling with bodyguards in Afghanistan."

I put aside as asinine that comparison of a Colorado high school with the barbarism of the unstructured Afghanistan battlefield where eight reporters had just been killed, four of them mutilated in the process. In the ongoing world war against radical Islamists, whether Taliban, al Qaeda, ISIS, or al Nusra, it is impossibly idealistic for reporters to feel they can still demand a sort of amnesty if captured.

The fate of the dead journalists in the early days of the Afghan War, like the later savage beheadings of Daniel Pearl and Steve Sotloff, and all the other reporters killed, belies that naive notion. To any journalist clinging to the old ways, the ISIS beheadings in Iraq and Syria are undeniable proof that, if it ever existed, the quaint notion that reporters are somehow beyond the fray is baloney.

Speaking of baloney, the PR guy for Fox News explained somewhat lamely to reporters seeking comment on my gun controversy that what I really meant to say was that we had armed guards traveling with us, who would handle any necessary gunplay. Nobody believed him, and the great gunslinger controversy set the stage for my career apocalypse at Tora Bora, but that was still a week away.

SALANG TUNNEL, NOVEMBER 2001

After a busy several days, we tried to leave Kunduz on December 3. All of northern Afghanistan was in the hands of the Alliance. The rout of the Taliban, which had begun three weeks before, was over. It started with a now-legendary cavalry charge, probably the last in the history of modern warfare, in which six hundred or so anti-Taliban horsemen accompanied by a handful of our special operators took the big northern city of Mazar-e Sharif. The battle is described in Doug Stanton's terrific book *Horse Soldiers* and the current movie *12 Strong*. The rout of the Taliban ended with the artillery barrages at Kunduz two weeks later and about a hundred miles away.

Since bad weather and the unavailability of aircraft prevented us from flying out, the most direct way to get to Kabul from Kunduz was through the Salang Tunnel. In peacetime, it is the main artery connecting north and south in Afghanistan. Burrowed through the ancient rock of the Hindu Kush Mountains, Salang was the world's highest tunnel when built by the Soviets in 1964. But when we needed it in December 2001, the tunnel was a postapocalyptic mess. Long closed to vehicle traffic, it looked like something straight out of the world of *Mad Max*.

As I reported:

> The mighty Hindu Kush Mountains cut across Afghanistan, dividing north from south. To facilitate the movement of their troops and tanks through those mountains during their ill-fated occupation, the Soviets built a mighty tunnel. But fifteen years later their broken tanks litter every highway and byway in Afghanistan. This tunnel they built is a wreck now, and if you want to pass through it, as we do, the only way is to walk.

Wrecked in savage fighting in 1997–98 between the Afghan Taliban and the Northern Alliance in their war before our war, it was impassable for vehicles. Gigantic fragments of cement from exploded and collapsed

At entrance to Salang Tunnel, elevation 11,200 ft. November 2001.

walls, blasted stone, and twisted metal blocked the roadway. Even on foot, the passage through the tunnel was a high-risk obstacle course, the approaches especially prone to Taliban ambush.

Desperate to move men and supplies, the anti-Taliban Alliance used Salang by driving to a loading zone about a half-mile from the tunnel entrance, off-loading, then hand-carrying cargo, first between the mine-fields on both sides of a narrow road to the tunnel entrance, then through the 1.6-mile chokingly claustrophobic hump to the other side. We had the added challenge of having to carry our two tons of television and satellite equipment.

We were anxious to meet Akbar bringing a Kabul-based team we had arranged to rendezvous with us on the other side. He had fresh vehicles and drivers waiting. Everybody and everything was awaiting our reemergence. The war was not waiting. Impatient to get through, I assumed the role of work boss, aggressively supervising the task of mounting our wartime safari.

Hiring two dozen local tribesmen on the spot as porters, I was a hurricane of horse-trading, rapidly sorting the fittest of those available, as Craig and the rest of the team worked hard to parcel our load into manageable bundles. It was a surreal experience; it was one of those "Damn, I am alive" existential moments.

Not believing in God or an afterlife, I am nevertheless a deeply spiritual man. Schooled in both my mother's Judaism and my father's Catholic faith, I am fatalistic about being a fleeting part of the great cosmos. As I mentioned, I feel we all spend our allotted days on Earth, and then we go back to where we were before we were born, nowhere, at least not anywhere physical. But before we go, we taste life, and live as long as someone living remembers us. Then, our essence is recycled, "dust to dust," even in death remaining part of the world.

On this deeply lived evening, we were 11,200 feet above sea level on a cold, dark, wintry night dominated by a harsh cutting breeze driving light snow perpendicular to the ground. The blacker shadows of the massive Hindu Kush peaks loomed up on each side. The valley below was a sharp, steep pit, those minefields on both sides waited hungrily for a misstep, and we faced a badly broken tunnel in front. I roared into the black night, alive and formidable, a fifty-eight-year-old Jew-Rican Tarzan.

We repacked everything down into the smallest units. There were about two dozen suitcase-sized, heavily built cases weighing between thirty and fifty pounds each. The toughest problem was the bigger of our two generators. The way through the tunnel was too tight and tortured for two men working together to carry a single heavy machine.

Momentarily stymied, the project was rescued when the biggest of the local guys said he would carry the generator through the tunnel alone. He rigged a canvas sling on his forehead, staggered momentarily, then gaining his balance, humped that two-hundred-pound beast through hell. This guy could easily have competed in one of those *Strongest Man Alive* shows.

The grueling two-hour transit accomplished, we set up a pay station in a recycled school bus our team had delivered to the other side. Giving each porter the grand sum of $40, about two weeks' salary, I made sure that nobody got paid twice by drawing a star on each man's hand with a Magic Marker.

A couple of guys tried double-dipping by washing my mark off and getting back in line, but a clean hand in that filthy place was a dead giveaway. I gratefully paid our Superman his promised double share. Even Akbar was impressed. Having kept his side of the deal by delivering the vehicles to the Kabul side of the tunnel, he was a whirlwind, urging his guys to get the vehicles loaded so we could get back to the capital as soon as possible.

Nightfall at wrecked, heavily mined Salang Tunnel, Afghanistan, November 2001.

THE *LOYA JURGA*, DECEMBER 2001

Events were rolling. In Kabul, everything was still shabby and broken, but there was a sense that the end was in sight. Bin Laden was uncaught, but the bad guys were everywhere on the run. We met again with Dr. Abdullah Abdullah, the suave, composed representative of the Northern Alliance, this time for dinner at his modest compound in Kabul. By then, December 3, less than two weeks after our first meeting, he was acting foreign minister of the entire de facto post-Taliban United Front government.

With the Taliban gone from the capital, entrepreneurs or their agents already crowded the now opened but dusty and barely functioning airport, bearing ambitious schemes ranging from establishing cell-phone networks to rare-metal mining to selling debit cards.

If that seems like putting the cart before the donkey, given the fact that bin Laden was still at large, consider that most Afghans viewed this conflict differently from the way we in the West did. The carnage of September 11 was our trauma, not theirs. Afghans are not a progressive bunch. Many still consider Christianity a capital offense and believe women should be confined to perpetual, invisible subordination. In Kabul, then and now, what is most revealing is that so many women completely hide their face and body, dressing in ugly blue burkas. They are invisible and indistinguishable from one another and have no public persona.

The ruling and educated class, at most 10 percent of the total population of 30 million, had been suppressed by the Taliban and understood that America's powerful military intervention was creating commercial opportunities, some involving sticky fingers. As I reported as I walked through a bazaar filled with contraband US military uniforms, canteens, endless boxes of rations, knapsacks, and other equipment:

> America is a great and generous nation, but sometimes our good intentions don't always end up helping those most in need. To get an idea, for example, of just how much US aid has been siphoned off or just plain, flat-out stolen, all you have to do is take a quick shopping excursion in Kabul's main bazaar. It's the Mall of American Aid.

Most knowledgeable Afghans saw this current turmoil as just another chapter in Afghanistan's long-running civil war, which had raged since the

"Afghans are not a progressive bunch. Many still consider Christianity a capital offense."

overthrow of the last monarch, King Mohammed Zahir Shah, by his own brother-in-law in August 1973.

But now in this heady time, the frail but revered ex-king came out of his long exile in Rome and returned to Kabul to preside over a *Loya Jurga*, a summit of the various tribal leaders. Later, my meeting with his former highness in his faded but still-grand palace in Kabul was a high point of my Afghan coverage. Living a good, if quiet, life in Italy, he was roused to answer his country's call as a symbol of continuity and order. He was too frail to make a difference, but America and our European allies liked the idea of the Return of the King. He died, still in Kabul, in 2007. He was ninety-two.

But in that December 2001, two energetic younger men had the inside track. They were hand-picked by the US State Department and appeared to be a match made in heaven to break the cycle of violence and lead Afghanistan to a new age.

With his powerful and deeply connected family and tribe based in the southern Kandahar region, Hamid Karzai was designated by the US to lead Afghanistan and unite the nation's various factions, now that the Taliban was beat up if not yet defeated. The fact that his brother would turn out to be a crook and a drug dealer was not yet known. The

With his majesty King Zahir Shah. He was overthrown by his
own brother. Kabul, Afghanistan, December 2001.

talk was that Dr. Abdullah would be Karzai's second-in-command in
a permanent postwar government. It was the Afghan equivalent of the
"Dream Team."

As I mentioned earlier, with a Tajik father and a Pashtun mother,
Dr. Abdullah was what the West hoped a "new" Afghanistan would be:
educated, secular, or at least tolerant, inclusive, and democratic. But our
trying to apply contemporary political science in the context of Afghanistan shows how hapless and ignorant we were of this pit of social regres-
sion. In this fifteenth-century environment where sect and tribal hatred is
instinctive and ingrained, the dream hatched at Foggy Bottom, the State
Department's headquarters in Washington, was impossible.

Dr. Abdullah is a noble soul, and at our dinner in Kabul on December
4, he gave me the scoop that changed my life, mostly for the worse. He told
me about Tora Bora.

"You have to get down there. It is near Jalalabad. We think bin Laden
is there." The news electrified me, as he knew it would.

"How do I get there?" I asked, my mind racing between panic and
exhilaration.

Meeting local leaders en route to Tora Bora, November 2001.

He gave that familiar small smile again. "I can arrange a helicopter to Jalalabad. Your team can prepare your supplies and security there. Tora Bora is just a few hours' drive away."

It was the biggest story of the war, and we had a head start. The killer of all those friends and neighbors, the man I had exuberantly, but sincerely, vowed to kill with my own hands if I had the chance, was within reach, making a last stand in a rugged valley not far from the Pakistan border.

JALALABAD, LATE MORNING, DECEMBER 5, 2001

We landed the banged-up chopper at the beat-up Jalalabad Airport on December 5. In a double irony, we were back in the city where we had begun our Afghan adventure two weeks earlier, and at the same airport from which SEAL Team 6 would launch the raid that finally brought back bin Laden's dead body from Pakistan. It would take almost a decade of fighting and dying.

Dr. Abdullah gave me a letter of introduction addressed to Hazrat Ali, a local anti-Taliban fighter who, as commander of a militia we were calling the Eastern Alliance, was leading the assault, such as it was, on bin Laden's redoubt in Tora Bora. We also benefited from our established relationship with acting governor Abdul Qadir, who, at the time, was Ali's ally in the fight.

We met at the Spinghar Hotel, the same one we stayed at on the way into Afghanistan in November. Like most semi-bandit militia leaders, Hazrat Ali played the angles, surviving by allying himself with whichever force had the upper hand at the moment.

Ali and other local leaders had coexisted with al Qaeda for several years. Indeed, a few years later he was sacked from his job as police chief because he was considered too close to the Taliban. But before al Qaeda took on the United States, alliances in that neck of the woods were fluid; everybody was hanging with everybody. The Arab and other foreign fighters living in the Tora Bora valley often owned their property and intermarried with the Afghans in the area. Bin Laden even had a home in Tora Bora, as well as the one in Jalalabad.

By this first week of December 2001, it was obvious to everyone that al Qaeda's time living in the open was over. The real issue was when, rather than whether, bin Laden himself would be killed or captured, that is if he was still there at all.

Morning bath. Base camp, Tora Bora, Afghanistan, December 2001.

First meeting with Afghan foreign minister Dr. Abdullah Abdullah, who became a great friend and ally. Panjshir Valley, November 2001.

Like most semi-bandit leaders, Hazrat Ali played the angles. December 2001.

Watching smoke plumes rise over the White Mountains
of Tora Bora from intense bombing raids.

The Americans had begun our intensive bombing of Tora Bora. We were using high-level, heavy B-52 and B-1B bombers based on Diego Garcia, an island 2,885 miles away in the Indian Ocean, and from about half as far away, more nimble F-15E fighter bombers, based on aircraft carriers cruising the Arabian Sea. We were pulverizing the valley and surrounding area, killing fighters and civilians alike. Raining death from above is often a messy and imprecise business.

As I scrambled to put together our convoy, my smartest move was hiring Hazrat Ali's son-in-law as head of our Afghan security force. Tall, slim, Omar Sharif–handsome, and obviously connected, he proved a perfect conduit for ensuring that Ali gave us the inside story as the climactic battle approached.

Chapter 5

MISTAKE IN TORA BORA

Our convoy made its way through a series of mud-walled villages until at the end of the winding road we reached the approach to Tora Bora and the first checkpoint, at midafternoon of December 5, 2001. Afghan mujahideen fighters, the good guys who were allied against the primarily Arab and Chechen fighters of al Qaeda, manned it.

The fighters belonged to Hazrat Ali's rival here in Nangarhar Province, a hustler of low repute named Haji Zaman Ghamsharik, who had just returned to Afghanistan from exile in France. Putting aside their differences for this final push against al Qaeda, Ali and Zaman were co-commanders of the anti-Taliban militia, which was now more grandly known as the "Eastern Alliance." Unlike the scene in Kabul or Kunduz, we were not too late to see action here. In fact, we were the first reporters on the scene of the biggest story in the world.

As we spoke with the militia leader, out-going cannon fire roared a short distance away. Farther off, we could see the smoke and flash of aerial bombs striking, and then hear the delayed blasts from the chains of explosions, perhaps five miles away.

We were in a valley looking south toward Pakistan. The area being targeted was at the base of the White Mountains, which separate Afghanistan from Pakistan, on the far side of the snow-covered ridges.

With militia fighter near Tora Bora, Afghanistan, December 2001.

At this junction, several country roads and trails come together and merge into the single dirt road running straight into the hamlet of Tora Bora. With a clear view of the action, bin Laden finally in our crosshairs, and no other reporters around, I was elated and spoke excitedly with the militiaman about the beast's finally being cornered.

His reaction was deflating. With fierce beard and demeanor, he lectured passionately about the deaths that morning of three of his fighters to friendly fire. Akbar translated as he complained of the imprecision of our air strikes and the fact that his men and innocent civilians were being killed by our negligence. He pleaded with me. I wrote down what he said in my reporter's notebook:

"First you do reconnaissance. Then send in the planes. We have no radio coordination with the aircraft. Can you help us speak with the aircraft?"

It was at that moment that I came to grips with the inescapable fact that as we killed our enemy, we were also killing our friends. Later accused of helping bin Laden escape Tora Bora, Commander Zaman survived this fight only to be assassinated by the Taliban in Kabul in February 2010.

Expressing my regret at the time for the losses to friendly fire, but indelibly committed to cheering from a front-row seat America's pursuit of bin Laden, the man who killed our thousands at the World Trade Center, I ordered our caravan down the road toward Tora Bora. The danger from friendly fire was firmly in my head. It would later tear out my heart.

FRIENDLY FIRE AT TORA BORA, WEDNESDAY, MID-LATE AFTERNOON, DECEMBER 5, 2001

We drove past scattered houses perched on the side of the valley as it dipped down to our left. Akbar told me these homes belonged to the foreign fighters of al Qaeda, mostly Arabs. Although most of bin Laden's troopers came from outside Afghanistan, many of their wives were local women, Sunni Muslims like them, with whom they had settled comfortably with their families into this lovely spot nestled at the base of the White Mountains, now just a mile or two away.

Smoke and dust plumes from aerial bomb drops erupted in plain sight in the valley in front of us. Driving down the road, we were soon close enough to see the orange-red flashes, not just the dark smoke plumes generated by the blasts. The time between flash and bang was less now, down to a second or two. It was like sailing toward a lightning storm at sea, the crack of thunder catching up to the searing bolts of light.

The main road dipped left toward the base of the mountains and in the direction of the action. A dirt trail split off to our right. We could see that the trail led up to a large plateau. On this inaugural journey, we drove past it until we reached a bend in the road beneath, curling under the plateau now rising a hundred feet or so up on our right. I made note of the plateau as a possible campsite. Leaving our crew and vehicles, we made the long walk toward the front lines deeper down in the valley.

Both Craig and Greg were shooting with their handheld DVD cameras. As we got closer to where the bombs were exploding just over the next ridge, our Afghan security and the mujahideen fighters nervously warned us that the gravest danger was not al Qaeda, but getting too close to the bombs impacting.

Akbar told me that bin Laden's summer home was farther down the road nearer the base of the mountain, but in an area still controlled by the bad guys. Unable to go farther because of the ongoing bombardment, and losing light, I ordered us back up the road to rendezvous with the satellite crew and find a suitable place to camp and set up our gear.

When we reached the trail going up off the road, we turned up to explore that big plateau overlooking the battlefield. Maybe two city blocks wide, it dropped off on the far side into another valley. About a half-mile long, it jutted toward Tora Bora. It was good ground, safe from direct fire from below, and vulnerable only to mortar or indirect rocket attack. At the far end, the plateau overlooked the battle like the front row of the mezzanine section of an outdoor theater.

FRIENDLY FIRE AT TORA BORA, WEDNESDAY EVENING, DECEMBER 5, 2001

We want to believe that America always fights clean, that only evil perishes by our sword. Modern war, especially from the air, is neither so clean nor precise, especially not in Afghanistan. The consensus number is that from 1,000 to 1,300 civilians and friendly fighters died countrywide in Afghanistan in the three-month-long Operation Enduring Freedom aerial campaign, from October 7, 2001, to January 1, 2002.

Chris Tomlinson, a solid, brave correspondent whom I ran into several times in Afghanistan including at Tora Bora, wrote for the Associated Press on December 3, 2001, "Afghan village riddled with bomb craters; 155 villagers said killed."

Philip Smucker, an excellent adventuring reporter, whom I also ran into at the wildest stretches of the Tora Bora battlefront, wrote in the *Daily Telegraph* on December 4, 2001, "Villages pay price as U.S. bombs go awry."

John Donnelly wrote in the *Boston Globe* on December 5, 2001, "Unintended Victims Fill Afghan Hospital."

Richard Lloyd Parry wrote in the *Independent* on December 5 that, "Civilians Abandon Homes after Hundreds Are Casualties of U.S. Air Strikes on Villages."

In the late afternoon of December 5, we set our camp on our big plateau overlooking the battlefield, choosing a location near an old Soviet-era tank the mujahideen were using as an artillery piece to lob shells in the direction of the enemy. In the fading light, our terrific satellite operators, Pat Butler and Pat Muskopf, finished setting up the generators and the big dish. The rest of us, including security personnel, worked to complete our base camp, rigging the tents and so forth.

In communication via satellite phone with New York for the first time since leaving Kabul and Dr. Abdullah about twenty-four hours before, we learned that earlier on December 5 there had been a tragic incident of friendly fire. One of our bombers mistakenly hit a large party of Afghans, including some of the anti-Taliban leadership. More painfully, we were told several of our US special operations personnel were also killed in the accident.

The names of the fallen GIs were released, but for reasons of security, the location of their deaths was not. With no word yet on where exactly the incident had taken place, I assumed this tragedy was the same one we had been warned about there in Tora Bora.

LIVE FROM TORA BORA, THURSDAY MORNING, DECEMBER 6

Our first live shot from Tora Bora was on the *Hannity & Colmes* show. Afghanistan is a weird nine and a half hours ahead, so for us it was 6:30 Thursday morning, but Wednesday night at 9 back in the New York studio. As I stood on the edge of the plateau where bombs had begun falling again at first light, Hannity introduced me:

"We're now joined by Fox News war correspondent Geraldo Rivera. He's reporting from a place in Afghanistan where very few journalists are willing to go, Tora Bora. Geraldo, I understand there's actually bombing going on right behind you."

"There is, Sean. If you just pan the camera over here, it looks like mist in the mountains. That's actually what's left of the—the impact from the bombs that dropped not more than six or eight minutes ago . . . The bombers have been coming over, I'd say at the rate of about every twenty minutes. At this rate, you know, during the course of your program, I'm sure they'll be back . . . We're actually on the outskirts, where we stand here, of Tora Bora. Tora Bora, the cave-and-cavern complex where Osama bin Laden has, with his hard-core fighters, set up what will be his—his last stand . . .

"There, another explosion! There! You can see it off on the—on the ridgeline. Can you see that? Another one. You'll hear the sound . . . There it is. There's the sound now. So we're—we're giving him hell. We're given him hell, Sean."

Cohost Alan Colmes was a wonderful colleague and fierce defender of liberal values on Fox News who passed away in January 2017. He asked the next question:

"Geraldo, it's Alan. We've heard reports that it's difficult for some reporters to get access to the front lines, a paucity of information. What was it like for you to get there? What was the process like? And are you one of the only reporters in that area?"

I answered, "We are the only—we are the only—here come the planes, right over us! Here they are. Alan, we are the only reporters here, Western or otherwise, as far as I can determine."

It was the answer I had left the plush, safe, high-paying NBC job to be able to give. We were ahead of the pack. Proof is in the pudding. Data talks, bullshit walks. Tora Bora was getting blown up, and we were the only ones to record and report it. Not only was my team on the front lines of the most important battle of the new twenty-first century, we were there alone. Then it was my buddy Sean again:

"Geraldo, just—just to be clear here—who's dropping those bombs there? And by the way, we see it very clearly. And the second part of my question is there—there's been a lot of press coverage, Geraldo, of you

"We are the only reporters here…" Tora Bora, Afghanistan. December 2001.

being over there, most of it very positive, an article in the *New York Post* today. I doubt you got your coverage while you were there, but —"

"B-52s coming! B-52s coming, Sean," I interrupted excitedly. Then addressing his first question, "It looks to us like you have naval air and the United States Air Force. You have both—you have the fighter jets coming in, tactically. They drop the one, the two, and the four. Then you have the B-52s. They're coming in. They're carpet-bombing."

At this stage I walked off the career cliff, conflating our local friendly-fire casualties with what we had heard from New York about the incident involving several of our Green Beret warriors killed the day before:

"I mean, that, of course, is—is how the three poor guys, Master Sergeant Jeffrey Donald Davis, Sergeant First Class Daniel Henry Petithory, and Staff Sergeant Brian Cody Prosser, got killed yesterday [December 5, Afghan time] in an incident of friendly fire from the B-52s. They're courageous guys. They called the big bombers in right on their own positions.

"So you've got the whole combined air might—you know, that tragedy, that awful warrior's nightmare of friendly fire aside, you've got the combined air might of the allied—allied forces striking at Tora Bora. And then on the ground, you've got four thousand of these mujahideen massed for the attack."

For whatever reasons, it never occurred to me that there were massive bombing and friendly-fire casualties going on anywhere else in Afghanistan. Without checking with my local sources, I had decided without even mentioning it to Craig that the three special operators who died by friendly fire must have been killed at the scene we witnessed in Tora Bora. In fact, they were killed three hundred miles away, in Kandahar.

It is not uncommon to assume in battle that the action you are seeing is the entire war. The ultimate conceit of war correspondents is that nothing important happens unless we are around. Reporters like me have the dangerous tendency to believe we are at the center of the universe and everything revolves around us. We aspire to be more Ernest Hemingway than Ernie Pyle.

Speaking of which, I then addressed the second part of Sean's question. Although I obviously had not read the *New York Post* story he was referencing, I was sure it concerned my earlier scandal about carrying a gun.

"As to the coverage about me . . . I'm just one of those lightning-rod kinds of personalities, and people like talking about what it is that I wear, or what my personal habits are, how I feel about the Second Amendment to the United States Constitution.

"All I say is I'm here doing a job. I'm reporting the facts as I see them. No one's criticized my reporting factually. And if they want to, you know, talk about whether I'm wearing a gun or not wearing a gun or wearing a six-shooter or a cowboy hat or whatever, you know, that's their problem."

What I should have said was that I was aware there was a big bull's-eye on my back and that every armchair reporter back in the States was ready to pounce on any misstep. In reporting about friendly fire, I had just given them a doozy. But for now, I was bathed in glory. Hannity concluded:

"Geraldo, you deserve a lot of credit. You've gotten closer than any other journalist there, very close to the bombing. You do have to arm yourself. We wish you Godspeed. Get home safe, buddy."

"Thanks. Thanks, man," I replied, the humble, six-gun-packing hero-in-his-own-mind.

LONG AND WINDING ROAD, THURSDAY MORNING, DECEMBER 6, 2001

The next live appearance, which is called a "hit," was about a half-hour later on the 10 PM show hosted that night by Rita Cosby. It was just past 7:30 AM locally, and full daylight bathed the contested battlefield.

Rita started her show with a sound bite from Pentagon spokesman Rear Admiral John Stufflebeem, who said, "Well, they're trying to determine locations of al Qaeda, and specifically, al Qaeda leadership and the remaining Taliban that might be in the area. The reports from that region are that many of these forces may have or have taken up refuge in caves and tunnels. So we're working to determine where these bad guys are and then to bring strikes on them."

Rita followed by assuring her audience, "And where those bad guys may be is Tora Bora, the suspected location of bin Laden's cave hideout and home to some of the most fanatical members of his murderous al Qaeda network. It's perhaps the most dangerous place in the world tonight, and you won't find any journalist with the guts to stand their ground and get the story. That is, any journalist except for Geraldo Rivera, who is standing by now in Tora Bora."

"We are standing here on the newest front line in the war against terror," I said, confident that we were where every war correspondent and daydreamer in the world longed to be. "You mentioned Tora Bora and you mentioned the cave complex, and I heard the admiral and the defense secretary mention it. It's right over here. You see the snow-covered mountains. The other side of these mountains is Pakistan. So you see strategically why bin Laden, the world's most-wanted criminal, wanted to locate here."

Then I compounded my earlier error about friendly fire, saying, "The mujahideen here really are very motivated. You know, that tragic friendly-fire incident that we had yesterday losing three of our own—three Special Forces—they lost a couple of their own guys in that same incident. Still, they're filled with a fire in their belly. They're amassing their infantry. We expect a big push that could come as early as today."

I referenced another of our scoops, soon obscured by the coming scandal. As far as I know, we were the first to confirm that bin Laden's mostly Arab foreign legion were in Tora Bora. We did it by intercepting their communications. On our handheld VHF radios we could hear them speaking to each other in Arabic, rather than in Pashto or Urdu, the indigenous Afghan languages. Fluent in all, Akbar translated.

"They have these very short-range walkie-talkies, Rita, and the amazing thing is that we can hear Arabic being spoken on their walkie-talkies. In other words, the bad guys—al Qaeda and these Arabs, the other foreign nationals fighting—are communicating in Arabic and using the same frequencies.

"So these guys who do not speak Arabic really hear that. They hear these foreigners in their turf. They get really motivated, very angry . . . they're ready, four thousand of them massed for an assault. I doubt they'll take the whole redoubt today, but they're certainly going to begin.

"It's going to be cave by cave, one against one, eyeball to eyeball, bayonet to bayonet. It's going to be brutal. It's going to be ugly, but it's necessary, because if they don't root out the approximately twelve hundred hard-core Arab and other foreign fighters that he's got up there, it's going to be a cancer that metastasizes and comes right back down infecting this valley all the way down into eastern Afghanistan. So, we're standing, I think, at a real hinge in history here."

It would have been "a hinge in history" if bin Laden had been caught there or killed. Instead, the words Tora Bora just became a shorthand, at least in my mind, for my deconstruction. Like Hannity, Cosby was generous with her sincere on-air goodbye: "All right, Geraldo Rivera, please stay safe, my friend, the only reporter tonight from Tora Bora. Thank you so much. Amazing pictures there."

Imagine if you were the news director of CBS, NBC, ABC, or CNN at that moment, watching the rival newscast up on the monitors, as they all do. Here I was, alone with my capable crew, live and right where they all wanted to be. To suggest they were frustrated is to understate the obvious.

For Fox News, the insurgent cable news channel charging down the right side of American society, it was a heady moment. All the publicity about my defection from CNBC led to this. Their man Geraldo was kicking butt. Ratings were soaring. Roger Ailes's gamble was paying off, big-time.

INTO THE ABYSS, THURSDAY MID-MORNING, DECEMBER 6, 2001

After the live shots were wrapped, we got ready for our real job, getting close enough to see if all the sound and fury of our bombardment was doing anything to win the war. Craig, Greg, and I, accompanied by Akbar and one of the local mujahideen bodyguards, put on our body armor and helmets, ready to hike down toward the action. That became our ritual for the next ten days. Home-base cameraman Pat Butler helped me tighten the straps on my vest, checked my rig, and wished me good luck as we marched toward the firing.

Getting near an ongoing battle in these circumstances is unforgettable. Every step you take toward close-in combat summons dread and elation. Your antenna is sharp and you are focused, at your best, and every veteran of combat knows what I am talking about. The battle and bombardment of Tora Bora dragged on so long that the odds of something bad happening to us kept increasing. My emotions went from eager confidence to resignation.

Pushing through physical fear is easy if you don't mind dying heroically in a good cause. I was filled with confidence. Despite being late to the war, I managed to bring my intact, competent, well-equipped, and now combat-tested team to the scene of the pivotal battle first. Even death could not defeat me now. If it did, my name would live forever bathed in the warrior ethos. Death would lead to secular sainthood, complete with a photo on the wall behind the bar at Elaine's or Ms. Elle's. This is why I took the Fox job, revenge and glory, and I was going to push even harder to stay in front of the pack.

As we advanced into no man's land that Thursday late morning, December 6, I wrote my script: "The frontlines are a deadly, dangerous place where weapons ranging from the giant B-52s to the AK-47 machine guns used by both sides are most evident by their ferocious sounds, from the big booms of the bombs to the rat-tat of the machine guns. The sounds of death are writ big and small.

"As mujahideen fighters filed past us, one was being carried on a stretcher, wounded by either shrapnel or a sniper's bullet. Another was bleeding, injured less seriously. At the base of the mountain, we tread more cautiously, aware that we were both in range and in sight of enemy sharpshooters."

Making our way up the first hill, we were acutely aware of enemy snipers on the ridge beyond. Leaving Craig and crew shielded behind a slight rise, I crawled out on my belly into the open to do an on-camera report about how the enemy was being pressed against the mountains. As I reported later:

We were alone in front-row seats for the biggest story in the world. December 2001.

Later in the afternoon, it appeared as if the Alliance lines were breaking under a counterattack by al Qaeda forces. But the commanders
explained to me that they have called in additional US air strikes
and were vacating some of their hard-won ground to avoid any more
incidents of friendly fire. Whatever the reason for the withdrawal, it
was temporary and the outcome here is inevitable, although as you're
about to see, this rat can still bite.

As I do my on-camera stand-up, a sniper's round cracks right over
my head, interrupting me in mid-sentence. For a war correspondent there
is no more unnerving or exhilarating sound in battle than the whistle of
small arms fire breaking the sound barrier as it zips past, especially when
all the sound and fury is caught on camera and nobody friendly gets hurt.

As the bullet zings by, I make a sound like, "Ohhh!" and then press
closer to the ground. I continue with the stand-up: "It can't last—it can't
last much longer. It can't last much longer. Their backs are literally to the
wall. They can keep sniping. They can—they can put up—they can put up
a fight, but they've got no place else to go."

My intense caught-on-tape near miss at Tora Bora on December 6,
2001, should have been the headline for posterity, the takeaway memory
of my undeniable walk on the wild side. Instead, it was investigated and
pored over for authenticity by skeptics, cynics, comics, and haters who
grabbed the legitimate controversy about my confusing two separate incidents of friendly fire, and perverted it into a nearly successful and enduring attempt to destroy an example of unflappable courage.

BREAKING THE FAST, THURSDAY
SUNSET, DECEMBER 6

Back at our plateau base, an extraordinary scene was playing out as the
sun went down. Below us, jogging mujahideen fighters were retreating in
scattered bunches.

"Where are they going?" I asked Akbar.

"It is Ramadan," he answered matter-of-factly. "They've been fasting
all day because of the holiday. They're going back to their homes to break
the fast with their families."

It was a revelation. I had covered war for decades, but this was the first where the warriors went home for prayer and dinner after work. Imagine if the Israelis had chosen to commemorate Yom Kippur instead of fight when they were attacked in October 1973. It seemed too casual for serious soldiers in all-out combat. The fire I saw in their bellies only burned from about 9 in the morning to 5 in the afternoon.

My near-miss moment at Tora Bora captured on tape made it on all the Fox News shows around the clock and beyond. It was a viral moment that had a huge impact commercially, one that helped reorder the cable-news hierarchy. By the end of this evening of December 6, insurgent Fox News reached a new plateau with a 2.0 rating that passed longtime leader CNN. (With rare exceptions, Fox News has stayed ahead of CNN ever since, faltering only temporarily when Bill O'Reilly got fired fifteen years later. That didn't last long, Sean Hannity soon retook the lead for Fox News, displacing MSNBC's Rachel Maddow whose brief reign on top during Summer 2017 featured a constant barrage of negative attention on President Trump's flaws, real and imagined. She was particularly obsessed with his purported collusion with Russia to rig the 2016 election. As of this writing, there has not been credible evidence implicating the president in any such plot. Conversely, as far as I know Ms. Maddow has never given Mr. Trump any credit for the economy, which has so far boomed under his watch). Back to Tora Bora.

NO ELITE WARRIORS, DECEMBER 7, 2001

At the beginning of our third day on the battlefield, at 5:30 AM Friday (8 PM Thursday back in the States), I was live on *The O'Reilly Factor*, which was beginning that generation-long run as the dominant, number-one show in all cable news. Bill expressed sincere concern for our safety as he introduced me on his broadcast.

Then O'Reilly asked about US special operators in our vicinity. I started to answer, then stuttered because we had seen only one, and he was the fellow up in Kunduz. We had pledged him confidence. We had not seen, nor would we see, any of the other elite warriors said to be directing the fight in Tora Bora. Nevertheless, I had leapt into the incorrect narrative that this was where three special operators died by friendly fire, and I was mentally stuck there, repeating the error for the next two days, obviously not realizing how destructively wrong I was. No one corrected me.

Bill O'Reilly: All right, how many US special ops are around you, and do you have any contact with them? Or what are they doing?

Geraldo Rivera: . . . I don't want to say, I tell you truth. I promised I wouldn't, and I won't. But I will say this, that yesterday we did walk over what I consider hallowed ground—yesterday my time, today your time—that area where the friendly fire hit. And it was—you know, it's just breathtaking, it's just so awful, the whole area kind of vaporized, little tatters of uniform everywhere.

Who would make this stuff up? Nobody would create that picture out of whole cloth. It was the truth. We saw and videotaped obviously fresh bomb craters, incinerated circles of scorched earth that the assembled fighters and our trusted guides told us was where our US aerial bombs had killed several mujahideen, anti-Taliban fighters.

"It was the saddest place I've ever been in my life. I stopped and I said the Lord's Prayer. It's just—it's the warrior's worst nightmare to be killed by friendly fire, to be killed by your own. Accidents happen in war, especially when it is as fluid as this conflict is here."

I saw the devastation and the carnage. I said the prayer out loud. I reported it, mistakenly thinking it was the same incident being reported near Kandahar. It was a stupid mistake. There were no Americans killed at the scene I saw. In fact, there were no Americans in Tora Bora on December 5, except us and, presumably, the sprinkling of special operators farther up the hill directing the aircraft. There were Afghans killed there, by our bombs.

Remember the now famous bullet whizzing through the air? After a series of widely viewed live appearances, everybody in the world knew my real location. Whom could I fool? Why would I want to? What glory is there in observing the remnants of a tragic friendly-fire incident? Did I just make it up because, as some later wrote, I wanted people to think I was in the midst of every substantive action for some psycho reason, that I cannot stand anything happening that is not happening to me?

At Fox News, it didn't seem to me that we cared much about Afghani friendly-fire casualties anyway. At least that was my impression especially then, just three months removed from the September 11 attacks. Fox was not unique in that regard. Three weeks later in a January 2002 FAIR (Fairness & Accuracy in Reporting), the progressive media watchdog group published a major article critical of war correspondents for omitting or downplaying reports of friendly casualties in Tora Bora and elsewhere. It stated, "When media portray reports of civilian casualties as an attack on America, it's hardly surprising that serious reporting on the issue [of friendly fire] is scarce. It is crucial that news outlets independently investigate civilian casualties in Afghanistan—not only how many there have been, but how and why they happened."

On *Hannity & Colmes* an hour later, Sean broke into his in-studio interview with a military expert, Robert S. Bevelacqua, to go to me at the front.

Sean Hannity: Bob, I got to stop you right there. We're going to go live to Tora Bora right now with Fox News Channel war correspondent Geraldo Rivera, who is there. Geraldo?

Geraldo Rivera: Sean, a B-52 coming in live. You see it right now. We just had one of the fighter-bombers come in and drop one of the precision munitions. Now comes the big B-52. This guy's going to unload big-time on the Tora Bora terrorist base right behind us in the White Mountains. We're watching virtually from underneath the bomb bay, actually, happily just clear of it. He's going to drop any minute. He may have already dropped.

This is now the second day of a ferocious assault on Osama bin Laden's terrorist base there in the White Mountains. You can hear—go back to the contrail (I instruct cameraman Pat Butler). Just show the—where the B-52—they should be impacting any second here.

The bombs were exploding right in front of our camp. Glamorous and just dangerous enough, this aspect of Tora Bora was also easiest. Up on high ground overlooking the pivotal battleground, our live cameras rolled as the action unfolded. And we were alone in front-row seats for the biggest story in the world.

Those other news networks with live capability were arriving in the area from Kabul and elsewhere, but initially they were not getting this close. Trailing us by almost two days, they were choosing to settle in the village we passed through at the entrance to the Tora Bora valley several miles farther from the action. To that point, Sean's sidekick Alan Colmes complimented me later in the show that I had scooped the world: "Geraldo, you have brought us the best pictures I've seen anywhere of this war, the backdrop day after day. You've really had some incredible graphics for us here."

As the Afghan War wore on, President Hamid Karzai would complain constantly about friendly fire and civilian casualties. He said the uncounted acts and many thousands of friendly casualties showed disregard for his people. But at this time, before his triumphal arrival in Kabul as the anointed face of the new Afghan government, like us Americans, he did not make a big deal out of what would later become his biggest issue with us. To me, because of the scandal that ensued, the terms "friendly fire" and "Tora Bora" have become obscenities, accusations, and attacks on my character.

THE BATTLEFIELD GRANDSTAND, DECEMBER 8–9, 2001

For the next several days we settled into an exhausting routine, up early enough to do the morning satellite hits, then donning body armor and venturing off the plateau toward the front line. Craig, Greg, Akbar, and I marching down into the scary unknown, shooting video all day then feeding the material via satellite to New York; grabbing a few hours' sleep between the 8 AM *Fox & Friends* hit at 5:30 PM local Afghan time; then up again before dawn for the live hits for evening prime time back home, beginning with O'Reilly at 8 PM, 5:30 AM local.

Aside from guts, in war reporting the three most important things, as with real estate, are location, location, and location. Ours was perfect. We were a mile or two from where gigantic explosions at dawn announced the start of the day's battle, on cue for the evening newscasts back in the States.

With the exception of a single barrage of RPGs—rocket-propelled grenades, i.e., shoulder-fired rockets—that were shot at us as we stood on the edge of the plateau looking down on the action below, our broadcast plateau was never directly attacked. Still, the constant threat of enemy infiltration initially kept the crowd of incoming journalists down to the hard-core.

For most of that first weekend, December 8–9, before the wave of the international press corps broke on Tora Bora, we patrolled farther up the ridge than even most mujahideen. Wearing our bulletproof vests and helmets, we marched into the unknown, dreaming of finding bin Laden's mangled corpse and returning with it before dark, in time for the next morning's hits.

The fact that the terror mastermind still had another decade to live was partially the result of our incompetent or at best unimaginative leadership's not committing ground troops and trying to run the Tora Bora air battle from far-off Central Command HQ in Tampa, Florida, nine and a half time zones away.

In the predawn dark as I prepared to go on live, tremendous explosions shook the earth around us. There was another, newer noise. The whooshing sound of Gatling guns hosing the area with deadly machine-gun fire let us know that close-in air support was also, finally, in action. How effective those attacks were in killing bad guys was another matter.

I was passing on resistance leader Hazrat Ali's casualty estimates, but needed proof, a Vietnam-style body count. By that point, several days into the aerial campaign, what was missing were dead bodies. A lot of bombs had been dropped, but not many human remains found, except for the shards of flesh at the friendly-fire killing field, the hallowed ground we had walked on December 5. Historians say that about two hundred al Qaeda fighters were killed in and around Tora Bora over the two weeks of bin Laden's last stand, but it was nothing like the pitched battles and fields of dead Egyptian and Syrian soldiers I reported on during the Yom Kippur War in 1973, in places like the Sinai desert and Kuneitra in the Golan Heights. Although the point is seldom made, during bin Laden's last stand in Tora Bora and environs, our bombing probably killed as many innocent civilians and friendly fighters as enemies.

I also wanted some news on whether the US-led coalition had managed to put a blocking force on the high ridges to prevent bin Laden from using the obvious escape route over the White Mountains into nearby Pakistan, a three-hour walk away.

Akbar got permission to accompany one of the forward-most mujahideen patrols to assess close up some of the damage wrought the night before. Taking a camera, he went up the mountain to see if any real damage was done.

He returned with footage of several dead terrorists apparently killed by the bombings, but told me there was no evidence of a substantial contingent of US special operators in front of us. If they were there, none of our Afghan good guys knew about them.

Subsequent books and testimony before the Senate Foreign Relations Committee in 2009 revealed that from December 3, when the aerial bombing campaign really began, until about December 10, the total US ground force in Tora Bora consisted of just "20 U.S. CIA NCS [National Clandestine Service] and Fifth SFG (A) ODA572 [Special Forces Group] team members, code name Jawbreaker," all inserted by helicopter; twenty against al Qaeda.

There were almost that many security personnel and techs working for my Fox News team. Adding in the CNN, NBC, and other crews who were arriving, the media clearly outnumbered the US Special Operations forces during the first crucial week of Tora Bora. Of all possible explanations as to how bin Laden was allowed to escape, the fact that only twenty GIs were assigned to trap him in Tora Bora is the most glaring explanation. However skilled or courageous they were, those twenty were obviously not able to do much on the mountain other than presumably spot targets for the warplanes.

It was a pitifully small number and insufficient to surround the al Qaeda positions. The notion put out by the Pentagon that we had skillfully inserted a substantial contingent of black-clad, bearded gringo warriors unseen even by friendly Afghans in the relatively confined Tora Bora valley as it was being pounded by B-52s turned out to be folkloric nonsense.

Another of the Afghan commanders, Muhammad Musa, later said, "There were six American soldiers with us, U.S. Special Forces. They coordinated the air strikes . . . My personal view is if they had blocked the way out to Pakistan, al Qaeda would not have had a way to escape. The Americans were my guests here, but they didn't know about fighting."

When they did finally arrive in force, some came by chopper, others more conspicuously in a convoy of SUVs on the one road into the valley, in plain sight of reporters. By the end, the force still consisted of only about seventy fighters from Delta Force, Navy SEALS, and Air Force STS, later supplemented by a handful of British commandos and even a sprinkling of Germans.

WHY THE FUCK DIDN'T SOMEBODY TELL ME? DECEMBER 11, 2001

Six days into the Tora Bora campaign, I did something rare: I checked some of the stateside reports of the war's progress that our techs had printed out. As I read one of the wire-service accounts, my throat constricted with the realization that I had been misreporting our friendly-fire incident, or rather that I had confused ours with a far more notorious event involving three US special operators and members of the Karzai family, which actually happened on the other side of the country in Kandahar.

Perhaps typically, my first thought was defensive, "Why the fuck didn't somebody in New York tell me?" That was followed by the less-savory notion that maybe nobody in New York had noticed, and that I could just correct myself without making a big deal of it. More than on most stories, war reporting is typically amended and rewritten on the fly, minute-by-minute, as facts replace initial impressions. Five died; no, ten died; no, it was thirteen, etc.

No such luck.

Preparing for the Hannity hit, I walked past our little equipment tent crammed with satellite gear. One of our two Pats, Pat Butler, innocently delivered my career death sentence. Looking up from his gear after reading the same report I had, he said, "You know they're saying that the friendly fire incident was in Kandahar, not here." A highly competent, thirtysomething, prematurely bald, solid-as-a-rock cameraman and technician with a wonderful temperament, Pat had no malice in his voice, but he was clearly concerned.

"I know," I muttered flatly as I took my mark for the live shot now two minutes away. As I stood next to the ancient mujahideen tank, which had become my signature shot at Tora Bora, explosions were shaking the valley below us. The high-altitude bombers were resuming their runs anew as daylight spread through the valley. They were right on cue.

The bombing was not my angle, though. However dramatic, it was already old news. My emphasis was going to be the arrival the night before of the Special Forces cavalry. It was Monday evening, December 10, in New York, about 6:30 AM Tuesday, December 11, local time. Hannity cohost Alan Colmes asked, "What's it been like the last 24 hours?"

The two Pats with Allister, our gutsy but awkward money man.
Craig, Allister, Pat, Pat, me, Greg. November 2001.

Geraldo Rivera: Well, Alan, let me start with the latest news, and I'm not talking about the bombing raid that just happened a minute ago because that's basically more of the same. Let me tell you what woke me up about three, four hours ago.

We heard the unmistakable sound of choppers, helicopters . . . It had the distinctive sound of American Black Hawk helicopters. And put that in conjunction with what sounded to us a lot like AC-130 gunships, not only AC-130 gunships, but that unmistakable sound from those Gatling guns that the AC-130s have.

I would submit to you, when you combine that information, what we heard with our own ears three hours ago, with information from local sources, that suggests that American military personnel are finally in the area here in eastern Afghanistan. To me, the conclusion that I get is that they mounted some kind of major special operations raid last night.

Now, let me tell you something else, Alan, that I find of great interest. Last night, a couple hours before we were awoken by the helicopter sounds, we got a call from Hazrat Ali. Hazrat Ali is the man who is in charge of the . . . Hear, another strike! Just got another strike up on the hill. You'll see the plume soon. We missed the flash . . . Haz-rat Ali called me to say . . . There it is! There's the plume.

They are convinced now that Osama bin Laden himself is up there, that their radio intercepts on the—you know, the short-range walkie-talkies and their human intelligence. They are—they tell us that they have—they have people inside. They have people who are pretending to be with the foreign legion of Osama bin Laden.

They are—they are telling us that the world's most wanted criminal himself is leading the defense with perhaps one thousand hard-core fighters, one thousand or more, many of them still, inter-estingly enough, Alan, with their families, certainly, at least with their wives.

They say that twenty-five of the terrorists were killed over the weekend, including one woman, in fact. So at that butcher's bill, how long can they sustain? We don't know. But it all suggests a tightening of the noose around Osama bin Laden, Alan.

Alan Colmes: So every time we see one of those plumes, as you call it, there is the hope that beneath that plume might be Osama bin Laden. The Pentagon, by the way, is saying that US special opera-tions forces are being resupplied, and that's what the helicopters are all about, and there's nothing more going on at this point with those helicopters.

Sean Hannity: Hey, Geraldo, it's Sean. Listen, I want to ask you about this. There you are in Tora Bora, and Fox News on its website has reported that within the last thirty-six hours that they dropped one of these fifteen-thousand-pound "daisy cutter" bombs. For those that don't remember, it's about the size of a Volkswagen beetle. That had to be fairly close to where you are. What can you tell us about that?

Geraldo Rivera: All I can tell you is my brother, Craig, and I awoke simultaneously last night, and Craig said to me—and I'm quot-ing—"That felt like a daisy cutter." I can't say that I felt what Craig did. I was half a second behind him in waking up. But Craig's pretty reliable and pretty conservative, so I would not at all be surprised if one of those, at least, was dropped maybe four hours ago . . .

IT HITS THE FAN, DECEMBER 11, 2001

After the live shot, I walked back past the equipment tent. Pat had a pained look on his kind face. "They want to talk to you. Rob Zimmerman, the PR guy. He's on the line," Pat said, handing me the bulky satellite phone.

Another competent new colleague, as the network's spokesman Zimmerman was riding the bucking bronco those days. A studious yuppie who left Fox News a few months later, Rob was the network's spokesman to the world during this heady, tumultuous period when the five-year-old news organization was rocketing to the top of the cable ratings.

Rob apologetically, almost sheepishly, explained that a reporter for the *Baltimore Sun* was aggressively inquiring about an "anomaly" in my reporting. He went on to explain the disconnect between my having reported on multiple occasions that I had walked the "hallowed ground" of friendly fire, when the actual incident being discussed back in the States happened three hundred miles from my location.

As my stomach dropped, I shot back defensively something like "but we had one here too." He listened sympathetically and then asked reasonably if I wouldn't mind talking to the *Sun* reporter, a guy I had never heard of, named David Folkenflik.

With about forty-five minutes until the next hit, I agreed, confident that I could quickly clear the matter up. As I recall, Rob punched in the reporter's number and conferenced us. In any case, I was soon explaining the innocent error to a gleefully skeptical representative of the most loathsome class of journalist, a newspaper media critic who had never actually covered war but who was an expert nevertheless. Here is how he described our encounter:

> Yesterday, in a twenty-minute interview peppered with profanity, Rivera railed against those who would question his work.
>
> "It's time to stop bashing Geraldo," Rivera said. "If you want to knife me in the back after all the courage I've displayed and serious reporting I've done, I've got no patience with this [expletive].
>
> "Have you ever been shot at?" Rivera demanded. "Have you ever covered a war?"

By this point the interview was clearly going badly. Pat listened as I railed against the smug reporter safe back home in Baltimore. In his initial account, Folkenflik paused in his written narrative about the friendly fire incidents to criticize my career shifts, characterizing my move as "a kind of pilgrim's progress from muckraker for a local station, to network reporter, to war correspondent, to syndicated showman, to liberal talk show host," to man with a mission. He wrote:

> Now, he has returned to the coverage of war. From the day of the terror attacks, Rivera, 58, spoke fervently of his anger with a nationalistic bent. He said the many deaths in his small New Jersey town led him to quit his anchor's desk at CNBC in November. He took a pay cut to travel to central Asia for Fox News. Since then, the television star that conservatives once loved to hate for his unabashed defense of President Clinton [during impeachment] is now featured as a leading example of how patriotism has resurfaced in American life.
>
> The veteran television war reporter angrily listed many of the hot spots he has reported from over the years. He also noted that he had won the Robert F. Kennedy award, a prestigious national journalism prize, last year for his reporting on conditions of women in jail.
>
> So far in Afghanistan, he said, he has been the first television reporter to have covered the fall of Kunduz and the fighting in Tora Bora . . . Here's what Rivera said last Thursday, a bit past 8:30 AM Eastern time [December 6, 6 PM local time], in a report filed from Tora Bora:
>
> "We walked over what I consider hallowed ground today. We walked over the spot where the friendly fire took so many of our, our men, and the Mujahedeen [anti-Taliban fighters] yesterday," Rivera said. "It was just—the whole place, just fried, really—and bits of uniforms and tattered clothing everywhere. I said the Lord's Prayer and really choked up."
>
> Although he had shown video footage from the Tora Bora ranges in other stories on Thursday, he did not identify where he had seen the site of the so-called "friendly fire" incident.
>
> A few minutes earlier, Fox News had run captions across the bottom of its screen describing the previous day's events, with some details about the deaths Wednesday of the three American special operations troops. The captions said they had been killed outside Kandahar.
>
> As Rivera had been seen live on the air from Tora Bora both Wednesday [December 5] and Thursday [December 6], journalists, Defense Department officials, and international aid workers

expressed skepticism that anyone could make a round-trip across such treacherous, distant terrain in that time.

It would take twenty hours to thirty-six hours by car across ravaged roads each way, people with knowledge of the region said. They said helicopter flights were almost unheard of and would have afforded dubious safety.

Because he was hell-bent on screwing me, Folkenflik spun the most obvious evidence that my mistake was innocent to make me both guilty and stupid. Does anyone reading this believe that I would be so dumb as to try to pretend I was three hundred miles from where everyone in the world knew I was?

Everyone knew my location because I was on live television, telling viewers hourly where I was. Precisely because of the logistical impossibility of being on two sides of Afghanistan at once, no one, however arrogant or dishonest, would try to pull off what he suggested I tried to pull off. Did he think my editors and news directors were ignorant of my travels?

I was with a team of twenty, including security. Were they all in on my fraud? What about the Fox News assignment desk in New York? Is the supposition that they were all part of a conspiracy to deceive the public?

Later, in anguish, I asked our lead technician, Pat Muskopf, why no one at Fox warned me that I was making a big mistake in conflating one friendly fire incident with another hundreds of miles away. He suggested, "You know, you are Geraldo. Maybe they were just afraid to contradict you."

Even as I write this more than a decade and a half after the fact, my blood boils. I made a damn mistake, innocent, however devastating to my life and career. The reason the entire press corps eventually seized on the allegation that I was a chiseler is that they wanted it to be true.

THE CORRECTION, TUESDAY MORNING, DECEMBER 11

By the time of my next hit an hour and a half after the shouting match, as I reported to Fox News host Jon Scott, I paused to clear up my transparent error about the friendly fire incident and cover my ass by setting the record straight:

But hopefully, with the news that I reported before the break, Jon, of the special operators on the ground, there'll be some land-air coordination. You know, I know that Kandahar is the place that suffered that dreadful friendly fire incident involving our special operators and some of the mujahideen.

But we had one here as well. You know, I walked that hallowed ground. At least three mujahideen fighters killed by our bombers because of the fluidity of the front line. One day, one side has the hill; the next day, the other side has the hill. And they're desperate to avoid repetition of those two friendly fire tragedies, the warrior's nightmare.

So hopefully, with our guys on the ground now—and I really do expect an escalation, a notching up of the quality of the combat. If our people are there, they have not—these Eastern Alliance fighters, God bless them—haven't gotten close to the cave complex yet. I would say we're at least a mile—three-quarters of a mile—away from getting there.

Confident that I had nipped any controversy in the bud, I swaggered from the live-shot location past the equipment tent and said smiling to Pat Butler, "That should take care of that. I was born at night, but it wasn't last night."

Pat nodded, but was otherwise noncommittal, clearly not as confident as I was that bygones were bygones. That was the last I heard about the friendly fire controversy for the entire time we were in Afghanistan.

GERALDO AND HAZRAT, DECEMBER 11, 2001

It is impossible to exaggerate the role Sheik Hazrat Ali played in my reporting. Unlike his double-dealing co-commander Haji Zaman, he was the military arm of the effort to capture or kill Osama bin Laden. Many later reports, written from far away, minimize Ali's stature and significance in the battle of Tora Bora. Some accuse him of being just another dope smuggler looking for an inside angle. I don't know about his other activities, but on the role he played here, the critics are wrong.

We had bin Laden in Tora Bora before anyone else. Our information was so razor-sharp, our access to the front lines so complete, it eventually created another near-scandal. A few days into the Tora Bora battle, as the broader press corps finally descended on this corner of Afghanistan, a reporter for the *Boston Globe* accused me of paying for information. The encounter came during a media gangbang, one of a handful of events staged by the authorities, such as they were, for the gathering press corps. The mujahideen put several al Qaeda prisoners on display. At the site of the sad mini-parade of POWs, a scrawny reporter from the *Globe* asked me to respond to "the charges." I said, "What charges?" Rather than answering, he asked straight up, "Do you deny paying for information?"

I said out loud in a voice full of attitude, "I deny it," and came close to punching his preppy face. We did not "pay for information." We got information from local people, some of whom we were paying for doing legitimate jobs like transporting and protecting us. In this world's most perilous place, our folks were doing the crucial job of keeping us alive.

We paid salaries. We did not pay in the way other news networks, desperate to catch up to us at Tora Bora, were throwing money around "to buy documents" (their lame excuse). I could name the reporters and the producers here and now, but what is the point? They know who they are.

It is impossible to exaggerate the role Sheik Hazrat Ali
played in my reporting. September 2002.

DAMNING COINCIDENCE, DECEMBER 2001

Stateside pundits far from Tora Bora jumped on the *Sun* bandwagon. They were also exclusively men who had never covered combat. They included Tunku Varadarajan, then a cultural critic for the *Wall Street Journal*, who was quoted as mocking "another Rivera report last Thursday in which the correspondent ducked in the face of apparent sniper fire. Rivera is 'really the subject of the story,' Varadarajan wrote Monday [December 10], 'Lest you thought, in a moment of stupidity that it was about Afghanistan.'"

"I think he is a clown, basically," *New York Times* columnist Frank Rich, at the time the ruling effetist, said about me on CNN. "His stories, with clear-cut morality tales of 'good guys' and 'bad guys,' reflect 'Rivera's self- aggrandizement,'" Rich is quoted as saying. "It's not about patriotism or anything else. It's about him trying to basically have reflected glory from the American military."

In truth, I did become enamored of my own sagacity and wisdom. If a thought occurred during one of my unscripted monologues, then it must be true. Once I started down the road to self-confirmation—and again, it's important to note, not being contradicted by my editors in New York—I became increasingly confident, and later paid a disproportionate price. I will never forgive myself the hubris, which led to my disgrace.

MAN-MOUNTAIN CRAIG, DECEMBER 12, 2001

As we traversed the bomb-gouged and cratered mountainside, Greg Hart and I found discarded Pakistani Army–style helmets that had recently protected the heads of now dead or missing al Qaeda fighters. I attached one to my belt. For one of our roaming patrols on the mountain, journalists from CNN and the Associated Press joined us. We began taking fire from snipers up the hill. Craig joked macabrely that he was most in danger because he towered over everyone else. Wearing combat boots and an old-style WWII US Army helmet, he was a mountain standing at least six feet four inches, a walking tall target for the snipers above.

The good news is that Greg Hart's camera was rolling as the volleys of shots began whistling past. The bad news is that Craig and the AP reporter got separated from the rest of us. They were farther up the hill on the upside of a dirt berm. The sniper rounds were either zipping past us or were thudding into the berm or the bomb-damaged adobe walls of the wrecked buildings behind which we had taken cover.

I kept calling out, "Craig Rivera!" worried about my intrepid brother up the hill, exposed to fire from above. As the rest of us crouched behind the berm, we were shocked and delighted when first the AP reporter, then Craig, tumbled over the berm to crash beside us. I was never happier to see my big lug of a kid brother.

As I described it later to Hannity: "It wasn't easy getting to the front, another one of those days where the snipers were obviously targeting foreigners, targeting Westerners like us. The bullets were zinging through the air all day long. My brother, Craig, the producer, had an incredibly close call, bullets whistled past his ear. All the journalists gathered there had to take cover, real salvo after salvo, fusillades fired at us."

During the time between when we taped our intense encounter with the snipers the afternoon before and the live hit with Hannity the next morning Afghanistan time, there had been the first political development of the Tora Bora fight. The Eastern Alliance had made a surrender demand.

As I reported,

They [al Qaeda] have until eight o'clock [AM] our time, ten-thirty PM Eastern time in the United States tonight . . . an hour and fifteen minutes from now, to surrender. If they don't surrender, then—the attack will recommence, and I fully expect that we'll be in the cave network today . . . And for any al Qaeda fighter—the reason two hundred to three [hundred] of them are said to be trying to flee to Pakistan on the other side of the White Mountains—the reason two hundred or more of these so-called suicide fighters are parlaying about surrender today is they know that they are a nineteenth-century army against a twenty-first-century Air Force and Army. They stand no chance.

I have no doubt that bin Laden, if he survived that attack, is deep in the caves. He's not going to give up. He's going to be Hitler in the bunker at the end of the Second World War. But we'll get him, too. By "we" I mean our guys.

At that point, with a flourish, I whipped out my confiscated helmet.

I have . . . a little token from yesterday—you know, I would never disgrace a warrior, but these guys were trying to kill us for no reason.

This was on the head of an al Qaeda fighter just twenty-four hours ago. Now I intend to give it to my friends at the firehouse at Sixty-Fifth Street and Amsterdam Avenue. They lost so much on September 11. I want to show them that . . . the guys that did this to them are now paying the price.

At this exact moment, my living, honest-to-goodness dream was me sitting alongside Erica on top of the backseat of an old Cadillac convertible for a World War II–style, confetti-showering victory parade through downtown Broadway's Canyon of Heroes. The only thing my glorious war story needed was a happy ending. I hinted to the anchors that one was just over the horizon.

I saw the ranks of the mujahideen, the good guys, swell yesterday as word of the victory, of the offensive, as the advance went forward. They came from everywhere. They seemed to come out of the woodwork, the volunteer army, as often happens when momentum shifts their way, so charged, so energized, that where I was watching two hundred, three hundred, four hundred guys fighting, suddenly there were a thousand.

But they do feel charged. They do seem energized . . . you should have seen the road up to the front lines yesterday. It was bumper to bumper with would-be volunteer warriors coming out of the woodwork to be part of the last big push against Osama bin Laden and what is left of his terrorist army.

I would estimate that there are less than five hundred of them left around him, if he still survives. It might have been that he's already incinerated, but my guess is that he's deep down in those caverns . . . he's someplace in some last bunker reserved for the boss. But it won't be long. The world's most hunted man is about to be—about to be nabbed, killed, or in some other ways, eliminated, guys.

THE FAKE SURRENDER, DECEMBER 11, 2001

The focus of the world during this tense day was the surrender deadline, which anchor Jon Scott brought up as soon as my next hit began.

"We want to get more now on that looming deadline for Taliban fighters in Tora Bora," said Scott. "Fox News war correspondent Geraldo Rivera is on the front lines in Tora Bora. Geraldo, we're twenty-five minutes away, any signs of surrender?"

And counting. I'm about to leave this position, Jon, as soon as I finish this broadcast to go back down the valley to the actual front line about three miles from this current position. If I were them, I would definitely take Hazrat Ali up on his offer. They have been pounded to smithereens. And it's—it couldn't happen to a nicer bunch, and it couldn't happen on a better day, the third-month anniversary of what the al Qaeda terrorists' network did to us on September 11.

Then, as we showed video, beginning with the cave, and later making special note of the tremendous bomb dropped during the night:

The scene of the daisy-cutter devastation: utter, utter destruction. It looks like a lunar landscape or a World War I battlefield. They're saying now that Osama bin Laden might have been in the area when this monster was dropped, and it was unbelievable what happened. This had to have, if it didn't kill them, oh, it had to shake their resolve and let them understand that there is no escaping, no escaping now from the firm resolution of the United States and our allies to perpetrate justice against those who perpetrated violence and mass murder against us . . . So, Jon, I think the end is in sight. It's D-Day, man. It's the beginning of the end. Back to you.

Every Johnny-come-lately reporter with or without credentials was arriving at the outskirts of town. Most were setting up camp at the entrance to the valley, but a dozen or more teams eventually found their way to our plateau overlooking the battlefield, which was filling daily with the arrival of the international press corps.

CNN was now there in force, with several correspondents and a score of technicians; NBC had also arrived in considerable strength, joining the French, German, Japanese, British, Canadian, Swedish, and other journalists on our plateau. We bought a half-pint of rum from a French team for fifty dollars US. Despite the steeply marked-up price, we were more than glad to pay it.

Anchor Brit Hume led into the taped version of my overview report that evening on *Special Report*: "Al Qaeda soldiers are cornered in a mountain canyon, and the US has been pounding the area with air strikes. Our war correspondent, Geraldo Rivera, is there."

(voice-over) The B-52s withheld their fire until the deadline for a negotiated surrender came and went this [Wednesday] morning. But when the forces of al-Qaeda did not turn up to turn in their weapons, the lumbering giants unleashed their fury on the remaining terrorist positions.

But even as the United States waged war from the skies, the mujahideen fighters, who yesterday had so successfully swept the enemy before them, withheld their fire, sealing off the front lines from fighters and journalists alike, as they attempted to salvage at least a partial surrender. Tense peace talks were held, we are told, in the same adobe huts where we had taken such intense sniper fire from just yesterday.

Based on another conversation with Akbar and the mujahideen around us, I concluded this report with an on-camera analysis of what was happening strategically, the big picture, and how a nonnegotiable demand had sabotaged the entire surrender process.

So essentially, the mujahideen agreed to allow two hundred of the rank and file al Qaeda members to go free. Their insistence, though, in the most important condition to accepting surrender, is that Osama bin Laden, if he is in there—and they don't know, but they suspect he might be—Osama bin Laden and twenty-two of his top lieutenants, all named and known in Washington, must surrender. Otherwise there will be no truce. If these conditions are not met by tomorrow morning, the war starts again.

Because it is extremely unlikely that they ever intended to turn over bin Laden dead or alive, in retrospect it seems al Qaeda used the negotiations as a ploy to gain a day off from yesterday's furious infantry assault. That ends at daybreak tomorrow. The B-52s are not stopping at all. From Tora Bora, Geraldo Rivera, Fox News.

SOCKS FOR THE SOLDIERS, DECEMBER 12, 2001

We arranged for a truckload of socks to be brought up to Tora Bora from Jalalabad for distribution to the ill-equipped mujahideen fighters. When Alan Colmes asked me what was going on, I told him how we were doing our humanitarian part.

Well, Alan, let me start with the small things first. I know how concerned you've been about the condition of the—of the mujahideen, the Afghan freedom fighters and their really—their clothing, so thin, so shabby, so ill-equipped for winter.

Well, the "Fox Patrol" [us], it's not much, but we've started our socks distribution. We had a truck come up from Islamabad bringing a hundred pair of socks, so we're going to start clothing these warriors from the bottom up, so they'll be—here's a couple more—so we can rest easy at least that their feet will be warm when they go into battle. So it's not much, but it's the beginning of our—our private, compassionate, you know, help for our allies.

These guys, the enemies of our enemies, they're fighting a wonderful fight here against a much more modern army. They're helping us. They're saving American lives by sacrificing their own. So it's the very—the very least I could do.

Recounting this incident more than a decade and a half later and remembering the audience response to this simple gesture of kindness, I am still impressed with the sincere patriotism of the Red State audience that is at the soul of Fox News. Over the years, they have reminded me that a vast, unjaded heartland lies between America's coasts. Denigrated and dismissed as deplorable rubes by some political and media elite, it is the population from which much of our armed forces hails. They are the crowd that fifteen years later saw something in Donald Trump that political pros missed, and elected him president.

Sean Hannity: Geraldo, Sean here . . . My great interest and the interest of many Americans is finding Osama bin Laden. After, as we've been reporting the last two nights, after they dropped the daisy cutter bomb, there apparently were numerous communication breaches on their part that gave every indication that Osama bin Laden was there, very close to where that daisy cutter blew up; any confirmation of that?

Geraldo Rivera: No confirmation yet, Sean, because that would really require, in my view, my eyeballs seeing the six-foot-five-inch Saudi lurking around back there, and I can't say that either mine or any other Western pair of eyes have actually spotted him. But I must say you're absolutely correct. The reports are consistent, sketchy if consistent, that bin Laden himself is still in there.

This was pretty ballsy reporting at the time. Pundits on television back in the States, especially beat reporters in the Washington-based defense establishment, were divided on whether bin Laden was ever really in Tora Bora. Eight years later, the US Senate Foreign Relations Committee confirmed that the best intelligence showed bin Laden to be in Tora Bora when I said he was.

Geraldo Rivera: When you think about it, maybe the easiest answer is the simplest answer. And maybe after preparing this last stand, this formidable cave and cavern complex, this last redoubt, he hightailed it there, thinking that he could buy temporary sanctuary, in the same way he underestimated American resolve and our anger—he underestimated, one, how successful he would be on September 11; two, how angry and how stirred to action the United States would be; three, how formidable our staying power and our invincible armed forces. And finally, he underestimated what his nineteenth-century fortifications could withstand against twenty-first-century munitions . . . I think that if it's not this afternoon, then it's tomorrow. We'll know what the hell and who the hell is in that—that Devil's Workshop.

Alan Colmes: Geraldo, thank you. Good reporting. Stay safe. Thank you for caring about the well-being of the soldiers, as well, and . . . keeping them warm.

AL QAEDA HOME MOVIE, DECEMBER 13, 2001

With the latest surrender deadline approaching in Tora Bora that Thursday evening, December 13, a sensational hour-long home video surfaced back in the States of bin Laden appearing to take credit for the 9/11 attacks.

Apparently not intended for public consumption, the tape records a meal shared by bin Laden and several key aides, including Ayman al-Zawahiri, the Egyptian surgeon widely regarded as bin Laden's principal deputy. If al-Zawahiri survives today, he does so despite the ravages of war, age, and a $25 million bounty, dead or alive.

In the video, an adoring radical Saudi cleric is shown serving the group sitting on the floor around a low table filled with food. A sheik, he is shown respectfully kissing bin Laden on the forehead as bin Laden describes watching the aircraft smashing into the Twin Towers at 500 mph, killing 2,606 innocent civilians, collapsing the structures, shaking American complacency, and ending the New World Order declared in 1991 by President George H. W. Bush after the end of Gulf War I.

US intelligence officers found the tape in a residence in Jalalabad on November 9, about fifty kilometers (thirty miles) from where I was standing and just three weeks before we got to Tora Bora. Hannity led his show with the bin Laden video, with the terror mastermind saying he underestimated the devastating force of the planes' impact.

Osama bin Laden (US government translation): "We calculated in advance the number of casualties from the enemy, who would be killed based on the position of the tower. We calculated that the floors that would be hit would be three or four floors. I was the most optimistic of them all. Due to my experience in this field, I was thinking that the fire from the gas in the plane would melt the iron structure of the building and collapse the area where the plane hit and all the floors above it only. This is all that we had hoped for." (End video clip)

Sean Hannity: Unbelievable. Joining us now from Tora Bora is Fox News war correspondent Geraldo Rivera. Geraldo, what's happening today?

Geraldo Rivera: Well, you know, it's so fitting when you hear . . . Osama bin Laden so coolly describing what he expected his body kill to be, so appropriate that, although it's not exactly accurate to say, "It's all over but the shouting!" because there's still some killing and some dying to do, Sean—I think it is fair to say that virtually every source here in and around Tora Bora suggests that when the Muslim holy month of Ramadan ends this weekend, there is a joyous celebration . . . There is a feeling Osama bin Laden is finally cornered in a place where he has no exit whatsoever. They have him surrounded . . . There is a feeling here of nervous expectation, a feeling here that this thing could be over by the weekend.

As I spoke with silly confidence in a happy ending, New York rolled video we had fed them earlier of a dangerous excursion Craig and I had taken that morning to work our way around the mujahideen roadblocks set up to prevent press access to the front during the crucial negotiations. As I reported to Sean that morning, "We decided to hike it. It was six miles uphill, very steep, with body armor and our packs, but it was well worth the walk."

What we saw was awesome devastation, chewed-up ground and gaping craters. There were also numerous caves bored deep into the mountainsides. What we did not tape, however, was a confrontation Craig and I had with the two local guys who were guiding us on this hump in the hills to get around the roadblocks. With Akbar off on another errand, the pair had convinced me that they could get us close to the surviving members of al Qaeda and the fight.

At one point, after taking us deep into no man's land, as I sat on a rock to catch my breath, both of them started shaking down Craig for cash. I watched as my brother excitedly argued with these two armed desperados, who were demanding $200 each.

They were gesturing with their weapons and getting red-faced pissed off. So was Craig. I fingered the pistol I was now carrying in the outside pocket of my coat. These were desperados and we were miles from Akbar at our home base. Finally, Craig agreed angrily to give them $100 each. As he stormed past me beginning the march home he spat out, "I wish you shot the motherfuckers."

On the air later with Sean, my live narration was interrupted by a bomb blast nearby.

> Oh, we just had a strike, just a strike over there, a strike just this second. We found what those strikes are doing . . . huge chasms in the ground, huge craters, and house-sized craters left by those B-52s. One of them destroyed absolutely a defensive position. It revealed in the destruction a small opening in the earth. When we peered inside, lo and behold, it was another one of those caves for which the Tora Bora camp in the White Mountains is so infamous.

As I spoke, producers were rolling the dramatic video of me inside the cave.

> Poked inside. It looked like a small cave. However, once inside, it was apparent it was a huge vault, at least a twelve-foot ceiling, maybe higher, the room itself at least twenty by twenty. I did not find any connecting tunnels in my very brief examination, my inspection. We couldn't stay long there. But it was again, I think, very characteristic of what we have been up against in our assault on this final strong-hold of Osama bin Laden.
>
> But by the look of the concussion outside that cave entrance, it was pretty apparent that whoever was inside was also concussed at least to death, maybe even incinerated, the way so much outside the cave entrance had been.
>
> Now, again, Sean and Alan, we hear the small-arms fire now, to go with the artillery and the aerial bombardment. It is pretty clear that if they're not eyeball-to-eyeball yet, they soon will be. And I think today really is the day, tomorrow at the latest.

That Friday morning in Afghanistan, I spoke on camera with Hazrat Ali the mujahideen leader, as Akbar translated. The late, great Tony Snow hosted from Washington, saying in his lead-in to my taped report, "Opposition forces in Afghanistan say they've advanced toward cave and valley hideouts in the mountains near Tora Bora. The US continues to support their mission with bombing raids aimed at forcing al Qaeda loyalists into the open. War correspondent Geraldo Rivera is there."

(Videotape of the Hazrat Ali interview begins.) Rivera: Will tomorrow bring victory?

Hazrat Ali (Akbar translating): I hope that at five o'clock, six o'clock, we will finish them.

Geraldo Rivera: Finish them—finished?

Hazrat Ali: Yeah.

Geraldo Rivera: Free Afghanistan?

Hazrat Ali: Yeah.

Geraldo Rivera: No Arabs?

Hazrat Ali (Akbar translating): He says he hopes that we will finish them tonight.

Geraldo Rivera: Evening time tonight?

Hazrat Ali: Yeah, tonight.

Geraldo Rivera: But maybe tomorrow?

Hazrat Ali (Akbar translating): No, tonight. He said he hope one hundred percent for tomorrow, twelve o'clock.

Geraldo Rivera: High noon tomorrow [Saturday, December 15]. As they say in Afghanistan and Brooklyn, "From his lips to God's ears." As far as bin Laden's whereabouts, the Alliance is saying they found evidence that he's occupied one of these recently discovered caves, but would not be more specific. But how much more specific than high noon tomorrow can you get? From Tora Bora, Geraldo Rivera, Fox News.

By sunset Sunday, December 16, and the end of Ramadan, the fighting was over. As the Senate report later said, "On or around December 16, two days after writing his will, bin Laden and an entourage of bodyguards walked unmolested out of Tora Bora and disappeared into Pakistan's unregulated tribal area. Most analysts say he is still there today." Issued on November 30, 2009, the Senate report was correct, as events leading to bin Laden's eventual takedown two years later would reveal.

I was the lead story on *Fox News Sunday*. Sadly, my news was not very good. Anchor Tony Snow began the broadcast network show with a reminder of Osama bin Laden's mocking tone on the captured video, and then cut to Defense Secretary Donald Rumsfeld.

Donald Rumsfeld: It is frightening and shocking to sit there and listen to him invoke the name of an Almighty to defend murder, to defend evil.

Tony Snow: . . . Good morning. We'll talk with our guests in a moment, but first there are major developments in Afghanistan. And for that we turn to Fox News war correspondent Geraldo Rivera live in Tora Bora. Good morning, Geraldo.

Geraldo Rivera: Tony, how you doing? Big news here, good news and bad news, a story of victory and disappointment; the victory first: The war in Tora Bora, therefore the ground war in Afghanistan, is over. Tora Bora has fallen to the forces of Afghanistan, the mujahideen, the freedom fighters. The army of the Eastern Alliance has captured the cave-and-cavern tunnel complex where Osama bin Laden was making his last stand here in Afghanistan.

The disappointment, the gross disappointment, is that the world's most hunted man, the world's master terrorist, is not there. When I asked the Eastern Alliance military commander in a world-exclusive interview, his first live interview, fresh from the battlefield, as Akbar translated he told me of this curious mix of elation and disappointment over these mixed results. Here is Hazrat Ali, the Eastern Alliance commander.

(Video clip begins)

Disappointment, happy, both today? He won the war but Osama bin Laden is not there.

Hazrat Ali (Akbar translating): We are very happy today because we finish our—the terrorist from our own homeland. But we are very disappointed because we didn't capture the Osama. Therefore, this is a day of both happy and—we are happy and also unhappy.

Geraldo Rivera: As to Osama bin Laden, when did he get out of here? According to Hazrat Ali, the commander, he said that it was during that phony cease-fire, during those thirty-six hours when the political wing of the Eastern Alliance insisted on giving the al Qaeda fighters the chance to surrender. They were asking, begging, for a chance to surrender over their short-range walkie-talkies.

Where are they now? They think either in the high passes of the White Mountains or that they've already made it successfully someplace into Pakistan, although, as you know, President Musharraf of Pakistan has mobilized a substantial chunk of his army on the Pakistan side of this very porous border. So now is the time to ask Pakistan for results. Back to you, Tony.

IT WAS OVER, DECEMBER 16, 2001

It ended with a whimper on that sleepy Sunday morning in the States. All of the buildup, the bombs, the tension and attention had come to this. Tora Bora was conquered, but so what? Bin Laden was gone. In those days, many questioned whether he was ever really there.

Despite my reporting, commentators and pundits argued passionately on that crucial point. Although he would later waffle, General Tommy Franks's second-in-command during the war, Lieutenant General Michael DeLong, was convinced that bin Laden was at Tora Bora, until he was not.

In his memoir, *Inside CentCom*, DeLong describes the massive, three-week bombing campaign aimed at killing al Qaeda fighters in their caves at Tora Bora. "We were hot on Osama bin Laden's trail," he wrote. "He was definitely there when we hit the caves. Every day during the bombing, Rumsfeld asked me, 'Did we get him? Did we get him?' I would have to answer that we didn't know."

Subsequent accounts were filled with scenarios under which an appropriate blocking force could have been placed between Tora Bora and the Pakistan border. On the question of whether bin Laden was in Tora Bora, there should be little doubt. Remember when bin Laden was discovered nearly ten years later, he was barely a hundred miles away in Abbottabad, Pakistan. Everything I heard, saw, and reported during that volatile period put him in Tora Bora. And as far as I know, every commentator with actual experience on the ground in the Tora Bora fight concurred.

For example, in his 2005 book, *Jawbreaker*, Gary Berntsen, a national-security analyst, who as a CIA officer based in Kabul in December 2001 directed a team charged with finding bin Laden, claimed that his operatives pinpointed the terror mastermind in Tora Bora.

"We needed U.S. soldiers on the ground!" he wrote emphatically. "I'd sent my request for eight hundred U.S. Army Rangers and was still waiting for a response. I repeated to anyone at headquarters who would listen: We need Rangers now! The opportunity to get bin Laden and his men is slipping away!!"

CNN National Security Analyst Peter Bergen, who produced the first interview with Osama bin Laden in 1997, wrote reliably in *The New Republic* in December 2009, in what the magazine called the definitive account of what really happened at Tora Bora: "At least five Guantánamo detainees have given eyewitness accounts of bin Laden's presence at Tora Bora."

Dalton Fury makes a similar claim in *Killing bin Laden*, in which he recalls how one of the CIA operatives at Tora Bora picked up a radio from a dead al Qaeda fighter.

"The CIA had a guy with them called Jalal, and he was the foremost expert on bin Laden's voice," Fury wrote. "He worked on bin Laden's voice for seven years and he knew him better than anyone else in the West. To him, it was very clear that bin Laden was there on the mountain."

In the words of the Foreign Relations Committee 2009 Report, "Fewer than 100 American commandos were on the scene with their Afghan allies, and calls for reinforcements to launch an assault were rejected. Requests were also turned down for U.S. troops to block the mountain paths leading to sanctuary a few miles away in Pakistan. The vast array of

American military power, from sniper teams to the most mobile divisions of the Marine Corps and the Army, was kept on the sidelines."

BIN LADEN IS GONE, DECEMBER 16, 2001

If not for the friendly fire mistake, I might have been honored when I got home by that ticker-tape parade I dreamed of, if not in downtown Manhattan, then at least at the VFW Hall in my modest New Jersey river town of Edgewater. None of that mattered on that Sunday evening, December 16. The chicken had flown the coop. Bin Laden was gone, disappeared into the White Mountains and into the belly of Pakistan to live almost another decade as Americans fought and bled in Afghanistan, and Iraq, expending trillions and alienating a huge hunk of the Muslim world. The mass killer upon whom America had sworn vengeance had escaped.

With adrenaline hemorrhaging, a deflating anticlimax gripped me. I wanted to get back to the States. I missed Erica and the kids and yearned for that hero's welcome and the beginning of a new career at Fox News. The big game was over, and although our home team played well, the match ended in a tie. I shed the gun and we headed home.

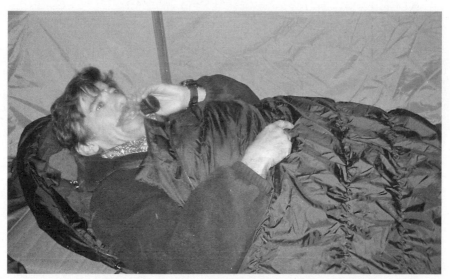

"I missed Erica and the kids and yearned for that hero's welcome and the beginning of a new career at Fox News." December 2001.

COMING HOME, DECEMBER 19, 2001

We caught a rickety (and dry) Pakistani Airlines flight to London and civilization. The initial inkling of utter career disaster came hours later, shortly after we settled into the lush first-class seats of the United Airlines flight from London to New York.

Over my long career as a roving reporter coming home from faraway places, that moment of first-class airline embrace is always the Big Sigh. The lush seat, the smiling attendants, the stiff drink . . . I had survived peril and discomfort, burnished the legend, and was heading back to applause and romance.

Given how big a deal it became in my life, it is surreal still that no one had even mentioned what was going on with the scandal brewing back home. It was about to blow up my life.

Having heard nothing about it for almost two weeks, I was stunned when I looked at the newspaper handed out by the flight attendant just before takeoff. There it was on the day-old front page of the *International Herald Tribune*:

GERALDO RIVERA DRAWS CONTROVERSY IN
AFGHANISTAN
    Dec 18 (Reuters)—It didn't take long after arriving in Afghanistan as a war correspondent for maverick broadcaster Geraldo Rivera to do what he is best known for—generate controversy.
    Days after nearly having his hair parted by sniper fire while filming a report for the Fox News Channel near Jalalabad, Rivera found himself the target of criticism in journalistic circles for carrying a gun on assignment, despite long-standing taboos against correspondents packing heat in war zones.
    Now the *Baltimore Sun* is challenging Rivera and Fox News on a dispatch Rivera filed about a deadly "friendly fire" bombing incident Dec. 5 . . . The apparent contradictions have raised questions from news executives and journalistic ethicists.
    "I believe that Geraldo Rivera and Fox News owe their viewers a substantive explanation of what this means, journalistically and ethically," Bob Steele, director of the ethics program at the Poynter Institute in St. Petersburg, Florida, told the *Sun*.

My first reaction was apoplectic horror. My head was about to blow off. I was being accused of the most hideous offense imaginable, perpetrating a wartime hoax on the American people. I was outraged; how dare they? I had explained the confusion. It was a classic "fog of war" mistake.

Thankfully we were back in the land of cell phones. Frantic, I called Roger Ailes before the airplane doors closed. With raised voice that alerted everybody in the first-class cabin to my distress, I explained what was going on. He told me to calm down and keep my mouth shut. His argument was that it was a minor flap that would soon blow over, and if I argued too loudly, I would only make matters worse. It was the worst advice he ever gave me, creating a breach that never totally healed.

DADDY IS HOME, DECEMBER 20, 2001

C.C. and the girls met me at JFK. I wept tears of relief at the sight of the children, who ran into my outstretched arms. "Daddy's home!"

In their eyes I was a returning hero. During their entire childhood, we had a routine whenever I was heading into danger. "Daddy always goes away," I would say. "But he always comes back," they would answer in unison, relieved and smiling through their tears. Over the years, parting from my children got harder, not easier.

On this original return from the front as a Fox News correspondent, I slunk through the airport. I remember being grateful that no one brought up my disgrace, which apparently had not yet made much of a splash in New York. I could not bear to look at the newspaper stands, for fear of what I would find. In those few days before my shame at Tora Bora became more widely disseminated, I could still picture myself the warrior journalist returning triumphant. Except, I was not.

Erica was waiting for me later at our small penthouse apartment on the West Side of Manhattan. In a minor historic coincidence, we lived in a Trump-branded building on Sixty-Second Street and Riverside Boulevard. As soon as the door closed behind us, we made love in the entrance alcove, not even waiting until we could reach the bedroom ten feet away. At least this part of my homecoming played out the way I had dreamed it a dozen times during the rugged journey just completed.

If only that passion was the enduring "coming home" memory of that first Afghan assignment. Instead, there is another tortured image from that first weekend home. It is a photo of me, a day later, standing in front of our home in Edgewater. By then the impression that I had faked the Tora Bora story was spreading all the way to late-night television. Conan O'Brien and Jay Leno were having a field day, mocking what they portrayed as my seemingly obvious misrepresentation.

Wearing an embarrassed, fake smile in the photo taken over the weekend of December 22–23, I am standing in front of our New Jersey house. It is festooned with an oversized "Welcome Home Geraldo" banner.

It was put there by our local contractor, a giant ex-cop and retired Marine named Tom McNiff, who had cheered my leaving NBC and going to war for Fox News and country. It was a gray, overcast day, and the banner had been soaked in an overnight rainstorm. Thinking we were coming back to the house, Tom hung the banner two days earlier, but I had opted to hide out in the New York apartment instead.

Whether in New York or Edgewater, by putting my head under the pillow I aggravated a disaster. Many of the same friends who just a month before had crowded Ms. Elle's celebrating my brave sacrifice were

With NYPD Marine Unit at my Edgewater, New Jersey, dock. Summer 2016.

now part of the chorus of ridicule, which was bounding and rebounding through the news business at lightning speed.

One incident I still remember vividly was running into Linda Sittenfeld, one of my closest, longest-running CNBC producers, so close that I considered her part of my brain. She asked me incredulously, "What happened?" I answered with a pained shrug, "I made a mistake."

"That was some mistake," she said almost contemptuously, her voice dripping disdain as she walked away, never to be heard from by me again.

With every media writer in the country choosing to focus on my dilemma instead of on the war itself, I was getting more ink than Osama bin Laden. Toby Harnden of the *London Telegraph* accurately saw what was happening in his story filed December 20.

GUN-TOTING GERALDO UNDER FIRE FOR THE STORY THAT NEVER WAS

. . . Sensing his difficulties, the American media has swooped with a vengeance. Having already had to defend his decision to arm himself, he is now being peppered with questions about the veracity of his reporting. The usual obscure academics and journalism tutors have been wheeled out to do him and Fox News down.

Geraldo's main crime, his defenders say, is his overnight switch from left-wing defender of Bill Clinton to a gun-toting, uber-patriot who warned that, if he found Osama bin Laden, he'd personally "kick his head in, then bring it home and bronze it." Critics hope Geraldo will be recalled in ignominy for crimes against journalism, while his application for a Pulitzer Prize is filed in the bin.

Steve Murray of the *Atlanta Constitution* was similarly evenhanded.

RIVERA IS EASY TARGET FOR CRITICS

These days, he doesn't have to get his nose busted by a white supremacist or open Al Capone's empty vault to grab attention. No, Geraldo Rivera—former tabloid journalist-turned-self-styled war reporter—has been grabbing headlines lately. But not the kind he'd like . . .

Geraldo "fessed up to [Folkenflik], it was a mistake," Fox News spokesman Robert Zimmerman says, referring to a follow-up interview Rivera gave a reporter at the *Sun*. He adds, *"The Baltimore Sun is trying to advance a story that was dead on arrival."*

Here reporter Murray made a fair point that it effectively took me years to follow up on.

The story doesn't end there, though. The only officially recorded incident of friendly fire casualties in Tora Bora happened three days after Rivera's report, when Afghan fighters were killed by a bomb. But that doesn't necessarily mean Rivera fabricated what he says he observed.

"It may well have been Taliban or al-Qaida guys he saw," says Lt. Col. Dave Lapan from the media office of the Department of Defense. "I have no way of telling what he may or may not have witnessed."

Which was fair enough as far as it went. The problem was that aside from my reporting and commentary, I had presented no hard, objective evidence that there had been friendly fire casualties in Tora Bora during that first week of combat. We never showed on air the video we had shot that day of the carnage in Tora Bora.

Murray concluded,

Rivera couldn't be reached for comment: On Wednesday he was en route from Afghanistan to spend the holidays back in the States. No, he isn't being called home early. Zimmerman says the seasonal furlough was always intended, and Rivera will return to report on the war later. "Right now the man has to come home and shower," Zimmerman adds. "He hasn't showered in three weeks." So it's official: Rivera stinks. But not the way his critics mean.

For days after returning home, I simmered with rage and embarrassment, wanting to fight back to prove my innocence.

At one point during that period, Jay Leno invited me on *The Tonight Show*. I was delighted and relieved finally to have a forum during which I could put the whole controversy to rest. But Roger refused my request to go out to the coast to do the show.

"Aren't you supposed to be on vacation?" he asked, coldly dismissing my frantic request just as he had earlier dismissed my distressed phone call.

CORPORATE RECKONING, FRIDAY, DECEMBER 21, 2001

There is another scene that aches. On Friday, December 21, my first full day back in the States, there was a meeting in one of the big conference rooms on the second floor of Fox headquarters on Avenue of the Americas, six or seven men in ties and shirtsleeves assembled. Lawyers and news executives present, this was my formal hearing to determine if the staging charges were true.

Did I intentionally misrepresent my location to make it appear that I was in Kandahar to walk "hallowed ground"? Did I lie to put myself near those slain by friendly fire incident? Faking news was utterly unacceptable.

News chief John Moody chaired the meeting. Short, with slicked-back black hair and a taut frame, Moody was Roger's powerful number two. In the post–Roger Ailes era he has been moved from the second-floor executive area to the seventeenth floor. Ironically, he is now next door to me. He was no friend at the meeting in December 2001. It was in a darkly lit, tastefully decorated conference room. I told my story as I have here, explaining my alibi to him and the other Fox News executives seated around an oval table.

There had been an incident of friendly fire in my location, I told them. We saw the aftermath. It was easy to confuse that Tora Bora incident in our location with the incident in Kandahar that everyone else was talking about back here in the States. Cut off from outside news sources, I explained how I made a flawed but innocent assumption.

Moody responded coldly in low, dramatic tones that rattled my nerves. "Our sources in the Pentagon say they know of no other incidents of friendly fire near your location on that date."

"I can't believe that," I responded defensively, my gut dropping out. "Every Afghan at Tora Bora was talking about the danger of friendly fire from the American bombers. Besides, it only matters that I thought sincerely that they were talking about friendly fire at my location."

Fox News cleared me of any intentional wrongdoing after considering the lack of communication with the outside world and the fog of war. "Based on Geraldo Rivera's thirty-year track record, Fox News has full confidence in his explanation and journalistic integrity," said the statement from Fox News. "This is not the first, nor will it be the last, mistake made in a war zone."

That boilerplate statement of support aside, I thought Moody's main goal was to make sure that I took the fall for the embarrassing blunder. Nobody wanted to confront a basic question: Why no one at the News Desk told me I was making a mistake.

Roger was not at the meeting. He had an expanding empire to run, and later said he sincerely believed that my flap would die down, like so many public relations crises he had steered his clients through in his political career. He ordered me to keep my mouth shut, and let the network handle it, which was the worst advice he ever gave me.

"LOOK, THEY'RE TALKING ABOUT YOU," DECEMBER 2001

Reporting on the Fox News statement, and no doubt empowered by my public silence, the *Baltimore Sun* attacked me again, this time more viciously. On Thursday, December 27, David Folkenflik reported that according to the Pentagon it was essentially impossible for me to have been confused. He added that although there was indeed a friendly fire incident in Tora Bora, it happened on December 9, three days after my mistake.

Most damningly, he wrote, "No journalist, international aid worker or Defense Department official interviewed could confirm the existence of another 'friendly fire' incident on December 5."

Note how carefully he couched his damnation, writing only that no one *he interviewed* could confirm the existence of another friendly fire incident on December 5. I tried to be indifferent, but it was impossible to ignore. Mainstream pundits were crawling over each other to appear on cable news decrying my blatant dishonesty. Wolf Blitzer devoted an entire hour-long program to the scandal; worse, it was on the monitor the first time I visited Roger alone in his office. "Look, they're talking about you," he said, his voice dripping disdain.

No one understood the depth of my humiliation, but I remained silent, becoming an obsession for reporters who chose to overlook the groundbreaking truth of my reporting from Tora Bora. Aside from being the first in the caves, as I said, I was also the first to report with confidence that Osama bin Laden had escaped, probably during or immediately after the phony truce engineered by local fighters.

Throughout 2002, I would spend half my energy making the case that the *Sun*'s reporting was based on a false accusation. Yes, I made a mistake. No, it was not intentional. Not many establishment types believed me, and the story continued to haunt everything I did. At one point Roger said to me, "I had no idea you had such a big bull's-eye on your back."

What I took away from that first meeting was that he regretted hiring me from CNBC, but as a loyal friend he was stuck with me. Like every executive and reporter in the building, he wanted my controversy to fade away to protect the network.

The pain it caused me could not be understood by anyone except Erica and Craig. By New Year's Day January 2002, Fox News had achieved ratings preeminence over CNN, a ranking that would run uninterrupted for a decade and a half. The last thing the flourishing operation needed was a credibility-draining controversy like mine.

NOWHERE TO RUN, JANUARY 2002

I thought of disappearing to escape the ridicule and even thought of suicide, but decided not to let my accuser off the hook that easily. The thought of critics remaining on Earth after me, garnering credit for revealing the shame that led me to take my own life, was what kept me alive. I could just see the nerd absorbing the quiet congratulations from the Geraldo-haters. "Oh I'm sorry he felt so ashamed that he killed himself to escape the truth." Bullshit.

Instead, I took a two-pronged approach to life after Tora Bora: one, to ignore the slings and arrows, vowing eventually to clear my name; and two, to fight the charges on their merits by proving there had been friendly fire deaths in Tora Bora during that first week of December 2001.

On December 12, an article had appeared on the website of FAIR, which billed itself as "the national progressive media watchdog group challenging corporate media bias, spin and misinformation." In other words it is an organization as ideologically far away from Fox News as possible. In the article, writer Rachel Coen did a survey of friendly fire incidents during the air campaign in Afghanistan.

Quoting the *Independent* newspaper, dated December 4, 2001:

From all over the countryside, there come stories of villages crushed by American bombs; an entire hamlet destroyed by B-52's at Kili Sarnad, 50 dead near Tora Bora, eight civilians killed in cars bombed by U.S. jets on the road to Kandahar, another 46 in Lashkargah, 12 more in Bibi Mahru.

. . . After U.S. bombing near Tora Bora destroyed two villages and killed over 100 people—reporters seemed surprised at Afghans' negative response to America's war on the Taliban and al Qaeda. CBS's Randall Pinkston reported that "at least 100 people" had been killed . . . He noted that the Tora Bora killings had provoked criticism of U.S. policy, and called this "a troubling new reaction." *CBS Evening News 12/1/01.*

Over the long years of this endless conflict, those friendly fire deaths strained our relations with the emerging Afghan government and put at risk all the blood and treasure that we shed there. The fact that our forces accidentally killed thousands of innocent Afghans in this longest war in our history is undeniable.

WALKING DEAD, DECEMBER 2001–JANUARY 2002

I kept myself crazy busy, seeking to prove with reckless courage that I had not deceived, because I was the bravest celebrity war correspondent ever to wield a microphone. It became my ambition to die in combat. Emotionally crippling, professionally, the flap destroyed my road to glory. On a fast track to being regarded as the preeminent combat correspondent of the age, I instead became a punchline. One cruel January 2002 television sketch on *Late Night with Conan O'Brien* cut deep. In it the character representing me is reporting an incident on a shipwrecked vessel. Because the faux Geraldo is far from the sea at the time of his report, a sidekick helpfully splashes "me" with water to make the scene more authentic. When Craig brought up the skit in the office the next day, saying I had to admit it was funny, I didn't speak to him for weeks. My team knew forever after they could not talk about Tora Bora. However vivid and important our memories of the caves, the bombs, the bodies, or the sense that we had been at center stage of living history, no one was allowed to mention the place in my presence.

As I wrote in my diary at the time: "Spent the entire month almost making history in Afghanistan only to watch it all turn to shit with the stupid story about friendly fire. It should have been great, but as Al Pacino said, every time I seem on the verge of a breakout 'they drag me back in.'"

Leaving Erica, who traveled home to Cleveland for the holiday break, I visited the girls at their seaside home in small picturesque Marion, Massachusetts. It was painful. The girls were still traumatized by my breakup with their mom C.C. the year before, and it did not help matters that I was damaged goods. A widely syndicated *Washington Post* article by Howard Kurtz appeared on Christmas Day, based on an interview I had given him before Roger Ailes shut me down. The headline was: "Geraldo Rivera is offering to resign from Fox News."

> Rivera acknowledges that he made an "honest mistake" by saying he was at a "friendly fire" incident in which three American soldiers were killed in a U.S. bombing raid. He was hundreds of miles away, near what he maintains was a second such incident in which two or three Afghan opposition fighters were killed.
>
> *Sun* writer David Folkenflik "has slandered a journalist who is an honest person and has contributed arguably much more to American society than he has," Rivera said. "This cannot stand. He has impugned my honor. It is as if he slapped me in the face and challenged me to a duel. He is going to regret this story for the rest of his career."
>
> Folkenflik said he was very careful in framing the story and could find no military official or journalist in the region who could confirm Rivera's account. "I don't know how many bites of the apple he gets to get a version that works," Folkenflik said. "There may be an explanation for this that bears up to scrutiny, but we haven't seen it."

Living in a semi-permanent funk, I became reckless, pushing as relentlessly toward danger as possible. Tora Bora was a low-grade fever, or a stain that could only be cleaned with glory. Time did nothing to alleviate the misery because the harder I tried to forget, the worse the memory got.

It felt impossible to walk the halls of Fox News. Although I had been in the news business for decades, these were people I hardly knew. With great fanfare, Craig and I had gone off to war within the first week we came to work with them. I could not meet anyone's eyes. They were strangers and I was notorious. My arrival was supposed to help bring the young network the credibility of long experience. Instead, I had brought ridicule and embarrassment to myself and, undeservedly by extension, to Fox News.

After a New Year's week with my sons, then twenty-two-year-old Gabriel and fourteen-year-old Cruz, and with Erica, spent mostly hiding out at our rented Malibu beach house, which felt like an enforced exile, we finally got back to New York from the coast during the second week of January 2002. Bill O'Reilly had me on his show first. In fact, he never faltered in his loyalty to me, always finding a once-a-week spot for me on his show throughout the fifteen years we shared at Fox News. Sometimes socially awkward, he was nevertheless a pillar of friendship, putting me on his show, and the two of us together making smart, tough, good TV. On this fraught occasion, he reverted to the Long Island blue-collar accent the network's first crossover star sometimes affected, blurting out the question I yearned to answer. "So what happened?"

I told the story as well as possible in the few minutes allotted, which satisfied the hometown Fox audience, but could not compete with the scorn being heaped by the outside world. It felt like the whole journalistic establishment was wagging its finger. They hated the ascendant Fox News Channel anyway, and I had given those critics the ammo they craved to attack and nearly destroy me.

Chapter 6

TOUR OF TERROR

The year 2002 became my year of living ever more dangerously. Stuck with me by contract and apparently still thinking the Tora Bora scandal would blow over before it destroyed my career or killed me, Roger made me senior war correspondent and host of a weekend show then called *War Zone*. The designation of *senior* correspondent was a letdown. The understanding I had with right-hand man John Moody was that if I returned home bathed in glory, I would be named the network's *chief* war correspondent.

Always with brother Craig and/or Greg Hart in tow, I vowed never to let any reporter out-risk me. Chasing institutional terrorism became my mantra and raison d'etre. After saying goodbye to Erica and the children, the crew and I headed for Kenya. I had not been there since 1998, just weeks after al Qaeda destroyed two of our embassies in East Africa, in its first major attack on US interests.

After doing a series of interviews with military and political experts in Kenya, the crew and I flew on to bordering Somalia. On Saturday, January 12, we landed in a pair of small, chartered twin-engine aircraft on a rolling grass field outside Mogadishu.

The trip was unusual even for that relatively free-spending era in foreign news coverage. We were lavishly equipped. We had a nimble airplane, a King Air, with us the entire time, and a second, less-elegant twin-engine cargo airplane available whenever we had to move the two tons of satellite gear needed to make television when we found something newsworthy. Nowadays, crews in the digital era need far less equipment to do the same job. I am convinced that eventually some tech genius will figure out a way to make our eyes able to transmit stories directly to home base with a coded blink.

Our King Air was owned and operated by a supremely knowledgeable and impressively connected black African pilot named John Mohammed. With him, we could fly confidently to every dusky, dangerous enclave around the Horn of Africa, secure that we had both local knowledge and a trusted go-between to negotiate access with whomever the power players happened to be at the moment. This man could have run a major airline or a big import/export firm.

The main Mogadishu airport, like the harbor and most of its infrastructure, had been destroyed by constant, careening, often-mindless violence. We drove into the lawless, ruined capital where no real government had existed for nine years. Back then, in 1993, our first military intervention into Africa, which was designed to prevent Somalia from dissolving into ethnic/tribal/religious factions, was ill-advised, short-lived, and tragic in its ending. The military disaster is now known by the radio call that signaled catastrophe to our commanders, *Black Hawk Down*.

Craig dresses down during a satellite hit from Kiwayu, Kenya, February 2002. Later the scene of a deadly terror attack.

The supremely knowledgeable and impressively connected pilot, Captain John Mohammed, January 2002.

We landed in Mogadishu in a pair of chartered twin-engine aircraft. January 2002.

It ended when President Clinton brought the troops home. We should have stuck it out, despite the disastrous loss of that Black Hawk helicopter and eighteen GIs. When Clinton and our international partners lost their nerve in 1993 and ordered our forces to pull out precipitately, we left a vacuum in East Africa that sucked law and order out of that corner of the continent, allowed anarchy free rein, and made room for al Qaeda, and later al Shabaab, the main Islamic militant group in the region, to take root.

The remains of the helicopter were still there when we arrived in 2002. Covered in street scum and dirt, it is a sick sort of tourist attraction. Any Mogadishu cabbie can take you to the half-buried, garbage-strewn remains. Ironically, the movie *Black Hawk Down* was playing in US theaters at the time we arrived at the actual scene of the crime. That coincidence was very much on the minds of Somalis. As I reported at the time:

"We visited the site of the real *Black Hawk Down* crash site over the weekend. It's all overgrown with cactus and covered with barbed wire now. And what the government here fears is that the movie will encourage American military planners to believe that Somalia is still an enemy of the US and make more believable the charge that Somalia is harboring al Qaeda."

In downtown Mogadishu we stayed in the bunker-like Central Hotel. With the constant rat-a-tat of gunfire outside the sturdy wall that surrounded the compound, the hotel was protected by huge iron gates and patrolled by heavily armed guards. For many years, it was a speck of stability in Mogadishu's cascading turmoil, frequented by what remained of Somalia's business and political elite and visiting media, who all treasured its security. That aura of safety suffered a blow in 2015 when al Shabaab militants blew it up, killing twenty-five.

WITH SKINNIES CHEWING KHAT, JANUARY 2002

After visiting ex-Somali president Hussein Mohammed Farrah Aidid, a former US Marine who was living in exile in Ethiopia, we flew to Luuq, an Italian colonial town on the Juba River in Somalia's western desert. We stopped there to spend some time with Western aid workers, part of the heroic crew of true humanitarians, who unlike the flabby poolside UN officials we had just seen at the hotel in Addis Ababa, really work selflessly for the greater good. In the next few years, many aid workers

With guides and bodyguards in Mogadishu, Somalia, February 2002.

would suffer abuse, kidnapping, and even murder at the hands of Somali extremists.

Less disciplined than the Afghan mujahideen, but just as fierce, Somali fighters are badasses. They are ebony stick figures, none tall, most around five and a half feet. They are kids with heavy weapons and extra ammo slung over bony bare shoulders, and are known locally as Skinnies or Technicals.

One of the reasons they are so lean, mean, and crazy is that most chew the narcotic leaves known as *khat*. These local extremists who came to be al Shabaab use khat to fuel their aggression. In fact, the leaf has been a fixture in the Horn of Africa for a thousand years. I confess to trying some. I am a sucker for local flavor. Chewing it numbed my mouth, increased my heartbeat, and reminded me of the times I had chewed coca leaves when covering another crusade, the War on Drugs in the South American Andes during the 1970s, '80s, and '90s, while working for ABC and later NBC News.

The main ingredient in cocaine, coca grows almost everywhere in the Andes. At 14,000 feet in Bolivia, it is all around you. Running hard to get the story, you can either chew the leaf or gasp for breath in the thin air of the High Plateau. I chewed and ran.

Less disciplined than the Afghan mujahideen, but just as
fierce, Somali fighters are badasses. January 2002.

Banned by the United States and Canada, khat is legal and widely
traded in Somalia. An amphetamine-like stimulant, in my case it ampli-
fied and aggravated my already reckless state. The leaf juice made me feel
bulletproof, had me running toward the gunfire rather than away from it.
I was snarling like an animal and belittling the concerns of my crew that
we lacked body armor or even basic security.

After "Black Hawk down" in '93 and the withdrawal of all US forces,
the fighting in Somalia turned stupid. Young men were getting their guts
ripped out by .50-caliber machine guns in daily gunfights in and around
Mogadishu.

By 2017, most Skinnies had become political and were fighting for
or against militant Islam in the jihad with the West. Back in 2002 these
kids were anarchists, not particularly religious, and fighting for nothing
more than bragging rights over which warlord controlled which block of
abandoned buildings in one of the world's most battered and bloodied
capital cities. Mogadishu is an aggravated, apocalyptic African version
of *Mad Max* gone truly crazy.

I have been in the company of scores of honored war dead, soldier
and civilian. During this 2002 trip we taped a guy dying in front of us.

In his midtwenties and dressed like a bank clerk, he was on a stretcher in a rudimentary field hospital and our camera rolled as his brains dripped out from a devastating head wound until he gasped and his heart finally stopped pumping blood onto the dirty floor.

Young men were getting their guts ripped out by .50-caliber machine guns in daily gunfights in and around Mogadishu, Somalia, February 2002.

ALPHA MALE SEEKS HONORABLE DEATH, JANUARY AND FEBRUARY 2002

That January and February 2002, I was a psychologically wounded man seeking an honorable death. There was gunfire and death everywhere in Mogadishu, which, as I said, I made a practice of running toward. During this malignantly obsessive, post–Tora Bora phase, I was self-centered, deeply hurt, and half-crazy enough to seek guns and gore to restore glory.

When heavy firing broke out as we were interviewing a local official near the wreck of the US Embassy, not far from our hotel in Mogadishu, I urged our crew to rush with me toward the sounds of gunfire even though we were unprepared. Our bulletproof vests and helmets were still in our rooms, precious minutes away. When Craig and Greg, who never refused to go into action, counseled that we should at least be properly equipped, I snarled, "If you're afraid, then go back to the hotel."

Needless to say, everyone followed me toward the action, although one of the members of the crew was so shaken by the tumult he left Africa as soon as we could arrange transport. The incident itself provided some of the most dramatic combat footage since Tora Bora. In one sequence, what must have been a .50-caliber machine gun blasted apart a street lamp just as Craig ducked under it.

Here's part of my report on Fox News:

We saw something today that provided us with a tiny glimpse of the horror and violence our GIs faced on the battle-scarred streets of Mogadishu in 1993. It was a bloody street fight between two sub-clans that ended with two militiamen dead and at least half a dozen innocent civilians seriously wounded.

Making a mockery of the government's call for the Mogadishu militias to disarm, the two sub-clans engaged in a fierce morning-long firefight, which began about a mile from the former American embassy.

By the time we reached the scene, it had escalated into a raging street battle, cutting down civilians and passersby alike with no regard for whether they were in one of the warring sub-clans or had any dog in this fight.

We later found that the origin of the violence was an absurd dispute over which group controlled a single ruined building in the devastated neighborhood. We discovered something even more distressing, that one of the dead was a driver for our hotel who had been caught in the crossfire.

At the hospital, the only working hospital in this city of one million, we saw the full extent of the grim reaper's tally. At least a half dozen were seriously injured, one was dead and one was dying right before our eyes. Chaotic, senseless, it was a bloody mess.

Later, I had nightmares of having to explain to Craig's wife, Cordelia, and his kids, Austin, then eight, and Olivia, age four, or to Greg's parents, that my recklessness had killed their loved ones.

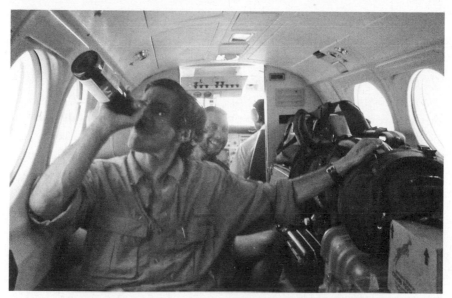

Celebrating when we left Somalia in one piece, February 2002.

BEIRUT, RUINED OASIS, JANUARY 2002

From the Horn of Africa, our next stop on the Tour of Terror was back in the Middle East. The crew and I arrived in Beirut, one of the planet's most unique cities, on January 27, 2002. It is five thousand years old, an ancient yet modern multicultural metropolis sitting at the rocky nexus of the Christian, Druze, Sunni, and Shiite worlds. Here East meets West, disco meets belly dance, and sharia meets sexy. How could it be otherwise given that the city has been held in turn by Phoenician, Greek, Roman, Byzantine, Arab, Crusader, and Ottoman rulers until fracturing along religious lines.

Still, until the mid-1970s, Beirut sported a wide-open, tolerant, cosmopolitan air that was a favorite of travelers from jet-setters to backpackers. The American University still attracts scholar/adventurers from throughout the Old and New Worlds. But beginning around 1975, a vicious, ten-year-long, sectarian civil war shattered the façade of harmony, probably forever.

I had covered Southern Lebanon from the Israeli perspective since Operation Litani, the 1978 Israel Defense Forces invasion whose purpose was to eliminate raids from Lebanese territory against Israeli coastal communities such as Haifa. Editorially, almost all my early reporting in the region was from an Israeli-American Zionist perspective.

Those were the Israel-can-do-no-wrong days, Israel as bastion of Western democratic ideals. Created by the scrappy underdog survivors of every persecutor from Goliath to the pharaohs, the Romans to the Nazi Holocaust, the Zionists were the underdog victors of desperate wars in 1948, 1956, 1967, and 1973, and worthy stewards of the Holy Land, protectors of the sacred ancient places and irrigators of the desert. The local Arabs, on the other hand, whether Sunni, Shiite, or Druze, were always portrayed by me and most others as shady, primitive, and generally up to no good.

I was totally wired into the Israeli government in those days, often getting editorial guidance from their powerful intelligence community, including the Mossad. That preference for Israel extended to their New Testament cousins, the Christians of the Mideast, whom I always described as "beleaguered" or "embattled." One vivid 1978 ABC News *20/20* piece, done with extensive Israeli editorial guidance, featured Major Saad Haddad. He was a gritty Lebanese Army officer who had formed his own militia of Christians and announced a military alliance with Israel.

Haddad occupied Southern Lebanon's strategic Beaufort Castle, which dates to the twelfth century Crusades. With Israel's logistical help, his forces were holding the castle's still-sturdy stone ramparts against a much larger Hezbollah militia in the midst of Shiite territory. In one vivid scene, my cameraman, old friend Anton Wilson, taped from a hilltop as I rode in one of Haddad's armored vehicles as it ran the gauntlet of Hezbollah gunfire, making the perilous supply run from Christian lines down a contested valley and then up to the castle. The audio of the ride is punctuated with the sound of small arms fire pinging as it hit the armored vehicle.

Curiously, Major Haddad also ran an American-funded Christian radio station out of the stronghold. The Voice of Hope played gospel and American country music. I scored the Haddad *20/20* profile with recent Christian convert Bob Dylan's just-released song, "Gotta Serve Somebody." It is a great tune about how he surrendered to the faith, although he has since returned to Judaism.

LEBANON'S GEORGE WASHINGTON 1980–1983

When I went to Beirut for the first time in 1980, ravaged by the savage, ongoing civil war, it was with the specific guidance of Israel's Mossad. An Israeli spymaster and former journalist named David Kimche put our team in touch with an up-and-coming Lebanese leader named Bashir Gemayel. A Christian warlord, Gemayel was promising to lead Lebanon away from confrontation with Israel once his faction won the war and he got elected president.

I came to love the guy. Sheik Bashir, as he was universally known, was dashing and courageous. He spoke effortless English (plus Arabic and French), orating expansively of a New Lebanon, one that would regain its central position in the Mideast and coalesce beyond its internecine cataclysm.

I had profiled him for an action-packed, bullet-whistling, April 1981 *20/20* hour-long special, "The Unholy War," which was more propaganda than journalism. As Jack G. Shaheen wrote in his book *The TV Arab* (1984):

> Consider the opening of the program in which host Hugh Downs says, "Geraldo Rivera goes behind the lines with PLO (Palestinian Liberation Organization) terrorists" and "the PLO has made the world its battleground." *War* continually calls Palestinians terrorists. There are over fifty references to terror, terrorism, and terrorist in all.

Given the strong, institutional, pro-Israeli bias that still exists among mainstream American media, the piece would not be out of place today, and certainly not on Fox News. My deviation from that Israel-can-do-no-wrong school of advocacy journalism would later get me into serious hot water and undermine my standing in the company, perhaps as egregiously as Tora Bora.

In one sequence of 1980's "The Unholy War" I follow as Sheik Bashir jumps from closely packed Beirut apartment buildings rooftop to rooftop, directing intense urban combat. Later, he speaks intensely on camera of his vision of a US-allied Lebanon helping moderate the region in cooperation with Israel.

With Lebanese journalists. Weeda, Ghassan, and team, Beirut, Lebanon, February 2002.

A charming, crafty leader, Bashir had a grand scheme, that if elected president, he would encourage Israel to invade Muslim-held areas of South Lebanon, humble Hezbollah, and force their Syrian and Iranian allies out. He was then going to use his relationship with the United States, enhanced by his personal connections with Americans like me, to encourage Israel to withdraw from Lebanon. To that end, he spent time in the United States to rally support, especially with the influential Lebanese community. He and I hung out socially in Washington, DC, and New York.

Sheik Bashir was indeed elected president of Lebanon on August 23, 1982. Having become a dear friend, he had promised me his first interview and, true to his word and despite the fact that I was four thousand miles away and he was in Beirut surrounded by the international press corps, he took my phone call from the United States and gave me his first interview.

Bashir was killed by a massive bomb blast along with twenty-six others three weeks later. The Syrians were later declared the culprits. They did not want a Lebanese leader friendly with Israel. His death enraged the embattled Christian community he had helped save and touched off an atrocity that foreshadowed the savagery of al Qaeda and ISIS.

A week after his murder, outraged Christian militiamen loyal to the slain sheik slaughtered as many as 3,500 Palestinians and Lebanese Shiites, including women and children, in what came to be known as the Sabra and Shatila Massacre, named for the village and refugee camp where the blood-letting took place during a night of wanton butchery. Since by that time the Israeli Army had invaded and occupied a huge chunk of Lebanon, the IDF and especially its legendary commander and later prime minister, Ariel Sharon, did not escape at least tangential blame for the atrocity.

The Mossad-inspired scheme of installing a pro-Israel, Christian-dominated government in Lebanon was in ruins. Instead, 850,000 Christians have emigrated, leaving the country forever. The Christian Lebanese diaspora is an underreported story. This proud and enterprising culture has spread its élan and enterprise throughout the world. Despite its travails, like the Jews and Jerusalem, they knew Beirut is their eternal home.

PISS OFF, FEBRUARY 2002

We ended this Part One of the 2002 Terror Tour in Sudan, where officials were as unhappy to see us as local officials had been earlier in Somalia. Dealing with the cancerous influence of foreign extremists, as well as homegrown Black tribal versus Arab, Christian versus Muslim civil strife, the Sudanese weren't eager for the international spotlight.

That has been one side story of my entire career. When I show up, it is generally bad news for the hosts. If they have anything to hide, I am the last person they want to see, and they frequently react accordingly. When we were trying to film the Nile River from a strategic bridge in downtown Khartoum, we were swarmed by fidgety, heavily armed soldiers who seemed on the verge of killing us as infidel spies. Briefly detained, we were released after a pledge to leave the country. Before flying out, we managed a brief visit to Osama bin Laden's onetime compound on the edge of the capital city, and another side trip to the aspirin factory President Clinton ordered destroyed in 1998, after mistakenly thinking it was a bomb factory connected to the African embassy bombings.

THE MURDER OF DANIEL PEARL, FEBRUARY 2002

After our 2000–2001 journey up the Amazon River onboard *Voyager*, I brought the old boat back from South America in stages. One of the last cruises I managed to squeeze between combat assignments was sailing her from Trinidad the six hundred miles to St. Thomas in the beginning of February 2002. Then it was back to real life, broadcasting the latest episode of *War Zone* from our New York studios. The weekend show on Fox News was now a regular part of the schedule and doing well in the ratings. I was already planning our next trip back to the conflict zone in Afghanistan when the awful news broke: twenty-eight-year-old *Wall Street Journal* reporter Daniel Pearl had been beheaded and otherwise mutilated in neighboring Pakistan.

He had been kidnapped by al Qaeda a week before, and the leaked video of his subsequent execution was chilling and infuriating. Years later, and only after waterboarding, Osama bin Laden's key terror aide, Khalid Sheikh Mohammed, confessed. He claimed at a closed military hearing in Guantánamo that he personally beheaded the journalist and cut him into ten pieces. Before he was brutalized, Pearl was forced to confess his Jewishness:

> My name is Daniel Pearl. I'm a Jewish American from Encino, California, USA. I come from, on my father's side, the family is Zionist. My father's Jewish, my mother's Jewish, I'm Jewish. My family follows Judaism. We've made numerous family visits to Israel.

His murder was dramatized five years later by the 2007 film *A Mighty Heart*, starring Angelina Jolie as Mariane Pearl, the crusading wife of the slain journalist. Aside from admiring the resolve of groups like Reporters Without Borders, which benefited from the gala New York opening of the film, and the thrill of meeting the glamorous yet down-to-earth Jolie and then-husband, Brad Pitt, at the premiere, I took Danny Pearl's death personally.

Remember how I got into major hot water for asserting that if the bad guys came for me, "it would be a gunfight, not a kidnapping"? With a Jewish Star tattooed on my left hand, I had chilling visions of what extremists like ISIS or al Qaeda would do if they had the chance.

The slaughter of Danny Pearl reaffirmed my decision three months earlier, in November 2001, to carry the pistol in Afghanistan, which came after the kidnapping, mutilation, and murders of the eight other Western reporters covering the early months of the war. Reporters have to protect themselves with deadly force if necessary. The fiction that reporters are above the fray and therefore a protected class, as I said, is naive and dangerous. I remember arguing with Jeffrey Gettleman of the *New York Times* at Baghdad Airport in the early days of the Iraq War about what to do if detained by extremists. I told him I was resolved to go down fighting.

At the time, an earnest, quietly daring thirty-three-year-old reporter, who five years later in 2006 became chief of the *Times'* East Africa Bureau, Gettleman replied passionately, "No, no, no . . . " before recounting how he had managed to extricate himself by talking his way out of just such a jam. He was adamant that a reporter should be neutral and not otherwise engage.

Those days are gone. This war on terror and Islamic extremism is way too dirty to expect rules to be followed by the bad guys. Just remember "Jihadi John" and his brutal beheadings of American journalists James Foley and Steve Sotloff and so many others beginning in 2014 with the ISIS reign of terror in Syria and Iraq.

In retrospect, while it was arguably practical for me to carry the gun in those chaotic early days of the war in Afghanistan, especially after the Taliban massacre of our colleagues there, I should have kept my mouth shut and quit the verbal swaggering. Nowadays, specifically on the issue of carrying a weapon, my rule is that if you do not have armed good guys watching your back, you do not go into the abyss. Let the pros carry the guns. If there are none available, don't go.

Chapter 7

WARRIOR JEW HEADS TO
THE UNHOLY LAND

Despite Danny Pearl's grotesque and outrageous murder, given the strain and tension I was feeling at Fox News' home base in New York because of the smoldering Tora Bora controversy, it was a relief to travel back to the Mideast war zone. Going first to Israel and Palestine, I wrote in my journal, "The warrior Jew heads for the Unholy Land."

Our hotel in Palestine sat on a ridge overlooking their de facto capital, Ramallah. On March 9 we had a front-row seat from the hotel balcony restaurant as an Israeli missile hit, with pinpoint accuracy, a vehicle in a convoy carrying Palestinian militant leaders. Like a lightning bolt it cut through the night sky. We later found it was righteous retaliation for a suicide bombing earlier that evening in Jerusalem, which killed eleven Israeli civilians and wounded scores of others in and around the Café Moment coffee shop near the prime minister's office in downtown.

During that time, provocations from both sides were constant. A couple of days after the Café Moment bombing, in one of the most poignant, painful incidents I have ever witnessed in a conflict zone, I watched as a Palestinian father and mother in traditional Muslim garb who had just given birth in an East Jerusalem hospital were prevented by soldiers at an

Israeli checkpoint from returning with their newborn to their West Bank home.

On this chill night, the new mother held her crying, swaddled newborn tightly in her arms. The parents had the appropriate identification and were pleading unsuccessfully to be allowed through to get their baby home out of the cold.

The inhumanity of the scene was exaggerated by the infuriating nonchalance of the IDF soldiers, who were brushing off the woman as if she were trying to sell them a bad watermelon. Witnessing it began a kind of emotional chain reaction. If it did not turn me against Israel and the side I had always taken, then at least it sowed doubt. I never felt the same about Israel after that night.

On edge because of the spreading anarchy and violence, the IDF was using quick-trigger muscle to quiet discord. We were heavily tear-gassed one afternoon outside Ramallah at Checkpoint Kolandia, and as we approached another checkpoint, shots were fired close over our heads from about a block away.

Aside from making you want to rip your eyes out to stop the burning irritation, tear gas does not bother me. A heavy dose of water usually does the trick, easing the irritation. Anyway, if you do not get gassed from time to time, you are not getting close enough to the action. What accelerated my doubts about Israel's moral supremacy at the time was a more troubling tactic. The soldiers had begun using magic markers to write identifying numbers on the forearms of the hundreds of young Palestinians being rounded up.

It reminded me of my Uncle Phil, a Holocaust survivor. Related to me by marriage, Phil was built like Popeye. He was a butcher with bulging forearms. What fascinated us kids growing up on Long Island was the faded but still readable numbers the Nazis had tattooed on the inside of Phil's arm. I remember running my fingers over the tattoo in disbelief at the inhumanity of it. The fact that Israelis had adopted an obviously more benign but arguably similar technique for keeping track of detainees made me sick.

I got understandably reamed for agreeing with Arafat's condemnation of the technique as "Nazi-like." Nothing compares to the Nazis, and shame on anyone, including me, who uses the comparison to make a point. But I have not changed my mind about the branding. Interestingly, the IDF dropped the technique soon after the controversy blew up.

My subsequent commentaries about Israel's oppressive occupation of Palestine had a profound effect on my standing at Fox News. My views were extremely unpopular, in a practical sense, affecting me almost as negatively as Tora Bora, although not in the same soul-rattling way.

Make no mistake, Israel, frightened, frustrated, and angry, was suffering abundant Palestinian provocation during what was becoming a full-fledged uprising. The Second Intifada was beginning. Civil order was being challenged. There were dangerous demonstrations, and insurrection was widespread, including suicide bombers. Most of the worst was still to come.

I remember how sincerely unapologetic Palestinian intellectual Hanan Ashwari was at dinner one evening in East Jerusalem, defending the suicide bombings. A high-level PLO official, she and I have known each other for decades. Usually I am sympathetic to her family's struggles with occupation and to the plight of her people. She has spoken to me of the humiliation of living in a territory totally controlled by an occupying force, and how not having a real passport caused complications for her family, involving everything from college to marriage. That night, though, she startled me when she told me with chilling frankness, "They [the suicide bombers] are our F-11s, our strategic bombers." Here, she used two-fingers walking to make sure I got the reference that the number eleven represented human bombs on legs; suicide bombers were Palestine's answer to Israel's superior weapons. As President Trump frequently trumpets, Israel's Great Wall, sitting astride Israel's version of the 1967 border with the Occupied West Bank, has virtually ended the practice.

Marine General Anthony Zinni, President George W. Bush's peace envoy, was visiting the region when I again appeared on *Special Report*, the network's signature show, Tuesday, March 12. Having heard my condemnation of the hideous new IDF practice of painting numbers on the arms of Palestinian detainees, Fox News principal anchor Brit Hume debriefed me after we resolved some technical problems.

Brit Hume: Earlier in the broadcast before we were rudely interrupted by satellite problems, Geraldo Rivera and I were talking about the change that some journalists undergo when they experience covering the Middle East firsthand. Geraldo, himself part Jewish, has been feeling some of that and he was telling me about that. Please continue.

Geraldo Rivera: The most insidious thing about evil, the most insidious evil about terrorism, I should say, is that because it is sometimes difficult to fight, you become something like the thing you are fighting.

You become someone who violates some of the basic concepts of your own fundamental democracy; who you are. That is the danger in the United States and a danger being realized in Israel.

When you use tanks and F-16s and these sledgehammers against thickly populated civilian towns and cities, that's not fighting terrorism; that is inflicting terrorism.

You may get some of the bad guys, but I walked down the streets of Bethlehem the other day. There were fifty-nine Palestinians killed, 367 injured by the Israeli action, and many were women and some were children.

You remember that infamous video of some months ago that showed a Palestinian father huddled with his nine-year-old son against the wall, caught in a crossfire between the Israelis and Palestinians, who were throwing rocks and shooting, and before it ended, the boy was dead and the father severely injured.

I would die for Israel. But watching the suffering of the Palestinian people, the real suffering, I've become a *Palestinianist* in a sense.

Like our president, like President Bush's stated United States policy, I believe the only solution is two states, living side by side with internationally recognized and maybe United States–guaranteed borders.

Brit Hume: When you come to see a certain equivalency, and you even used the word terrorism to refer to what Israel does, Israel inflicting terrorism. Do you really think that Israel is intentionally killing civilians or are they in a sense collateral damage?

Geraldo Rivera: I think that—it's more than collateral damage. There's an expectation when you use a jet fighter they're flying at five hundred miles an hour to get a terrorist nest, although the Israelis are the best at it, as precise as any of our guys, there is an inevitability that there will be civilian casualties.

They do not intend to hurt the Palestinian civilians. I don't mean to suggest that at all. That's not the case. The tactics they're employing, that Prime Minister Ariel Sharon over the severe objections of his defense minister, as we at Fox News broke the story of the secret argument about the incursion into Ramallah on the eve of General Zinni's visit. You cannot do those things. You cannot round up Palestinian young men and put numbers on their arms to make it easier to identify them in the future.

What does that remind the world of? That reminds the world of what Hitler and the Nazi pigs inflicted on the Jewish race during the Second World War. Maybe the comparison is not precise or exactly parallel, but the echoes of it are unmistakable. It's indefensible.

These people, the Palestinians, they bleed just like we do. They suffer just like we do. They have the same aspirations. They want to make a living. Yes, there are terrorists among them. Yes, there are young people who would strap explosives to their body and on the promise of something in heaven, blow themselves up. We cannot become the thing we loathe. That is indefensible and non-Jewish.

Brit Hume: Geraldo, very interesting. Great to have you. Geraldo Rivera, having a change of heart on this issue not unlike that which many other journalists have had in that region. It is striking.

THE WRATH OF THE JEWS, SPRING 2002

Roger Ailes later told me how he and our boss of bosses, Rupert Murdoch, watched my Brit Hume interview together, and how at one point Murdoch asked him incredulously, "Is he [meaning me] pro-Palestinian?" Roger told me his reply was, "The Israelis think so."

The viewer reaction to my remarks was much more intense. It blew up the Fox News audience email system and main switchboard in New York, as supporters of Israel heaped scorn and outrage. It was not just that Israel was being criticized, but that in the midst of another Intifada someone who had consistently supported the Jewish state was criticizing it and doing it on the most conservative news network in America.

Doing a live shot later outside the Café Moment bombing site, I was berated by a middle-aged, potbellied, gold-necklace-wearing Russian Jewish cab driver who pulled over to lecture me about being dangerously naive. "Do you see what these people are doing?" he said, gesturing dramatically at the scene where eleven Jews were murdered three days before. He gave me a disdainful sneer as he got in his cab, slammed the door, then spun his wheels leaving rubber as he sped off.

As is my custom, I stayed at the King David while in Jerusalem. Built in 1931, the deeply historic five-star hotel overlooks the walls of Old City and hosts endless conventions by the JCC, B'nai B'rith, ADL, Federation, countless aliyahs, bat and bar mitzvahs, weddings, class trips, and reunions.

The hotel was not immune from violence, the deadliest attack coming from militant Zionists. In 1946, when it was being used as a headquarters by occupying British forces, it was severely damaged in a bombing that killed ninety-one people. Future prime minister Menachem Begin's Irgun Gang carried out the lethal attack. Its aim was to terrorize the British authorities and make them eager to end their rule, called the Palestine Mandate, which the League of Nations granted Britain following World War I. The Irgun and its similarly violent adversaries wanted them to leave and let the Jews and Arabs fight it out among themselves, which they have predictably done for seventy-five years and counting.

Over its long reign as the best hotel in the country, the King David has housed everyone from the dowager empress of Persia to the emperor of Ethiopia and virtually every world leader who has ever visited modern Israel. The 1960 film *Exodus* was shot there, and if it was good enough for Hollywood royalty Paul Newman and Emperor Haile Selassie, it is good enough for me. And, because I use my hotel room as both road office and VIP interview location, my suite tends to be among the best in the building.

On the weekend following the Brit Hume eruption, I was visited in my room by once and future Israeli prime minister Benjamin Netanyahu. Bibi and I met during the taping of the 1980 "The Unholy War" special for *20/20*, getting along great, hanging out in New York and Israel over the years, before drifting apart as his career soared and mine soldiered on.

Even though he was not formally in the government at the time, I had the distinct impression when Bibi showed up in my room on short notice that he had been dispatched as part of a charm offensive by the Israelis. The government seemed to be operating on the assumption that if it just treated me better, my reports would be more favorable to Israel's position.

Skiing at an unlikely resort outside Beirut, Lebanon, April 2002.

A few years earlier, Netanyahu had been Israel's youngest-ever prime minister and the first to be born there. At the time of our meeting at the King David, he was no longer in the top job, having been crushed by former IDF commander Ehud Barak in a reelection bid in 1999. When Ariel Sharon defeated Prime Minister Barak a few months later, in November 2002, Bibi was appointed Sharon's foreign affairs minister and later finance minister. Bibi later returned to the premiership, getting reelected a record three consecutive times. As of this writing, he is still prime minister, although various corruption controversies swirl around him and his wife, Sara.

More than any Israeli leader in history, Bibi is an inflexible hard-liner against independence for the Palestinian territories. He calls the West Bank "Judea and Samaria" in deference to their Old Testament roots as Jewish states, and his mental map of Israel includes them as a biblical imperative. An MIT and Harvard graduate, he is hugely popular among American conservatives. He also became the first Israeli leader to choose sides in terms of American politics, bluntly and boldly campaigning for Mitt Romney in the 2012 presidential election against Barack Obama. Arrogant and self-assured, Bibi also had the audacity to come to Washington, DC, uninvited by President Obama, to receive the adulation of the Republican-led Congress in 2015.

I feel about Bibi the way I feel about President Trump as I write this. Both are undeniably powerful, charismatic, and charming, while both propose policies I sometimes detest. Perhaps the Trump administration will have more success in promoting peace between Palestinians and Israelis. Early signs are not encouraging—the announcement that President Trump is moving the U.S. embassy from Tel Aviv to Jerusalem seems fraught, but you never know with Donald Trump; he may pull off another miracle.

When I opened the door to my big duplex suite in the King David, Bibi sailed in, lit a big cigar, pulled up a chair, which he spun around, sat down, gestured to a second chair, and said bluntly, "We've got to talk."

He then lectured me for the next hour on the impossibility of the two-state solution, and more generally, on trusting the Palestinians on anything. Remember, at this time the Intifada was escalating dangerously, and day-to-day life in Israel was being profoundly disrupted by horrible acts of mass violence. Fear stalked Israel's streets.

Bibi was scornful and dismissive of the current, frantic, and ultimately fruitless efforts of the Bush administration to get traction on the peace process. Bush 43 had taken to referring to the territories for the first time as *Palestine*, which took guts. President Bush also dispatched Vice President Dick Cheney on a diplomatic offensive to the region, having already appointed Vietnam War hero Zinni as special envoy to Israel and the Palestinian Authority.

"Do you know what the sum total of my concessions to the Palestinians was when I was in office?" Bibi smirked, as he gestured broadly with his lit cigar in our hotel room confrontation.

"A casino in Jericho," he said, barking a short laugh. He went on to explain that his sole concession to the peace process was allowing the Palestinians in 1998 to open The Oasis casino in Jericho, the world's oldest city. Located deep in Palestinian territory and frequented mainly by Israelis, the casino was closed two years later as a security risk.

Bibi was pushy in suggesting that I resume backing Israel unambiguously, but he was not unpleasant, granting me a formal sit-down interview on the security situation the next day, Sunday, March 17. Unlike Bibi, many of those phoning my room that week were intensely disagreeable, even threatening my job. Some were leaders of various Jewish groups in the States, others just regular civilians, and they were barraging my suite at all hours, until I put a do-not-disturb order on the line, something a foreign correspondent on assignment abroad rarely did in those days before reliable international cell phones.

We pulled out of Jerusalem for Tel Aviv the next day, ultimately making the difficult border crossing into the Gaza Strip to do several confrontational interviews with assorted radicals, including the leader of Islamic Jihad. One of their terrorists had just killed seven more Israelis, including four IDF soldiers, while injuring twenty-seven others when he blew himself up on a bus going from Tel Aviv to Nazareth in northern Israel.

Despite the Intifada's accelerating descent into full-scale religious warfare, newly elected warrior prime minister Ariel Sharon was struggling to maintain some semblance of a peace process, and the government wanted me to know that.

Their relatively liberal defense minister in the new and still-shaky coalition government, Binyamin Ben-Eliezer, an Iraqi Jew, gave me an intimate briefing suggesting that if only the Palestinians would toe the line of civility, peace was still possible. He also told me there was some positive stirring in the Arab world that I should watch, in Beirut.

PASSOVER MASSACRE, MARCH 2002

With little advance planning, but now informed that the Arab League was meeting in the Lebanese capital to propose something dramatic to resolve the Israeli-Palestinian conflict, we set out immediately.

It is only 125 miles from Tel Aviv to Beirut, but you cannot get there from here. There is no direct air, sea, or land traffic between Israel and Lebanon. You can fly to the island of Cyprus and then change planes to fly to Lebanon. Or, since Israel's heavily fortified northern border is impassable, closed tight, you can drive the long way around through Jordan, which is what we did this trip, driving across Israel and Palestine, across the tightly guarded Allenby Bridge spanning the Jordan River, across the desert to the capital city of Amman, where we caught the short Royal Jordanian Airlines flight to Beirut.

I was thrilled to be back for such an auspicious occasion. The summit conference marked the first time the Arab nations were officially throwing their weight behind a comprehensive peace plan that recognized Israel's right to exist as a nation. They were scheduled to vote on the Saudi-sponsored resolution the next day, which coincidentally was the first day of Passover, March 28, 2002.

Certain to have unanimous support because of its Saudi imprimatur, the resolution coming out of the summit called for Israel to withdraw from Syria's Golan Heights and from the Palestinian West Bank and Gaza Strip in return for normal relations. It was to be "Land for Peace," and I was practically dancing in the streets of Beirut.

During that groundbreaking conference, I met and interviewed the most reasonable Sunni Muslim leader in the Middle East of the era, Lebanon's prime minister, Rafik Hariri. There will never be peace in that troubled region without the help of people like him. Though a devout Sunni Muslim who specialized in building mosques for the faithful, he was another confident, self-made billionaire businessman. This one, though, wanted to help steer the Arab world into the modern era.

Hariri, always dressed in sharp, shiny business suits, black-gray hair slicked back, and sporting an ample mustache, reminded me of an Arab Prince Rainier, Princess Grace of Monaco's husband. The prime minister's opulent palace in Beirut, personally refurbished by him, made him seem royal despite his humble birth.

Prime Minister Hariri told me that the Arabs were ready to take a chance for peace. But he complained bitterly that the Israelis were "stealing Palestinian land" with their continued expansion of settlements in the West Bank. Still, he told me passionately, the Arabs were ready to make their historic proposal, if only Israel was ready to compromise.

Then hell was unleashed back in Israel by a Palestinian suicide bomber. Disguised as a woman, Abdel-Basset Odeh entered a big Passover Seder celebration in the Park Hotel in suburban Netanya outside Tel Aviv. Inside were 250 guests, many of them elderly Jews in Israel without family. The Seder was a hotel tradition for the lonely who gathered for conversation and company at its annual party on this festive holiday.

Detonating his powerful explosive vest, the bomber ripped apart twenty-eight of the innocent old folks and injured 140 others, many of them Holocaust survivors. The Palestinian terror group Hamas claimed responsibility. The fury in Israel was raw and understandable. My lesson for then and now is clear and indelible. Never bet on a happy ending in the Mideast. Violence always wins.

"ARE YOU JEWISH?" APRIL 2002

With this mass murder, Hamas killed the peace process for my lifetime and beyond. I was bereft. It was the end of hope, the last best chance for peace in the Mideast. Even today I look back on that singular atrocity, the Passover Massacre, as the moment disorder finally routed hope. It is over. We will never get that close again. Trust me, never.

The next day, after reporting at a Palestinian refugee camp in Beirut, I cornered the highest-level Hamas official attending the Arab summit. I fired off a rapid-fire series of angry, condemning questions about the immorality of slaughtering innocent elderly civilians. The smug creep responded coldly with a question, "Are you Jewish?"

I was flustered. To say yes would be to make my righteous anger parochial, as if only a Jew would think the bombing was a disgusting atrocity. So I picked the middle road, avoiding the question.

"What the hell difference does that make?" I responded angrily. "Why did you ask me if I was Jewish?"

"Just a question."

"Why?"

"Just a question."

"Why?"

"Because you were talking about them as if they were innocent people."

"They are innocent people."

"No, they are not."

The next evening, I was on with Sean Hannity and cohost Alan Colmes.

Sean Hannity: We continue now with Geraldo Rivera reporting from Beirut tonight. This is why—I got to tell you something; it's your reporting that—and I'm an optimist by nature—that causes me not to be optimistic.

When you have people sworn to the destruction of the State of Israel like the leader of Hamas you showed us last night—I want to remind our audience—I don't know how there could ever be peace . . . They're not going to be happy even if we went back to the pre-1967 borders. They won't be happy with that mind-set until Israel is pushed into the sea. Correct?

At which point I made a pitch for Palestinian sovereignty, if only to have a political entity that could be held responsible for atrocious acts of violence. Alan, a sharp observer, brought me down to earth.

Alan Colmes: Geraldo, he wanted to know if you were a Jew because he clearly felt that you had an agenda. That was a very scary question.

At this point in the live shot I described and demonstrated how the Hamas confrontation had unfolded.

Geraldo Rivera: This is what happened—we did the interview here. Right where I'm standing. We started walking over here. And it was over here where I finally got the kind of rage in me where I said, "Why in the world would you ask me if I was Jewish?"

By the time we got to this light-stand over here, Craig and I are united [indicating my brother as the camera panned over to show him]. You know, we're Jewish, our mom, our dear mom is watching right now in Sarasota [Florida], Jewish, our dad Catholic. And right here, both of us wanted to thump that guy. Both of us wanted to give him a couple of overhand rights and say, "How dare you? You're a pig, you're an animal, and you don't deserve to . . ." And then I bit my tongue at the very end because I didn't want an international incident. I didn't want to fight my way out of Beirut.

I understand that these are devilish, terroristic kinds of people. But Arafat can—listen, the sainted former prime minister of Israel blew up the British in the King David Hotel in 1946. He was then considered a terrorist, and then he became a statesman. Give the guy [Arafat] a chance. He's a better—it's better to make friends with these people. You can't—Palestinian and terrorist are not synonymous. That's my basic point.

Sean Hannity: Alright. We'll give you the last word tonight. I say he's still a terrorist. I hope you're right. Great reporting.

THE ELEVENTH COMMANDMENT, MARCH 2002

I left Beirut for JFK via Paris on Air France the next day, flying to meet Erica and her family in her hometown of Cleveland for Friday Seder dinner. During the long flight, I penned a blog to my Jewish viewers explaining how hurt I was by their continuing rage.

It was a weird and troubling experience. In the thirty-two years I've been in the television news business the response to my work from viewers of the Jewish faith has been unswervingly positive. The walls of my den in Rough Point were lined with plaques, a large percentage of which were given by Jewish organizations for work like my 1980 ABC News documentary *The Unholy War.*

After my televised battles with neo-Nazis and skinheads, and with the Star of David tattoo on my left fist, I've been one of America's most highly visible, tough-guy Jews.

Now, all I'm getting is hate mail from my old admirers, 18,000 angry emails and still counting. The problem is that I broke the 11th Commandment: I publicly criticized Israel. The issue is Palestine.

On the eve of Gen. Anthony Zinni's peacekeeping mission to the region, in February I traveled there with my TV crew. It was clear even then that the administration of George W. Bush had become convinced that America's strategic interests required it to resolve the issue, and that the resolution required nudging the parties into meaningful peace talks.

For Yasser Arafat and the Palestinians, that meant at a minimum stopping the suicide bombing. For Ariel Sharon that meant negotiations the end result of which would be the creation of an independent (Palestinian) state. Over the bloody weeks and months that followed it became clear that neither side was willing or able to do it. The result was more chaos and violence and an escalating conflict, despite the further visits of Vice President Dick Cheney and Secretary of State Powell.

My break with my traditional Jewish allies came when I began warmly endorsing America's calls for an Israeli withdrawal from the West Bank and the Gaza Strip, territories Israel has occupied since the 1967 War.

While constantly hammering the Palestinians for their hideous use of suicide bombers and the targeting of innocent civilians, I also criticized Israeli abuses of Palestinian human rights. One specific tactic I found particularly offensive was the rounding up of all men between the ages of fifteen and forty-five, stripping them, and then painting numbers on their arms to better administer the incarceration and interrogation process. When I commented about the world seeing this kind of thing before and that if the roles were reversed, can you imagine Jewish reaction? The stuff hit the fan.

First there was the deluge of angry phone calls, hundreds of them, followed by the email avalanche. My new bosses at Fox News were soon shell-shocked. When I refused to back down, citing the fact that I was merely stating support for express U.S. policy as set forth in a recent U.S.-sponsored UN Security Council resolution, the situation calmed, only to flare whenever I pointed out that Israeli-occupation of the territories had to end.

No amount of lobbying can change that fact. Occupation and terror are organs of the same beast. They feed off each other. Arafat may be the savage Ariel Sharon portrays him as. Still, as long as Israel remains one of the few countries occupying the land of another, the violence and misery will continue. It might continue in any case. But at least Israel will be fighting from the moral high ground, as a democratic nation intent on protecting its people and its recognized borders. Not as a military occupier intent on inflicting its will on others. Please, keep your cards and letters.

WE'RE MAKING ALIYAH! MARCH 2002

I came up with a flamboyant fix for my specific "Jewish Problem" on my way to Seder in Cleveland. The brilliant idea was that Erica and I would marry ASAP and resettle in Israel. Here is the good part: Having established residence, I would then run for the Knesset, Israel's parliament, from Herzliya, an upscale neighborhood on the north side of Tel Aviv, popular with expat American Jews. How better to prove that I loved the Jewish State than to move there and become part of the government?

After my hotel-suite confrontation with Bibi, and after many long phone calls to Erica in New York, I went so far as to apartment-shop in Herzliya. My dear friends Hanani and Naomi Rapoport live in Tel Aviv. She was a real estate agent, he an Israeli television-news executive who worked with me as a producer on *20/20* when the couple lived in the States.

Our families are still close. They provided the ten men or minyan for my son Gabriel's bar mitzvah in Jerusalem in 1993. Their baby daughter, Dana, grew up to be a producer of mine at Fox News. We have known and loved each other since Hanani's dad, Azaria Rapoport, was Israel's consul general in New York. Consul General Rapoport was instrumental in getting me embedded with the IDF during the 1973 Yom Kippur War.

Holding public office was something that always appealed to me. My dream growing up was to be mayor of New York. As a representative of two of the big city's most important ethnic groups, Jewish and Puerto Rican, I felt born for the job. In 2000, when two-term mayor Rudy Giuliani was set to leave office, I went so far as to commission a poll to determine my chances running as an independent. It would have required moving my voter registration back into the city from New Jersey, where I was still living at the time, but I was keen on making the race.

As expected, the poll showed the probable Democratic candidate, a lifelong politician named Mark Green, winning easily, with me as the independent tied with the probable Republican candidate, Michael R. Bloomberg, a little-known rich guy from Boston. When Bloomberg announced that he would spend up to $50 million to win the office in City Hall, I pulled out. Now a billionaire and one of the world's richest men, Bloomberg spent that $50 million and about $950 million more in winning three full terms in City Hall.

The political bug kept buzzing in my ear. Years later, in 2013, I came within minutes of filing to run as a Republican against then-mayor Cory Booker of Newark for the US Senate seat vacated by the death in office of long-serving senator Frank Lautenberg. In contemplating making the long-shot run against a powerful celebrity Democrat in a hard-blue state, I consulted various, very connected experts, beginning with Roger Ailes, who was skeptical. I also spoke with Kellyanne Conway, the brilliant pollster and frequent guest on my CNBC *Rivera Live* show, who later became President Trump's mouthpiece and White House consigliere.

Mayor Booker is a camera-ready media darling, well known for frequent appearances on Bill Maher and other celebrity talk shows. A tireless self-promoter, he got a ton of press for getting Facebook's Mark Zuckerberg to donate $100 million to Newark schools. The money was squandered on thousand-dollar-per-day consultants, changing next to nothing in the school system. The mayor also attracted attention driving around Newark searching for crime, and for running into a ghetto house fire to rescue a family pet, like an action hero. Kellyanne advised me to tape my campaign spots in the wrecked heart of ghettoized Newark, where Mayor Booker had long held sway. "Your spot could say, 'In the Senate, Corey Booker will do for New Jersey what he did for Newark.'" Ouch.

I pulled out of that Republican primary race literally a few minutes before a midnight deadline for filing. Again, it was about the money. The immediate reason was the just-announced support for my primary opponent, a hard-right-wing, small-town mayor named Steve Lonegan, by the fabulously wealthy Koch brothers. They were said to be willing to invest $5 million to back Lonegan, the truly conservative candidate, which I was obviously not. Running against him would have busted me in the primary alone. My argument that a rigidly conservative GOP candidate had no chance in relatively left-of-center New Jersey fell on deaf ears. Booker won easily, as expected.

In 2002, the possibility of the far more exotic run for Israel's Knesset did not even last as long as my Jersey US Senate dream. When we arrived at the Levy home in suburban Shaker Heights, Ohio (where we now live), a distinct chill was in the air, and it was not all coming from the notorious lake-effect snow on the lawn. Although her parents had been remarkably accepting of Erica's and my relationship despite the enormous difference in our ages, they were firmly opposed to our moving to Israel, especially as an Intifada raged.

Erica's dad, Howard A. Levy, was an excellent labor lawyer who handled discrimination cases and did precedent-setting work on the limits of electronic discovery. Discovery in this context is what opponents during a lawsuit are permitted to see of the opposition's emails, text messages, and so forth. He was also a highly regarded official in the Anti-Defamation League, the ADL. Her mom, Nancy, taught preschool and English to immigrants and was active in the heavily Jewish east-side Cleveland community where Erica was born and raised and that, fifteen years later, we now call home.

Both a couple of years younger than their notorious son-in-law-to-be, they were invariably kind, defending me to their close-knit group of friends in Shaker, many of whom were following our very public romance. Afflicted by the prostrate cancer that would kill him five years later at age sixty-two, Howard was not remotely amused by the prospect of his daughter's moving to violence-torn Israel. Usually deferential, he dismissed this notion and refused to hear another word. Eventually, I felt foolish enough that I dropped the subject. Over the years, Erica and company have had a few laughs at my expense over that Knesset scheme.

RUNNING BACK TO WAR, APRIL 2002

Having celebrated the tail end of Passover with my future in-laws in Cleveland, and soon to celebrate the Catholic confirmation of my then-fifteen-year-old son, Cruz, in his hometown of Dallas, I completed my ecumenical family travels when I went to ultra-Episcopalian Marion, Massachusetts, to be with the girls and their mom, C.C., on Easter Sunday.

Like every man who ever left his family, I was weighed down by guilt, but I was soon heading back to the Middle East. That is one of the fringe benefits of being a globe-trotting correspondent. Whenever dealing with real life gets uncomfortable, you leave. Before returning to the Intifada, though, the immediate plan was to sail *Voyager* to New York Harbor from her current berth in picturesque Beaufort, North Carolina, where she had spent the 2001–2002 winter getting a new engine installed after the grueling trip up the Amazon and back. She was coming to the new home I was building on the Hudson River just south of the George Washington Bridge in Edgewater, New Jersey. Designed as the ultimate bachelor pad, it was being converted in a hurry to a family home now that Erica and I had fallen in love and planned to marry.

The trip on board *Voyager* did not go as planned. What I hoped would be a pleasant early-spring sail up the coast instead turned out to be a crashing, smashing several days of fighting a full gale on the nose in the area known as the "Graveyard of the Atlantic." I described it at the time as "Cape Hatteras fucks us again, freezing, awful, true shit, but nonetheless a vivid experience."

After we had passed the cape, slowed by the wicked weather, the much-longer-than-expected journey was aborted after I was summoned to New York to do a special episode of *Warzone*. I left *Voyager* with the crew in Norfolk, Virginia, and flew home, before heading back to the Mideast on April 16, 2002. Israeli forces had just occupied the biblical city of Bethlehem in the Palestinian West Bank, and the region was on the brink of all-out war.

As the Israeli Army (IDF) continued to sweep up thousands of suspected Palestinian militants, dozens took refuge in the Church of the Nativity, the traditional birthplace of Christ. When they sought sanctuary, the Franciscan monks had no choice but to grant it. The church was surrounded, IDF snipers were in place, and a tense standoff was attracting the attention of the world.

Gambling that the situation at the church would hold, we went first to Southern Lebanon, where I planned to meet with bitterly anti-Israeli UN Special Envoy Terje Larsen. As I reported, "With escalating exchanges of fire coming on the eve of Secretary of State Colin Powell's scheduled visit here to Lebanon and to neighboring Syria, the fear is of a second front in a full-scale shooting war."

Ground zero in Southern Lebanon was an area called Shebaa Farms, a disputed hamlet-sized pocket of land located in the border corner where Lebanon, Syria, and Israel meet. Israel claimed that the farm was under its control as part of its occupation of the Syrian Golan Heights since the 1967 War. The Lebanese, led by Hezbollah militants, claimed Shebaa Farms as its historic territory and had mustered their army, threatening war, if necessary, to get Israel out.

"On a day as stormy and miserable as the current political situation here in the Middle East," I began my live show from the edge of a minefield on a black, wet night.

The sign says it all, "Danger, Death, Minefield." I'm standing right now on the border between Lebanon on this side of that fence and Israeli-occupied (Syrian) territory on the other. And between here and there, as the sign says, is a minefield that promises to kill anyone foolish enough to tempt it. Less than a week before, fierce fighting between Israelis and Lebanon's Hezbollah guerrillas ripped through Shebaa. The fighting was so intense it seemed on the verge of becoming a second front in an expanding Arab-Israeli conflict. The fact that it has not yet happened is one of the few bright spots in this tortured region.

BEIRUT, MARCH–APRIL 2002

On this trip, I interviewed Lebanese prime minister Rafik Hariri for the second time. Welcoming me to his palace like an old friend, this gregarious man was beset by melancholy, holding little hope that a pending visit to the region by Secretary Powell would do any good. Although he was deeply concerned about the standoff at Shebaa Farms in his own country, events in Palestine were foremost on his mind. Bloody fighting in the West Bank town of Jenin horrified the prime minister, and he was fearful the incendiary standoff in Bethlehem would explode in full-scale war.

Underlying his pessimism, Hariri told me on camera, was the fear the Israelis had been emboldened by the 9/11 attacks on the United States, with Americans now regarding all Muslims as enemies. Long before the advent of Donald Trump on the political scene, the prime minister said woefully, "Now to American eyes we are all terrorists. If President Bush doesn't step in, things will get worse."

The next day the crew and I flew from Beirut back to Amman, Jordan, en route to Bethlehem and the standoff at the Church of the Nativity. As it entered its fourth week, Israeli snipers began picking off Palestinian militants foolish enough to poke their heads out the windows of the old church.

ALLENBY BRIDGE, APRIL 2002

I was anxious to get to the action, which brought the region back to the front page, leading news shows in the United States. But the tension in the region made getting across the historic Allenby Bridge over the Jordan River into the Israeli-controlled West Bank more difficult and interminable than usual. Even in the best of times, Israeli security is not like our TSA. They are humorless, ruthlessly efficient, and meticulous, going through every crevice and wrinkle of every bag. Rather than waste time waiting for stern-faced IDF reservists to sift through our two tons of stuff, I wrote a short essay based on my conversation with the Lebanese prime minister.

Allenby Bridge, Jordan River Crossing, Occupied West Bank, 22 April 2002

An old rabbi once described the Middle East as a dark basement in which all kinds of horrors were being perpetrated: human rights abuses, torture, suppression of women and ethnic minorities, etc.

Israel, he said, was the one small corner of that basement where the light of democracy, free speech, and freedom of the press shined. But because it was the only place in that dark basement light enough to see anything, critics were always saying, "Look at this problem or that with Israel."

I relate the old rabbi's story to suggest that since its creation in 1948, Israel has suffered unfairly from criticism made possible only by its open and democratic nature. And that virtually every other country in the region experiences far worse abuses.

But Israel's relative goodness is no longer enough to shield it from being raked over the coals of public disapprobation. Her harsh and unfocused military response to the suicide bombings has made sure of that.

"How can any Arab ignore what is happening in Jenin and the West Bank?" asks Rafik Hariri, the Lebanese Prime Minister, his voice cracking with emotion, his arms spread wide. "It's on every television station, American, British, Lebanese, and the Gulf States. You can't avoid the images of destruction and suffering. My daughter called me from Paris. She heard that I had arrested four Palestinians trying to cross our southern border to attack Israel. 'Dad,' she asked me. 'How can you arrest people trying to struggle for their freedom?' I explained how Lebanon has laws and that they were breaking our laws and if we don't follow the law, how can we criticize the Israelis for their illegal acts in the West Bank?"

In this anecdote, more of a loving father and his daughter, than of a political figure explaining policy, I found some scant hope in an otherwise bleak landscape.

Lebanese prime minister Rafik Hariri, the most reasonable Sunni Muslim leader, later assassinated by Syrians. Beirut, Lebanon, 2002.

A consistent voice for reasoned accommodation in the Middle East, Hariri was murdered in a massive February 2005 bombing in Beirut, engineered by the Syrians. The longer I live the more alarming becomes the number of dead friends and the prospect of joining them. The explosion wiped out his motorcade, claiming twenty-two lives, wounding hundreds of others. Rest in peace, Rafik Hariri, a fine man.

CHURCH OF THE NATIVITY SIEGE, APRIL–MAY 2002

The Israeli offensive in the West Bank and the subsequent siege of the Church of the Nativity were making a mess of the ancient city of Bethlehem. While driving to the scene past destroyed buildings, burned vehicles, and garbage-strewn, smoke-filled streets, I reported:

> Given the awful provocation of the murderous suicide bombing attacks against innocent Israeli civilians, when you look at the widespread damage and devastation here in Bethlehem, it is hard to avoid the conclusion that a kind of collective punishment has been meted

out on the Palestinian people, and it is hard to avoid the conclusion that the seeds are sown for future conflict.

The Church of the Nativity and its host city of Bethlehem are an island of Christianity in a Muslim sea, unique in Sunni-majority Palestine. For various reasons including religious intolerance, as in Lebanon and throughout the region, the religion of Jesus is fast diminishing in this land. Holy places are profaned and antiquities destroyed, especially with the coming of al Qaeda and later its savage progeny ISIS and al Nusra. Religious oppression threatens to make Christianity a relic, like the ruins of past civilizations that dot the ancient landscape.

I have Palestinian friends in Bethlehem, families I have known for generations. I met Joseph and his family in the 1970s. Long-established in Bethlehem, his dad was my fixer when I worked at ABC News during and after the Yom Kippur War. His namesake son worked with me at Fox News despite the obvious bias of my network in favor of the Israeli point of view.

A couple of years ago, we put together a mini-rapprochement when I brought my assistant, Israeli-born Dana Rapoport, to a family dinner in Bethlehem. Although her parents' home in Tel Aviv is just fifty miles from his, it was the first time Dana had ever been in the "Territories," which is the sanitized way Israelis reference occupied Palestine. I am convinced that if native-born Israelis, known as Sabras, and native-born Palestinians spent more time together, they would see how close they are, cousins really, at least genetically/DNA-speaking.

The situation is worse, and the future bleaker, today in 2018 than it was in 2002. Nowadays there is not even a legitimate attempt to bring the sides together. Outsider peacemakers have given up. President Trump openly and enthusiastically embraces Benjamin Netanyahu and his hard line. The Palestinians simmer and can burst into another full burn at any time. When President Trump made the announcement that he will move the US Embassy from Tel Aviv to Jerusalem, and that we recognize Jerusalem as Israel's capital, the world condemned it as one-sided and unproductive. Worse, the US is tacitly allowing Israel to continue expanding settlements in the West Bank. If there is no land left for a viable Palestinian state, what will happen with the Palestinian people? Will they be vassals of Israel forever, living in isolated enclaves in a Greater Israel?

In 2002, the ancient Church of the Nativity was plunged into this heart of Muslim discontent when Palestinian rebels occupied it. The church lies at the end of a broad, tree-lined plaza across from a town square lined by two- and three-story buildings, with restaurants, small hotels, and shops selling Nativity trinkets on the ground floors, Palestinian Authority and other offices above. During Christmas and Easter celebrations, Manger Square is traditionally filled with Christian celebrants, although because of the Intifada it was not in 2002.

The sacred church structure is a patchwork that reflects the changing fortunes of the region, going from pagan to Christian to Islamic, back to Christian, then back to Islamic. Built during the Roman Empire, and then lost to the Muslim conquest of the seventh century, the original building sheltering the manger was largely destroyed. But some of the fortress-like, massive stone walls and towers have stood since the very beginning of this formal church in the fourth century.

The European Crusades of the Middle Ages liberated this traditional birthplace of Jesus for eighty-eight years, from 1099 until 1187, when the conqueror Saladin recaptured Palestine for Islam. Now, during this siege of April 2002, 815 years later, Muslim militants protected by Christian clergy sought refuge behind its walls as a Jewish army laid siege. All eyes were focused on "Humility Door," the main entrance, a single heavy wooden door clearly visible across the empty square.

As I reported:

According to various sources, the negotiations for ending the impasse at the church, now in its fourth week, while stalemated over the larger issue of what to do about the Palestinian militants wanted by Israel, have agreed on something.

While the standoff and siege of the 1,700-year-old Church of the Nativity promises to drag on, today the expectation is that the Israelis will allow the two dead bodies inside to be removed. They've been inside now for days, and are said to be decomposing.

We're told that the teenagers inside the building, or at least some of them, will also be coming out. The young people have been a point of considerable controversy. The Israelis allege that they're being held by the Palestinians against their will, the Palestinians countering they're in there because they want to be.

BE NICE TO GERALDO, APRIL 2002

Defying bitter complaints from journalists gathered from dozens of the world's news networks, the commanders of the besieging Israeli forces, including IDF spokesman General Ron Kitrey, gave us preferential treatment. The Be Nice to Geraldo – So He'll Be Nice to Israel strategy was clearly still in place.

All press, including us, were kept at a distance of about a football field from the church door, but even though we had just arrived in Bethlehem and our rivals had been covering the siege for four weeks, we were taken to the head of the line and given the best vantage point, on the second floor of a building called the Peace Center, a sweet spot from which we could broadcast Humility Door on live television.

Remember, in those days, spring 2002, to be live on TV required a cable from the camera to a satellite uplink, which requires substantial equipment. It was neither easy nor convenient, not like today's lightweight, handheld wireless devices. In any case, we were in the perfect spot to watch the excruciatingly slow surrender process take place. On Sunday, April 28, I reported:

> Now in its second month, the bitter and bloody standoff here at the birthplace of Jesus seems headed for a conclusion sooner rather than later. Another melancholy, empty Sunday for what has become the most watched entrance in the world, Humility Door, the Church of the Nativity's main entrance facing Israeli troops occupying Manger Square.

On May 1, the sanctuary seekers finally began emerging in a steady stream, twenty-six of them, but as they were leaving, American and European peace activists were using the commotion to sneak past the Israelis and join the besieged inside the church. The damn standoff seemed endless. Even the kindness shown me by the IDF could not alter the fact that the stalemate went on long enough that we were forced to move when the Peace Center closed for security reasons.

At our new location, we found ourselves spending a cold night clinging to a slippery steep roof overlooking the church square, not knowing when the siege would break. This waste of time is why I hate stakeouts.

They are the hardest part of original reporting. You wait around for something to happen, and if you take a bathroom break or grab a bite, you might miss the money shot.

The hang-up prolonging this crisis was the ultimate fate of the militants inside. All were required by Israel either to go to jail or at least be exiled from the Middle East. Would they get asylum in friendly countries or be deported to the Gaza Strip?

SHARING HUMMUS WITH ARAFAT, MAY 2002

Under intense pressure from America and Britain, the Israelis lifted a weeks-long blockade of Yasser Arafat's Mukata walled compound in the West Bank city of Ramallah. As I reported:

> That would pave the way for the Palestinian president to be released from his house arrest, and for the Israeli army to release its iron grip, its siege of the devastated compound as early as tonight. The fear among all the parties is that the sort of fighting we've been tracking from that fierce fight we witnessed last night that lit up the sky over Ramallah would spread even wider.
>
> Emerging from his 34-day-long confinement under Israeli siege, Yasser Arafat is one of the most enigmatic people on the world stage. Branded a terrorist by the Israelis and those who support them, he is hailed here as a hero by most Palestinians, a kind of Founding Father.
>
> The 73-year-old Arafat has been part of the public dialogue on the Middle East for most of the last four decades. Credited with giving the Palestinians a national identity, he also stands accused of consistently choosing confrontation over conciliation. But who is this frail strongman whose face has been featured on so many front pages and so many cartoons?

To answer that question, I used sharp elbows and a determination not to be beaten to scoop an exclusive interview with the Palestinian chairman, beating every other reporter crowding around him. Apparently impressed by my aggressive performance, Arafat, through an aide, later invited me to spend time inside his still-surrounded West Bank compound.

"Yasser Arafat was one of the most enigmatic people on the world stage." April 2002.

What he did not seem to remember was that this was actually our second encounter. I had first interviewed Arafat nineteen years earlier in June 1983 in Tripoli, Lebanon, as his encircled followers were being forced to surrender to a dissident Palestinian faction backed by a surrounding Syrian army. It was a low point in his life. He was being deported from the Holy Land. As he emerged from a bunker in 1983, I asked him if this was "the end of the Palestinian Revolution."

"Of course not," he replied curtly, his eyes bulging in anger and frustration, as he headed under heavily armed Syrian escort by convoy to Damascus and from there to be flown to exile in Tunisia, where he would spend the next decade.

Flash forward to May 2002 as he was released from confinement in his compound in Ramallah. But in any case it was a compound no more. The Israelis had torn down the adobe wall that long encircled his headquarters and were driving their military vehicles around it like Apaches attacking a wagon train in our Old West.

Arafat seemed unperturbed by the provocation. He was just relieved to be free from house arrest and able to speak to comrades and the gathered world press. In a buoyant and reflective mood, he shared a lavish Lebanese mezza consisting of heaps of tabbouleh, hummus, and kebabs with Craig and me. I didn't bring up the fact or the circumstances of our first meeting in Tripoli, and he didn't mention it, either. At one point, he was so keen on making friends he hand-fed us an elaborate pita sandwich piled with cucumber and hummus.

"Taste this," he insisted as he daintily put the food in our mouths.

We took pictures, and he quietly reflected on his greatest disappointment, making news when he confessed that his biggest mistake was not accepting the 1999 Clinton two-state peace initiative, which came closer than any other to resolving the intractable Israel-Palestine conflict. Arafat balked because he did not feel an impeachment-wounded President Clinton could deliver on his promises. When I later shared with Prime Minister Ehud Barak after he was out of office and visiting New York what Arafat had told me about the near miss of the Clinton peace process, Barak, a former fighting general, replied earnestly, "I wish he [Arafat] had told me that."

As I reported from Ramallah:

In a wide-ranging interview with the Palestinian president on the very night he regained his freedom of movement, we spoke of many things, including his willingness, indeed his eagerness, to have an international peacekeeping force inserted between his people and the Israelis.

Conducted before Israel released its latest intelligence claiming Arafat personally approved acts of terror against Israeli civilians, I did press him during the interview to denounce suicide bombing.

It is doubtful that Chairman Arafat's statements will change any minds, certainly not [then-prime minister] Ariel Sharon's. The Israeli leader is scheduled to meet with President Bush this weekend.

From that day, I felt more sympathetic to Arafat than almost any of my colleagues. He should have trusted President Clinton, regardless of Monica Lewinsky. The deal Bubba proposed was so specific it defined the exact borders of the proposed "two states living side-by-side in peace" down to named streets and landmarks. Arafat did not take the offered deal, in my opinion, because he had no faith given impeachment that Vice President Al Gore could win the 2000 election and be able to implement the fragile deal.

Meanwhile, the Church of the Nativity siege finally broke a week later when the remaining militants, and various civilian sympathizers, slowly began emerging to go either into exile abroad or a local prison, or to be released. We were there as it happened. Fox News interrupted a taped episode of the *O'Reilly Factor* to go to me live.

I reported,

> The negotiators accompanied by the monks have just come out. Eight men have just come out of the Church of the Nativity. They are gathered at the lower left of your screen . . . There you see them. They are apparently waiting.
>
> It seems as if they are waiting for the others to come out of the church to leave Humility Door, the main entrance of the 1,700-year-old building built over the birthplace of Jesus. We understand the two groups to be coming out with the civilians—the seventy-five to eighty or more people who are relatively innocent and of whom the Israelis said they will be able to go home, go free. It seems inevitable now. This is Geraldo Rivera standing by live at the Manger Square at the Church of the Nativity.

ABE MEETS GERALDO, SPRING 2002

In the right place at the right time to record the historic moment of surrender, I noted at the time, "We kicked CNN's butt." But the Arafat/Nativity scoop was a small triumph in the scheme of things, and had no enduring impact either on this highly charged saga or on my career.

Rather than propel me to greater heights inside the Fox News hierarchy, this April 2002 trip was essentially the end of my uncensored criticism of Israel. Like former president Jimmy Carter, whose 2006 book *Palestine: Peace Not Apartheid* made him a pariah among Zionists, for years after Bethlehem, like so many other commentators who do not toe the pro-Israeli line, I too was intimidated into silence. It's one thing to stare down Islamist terrorists or gangbangers or ghetto muggers. It is another to take on the Jewish establishment, which truly never forgets.

Hoping to repair my rift with the pro-Israeli world, my future father-in-law, Howard Levy, later arranged a dinner with Abe Foxman, the fiery head of the Anti-Defamation League, the ADL. As I mentioned, Howard was a ranking ADL official representing the Midwest from his base in Cleveland. The lunch in New York's Plaza Hotel did not go well.

During an afternoon none there will ever forget, all conversation ceased when red-faced and veins-popping Abe exploded at me, demanding to know who the hell did I think I was to criticize Israel? How dare I? And so forth. I responded calmly, knowing by this time that I was not going to change his mind on the subject. The Levys, although they generally agreed with Abe's position, were mortified by his rudeness and ill manner. We made up years later, when Abe and I shared a stage doing a marathon reading of Eli Wiesel's *Night* to benefit the Museum of Jewish Heritage in Lower Manhattan.

Abe won our battle in 2002. After Bethlehem, Arafat, and the Intifada, I did not allow myself to speak of Israel's transgressions on the air with the same courage and frankness that I showed that spring 2002. For one thing, Fox News stopped sending me to the Middle East. In the August 2006 war between Israel and the Lebanese-based Hezbollah, I was not asked to go, and chose not to volunteer. I knew that almost everyone assigned would cover the war from the Israeli side, and that because the IDF made access easy and relatively safe, many desk-jockey anchors would jump at the chance to play war correspondent.

In any event, the fierce border skirmish between Israel and Hezbollah ended inconclusively. One hundred eighteen IDF soldiers were killed in combat in Southern Lebanon. About thirty-five Israeli civilians also died, killed by Hezbollah rockets. The number of casualties on the Lebanese side was far larger, but in no sense was this battle a victory for Israel.

Despite having a force numbering 20,000, the vaunted IDF's failure to destroy Hezbollah led to the collapse of the government of Prime Minister Ehud Olmert and a shakeup in the Israeli army command. If anything, it revealed how powerful the Shiite militia had become, and how vulnerable Israeli civilians living in the north were to attacks by cheap, easily handmade, unguided missiles.

By 2014, in the similarly vicious mini-war in the Gaza Strip against Hamas, the Sunni militia widely considered a terrorist group, Israel was ready for those unguided terror rockets, deploying the American-supplied "Iron Dome" anti-missile system. I covered that deployment of the Iron Dome in Gaza, but that assignment was an exception.

For the ten years beginning in 2002, I focused on the wars raging in Iraq and Afghanistan and seldom visited Israel, except to pass through coming and going from Jordan. I avoided Israel to avoid the "Palestinian Problem" and my conscience. From the encounter with Abe Foxman until relatively recently, the last couple of years really, I muted my public criticisms of Imperial Israel in a way that now feels cowardly.

Chapter 8

FACING TORA BORA

By April 2002, Tora Bora was back in the news. Some of it was good, as several reports and quickie books confirmed our scoop that bin Laden had been there, and had been allowed to escape under the guise of the phony cease-fire.

Unfortunately, I was not getting the credit for the original reporting of his escape, and, worse, I was still getting reamed for faking the friendly fire incident. By avoiding the issue, I had made the situation worse. To the journalistic ruling class, my name was now synonymous with cheater. Sitting in Royal Jordanian Airlines's modest first-class lounge at the Amman Airport, and having just been asked for the umpteenth time by a radio correspondent who was there from another network what "really happened" at Tora Bora, I decided I had to face it.

I went outside and, taking advantage of the fact that Jordan had something Afghanistan and most of the Mideast at the time did not, cell phone service, I called the Chicago home base of the Tribune Company, which owns the *Baltimore Sun*.

Although we had not spoken for a year, my former partner on the successful syndicated talk show and Tribune's chairman Dennis FitzSimons was a trusted friend, and was sympathetic. "What took you so long?" Dennis asked when he got on the line, his voice kind and concerned. He explained that the public pummeling I had been receiving from one of his newspapers troubled him. I made my case to Dennis over the phone that I had made an innocent mistake. He promised to have his corporate ombudsman check out the *Baltimore Sun*'s account, and to do the right thing.

At the urging of that Tribune corporate official, the editors of the *Sun* agreed to hear my side of the Tora Bora story when I returned to the States. I eagerly looked forward to confronting my accusers at the paper. To help prepare my case, I hired Charlie Thompson, one of my best producers from our days together at *20/20*, as my investigator. A gun-toting Vietnam War veteran, Charlie did some great reporting with me for ABC News. He produced our giant hour on Elvis and a series of reports on the lingering effects of Agent Orange on our Vietnam GIs.

We had some rollicking times together, near and far, including a blockbuster fistfight with a mean-spirited Missouri cowboy who was trying to prevent our reporting on the use of Agent Orange as a defoliant on his dioxin-contaminated ranch. When he smashed my camera, I punched him so often in the teeth that my fist got infected. I did the voice-over narration for our subsequent special report on the prevalence of toxic human carcinogen with an IV of antibiotics attached to my arm in Lenox Hill Hospital on New York's Upper East Side.

Our team strode into the conference room at the *Sun* confident that the half dozen or so newspaper executives gathered would soon declare my mistake about the friendly fire incident an innocent one. We were greeted coolly but politely and were allowed to screen our videos, but we may as well have been speaking Pashto. They were not budging. Also, I confess to being disappointed that the video evidence we brought with us did not specifically show the "hallowed ground" where I alleged the friendly fire had happened in Tora Bora.

Although I was sure we had taped it, the scene was not among the tapes we showed the newspaper people. Having only arrived the night before from Israel, and having spent the morning before this confrontation at my daughter Simone's piano recital in New York, I did not have a chance to screen the videos, which Craig and Greg had hurriedly put together upon their arrival home. Of all my self-inflicted wounds, this one takes the cake. My video vindication would wait another fourteen painful years.

We had been refused the chance to talk directly to the *Sun*'s TV critic David Folkenflik, but Charlie Thompson had earlier spoken with Steve Proctor, the paper's assistant managing editor for features and the reporter's immediate superior. Charlie told Proctor that, according to Major Brad Lowell, the spokesman for CentCom, Central Command down in Tampa, there had been between twenty and forty civilian and mujahideen fighters killed by friendly fire on or around December 5, 2001. "We won't agree to the hundreds some are claiming happened that day, but are willing to live with twenty to forty," Charlie quoted Major Lowell, but to no avail.

"DEAR BILL," JUNE 3, 2002

In the case against me, Folkenflik had a single military source, a Pentagon spokesman, Marine Lieutenant Colonel David Lapan, who said there was no friendly fire incident in Tora Bora until December 9. In other words, I could not have confused the friendly fire incident I reported on December 5 with the friendly fire incident in Kandahar that day because there was no friendly fire in Tora Bora until several days after my report. *Sun* editor Bill Marimow wrote me that, "Marine Lt. Col. David Lapan said he did not recall any friendly fire incidents in Tora Bora around December 5, the day before your report."

In a Dear Bill letter pleading my case to Marimow, I wrote on June 3,

> Without belaboring the point, it is crystal clear in retrospect that the *Sun* television critic's reliance on the Pentagon's denial of a specific friendly fire incident in the midst of a raging conflict was at best naive . . . Pentagon denials [of friendly fire] were as routine as they were later proven inaccurate.

There have been many hundreds of friendly fire tragedies in Afghanistan, some documented, some not, that have inflicted widespread death and destruction, straining our relations with the government and putting at risk all the blood shed and treasure spent there. The AC-130 gunship's destruction of the MSF hospital, killing scores in Kunduz in November 2015, was the worst recent example. In my letter to Marimow, I laid out some specific reports concerning Tora Bora during our intensive bombing campaign. This one, from Paul Salopek at the *Chicago Tribune* from December 28, 2001, is typical:

U.S. BOMBS LEAVE WASTELAND . . . FIERCE ATTACKS
ANGER VILLAGERS, RAISE QUESTIONS
According to death tolls gathered from elders in four communities
in the area in recent days, at least 87 farmers *and anti-Taliban soldiers* appear to have died in intense U.S. airstrikes on Tora Bora, the
cave-riddled mountain stronghold of Bin Laden ... For its part, *the
Pentagon at first categorically denied the bombing reports* (emphasis added).

An unnamed Pentagon source told reporters earlier this month
that the attacks *"never happened."* More recently, however, the U.S.
military has softened that view. "It is certainly possible that there were
civilian casualties who were not Taliban and Al Qaeda that we're not
aware of in Tora Bora," said Colonel Rick Thomas, a spokesman
for the U.S. Central Command in Tampa, the headquarters of the
Afghan campaign.

After reviewing the available articles and screening the videotapes
we provided, editor Marimow did write me privately praising my "courage and grit" getting "to the front line at Tora Bora, and under those
extremely difficult circumstances, I can understand how any reporter
could make a mistake." Further, he assured me that he did not believe I
intended to deceive our audience. Adding, "I personally do not believe
that, despite the erroneous foundation of your story, you intended
to deceive your viewers," but he refused to say so in the pages of his
newspaper.

There was also another piece of evidence that the editor and his folks
chose to ignore as irrelevant. While Greg Hart was taping the killing zone,
he spotted a longish piece of metal in the scorched earth. After he finished shooting, he retrieved the metal shard, which turned out to be shrapnel. It bore US identification, and was later identified as being part of a
two-thousand-pound bomb, clearly dropped by a B-52.

THE *SUN* NEVER RISES, MAY 2002

After a month-long review process, the paper decided not to retract or clar-
ify its report publicly. The paper also insisted that, while it might be unfortunate, it was not responsible for the fact that other critics and journalists

were inferring from the *Sun*'s reporting that I willfully misrepresented the facts, rather than just got the story wrong.

As a result, critics kept piling on. Contrary to Roger Ailes's confident prediction that the story would eventually go away, it showed no signs of doing so. An article in *Variety* in June 2002 tore into me. As I wrote to Kevin Magee, who was Roger's number-two administrator at the time,

> I understand what a pain in the butt my obsession with this Tora Bora controversy is, but it is like cancer to me. My silence on the issue will not help it disappear. In retrospect, I only wish that I had followed my initial instinct to challenge the slanderers earlier. My continuing frustration with the story is that everyone who repeats it, like today's *Variety*, writes as fact that I had been "charged with and found guilty of unethical conduct." Not only is that false, but my principal accuser now says for the record (but not in his newspaper) that I am innocent of it.

The *Variety* story was the type that editor Marimow supposedly found regrettable, but brushed off. "I know that we disagree about whether [our] stories were 'fair' and I believe that we agree that some of the stories in other publications, which followed the *Sun*'s stories, were not fair." But too bad.

Reporter Folkenflik's career flourished, much of it at taxpayer-supported National Public Radio. He was the man who successfully cut Geraldo Rivera and Fox News down to size. In June 2002, he got $10,000 for his efforts, winning the Paul Mongerson Prize for Investigative Reporting on the Media, administered by the Center for Governmental Studies at the University of Virginia.

Adding insult to injury, I found out about the ten-grand prize from Roger, who told me as a "by the way" one afternoon in his office, saying, "Did you hear your boy won an award?" I didn't even know Folkenflik was up for an award. The stay-at-home critic who risked nothing gets the cash prize, while the swashbuckling hero who gave up so much, risking life and limb, gets ridicule. I complained bitterly to Professor Larry Sabato, the well-known television pollster who runs the UVA program, that they could have at least reached out to me for my side of the story. He never responded.

After I simmered down, I had a Eureka! moment. The pending award to Folkenflik was why the *Sun* refused to say publicly what editor Marimow was saying to me privately. It was the fact that their reporter was up for the Mongerson award in the first place that kept editor Marimow from publishing in his newspaper the mitigating words he put in his letters to me. The editor denies the charge.

"A GOOD GIRL?" JUNE 2002

Professionally and personally, I stayed busy after the *Sun*'s devastating 2002 decision. Roger's affection and loyalty to me seemed undiminished by the scandal. Linked at the hip, he named me to the cast of a new, though short-lived, Fox Broadcast Network show called *The Pulse*, hosted by Shepard Smith. It failed after a few episodes, but it got me back on the publicity circuit promoting the program. After I made several appearances, Craig referenced how cheerful I was on tour in comparison with my dour mood since Tora Bora. "I forgot how charming you could be," he said.

On the personal side, Erica and I were swooning over each other hot and heavy, as our improbable relationship careened toward marriage. I used appearances on Jay Leno's *Tonight Show*, Billy Bush's *Access Hollywood*, as well as visits with the funny and charming Regis and Kelly, irreverent Howard Stern, along with Carson Daly and Dennis Miller to introduce Erica—and the notion that we had fallen in love and were going to be spending the rest of our lives together—to the American people.

The only personality to scoff publicly was Joy Behar on *The View*. She was openly scornful and said as much on the air, essentially accusing me of being just another old man who dumps his age-appropriate mate to troll for naive postgrads. Cohost Star Jones was also cold. I do not blame either. Judging from appearances, I was the stereotype. Seventeen years later, no one is skeptical. Joy always remembers Erica's name, and is totally respectful. We love her and Star, cohost Whoopi Goldberg, and, of course, the one and only Barbara Walters, who has withdrawn from the show she created after an incredible career spanning more than sixty years. Dear, diamond-tough Barbara was also passive aggressive when I first brought Erica around. Barbara simply refused to look at my shining star in the green room, even though just a few feet separated them. Nowadays, whenever we see any of them in public, our encounters are marked by kindness and caring.

Those few exceptions aside, even back in the day, most commentators were supportive of the relationship. *Tonight Show* host Jay Leno was especially loving and welcoming. He was so protective that he went so far as to edit out something I said on the show that offended Erica. When he asked on the air about my feelings for her, after telling him how I adored her and bragging on her professional competence, character, looks, and quality, I clumsily said, "She's a good girl."

After the show I found Erica in angry tears in the green room. "What's the matter?" I asked. "A good girl?" was her sharp, pained response. "I'm not your child!" It was our first crisis. I had put my foot in my mouth. Worse, the statement made credible the old man/young lover stereotype. Leno saved me. Back in the Bel Air Hotel as Erica and I watched the taped show airing later that night, we realized that the excruciating scene did not appear. Unprompted by me, Jay had cut the offending phrase out of the interview. He got me off the hook, and I will always appreciate it.

Whenever possible, I used our downtime to bring Erica and the girls together, often on board *Voyager*. On one cruise, I wrote in my journal: "The sail was great. I just love being out there with the crew and the structured casualness and the magnificent vessel. It's the best life. The family reunion went OK once I profusely apologized for breaking the news of our engagement on television, which really was déclassé."

At this point inseparable for twenty-one months except for my travels, Erica and I were hurtling toward permanency. We spent a week with all four kids at our Malibu beach house. Cruz, then fifteen, and Gabriel, twenty-two, were more or less blasé about the unfolding soap opera. Isabella and Simone were OK with Erica, but cautious, skeptical, and embarrassed by the age-inappropriate match. Many of our old friends were regularly ridiculing the age difference, and the preposterous possibility that I was going to add a fifth notch to my tally of marriages. Then stuff really hit the fan when *Page Six*, the notorious gossip column in the *New York Post*, ran the following item:

> You'd think that a cynical old journalist like Geraldo Rivera would
> be out of the marriage stakes after four attempts. But Geraldo, who

covers war and mayhem for the Fox News Channel, is heading for the altar again. His former assistant Erica Levy, 29, is the lucky girl, according to the upcoming issue of *Star* magazine. The supermarket tab says Rivera popped into Harry Winston the other day and put down $280,000 for a five-carat ring. Erica is apparently unaware of what's coming her way because Geraldo is waiting for the right moment in the next week or so to make his formal proposal.

The right moment came on board a flight to Edinburgh, Scotland, on August 21, 2002, where I was to make a major speech about advocacy journalism at the historic city's Fringe Festival. As we snuggled, shortly after takeoff from JFK, I handed Erica the complimentary toilet kit. It contained the big ring, which cost almost ten times more than my modest first home on Avenue C in New York's Lower East Side.

"I just love being out there with the crew and the structured casualness and the magnificent vessel." Winter 2007.

FIFTH TIME'S THE CHARM, AUGUST 2002

When we got home from Edinburgh and our formal engagement was announced, I was distraught. The persistence of the Tora Bora issue convinced me that I would never be free of the emotional load until I proved my innocence of that charge of fakery. Contributing to my fragile emotional state was the fact my accountant was near panic.

From the journal:

> Another emotional rollercoaster all centered around the very public engagement of Erica and me . . . Then there was my psycho breakdown in Scotland over money and age and Erica, then the buildup to the house and party, and the revelation of our finances all going to hell in a hand basket. The nightmare scenario is ending up old and broke. Won't happen of course, but the thought of it is still very unsettling.

Statistically speaking, our coming marriage faced an actuarial bump down the road. At the rate I was spending money, how was I going to provide for my life after television, and for a wife who would survive me by half a century? Putting doubt aside and a smile on my face, I acted the Puerto Rican–Jewish Great Gatsby for the engagement party of the summer. Along with the tents and decorations, I temporarily added two hundred feet to our dock so that a deep-draft ferry could shuttle guests from the West Seventy-Ninth Street Boat Basin in Manhattan across the Hudson to our newly refinished home in Edgewater, New Jersey. It was unfortunately a dark and stormy night, the wickedest August weather in memory. Nevertheless, hundreds attended, including our families and numerous friends and friends-of-friends. Many of my former colleagues at NBC News came, as well as Roger Ailes and the entire Fox News crew, who improbably mixed with Reverend Al Sharpton and others from our earlier lives. I left shortly after the party, bound for Afghanistan.

AKBAR REUNION, SEPTEMBER 2002

Despite my chronic self-indulgence as a younger man, nothing is more important to me than family. My wife, siblings, and children command my unshakeable loyalty. Akbar Shinwari, about five feet seven inches with a mustache over a perennially smiling face, is de facto family, and seeing this cherished friend again was like seeing a too-long-absent brother or son.

I put my life in his hands during the first battles of the never-ending Afghan War and would many times over the years. He came to stay with us in New Jersey, and I knew he could be trusted to keep us safe anywhere on earth that his Sunni Muslim Pashtun cousins held sway.

Akbar gave me a deep and abiding respect for the sincere power of his faith. He had proudly made the Hajj, the ritual pilgrimage to Mecca, several times, and regardless of the state of combat raging, sometimes with bullets zinging around us, he dutifully prayed the requisite five times facing toward his holy city.

On this journey back to Afghanistan to mark the first anniversary of the 9/11 attacks, the worst sneak attacks on America since Pearl Harbor, he knew I had two goals. One was to prove Osama bin Laden could easily have escaped the ridiculously imperfect trap our forces tried to set for him at Tora Bora in December 2001. The other, more personal, was to prove that there were friendly fire casualties where and when we said there were.

We drove the depressingly familiar thirty miles of bad road from Jalalabad, arriving back in Tora Bora, scene of bin Laden's great escape and where my fate as a war correspondent was sealed. It was exactly as we had left it nine months and a lifetime ago. The Arab fighters, their wives, and consorts were gone, but everything else was the same.

The next morning we broke camp and set out first to visit bin Laden's home in Tora Bora. A gigantic bomb had leveled the one-story cement structure, but you can still see how nicely the property is situated, with a swimming pool looking out at the majestic snow-peaked White Mountains and Pakistan beyond.

With widespread doubt still attached even to the issue of whether bin Laden was here when and where I said he was, and how and why he was allowed to escape, my goal on this return as I said was to confirm my reporting once and for all. Using footage from December 2001, I reported:

Not many observers had a better front-row seat to the fight at Tora Bora than we did. We were close enough to get shot at [video showing

With Greg, Craig, cameraman Carl Glogg, and Akbar, who gave me a deep and abiding respect for the sincere power of his faith. March 2003.

ducking and grunting] . . . We were close enough to watch the sound and fury of U.S. airstrikes [video showing boom booms]. We were close enough to witness the advance of our Afghan allies [video] and we were close enough to watch their occasional retreat [video]. And if he was there—and we have still heard no reliable evidence to the contrary—then we think we know when, how, and to where Osama bin Laden escaped.

It is the second week in December 2001 and al Qaeda is on the ropes. We hear them on the radio speaking in Arabic about laying down their arms and surrendering. The U.S. strongly suspects the obvious, that the requested cease-fire is a hoax, a hoax to allow the beaten terrorists some breathing room in which to escape . . . Yet over the objections of Hazrat Ali, the brave Afghan military commander on the scene, local Afghan politicians grant a twenty-four-hour cease-fire, later extending it to thirty-six hours.

So even as our mighty B-52s circle overhead cutting back on their bombardments, and honoring a cease-fire that the U.S. had warned against and does not believe in, many Afghans believe the al Qaeda chief escapes.

Militia commander Hazrat Ali met us on this return to Tora Bora and granted a new interview at the scene, with Akbar translating: "When I found out about the cease-fire, I said to my commanders they just want to betray us."

Here is what the Senate Committee on Foreign Relations reported in November 2009, eight years later: "On or around 16 December 2001, two days after writing his will, bin Laden and an entourage of bodyguards walked unmolested out of Tora Bora and disappeared into Pakistan's unregulated tribal area. Most analysts say he is still there today (2009)."

OSAMA BIN LADEN'S ESCAPE ROUTE REDUX, SEPTEMBER 10, 2002

If partisan-cheerleader war correspondents like me had had the courage or insight to report it, we would have said that the war in Afghanistan started unraveling almost immediately with bin Laden's escape. As our high-altitude bombers pounded the bunkers and caves thought to be hiding the architect of the 9/11 attacks, he snuck out the back door. As we boasted of "America Triumphant" on live TV, showing the world what real resolve looks like, the mastermind, the world's most-wanted man, just walked away unscathed.

It should have been vexing news, but its impact on American self-esteem was muted by the prevailing "we can do no wrong" patriotism that followed the brutal attacks on the Pentagon and World Trade Center; and by the newness of this war, wars always being popular in the beginning. Buoyed by our counterattack, no one wanted to view bin Laden's escape as anything more than a temporary setback. We will get him. It is just a matter of time.

In my return to Tora Bora in 2002, it was with great pleasure that I pissed on what remained of bin Laden's residence in the rugged but lovely valley. Then, as the crew filmed from the valley floor, I frantically scaled several cliffs, sometimes with Akbar by my side, to peer inside to see whether there was any evidence left behind. I was manic the entire time, restlessly tracking down every lead as to the whereabouts of bin Laden. Here is how we solved the mystery of bin Laden's disappearance in 2002, almost eight years before Congress came to the same conclusion:

"We follow a small river coming down out of the White Mountains of Tora Bora on the lookout for yet-undiscovered al Qaeda hideouts. In a Fox News exclusive we find something else instead. After a three-hour march we discover an ideal escape route out to Pakistan."

If you were around to follow the news from Tora Bora, you heard the refrain on countless talk shows: How could a caravan led by bin Laden, a six-foot-five-inch Arab on kidney dialysis, traveling with his extended family, walk out from under the noses of the world's most formidable military? It was easy. The most formidable military in the world had virtually no soldiers on the ground.

We had that handful of special operators but, as I mentioned earlier, no plan for creating a blocking force, and were utterly incompetent in our plan of action. The United States endured the consequences of bin Laden's escape for years to come. It emboldened his fellow Sunni Muslim extremists and proved that even the vilest crime could be committed against the United States and (for too long) go unpunished.

After our march, I ended the report by reading our location from our handheld GPS device. Our coordinates proved that in just three hours we had walked from the Tora Bora battlefield in Afghanistan across the unmarked, undefended international border into the tribal territory of Pakistan. We could have easily kept marching deeper into Pakistan until we reached a town or city or railroad station and disappeared into the teeming populace, as bin Laden manifestly did. I showed the reading on the GPS to the camera. We were live on *Fox and Friends.*

> That would make our position right about here, 070 degrees 11 minutes east longitude, 34 degrees 05 minutes north latitude; that would put us right about here. This white [on the map], this is Pakistan. If we could make it into Pakistan, certainly Osama bin Laden could.
>
> Although the crucial question of Osama's current whereabouts is impossible for us to answer, he clearly had the means and opportunity to make good an escape to Pakistan.

Tora Bora was and remains a rough neighborhood for outsider infidels. As far as I know, no other reporter replicated our relatively simple exercise, exploring the immediate environs. No one picked up on either our original December 2001 reporting of bin Laden's probable escape date or on this September 2002 report of his likely route out. Though every historical account now confirms that our reporting was accurate, even groundbreaking, critics were less interested in bin Laden than they were in taking shots at me, and, through me, at Fox News.

Returning home to the United States, I wrote,

> Coming back from Afghanistan, I head home with an almost perfect performance under pressure and duress. It is unusually low pressure, really. Danger is not pressure. Getting close enough to danger is pressure. Weird how Tora Bora still rankles. If only. Yet the only way to remove the stain is by consistent brilliance under fire. And surviving.

In presenting my case to friends and colleagues at Fox News once I got back from this second trip to Afghanistan, I chose a letter addressed basically to all the reporters and producers at our bureaus across the country and abroad.

> Despite risking everything in many violent encounters from Afghanistan to Somalia to the Palestinian territories, for the first time in my thirty-two-year career I stood publicly accused of combat chiseling. For war correspondents, there is no graver charge. It has been a humiliating and frustrating experience.
>
> But because we saw what we saw in Afghanistan and taped it, I knew the truth would eventually clear us. And here comes the truth.

Then I described our return to Tora Bora.

RETURN TO HALLOWED GROUND, SEPTEMBER 2002

It was relatively simple to track down eyewitnesses to the widely remembered friendly fire tragedies, including the one that happened during the first week of the critical offensive in December 2001. On the same "hallowed ground" where tragedy struck, I interviewed a twenty-five-year-old fighter named Sheer Ahbad, who described three of the victims on camera with Akbar translating. "They were mujahideen [anti-Taliban fighters]," Sheer Ahbad says on tape.

After taping the interview and doing several live shots during our dramatic hike from Afghanistan to Pakistan, we pulled out. Resentment over the bombings and the disruption from the war, along with a general lawlessness and opposition to authority, made it too dangerous to hang out. But as a trusted insider and member of the dominant Shinwari clan, Akbar had free rein, so I left the task of further evidence-gathering to him, our Afghan brother.

Akbar taped several more interviews with eyewitnesses. One was with another mujahideen fighter with the regal name Sultan Mahmood, a member of the provincial military commander Hazrat Ali's staff. Sultan was one of our guides at Tora Bora during the original December 2001 trip.

The interview was conducted at the Jalalabad Airport where Mahmood was the head of security for the US Special Forces base there. As the tape shows, his US-issued identity card reads, SULTAN/ALPHA COMPANY/1st CORPS/RANK: COMPANY XO/No. 86.

Mahmood told Akbar on tape that he remembered the incident of the mujahideen fighters accidentally killed and injured on the first day of our coverage of the assault on Tora Bora. "They were mujahideen from our side," he recalled. "These people were killed by the B-52 bombing on Tora Bora." Mahmood recommended that Akbar then visit the nearby village of Agam, near the Pakistani border, to speak with other eyewitnesses.

In Agam, Akbar found and later interviewed several, including Sayed Alam and Abdul Sapar, both twenty, and both mujahideen fighters near the front line at the time of the bombing. Sayed recalls during the videotaped interview done at the scene, "This was the front line where we were fighting against Taliban and al Qaeda and we were here when a B-52 dropped a bomb here and three of our mujahideen were killed here and more of them were injured."

Forgive my obsession with this incident, but understand that it is the only time I have been formally accused of faking a wartime report, the one persistent stain on my reputation. It changed my life.

SHOCK, AWE, AND DRINKING HUSSEIN'S BOOZE, BAGHDAD, MARCH 2003

The world's attention was about to leave Afghanistan, despite my feeble efforts to keep it in the headlines. We missed the beginning of the March 2003 Iraq invasion because my team and I were 1,645 miles away in Kandahar, Afghanistan. We were with the First Brigade Combat Team of the Eighty-Second Airborne Division when the Iraq War started with the massive "shock and awe" bombing of Baghdad. I had committed to then-Colonel John F. Campbell, my war buddy and the commander of the Fort Bragg, North Carolina–based First Brigade, that we would cover a major offensive his fighters were waging in Afghanistan against the Taliban. When he was forced to retire in 2016, Campbell had leaped five ranks and was a four-star general, having received the fastest promotions of any other flag officer in decades.

General John F. Campbell retires after a brilliant career that saw him
rise from colonel to four-star general in record time. April 2016.

We knew the Iraq invasion was coming, having covered the run-up to the war from nearby Turkey and Cyprus, including the frantic efforts of the International Atomic Energy Agency (IAEA) investigators to prevent it. We gambled that we could wrap the Afghan assignment before the Iraq battle began, but were a week off. The administration of President George W. Bush was beyond eager to launch the Iraq invasion despite only sketchy evidence that Saddam Hussein had weapons of mass destruction. The WMD were only just an excuse to oust the Iraqi dictator, anyway.

Colonel Campbell arranged to have us flown from Kandahar in one of his C-130 cargo planes heading to Kuwait, the staging area for the Iraq invasion. At the sprawling base outside Kuwait City, we loaded our gear onto a flight of Black Hawk helicopters, embedding with the First Brigade of the 101st Airborne Division, Air Assault, the famed Screaming Eagles, at their front-line base in the blowing sands of Iraq's western desert. From there, the Apache attack choppers of the Air Wing of the division were launching furious attacks against Saddam's rapidly deteriorating forces, but not without casualties. Three of the warbirds were lost trying to land in the intense, blowing sand of Iraq's desert.

Preparing to embed with the 101st Airborne Division during
an Iraqi missile attack. Kuwait, March 2003.

As the division and the rest of our massive invasion force swept unstoppably into an upscale suburb of Baghdad, our unit made its camp in the abandoned estate of a cousin of Saddam Hussein. The lush compound had a swimming pool and a private helicopter hidden under a camouflage awning. It also had a full bar, which made the two-day stay particularly luxurious. The Hussein family thus bought this correspondent a few drinks. Funny how many supposedly devout Sunni Muslims, from Morocco to Saudi Arabia, Kuwait, and the Persian Gulf, are some of the biggest party-hearty players on the planet.

As we rested after the grueling sprint across the desert and into the outskirts of the city, then two-star Major General David H. Petraeus, code-named "Eagle 6" and commanding the 101st, visited our company. What I remember most about his demeanor was that he was all business. He led the division into battle from the front, issuing the stirring battle cry of the Screaming Eagles when the war began:

"Guidons, Guidons [Battle Flags, Battle Flags]. This is Eagle 6. The 101st Airborne Division's next Rendezvous with Destiny is north to Baghdad. Op-Ord Desert Eagle 2 is now in effect. Godspeed. Air Assault. Out."

You do not want to mess with this war-fighting man. Despite the suffocating heat and choking dust, General Petraeus's uniform was immaculate, and we watched as he chastised several troopers for not being shaved and for having their uniforms out of order. When one NCO stated mildly defensively that they had just finished a long, hot march, the general shot back, "So have I."

It was clear that Petraeus was going places, and as with eventual-General Campbell, it was an honor to track his meteoric rise from two- to three- to four-stars. In my cluttered Fox News office, which is festooned with memorabilia from far-flung assignments, right next to the dead al Qaeda guy's helmet from Tora Bora, which I never got around to donating to the firehouse because of embarrassment over the controversy, I have an array of signed pictures taken with battlefield commanders I have had the honor of covering, including General Petraeus after he engineered the Surge, which, for a time, vanquished our radical Islamist enemies in Iraq.

The photo was inscribed, "20 October 2010, For Geraldo—With respect and with thanks for sharing hardship and risk with our troopers over many campaigns and many years. Air Assault! Dave Petraeus."

With honored war buddy General John F. Campbell,
"America's Spartan." Baghdad, Iraq, 2007.

Another photo is with the indefatigable warrior I by then had dubbed "America's Spartan," General John F. Campbell. We are standing outside Saddam Hussein's parade grounds in the Green Zone in the battered Iraqi capital, where the general had command during hard, ugly fighting that claimed many GI lives.

Petraeus retired first, leaving the military in 2011 to assume the directorship of the CIA. A year later, our generation's greatest general got into the much-hyped scandal that ended his career. It involved an ill-advised affair (aren't they all?) during which he told tales out of school to his biographer-mistress, Lieutenant Colonel Paula Broadwell. It was stupid and shortsighted on his part, but having often thrown caution to the wind under similar circumstances, I can relate. Boners make boneheads out of the best of us. Petraeus is a great patriot, and his forced resignation was a tremendous loss for the country.

Speaking of hype, let me tell you a bit about my second wartime scandal, the infamous "Line in the Sand." This one generated far more negative press than Tora Bora, but did not bother me nearly as much because

It was clear that Petraeus was going places. Brilliant war fighter. Baghdad 2007.

it was an attack on my judgment, not my character. In broad strokes, as I explained the state of the battle during a live shot from our desert base, I used a stick to draw a map of Iraq in the sand. The purpose was to demonstrate generally where our unit was relative to Baghdad, the Iraqi capital.

Check out the tape of the incident. There was never any actionable intelligence in that crude, stupid map. I would never give away military secrets or put our beloved troops in the field at risk, two of the most frequent and annoying charges at the time. Military experts in studios in New York and Washington, DC, were using far more detailed electronic maps of the unfolding action in real time.

As I said at the time, aside from my dopey drawing of the dumb map in the sand, grossly aggravating my dilemma was the fact that Fox News was engaged at the time (2003) in a publicity war with our desperate cable-news rivals at CNN and especially at then-fading MSNBC, whose parent network, Big NBC, came after me with all PR guns blazing. Remember, I had jilted them by leaving my top-rated show to jump to Fox two years earlier.

It was, as several key participants later admitted, an organized, network-sanctioned "Get Geraldo" campaign, for which, as I said at the time, they used their "neo-Nazi ex-congressman [Joe Scarborough] and psycho ex-sportscaster [Keith Olbermann] as their hatchet men." I promised to beat the hell out of both men when I caught up with them, but never got around to it, although I came close with Scarborough in a Washington, DC, bar while in a tequila haze after one of the White House Correspondents' dinners.

In fairness, their attacks on me were a tit-for-tat for our attacks on them. At the time, our guys were mercilessly mocking NBC's Pulitzer Prize–winning war correspondent Peter Arnett for "giving aid and comfort to the enemy." His sin was granting an unauthorized interview to Iraqi state television in the first few days of our invasion, in which he questioned US policy.

"It is clear that within the United States there is a growing challenge to President Bush about the conduct of the war and also opposition to the war," Arnett told the interviewer. "So our reports about civilian casualties here, about the resistance of the Iraqi forces, are going back to the United States. It helps those who oppose the war when you challenge the policy."

Despite the fact that he was technically correct, the timing and the venue of his interview were indefensible. One of the few Western correspondents reporting live from Baghdad, Arnett was soon cable-news history. Fox News and most congressional Republicans came after him. Former New York senator Al D'Amato accused Arnett of treason in wartime, for which the penalty can be death. Unlike my crude line in the sand, Arnett's sin was not forgiven, and he was summarily fired by NBC.

In June 2005, in describing the overreaction to my incident to Sridhar Pappu, the fine writer for the *Atlantic* magazine, I said,

Attacks like this are more illustrative of the people who hate me than they are in any way of me—because action talks and bullshit walks. That's why I said [then-CNN anchor] Aaron Brown would shit in his pants if he had been in some of the places I was. That's true. That's absolutely true. It's the same way about all of them—every one of those Geraldo detractors. How many times have you been shot at?

Reporter Pappu wrote in that issue of *Atlantic* what I consider the most intellectually honest biographical summary of me, saying,

He is a cultural phenomenon and often, it seems, the punchline to some pop-culture joke. He broke major stories as far back as thirty years ago, and there is no more fearless war correspondent around. This is hard to remember, however, when seeing footage of him having fat from his buttocks injected into his forehead, or contending with brawling neo-Nazis on his talk show, or vainly searching "Al Capone's vault" for two hours on live TV, or promising to personally kill Osama bin Laden, or simply strutting and preening and boasting the way he does.

Some smart, prominent people (Harvard professors, high-powered lawyers, distinguished journalists) who know Rivera well call him brilliant—and yet he can't seem to escape the larger-than-life circus act that is "Geraldo."

Guilty as charged. But there is much to be proud of in the last five decades, like the Willowbrook crusade, which changed the fate of so many of the disabled; my work on behalf of migrant farmworkers, the urban poor, the drug-addicted, the wheelchair-bound, cheated consumers, storm victims; the many televised confrontations with the KKK and racist skinheads; and the fact that few high-profile correspondents have spent more time marching into harm's way alongside members of our military.

I doubt any correspondent has taken more pictures with deployed service members, attended more memorials, fundraisers, and promotion ceremonies, or has pictures alongside GIs later killed in combat sent to me by their families after the tragedy.

WARRIOR JOURNALISTS, NOVEMBER 2003

It has taken several years, but the cynical attitude and skeptical vibe toward me has definitely diminished as I evolved toward senior citizenship. Still, it remains a wound on the body of my career, not the whole run as a larger-than-life persona, but the war reporting specifically. In my case, every accusation of dishonesty is baseless. Whatever you think of my style or grandstanding, no one can deny that over the last four-and-a-half decades I have been around more hostile gunfire from closer up than any other "celebrity" reporter.

In Israel, Egypt, Gaza, the West Bank, the Golan, Sinai, Syria, Egypt, Mexico, Lebanon, Somalia, Sudan, Afghanistan, Pakistan, Iraq, Kosovo, the Philippines, Colombia, Bolivia, Peru, Venezuela, Guatemala, Nicaragua, Libya, and elsewhere, I have always behaved admirably under fire or extreme duress, as gutsy as any war correspondent in the half century beginning in 1973.

I am not alone. In the late War on Terror era (2013–2017), which I played no role in, there were brave beat reporters who matched my earlier exploits, while getting a lot less attention. More recently, women like CNN's Arwa Damon and Clarissa Ward have taken the lead in covering the fight against ISIS in occupied Iraq and especially in the bloody Syrian Civil War, which began in 2014. Because not many American forces were initially involved on the ground, the reporters' superb efforts under fire attracted far less intense public interest than the giddy early days in what we called the War on Terror.

Despite the relative lack of attention, those conflicts are still grinding out death, misery, and refugees as I write three years later, although the end, or rather the latest version of the end, may be in sight. All of Iraq, including Mosul, has been retaken from Islamic State, as was the "capital" of their self-proclaimed Caliphate, Raqqa, Syria, which fell to a U.S.-backed

My fierce face. Iraq, 2007.

alliance in October 2017. There were still scattered pockets of resistance along the Euphrates River, but ISIS no longer exists as a geographic entity.

Let me further amend my statement about having been Top Gun among celebrity reporters, which I define as public personalities whose fame exists beyond the boundaries of the news business, men like Hemingway and Ernie Pyle in WWII, and Dan Rather and Morley Safer in Vietnam. In that exclusive crowd, there is a gutsy chick who is the heir to glamorous World War II icons Oriana Fallaci and Martha Gellhorn. Even after she got brutally assaulted in Tahrir Square, Cairo, in 2011, CBS *60 Minutes*' Lara Logan, a sharp, smart, beautiful woman, also had the biggest balls in the modern war-reporting business, gender ceiling notwithstanding.

I saw her courage up close in Afghanistan. Craig, Greg, and I were riding a few vehicles back in the same military convoy as Lara and her CBS team on November 23, 2003. She was in the lead truck because the military loved her, a lioness's heart with a face from *Vogue* magazine. Our convoy was driving along a desolate dirt road close to the Pakistani border, just below a trouble spot called Lozano Ridge, outside the Shkin base in Paktika Province.

Embedded with the 504 Brigade, 82nd Airborne Division.
Paktia Province, Afghanistan, March 2003.

The ridge had been the scene of several fatal ambushes in recent months. Everybody was on edge, GIs scanning the ridge, fingers on their triggers, when all hell broke loose. I watched as the lead truck Lara was riding in hit an IED. She and her cameraman, who were both riding in the bed of the truck, got tossed as the vehicle was rocked and overturned in the violent blast. The soldier riding in the front passenger seat of the truck lost his leg as the wrecked vehicle rolled and twisted.

Cameras rolling, Craig, Greg, and I ran toward the truck; the GIs that formed a protective circle around the wreckage were unleashing furious suppression machine-gun fire aimed at the ridge above. Lara, her cameraman, and David Rohde, a *New York Times* reporter who had been traveling in a second vehicle, were sheltering in a huge hole blown in the road by a previous explosion. (A two-time Pulitzer Prize winner, Rohde was later captured by the Taliban, and dramatically escaped after nine months of captivity.) As we taped the wounded GI being evacuated by helicopter, I interviewed Lara, who gave a breathless, but otherwise incredibly calm, professional account of what happened when the bomb blew up under her. When it became apparent that her camera had been smashed in the blast and that she had no tape of her own near-death experience, I offered to provide her all the footage we shot of

At Shkin Base, "The evilest place in Afghanistan." Paktika Province, November 2003.

her harrowing ordeal. She accepted gratefully, later using our video in
her report for CBS News.

As long as I'm acknowledging ballsy colleagues, there's also ABC's
Pentagon correspondent Martha Raddatz, who broke the news in 2006
that bin Laden's main man in Iraq, Abu al-Zarqawi, had been killed; and
CBS correspondent Kimberly Dozier, who was brutally wounded in an
IED attack that same year in Baghdad. She fought her way back to health
and work. She reports now for the *Daily Beast* and I ran into her when we
shared a military C-130 relief flight down to hurricane-stricken Puerto
Rico in 2017. Others include NBC's excellent Richard Engle, who came
to fame by getting to Mesopotamia as a freelancer and sticking it out as
war started all around him in Iraq in 2003. Now he's the network's chief
foreign correspondent. CNN's Ben Wedeman, like my excellent Fox News
friends and colleagues Steve Harrigan, Christian Galdabini, and Rick Leventhal, is cool, unflappable, and deeply impressive. Ben also speaks Arabic. I give kudos as well to CNN's Anderson Cooper, who despite his
status, high style, wealth, and fame, often went the extra step toward peril
to get the story, as in the Cairo uprising of 2011.

In front of a Humvee severely damaged in an IED attack.
Paktika Province, Afghanistan, November 2003.

A THOUSAND MILES OF BAD ROAD, MARCH 2004

Having covered war during five different decades, I subscribe heartily to what British prime minister and serial war hero Winston Churchill said about surviving close combat: "Nothing in life is so exhilarating as to be shot at without result."

That is why soldiers go to war. Everyone thinks the other guy is the one who is going to get shot, not you. To quote perhaps our greatest World War II fighting general, George S. Patton, who said before leaving North Africa to begin the invasion of Nazi-occupied Sicily in 1943, "I want you to remember that no bastard ever won a war by dying for his country. He won it by making the other poor, dumb bastard die for his country. We want you alive!"

Thankfully, while my brother, Craig, and other brothers-in-war like Greg Hart have endured hardship, loneliness, and danger at my side in combat, in my forty-eight years as a television correspondent, my crew-mates suffered only a single combat injury. In 2004, one of my drivers was wounded when our convoy was ambushed outside Mosul, Iraq.

Ambushed in Mosul. Our driver Hussein took a bullet in
the arm. Probably a ricochet. Iraq, 2004.

We were taping an action-packed, hour-long Fox News special report called *A Thousand Miles of Bad Road*, which chronicled a perilous tour of war-ravaged Iraq from south to north, bottom to top. We began on the Kuwait border in the southern city of Basra and made our way north through the tense Shiite strongholds of Najaf, Karbala, and Sadr City, to the Sunni Triangle towns of Ramadi and Fallujah.

In Fallujah, we videotaped a pickup truck filled with dead bodies in the same community where eleven years later bloody battles were still being fought. As I reported on February 15, 2004, "Tension was razor sharp near the embattled Fallujah police station. Evidence of day-old violence was everywhere, following a guerrilla raid that took the lives of twenty-two cops, left others wounded and dazed, and resulted in a jail-break that freed dozens of anti-government prisoners . . . Still, they put up a hell of a fight, as indicated by the four dead attackers piled in the back of a police pickup truck, bound soon for coalition headquarters in Baghdad. This is the grim carnage, the reality of what happens, this is what Iraq looks like far too often."

Few journalists saw more death than our team in those years 2001–2012. Because I saw my role as part goodwill ambassador, I gave these battered Iraqi cops in Fallujah a pep talk. As I noted at the time, "Because under those circumstances it took guts and grit to stand and fight and not to cut and run, I let these men know how they earned my enduring respect." I exhorted the dispirited government cops through our transla-tor: "Tell them we appreciate their courage. They are brave fighters, fight-ing for a free, independent Iraq. Don't be discouraged by this, don't let them frighten you away."

After a few days of high-tension work in and around then deadly, dan-gerous Baghdad, we continued north, making a stop in Saddam Hussein's hometown of Tikrit on the historic Tigris River. There we met General Ray Odierno for the first time. Big, bold, bald, and confident, he was then the newly anointed two-star commander of the Army's Fourth Infantry (Iron Horse) Division, the crew Hemingway attached himself to in the fighting around the Ardennes in 1944, submachine gun in hand.

Odierno was an aggressive war fighter in the heartland of the Sunni resis-tance in the early days of the Iraq War, and he was a far more realistic admin-istrator than our charismatic ambassador-dud, Paul Bremer, a Yale-educated Yankee who made the disastrous decision to dismantle the Iraqi Army after the invasion, thereby destroying the one integrated Iraqi entity that might have prevented the nation's vicious spiral into chaos and anarchy. As Bremer scrambled desperately to keep Iraq from unraveling, I was in his office when he handed a shady-looking Sunni sheik a suitcase jammed with Benjamins, as in fresh, stacked $100 bills. I did not see him get a receipt.

General Odierno, on the other hand, had supervised the efforts of his First Brigade Combat Team to capture Saddam hiding in a rabbit hole near his hometown of Tikrit. We watched, over the years and through many interviews, as Odierno ultimately became the four-star Army chief of staff before his retirement in 2015.

Leaving him, we headed up to the Kurdish communities of Kirkuk and Erbil, until we finally met our near-death experience in Mosul, the northern Iraqi city that is a perfect example of how frustrating the wars against militant Islam have been for the United States. Even back then in 2004, I said of the city, "Mosul is a former Saddam stronghold, overwhelmingly Sunni Muslim. Former regime elements are still strong here." They were strong enough to capture the city and surrounding countryside. Between 2014 and July 2017, thirteen years after the incidents described here, ISIS controlled Mosul. Iraq's second-largest city was recaptured from the militants only after months of ferocious fighting that left much of it in ruins.

General Raymond T. Odierno, retired chief of staff of the Army. June 2015.

Our destination in 2004 was the big base in the city that had recently headquartered the legendary 101st Airborne Division (Air Assault) when it was under the command of one of our best-ever warriors, the afore- mentioned General David Petraeus. After he received a big promotion to three stars and the division was redeployed back to Fort Campbell, on the Kentucky-Tennessee border, the Mosul base was taken over by a smaller and much less effective fighting force out of Washington State called Task Force Olympia, centered on the relatively new and untested Stryker Brigade.

We were en route to an interview with the task force commander, Brigadier General Carter F. Ham. Later in his career, General Ham was commander of all our forces in Africa during the time of the tragic 2012 attack on our consulate in Benghazi, Libya. He is a good guy, charming and charismatic. Back then he was working hard to get the kinks out of his just-deployed unit.

Among their Herculean tasks was to make sense of the new multi-wheeled, but lightly armored, Stryker combat vehicle, from which the brigade took its name. Ultimately, it proved not up to the task of deal- ing with the wickedly powerful improvised explosive devices, the IEDs that wreaked havoc on our forces, and which required the much heavier Mine-Resistant Ambush Protected (MRAP) vehicles to defeat. Ham had the additional task of getting the Sunni tribal leaders to respect him. Unlike Petraeus, who exerted a tremendous authority over the wily sheiks, Ham had no such status among the tribesmen, many of whom would later turn on the United States and support the ISIS occupation.

As we approached the base, Craig and I were riding in the backseat of a hardened SUV that was just behind our security guys leading our four-vehicle convoy. Hardened means it was armored strongly enough to deflect most bullets, but not anything bigger. A rocket-propelled grenade (RPG), for example, would tear it to shreds.

Picked by a bushwhacker as the highest-priority target, our vehicle was suddenly hit by fourteen shots on Saturday morning, February 28, 2004. Each shot from what was probably an AK-47 felt like a hammer blow on the armored doors and bulletproof windows. We got most of the incident on tape. In those days Craig and Greg both drove around holding a digital camera in their laps, fingers on the trigger.

"Roll tape!" I yelled to Craig, unnecessarily. He was already rolling as the rounds smacked into the SUV. Then I said breathlessly to Craig's camera:

Craig caught the attack on camera. "Roll tape!" I yelled to Craig, unnecessarily.
He was already rolling as the rounds smacked into the SUV. Mosul, Iraq. 2004.

"We've been hit. Ladies and gentlemen, we have just been attacked. We've just been sniped. We've been hit! Go, go, go! We've been attacked. We've been hit."

After scrambling a few blocks to reassemble our convoy, I got through on the security guard's radio to the US base, "We've been hit as we were about to enter your base. We have a wounded man. Our driver has been wounded. We're going into the university area; can you give us instructions?" Not getting a reply, we pulled into what seemed a safer area. As I reported, "Seeing the four-man security detail guarding the university hospital, we pulled behind their strong gate to await help from the Army base nearby."

Then on camera: "Now, we're inside the grounds of the university hospital. There are cops here, situation relatively stable. Actually, we've got a good place because we've got that injured driver also. He's been hit in his left shoulder and hand. Right wrist possibly fractured."

Aside from tending to our wounded man, the first thing we did when we were safe was to screen Craig's tapes. "He got the shots," Greg confided with quiet jubilation after seeing that Craig had captured seven of the fourteen bullet impacts on tape. As I said quoting Churchill earlier, there is no greater sense of satisfaction for a war correspondent than surviving close calls. I reacted by smoking a cigar offered by cameraman Carl Glogg and strutting around like I was General Patton.

Protected by fate, our armor plating, and good luck, we suffered just that lone casualty, our longtime driver and friend, forty-year-old Hussein Ali Farhan. He was driving the unarmored equipment bus behind us when he was hit by a single shot, maybe a ricochet off the side of our vehicle. The round pierced his right shoulder, running down his arm and fracturing his wrist before exiting his body.

"Who loves you, baby?" I kidded Hussein, as our security guys stopped the bleeding and stabilized his wound. Then after puffing on that celebratory cigar, I did a show-and-tell describing how the rounds had struck our vehicle.

> They [the bullets] came sweeping down, obviously on this side. The shot—this is the first shot. I heard the first shot. It hit here—then the bullets—got in front of us, turned back, sprayed us again—then he—then he went to the next vehicle. Which has—the glass is not bulletproof, it punctured his [Hussein's] window and put the rounds into the glass. We're OK. Thank God. Thank God.

Pointing where bullets struck our armored vehicle, which
likely saved our lives. Mosul, Iraq, 2004.

We later pried out the crushed bullets and kept them as souvenirs. Hussein was fine after being treated at the then-still-functioning university hospital, never losing his good nature as we completed our taping at Task Force Olympia and eventually made our way out of Iraq via Turkey, eighty long miles away.

I personally drove our SUV for the rest of the journey, resolved that if we came under fire again I would use our hardy, now-tested bulletproof vehicle to squash any attacker. Typically, no other media picked up the story of the breathtaking, caught-on-tape ambush. I said bitterly at the time, "Imagine if this had happened to any other network correspondent?"

After a few days home, I wrote in my journal, "Coming back from Iraq after that violent trip, filled with death and still stunned by the attack in Mosul, I went through an unprecedented decompression. I was in shock, my bravado stripped, nerves shaken. It was deeply unsettling." Again, in retrospect, I am fortunate that my wild post-9/11 reporting did not get Craig or Greg or somebody else killed along the way.

NEW YORK HARBOR, SEPTEMBER 2004

A steadfast friend from our initial meeting in Afghanistan in November 2001, Dr. Abdullah Abdullah, a man of impeccable character I described earlier, is one I continued to rely on to get a firm, fair idea about the war and his nation's progress. Sadly for him and Afghanistan, neither has gone well. In fact as I write this, more than sixteen years after our war in Afghanistan began, the nation totters on the brink. The Taliban is resurgent and the future bodes ill. President Trump has authorized a mini-surge to reverse the downward slide, but I don't expect his efforts to do more than prolong the endless fight.

Several years after we met in Panjshir Province, I had the pleasure of hosting Dr. Abdullah in New York. By then representing his nation as foreign minister, which is comparable to our secretary of state, he was in town to attend the United Nations General Assembly of 2004.

I picked him up by boat at the West Seventy-Ninth Street Boat Basin in Manhattan, and, with brother Craig and Greg Hart, took the foreign minister on my well-practiced tour of New York Harbor. It is a boat ride I have done so many times, I consider the harbor my backyard and know every buoy and navigational marker. Tugboat crews and police and Coast Guard personnel wave friendly greetings when they see my familiar boat *Belle*, an old thirty-six-foot Hinckley, a stylish but modest vessel, which is a cross between a traditional Maine lobster boat and a classic, varnished-wood runabout.

In *Belle* I gave Dr. Abdullah my "Why We Fight" harbor tour, which since 9/11 includes stops at the Statue of Liberty and Ground Zero in Lower Manhattan. I later gave an on-camera version of the same tour during *Celebrity Apprentice*, narrating the highlights and capping the task by yelling, "Screw the terrorists! We have rebuilt the Trade Center bigger and bolder than ever!"

The NYPD freaked when we told them the Afghan foreign minister had accepted my invitation to tour the harbor. They assigned a police boat to shadow our cruise after reminding me that Dr. Abdullah was a "Class One Target" for terrorists. Our boat ride ended with dinner with Erica at our home on the Hudson River near the George Washington Bridge. We catered it from the local Afghan restaurant on nearby River Road.

After being twice cheated out of the presidency of his country, Dr. Abdullah has served as chief executive of the Islamic Republic of Afghanistan since 2014. The position is a kind of co-presidency. He, at the highest level, and more modestly, other solid friends like Akbar in the middle, represent the best of Afghanistan. Unlike the more outwardly sophisticated Iraqis or Iranians, the down-to-earth Afghans I have met are fiercely loyal and reliable friends, but they are captives of their history.

Despite Abdullah's unfailing honesty, courage, and patriotism, political cronyism and endemic corruption, plus the spreading cancer of Sunni Muslim extremism and the undefeated Taliban's eternal war on women and modern life, all conspire to keep the country stuck in the fifteenth century. The population rejects outside ideas instinctively. That cultural and now harsh religious intransigence drained the energy of Alexander, and of the Persian, Sikh, British, and Soviet empires, and will do the same to ours if we over-commit to trying to change it. Afghanistan will break President Trump's heart as it has all the others'.

PETER JENNINGS'S LAST PATROL, IRAQ 2005

Because of my own experiences with the Tora Bora controversy and the "line in the sand" in Iraq, among other professional crises, I had some sympathy for NBC anchor Brian Williams when he got into that jam for puffing war tales. As I mentioned earlier, he spoke repeatedly about how his helicopter had been hit by enemy rocket fire, when the RPG had actually hit another helicopter from the unit. Despite that obvious unforced error, you should know that Brian is a brave reporter. Notwithstanding his unfortunate exaggeration, he had the guts to be in Iraq during the most dangerous period, pre-Surge, when we were losing three or four or more GIs a day.

We shared a flight on a C-130 military transport plane from Baghdad to Mosul during 2005, a really violent year when the insurgency made flying truly perilous. Our aircraft was forced to execute extreme evasive action, banking sharply to the left after takeoff following an incoming missile alert. We were fine, but I am just saying those were bad times, and he was there, unlike most of his critics.

Also on board that flight, coincidentally, was ABC News anchor Peter Jennings, who at this point in his distinguished career rarely made his way to the front lines. As senior men, Peter and I sat in the cockpit jump seats. Brian sat with the crews and GIs in the main cargo compartment. Before boarding, Brian and I had a whispered conversation about how nice Peter was behaving to everyone, signing autographs for the crew and being extremely gracious to all the soldiers and to us. Since he was often overly formal and stuffy during the fifteen years I worked with him at ABC News, his egalitarian behavior now was as refreshing as it was unexpected.

Not long after that trip, back home in summer 2005, Peter died of cancer, and I wondered if he knew he was sick while in Baghdad, and whether that influenced his mellow mood and gracious conduct.

Hopefully, by the time you read this, Brian Williams's career will have been restored. Although he necessarily lost his big anchor job at *NBC Nightly News* to Lester Holt, who by the way is terrific, Brian made a good start at rehabilitation at MSNBC with his skilled, professional election coverage in 2016. Subsequently, in 2017 Brian got his own show on MSNBC called *The 11th Hour* (and his scandal became small potatoes compared to what happened to Matt Lauer and the other men drummed out for sexual harassment), but everyone makes mistakes. It is easy to puff, brag, and misremember a war story, especially in a barroom retelling. But the shaming that accompanies innocent puffing in this one area can be disproportionately egregious.

One extreme example from 1996 involves the Chief of Naval Operations, Admiral Jeremy Borda. The first CNO to rise from the enlisted ranks, he killed himself after a *Newsweek* reporter questioned why he was wearing two Combat Distinguishing Devices from Vietnam that were not earned. I mention Borda's suicide because, at times during the Tora Bora scandal, as I said, I contemplated my own. If you hear some snot savaging someone you trust, remember what Teddy Roosevelt said: "It is not the critic who counts; not the man who points out how the strong man stumbles, or where the doer of deeds could have done them better. The credit belongs to the man who is in the arena . . ."

VINDICATION, THE LOST TAPES, MAY 11, 2016

As I was about done writing an early draft of this book in May 2016, before the harassment furor at Fox over Ailes and O'Reilly, I asked Greg Hart to have one more go at our video libraries to see if there was anything from Tora Bora that we might have missed. Although nowadays most news cameras are digital, with archives stored in the cloud, we still keep a vast archive of all the pre-digital field tapes. The storehouse also contains random memorabilia, such as the studio chair the racist skinhead used to break my nose in 1988.

Now fifty-two, Greg has worked with me since the day thirty years ago he graduated Fordham University in the Bronx. Erica, Craig, and I attended his wedding to Andrea at their new home on John's Island, South Carolina, in June 2017. As his brother said during his wedding toast, "Here's to the last never-married straight guy in South Carolina." With the tightly built body of a jockey, Greg is a perpetual-motion machine who has an understated way of delivering good news, like when he told me that Craig had captured on tape the bullets hitting our car during the Mosul ambush of 2004.

This time, Greg told me that he had found previously untouched outtakes from Tora Bora from the days in question, December 5 and 6, 2001. It was like the past decade and a half of cloudy skies parted and the glorious sun shone through. My life was redeemed. On May 12, 2016, I sent the following email to former *Baltimore Sun* editor William Marimow and former Pentagon spokesman Colonel David Lapan, to then Fox attorney Dianne Brandi, Fox executive Bill Shine, and to my immediate Fox supervisor back in 2001, John Moody. Later that day I sent it to television critic David Folkenflik himself.

From: Rivera, Geraldo
Sent: Thursday, May 12, 2016 9:14 AM
To: Marimow, William; David.Lapan.com; Moody, John; Brandi, Dianne
Cc: Shine, Bill; Rivera, Geraldo
Subject: Urgent: Lost Tapes Found

Gentlemen and Lady,

In vetting the final draft of the manuscript for my war memoir, we found the raw tapes in storage from Tora Bora from 5–6 December 2001. Those tapes belie the then *Baltimore Sun* reporter David Folkenflik's destructive characterization of my work as fraudulent. They also disprove then Pentagon spokesman Lt. Colonel David Lapan's statement that there were no incidents of friendly fire until 9 December 2001 in Tora Bora. Obviously in the heat of combat Pentagon statements on friendly fire have been wrong before, at least until corrected by the facts. I herein offer you the facts of what I saw and reported.

In your defense, it does not appear that we presented these tapes to you when we visited the offices of the *Baltimore Sun* on 15 May 2002 in the vain attempt to prove to you that I made an honest error rather than intentionally reported that I was somewhere I wasn't. What we presented to you that day 14 years ago was what we *aired* on Fox News. The following on camera statements were *never aired*. Obviously, since I present them to prove my statement that I witnessed the immediate aftermath of an incident of friendly fire in Tora Bora on 5–6 December, the fact they never aired is irrelevant.

Since we had two cameras rolling, the incident is captured on both the camera operated by Greg Hart, and a second camera operated by Craig Rivera.

Late on 5 December local time, as the tapes which we have now recovered and which are available for viewing show, I reported on both cameras as we walked across a battlefield in No Man's Land:

(51:25 in on HART #16 tape)
(12:18 in on CRAIG #22 tape)

That smoke over the rise is from our air strikes, you can tell that these guys are a little edgy about getting on the other side of this thing (indicating the nearby ridge. A bomb hits nearby as I speak, the explosion is caught on tape). They don't want another repetition of friendly fire, the forces are so fluid, they are moving so quickly it is almost impossible I would imagine for U.S. Central Command to know exactly where the good guys are. They are moving. They are sweeping.

Early on 6 December local time (and before the appearances that doomed me to a decade and a half of ridicule), I report the following graphic scene on both cameras:

(22:14 in on HART #17 tape)
(47:58 in on CRAIG #22 tape)

This devastated moonscape here is where at least one incident involving friendly fire happened. There are the bits and pieces of Mujahedeen uniforms, even body parts. It's obvious that some American bombs were dropped here, inadvertently. I told you how fast the Mujahedeen were advancing. The intelligence back at the Central Command simply could not keep up with it. This is the result, a tragic accident of war; a warrior's worst nightmare, death by friendly fire.

The shards of body parts and the shreds of clothing are clearly visible in the huge bomb craters. Then, on tape, I said the prayer, the reporting of which I was widely mocked as being fraudulent.

(48:49 in on CRAIG #22 tape)

Our Father who art in heaven hallowed be thy name. Thy kingdom come, thy will be done, on earth as it is in heaven. Give us this day our daily bread and forgive us thy trespasses as we forgive those who trespass against us. And lead us not into temptation, but deliver us from evil, for Thine is the power and glory forever, Amen.

It is on tape. Then I do another on camera, which says,

(57:55 in on CRAIG #22 tape)
So the butcher's bill is in for today's fighting, three Muja-hedeen fighters killed, two wounded, but they ended up killing nine, they killed nine of their enemies, al Qaeda. Now they have come down off of the mountain. They have called in air strikes to get rid of some of the Rats Nest up there, so they have come down off of the mountain to avoid any of those terrible friendly fire incidents. So from Tora Bora, the Rats Nest itself, and the battle raging around it, I'm Geraldo Rivera, Fox News.

It is on tape. We are ready, willing and able to show these tapes to anyone you suggest. I will follow any timely instructions you have to allow you to view these tapes. I want you to admit what these tapes prove, that you made an honest mistake in portraying me as dishonest.

Please pass this message to David Folkenflik. I await a response from all of you. If you would like to designate anyone, including a forensic expert, to come to Fox News to screen these tapes please so indicate as soon as possible.

Thank you,

Geraldo Rivera

Neither of them answered, not former Pentagon spokesman Colonel David Lapan nor editor Bill Marimow. Speaking for Fox News, attorney Dianne Brandi was generally supportive, but cautioned against my counting on my antagonists suddenly reversing themselves. Folkenflik, to whom, as I said, I sent his own copy of the message, and much of whose career since December 2001 has been based on this lie, did say he was interested in seeing the lost video from Tora Bora, but has not been heard from since.

Marimow and Folkenflik gave lame statements to *Page Six* of the *New York Post*, standing by their stories, but have otherwise remained silent and have not responded to my request to have our grievance arbitrated by a panel of journalism-school students.

The awful irony is that I am bringing this long-dead incident back from the grave of obscurity. My obsession with it is probably more interesting to most than whatever happened at the time. But I could not let this black mark go unchallenged for the obituary writer at the *New York Times* or Wikipedia to gloat over when I'm gone.

Chapter 9

GERALDO OF ARABIA

Although it hurts worst, my work as a war correspondent was not the only aspect of my long career subjected to ruthless criticism and unfounded allegations. Hurricanes Harvey, Irma, and Maria raked Texas, Florida, and the Caribbean in 2017, causing uncountable misery and devastation, but the granddaddy of them all was Hurricane Katrina in 2005. It was the deadliest, most-costly natural disaster of the modern era. Sent down to New Orleans five days after the Category 5 killer storm crashed ashore, we arrived to find a city flooded and many of the 1,245 dead still uncollected.

Craig, Greg, and I set out into the flooded, ruined Ninth Ward of the city, where we watched as rescue workers evacuated stranded residents. We later set up our live shot in front of the otherwise ruined Convention Center, which was at least on higher ground with an intact roof under which the refugees from the storm were seeking shelter. I remembered the center from the glory days of my talk show when it hosted the NAPTE (National Association of Television Program Executives) conventions, during which I did deals and partied with syndicators. Remembering those extravagant times in this building in this city made this horrible, grim time even worse. The other intact structure, the Louisiana Superdome, was similarly ravaged, wet, and inadequate in the chaotic aftermath of the epic storm.

The shocked and shattered residents were not being fed. There was no child care, no medical supplies. The situation was desperate. The worst thing was that the mostly black and poor residents were being prevented from leaving the city. There were roadblocks on all the main bridges and highways leading out. The white suburbs were insistent that this poor, black, hungry horde not be allowed to enter their towns and neighborhoods.

The reaction to the relief effort in New Orleans broke down along strictly partisan lines. Republicans and many of my Fox News colleagues publicly supported the Bush administration. Democrats were vehement in their criticism of what was clearly an unfocused, incompetent, even racist response. But those who expected my friend, Fox News anchor Shepard Smith, or me to toe any political line were to be quickly disabused of the notion.

Standing astride the blockaded elevated highway out of town, Shep was wickedly critical of the grossly inept FEMA, Federal Emergency Management Agency, and the Bush administration. My criticism was equally blistering. Choked with emotion and surrounded by destitute mothers and children, I said to anchor Sean Hannity:

Geraldo Rivera: Sean, I can't emphasize what Shep just said enough. He said it exactly right. There's no earthly answer that anyone can understand to why these people after six days are still in this filthy, filthy miserable Convention Center. Why are they still here? This is the freeway here. I tell you what I would have done. And what I would still do. I would say let them walk out of here! Let them walk away from the filth. Let them walk away from the devastation; let them walk away from the dead bodies in here.

I'm telling you, Sean and Alan, this is . . . you cannot deny that it is six days since this natural disaster befell New Orleans. What has happened since is as bad or worse than what Mother Nature did. It's just . . . I mean I can't understand it. I've only been here in Louisiana for less than a day. I left New York yesterday, but coming to the Convention Center, it is as if time stopped. It's as if I'm back and it's Wednesday.

I saw Fox News on Wednesday and people were here at this building, the Convention Center, saying, "Get us outta here. Help us; help us," and now it's forty-eight hours after that and the people are still here . . . They're all still here. Why is that? God, I wish I knew. I wish someone would tell me. Where are the buses? There are so many buses but they're all still here.

Why is that? Look at this . . . look at this little baby. So many little babies. [I pick up a baby.] How old is this baby?

Mom: Sixteen months, okay.

Geraldo Rivera: Sixteen months, okay . . . I got a baby. [My daughter Sol was one month old at the time. I start crying as I hold the child.] You know, I have a baby. You see, there are so many babies here . . . it's just not . . . I mean it's just not . . . it's not, you know . . . it's not a question of objectivity; it's a question of reality. This is . . . how do . . . I don't, I don't know, man.

Let them walk out of here. Let them walk the hell out of here. Let them get on that interstate and walk out, walk someplace. Walk to the Wal-Mart on the other side of the river. Walk to some other town. Walk someplace where you can help 'em. What you got here is thousands of thousands of people who have desperate, desperate needs six days later. These people are still in the same clothes. Where do you think they go to the bathroom? They don't wash their hands; they don't wash their face . . . these babies. What the hell? It's, it's, it's . . .

Shepard Smith: They won't go anywhere because I'm standing right above that Convention Center, and what they've done is they've locked them in there. The government said you go here and you'll get help, or you go to that Superdome and you'll get help and they didn't get help. They got locked in there. And they watched people get killed around them and they watched people starving and they watched elderly people not get any medicine. And now they know it is happening because we've been telling them.

At that point, enraged that Shep and I were excoriating the Bush administration's bungled response to the crisis in New Orleans, Roger pulled the plug on my coverage for the night. He later told me, "Passion is one thing. Incitement is another." I suspected Roger's reason was bogus, and my passion totally appropriate under the extraordinary circumstances of Hurricane Katrina. He was being protective of his longtime friend President George W. Bush. "We did a 4.9 rating that night," Hannity recently confided, "but Roger hated your coverage." I kept my mouth shut until the next morning when I was allowed back on the air to celebrate the arrival of the US military into the city. They began mass evacuations and bailed out the grossly incompetent FEMA and its administrator, the hapless Michael Brown, who soon resigned.

The otherwise pleasant and engaging president failed utterly in his role as Healer-in-Chief. To add insult to injury, Bush 43 did not cut short his vacation on his Crawford, Texas, ranch. His only visit to the devastation wrought by the worst hurricane in US history was to overfly New Orleans in Air Force One en route back to Washington, DC.

Cruel comparisons were soon drawn between his apparent lack of compassion for the poor black folks of New Orleans, compared with his lavish generosity toward the more upscale victims of the hurricanes that had hit his brother Governor Jeb Bush's Florida the year before. Kanye West sealed the Republicans' defeat in the next year's midterm elections when he said, "Bush doesn't care about black people."

By not following the company line, and with our unflinching coverage of the meteorological, human, and political disaster in New Orleans, Shep Smith and I saved the honor of Fox News.

After our tour of duty ended in New Orleans, Craig, Greg Hart, and I drove up to Baton Rouge, the battered state capital, to assess the belatedly mobilizing rescue effort. During an interview with Hannity for his radio show, my friend Sean blindsided me, asking about an article in that day's *New York Times,* which I had not yet read. Sean told me the article alleged I had staged my coverage. It was devastating and outrageous. Specifically, the paper's chief television critic, Alessandra Stanley, wrote that I had "nudged" an Air Force rescue worker out of the way so I could appear a hero, carrying an elderly nun to safety from the storm.

Here is what Stanley wrote: "Fox's Geraldo Rivera did his rivals one better: yesterday, he nudged an Air Force rescue worker out of the way so his camera crew could tape him lifting an older woman in a wheelchair to safety."

I was furious, sputtering as I told Sean it was a total lie. And I was hellbent on proving it. As soon as our team returned to New York, we made all the video from the incident available to the newspaper's editor,

Bill Keller, and demanded a retraction. Despite the unequivocal video evidence, Keller and company refused to correct their patent error. That did not sit well with the paper's own public editor, Byron Calame, however, who decided after receiving dozens of complaints from readers, some of whom were not particularly fans of mine, that the paper was being unfair.

In a column headlined, "Even Geraldo Deserves a Fair Shake," after saying that "one of the real tests of journalistic integrity is being fair to someone who might best be described by a four-letter word" (which is a hell of a way to begin a correction), Calame concluded that "the *New York Times* flunked such a test in rejecting a demand by Geraldo Rivera of Fox News for correction of a sentence about him in a column by the paper's chief television critic.

"My viewings of the videotape—at least a dozen times," continued Calame, "including one time frame by frame—simply doesn't show any 'nudge' of any Air Force rescuer by Mr. Rivera . . . a nudge is a fact, not an opinion. And even critics need to keep facts distinct from opinions."

The bottom line is that even the newspaper of record has its own good guys and bad guys when covering people in the news, and it is willing to abandon any pretense of objectivity and fairness when it suits its political agenda. The distorted way the paper covered Donald Trump during the 2016 presidential election and the way it covers him now that he is president proves beyond a doubt the *NYT* is exactly what it criticizes Fox News for being: partisan. They hate the 45th president, and the feeling is mutual.

The paper and its rival the *Washington Post* also hated Richard Nixon. The difference between Tricky Dick and The Donald four decades later is Fox News. If Fox News had been around in 1972–73 to defend Nixon and savage his critics, the thirty-seventh president would never have been forced to resign. Just as I helped save Bill Clinton during impeachment by berating his nemesis Ken Starr night after night on CNBC's *Rivera Live*, formidable Sean Hannity would have wrapped his arms around Nixon and battled Woodward and Bernstein to a draw.

INCONVENIENT TRUTH, 2006

In the early years at Fox News, I was often asked whether I regretted leaving NBC to go to work for a network whose politics and philosophy are so different from my own. My answer was and remains that I am the same person, true to the same values I have always had. Some remain skeptical. One particular incident still rankles.

In the summer of 2006 as I was entering the Fox News World Headquarters on Avenue of the Americas, I ran into former vice president Al Gore and former *Saturday Night Live* comic Al Franken, who had not yet announced that he was leaving comedy to run for the United States Senate from his home state of Minnesota. Franken would narrowly win the race despite the best efforts of Bill O'Reilly, who absolutely hated him.

The ultraliberal pair had just screened Gore's controversial Oscar- and Nobel Prize–winning documentary, *An Inconvenient Truth*, in one of 21st Century Fox's screening rooms upstairs. It seemed an ironic incongruity, these two high-profile Democratic activists viewing a film widely derided and ridiculed in that particular building, which housed perhaps more skeptics on climate change than any other, your humble correspondent excepted. To them, it must have felt like going into the heart of darkness.

When I greeted both men, whom I had previously met and interviewed, and both warmly responded, Gore with a smirk asked me, "How can you possibly work for Fox News?"

I gave him my standard answer about being the same man, just in a different building. Gore shook his head, never losing the smirk, and added, "I guess you can't bite the hand that feeds you." When I protested his cutting remark, he kept that maddening smirk, saying goodbye as he walked through the security gate with soon-to-be-senator Al Franken in tow.

The vice president's air of moral superiority was insufferable, especially when you consider what a hypocrite he later became. In January 2013, it was announced that the former presidential candidate had sold his principal business, a cable network called Current TV, to Al Jazeera, the Qatar-based broadcaster owned by the Qatari royal family, for about $400 million. So here is smug Mr. Gore, who pinched me for working for Fox News, making a cool profit selling his network to an oil-soaked emirate, which makes its billions pumping and selling dirty oil, the use of which is warming the planet and causing the very "Inconvenient Truth" the former vice president rails about.

Senator Franken had worse karma. In his second successful term he was forced to resign when the infamous photo surfaced of his pretending to grope the bullet-proof protected breasts of a sleeping radio talk show host with him on a USO tour in 2006. His presence is missed by many progressives who worry about losing sight of the big picture.

LOSING MY SWAGGER, SPRING 2010

Aside from its emotional baggage, by 2010 a decade of hard-marching war coverage had taken a toll on me physically. I was in a spiraling funk. The cause was severe complications following surgery on my lower back. The devastating aftermath of that surgery was made painfully clear one weekend afternoon in 2010. I remember looking out at trusty old sailing vessel *Voyager* riding comfortably on her mooring in front of my home in Edgewater. That was the moment when it hit me that I was not working.

For the entire nine years I had by then been at Fox News, Saturday and Sunday was "show day" for my Fox News program, first called *Warzone*, later *Geraldo At Large*, and still later *Geraldo Rivera Reports*. This was an especially pretty April day on the big river, and I was feeling guilty about missing work because I had done something unthinkable: called in sick.

Sick days are not part of my nature. In four-plus decades of hard marching, field reporting out beyond the wire from some of the grimmest places on the planet, plus the often nerve-jangling experience of doing studio and location shows by the thousands, I honestly do not remember ever taking a sick day. I had never been so incapacitated that I could not drag myself in and get the job done, all the while being secretly scornful of weaker souls who beat it out of the office at the first sign of a sniffle.

Generally fearless and combat-tested, I described myself with clichés, as a damn-the-torpedoes personality always ready to answer the bell, and if push came to shove, able to handle crises with confidence that I could still kick most asses. Until that moment in 2010, that is, when excruciating pain from my otherwise dead foot rendered me incapable of working—wounded, mortal, and a shadow of my former self.

The experience of forced inactivity yielded some undeniable truths. First, that getting old sucks. Even if you're not sick, vital moving parts are wearing out. My left knee was replaced in October 2009. That irksome recovery was nothing compared with this complication following back surgery I felt compelled to undergo.

The catalyst for the surgery was my poor performance on the ground earlier in 2010 in southern Afghanistan. That was two tough weeks in mid-February, when I could hardly keep pace with the rugged young Marines patrolling the dangerous, opium-poppy-laden, IED-plagued, Taliban-infested, semi-ghost town of Marja and similar dusty shitholes up and down Helmand Province, the world's heroin capital.

On foot patrol with the Marines, I had to bend over every hundred meters to stretch my weak back or even sit down for a minute or so to relieve the pain and catch my breath. Walking at the rear of the column, I tried surreptitiously to touch my toes unnoticed, but out of the corner of my eye, caught the surprised, concerned glances of the young war-dogs shocked by the surprisingly fragile icon in their midst. As I wrote at the time in Afghanistan, "To be so handicapped after being so active is deeply upsetting. All the Marines saw it. I had to sit and/or stretch every hundred meters. Only sitting down relieves the symptoms. No more marches for me."

It happened all of a sudden a couple of days after the surgery. The recuperation from the back operation was going smoothly, and I strutted around the sixth floor of New York's elite Hospital for Special Surgery at a crisp pace, climbing and reclimbing the steps in the physical therapy room, demonstrating my flexibility and growing strength to the fine rehab staff. At that point disaster struck.

Late one Saturday, my third night in the hospital, I was surprised by an unwelcome guest, an ex-con doctor who insisted on staying to talk about his legal problems involving insurance fraud until the last second of visiting hours. To show him through body language that I was not pleased with his persistent presence, I slammed the room's refrigerator door closed with my foot, while leaning over still attached to the IV on my bed. The result was a popped sciatic nerve that was painful and debilitating and wrecked my right foot, leaving it as numb as a peg-leg pirate's. Something neurological had been busted.

Despite shooting pains that were like a Taser shot, after I got home I did drag my lame, sick-day ass and numb foot off the couch and out of the house to make a little speech to a big group of local kids marching against breast cancer. Then I spent another post-op day back in the hospital trying to figure out what was going on with my broken body. But I was clearly screwed, and it would affect the rest of my life.

In the days following his own hobbling heart condition, former president Bill Clinton increasingly referenced our cycle of life, that journey from youth to puberty, maturity, old age with its escalating infirmities, and death. Among older Baby Boomers, it is common to infuse any conversation with updates on the various maladies afflicting us. "How's it going?" we quietly ask those with heart problems or prostate or colon cancer, perhaps finding comfort in the struggle and triumph of others. My rule is to limit such discussions to the first two minutes before moving on. Otherwise it is all we talk about.

Here is my two minutes: The complications following my back surgery are not life-threatening, but the busted sciatic nerve adds a dimension of physical and emotional discomfort and vulnerability that I have been unable to purge. To add insult to injury, my back pains are back, worse than ever. My sidekick, brother Craig, younger (by eleven years), taller (six foot one to my five foot nine), better looking (check Wikipedia), laughingly encourages me with mock seriousness. Playing on the unwaveringly upbeat rhetoric of the rehabilitative community, he says, "You're not handicapped. You're handicapable."

LIMPING IN LIBYA, APRIL 2011

As a kid in the 1950s I loved a TV series called *Gunsmoke*, which featured actor James Arness as the understated but nevertheless dependably competent and courageous hero, Marshall Matt Dillon. In the days of my youth, I identified with his wise, brave character. Now, I more resemble his loyal sidekick, Chester, played with wry humor by Dennis Weaver. Like Chester, I limp now, but that did not stop me from dragging my sorry foot through some final hairy combat assignments, including one in eastern Libya in April 2011, memorable for the intensity and proximity of the combat we captured on tape.

The fight involved some of the same double-dealing, low-life Sunni Islamist scum, which the Obama administration sixteen months later tragically entrusted with keeping safe our diplomatic compound in Benghazi, Libya, resulting in the death of our ambassador and three other American heroes on September 11, 2012.

The violence I recount here happened a year before the ambassador's death, just after the United States and France militarily intervened to oust the dictator Muammar Gaddafi. He fled Tripoli, his capital in the western part of the country, and was on the loose. His loyal forces in eastern Libya were outnumbered. Far from their home base, they were fighting against a ragged and undisciplined group of rebels. Supposedly the good guys, the rebels sucked in every regard: competence, motivation, honesty, and morality. In broad strokes, we were supporting the scum of Libya, lowlifes worse than Gaddafi ever was. With North Africa in chaos and turmoil from Tunisia to Libya to Egypt, I dragged my crew and myself into a fierce gunfight, which turned out to be my last.

THE FIREFIGHT AT BREGA UNIVERSITY, APRIL 2011

Our team got caught in the crossfire between what was left of Gaddafi's army and the unprincipled Islamist militiamen who would replace his despotic rule with vengeful anarchy. As a result, we got some of the most vivid, high-intensity, close-up combat footage of the modern era. You can still see it on Geraldo.com.

Outside the town of Brega, west of Benghazi, along the North African coast, I reported:

> Most of the "freedom fighters" are a ragtag hodgepodge of civilians that has less discipline, training, experience, and organization than a Chicago street gang. They are hapless, clueless, and frequently seen retreating at the first shot. They cannot even tell the difference between incoming or outgoing fire; they shoot with little or no idea of what they are aiming at; and they are as dangerous to themselves or to civilians in the area as they are to Gaddafi's forces.
>
> Driving through the old section of Brega early Sunday morning, I was surprised at how lightly manned the road was. Where was the rebel army? Later, I learned that they usually show up for work after breakfast in Benghazi. Then they call it a day in time to get home for the evening meal.
>
> After a series of rolling hills, we could see the University of Brega on the next rise. There was a small group of rebel fighters

crouched by the side of the road, maybe four of them, lightly armed with AK-47s and an RPG. "Gaddafi! Gaddafi!" they said, urgently pointing toward the university.

Because they tend to see Gaddafi soldiers under every tree, I discounted their shouted warnings. We got out of our vehicles, and I started walking up the slight rise toward the university buildings, Greg Hart walking alongside, camera in hand, taping everything.

Then the first shot whistled over our heads. What followed was a cacophony of firing from the Gaddafi forces holed up at the crossroads less than a half-mile ahead. They started firing at us with everything from RPGs to heavy machine guns. The shots cut through the air with that zinging sound that terrifies the soul. The worst part came when enemy mortar rounds started landing behind us. Retreat then had to go through that zone already bracketed by their firing.

On our side, opposing the Gaddafi forces, were the rebels.

The Libyan rebel army is the most ill-disciplined, inexperienced, and unreliable I've ever seen in a combat situation. Their level of incompetence is so shocking the very notion of heavily arming them gives me nightmares of dudes walking around with machine guns, looking to settle personal scores that have nothing to do with their revolt in the desert.

On this eastern front in Libya, the rabble rebel army roars with bravado until confronted. They fire their weapons wildly, and shout *Allah Akbar* as if Allah cared about their macho posturing. Then, at the first sign of a determined counterattack, they run. Their whining incompetence makes them unfit to wear the title "freedom fighter"; even "rebel" sounds too grandiose for these poseurs. These gangsters should not be armed by NATO; they should have their asses kicked into shape by French, Italian, and British noncommissioned officers who can teach them not to run away when fired on, but to dig in, form a defensive line, send forces out to the flanks, and scouts up forward, and to shoot horizontally, not vertically.

When we got caught in that crossfire, it revealed that what this mob needs is a few good Marine Corps drill sergeants, not more or heavier weapons. Picture this: In front, a fortified enemy position; Gaddafi loyalists have dug in behind the brick or cement walls of the town's university. Actually, it's more of an oil-related trade school, called Bright Star Petrochemical University.

What deeply impressed me was how much more admirable Gaddafi's forces were than the rebels opposing them. They are out-numbered and far from home; they know that if they surrender their fortified positions and attempt to flee westward toward the remain-ing Gaddafi stronghold of Tripoli, they will be exposed to harassing attacks and possibly more allied air strikes. So they are not going anywhere, and they have no choice but to fight.

Coming down the road from the eastern side is the vastly larger rebel force of at least 1,500 or 2,000. They are armed with rocket launchers, RPGs, heavy machine guns, twenty-millimeter anti-aircraft guns mounted on the backs of Toyota pickups, and other assorted lethal weapons.

The rebels drive toward the fortified position essentially in sin-gle file. In other words, only a few of their formidable arms can be brought to bear on the target they are attacking. No effort is made to spread out the line. No effort is made to protect either the north or south flank. No scouts are sent ahead to pinpoint potential targets within the Gaddafi stronghold.

Instead, the lead elements begin firing wildly. In vehicles back farther in the line, weapons are also let loose. Rounds fly dangerously close to the heads of the rebels in front. To avoid killing their com-rades, the rebels aim high. Clearly the fact that they are shooting the sky does not occur to them, as they are made euphoric by the sheer power of their weapons igniting, however harmlessly. Many shout *Allah Akbar* as they fire.

The Gaddafi forces endure this assault for several minutes before letting loose their own barrage, better aimed. Several rounds land among the rebel column. This sets off one of their typical mad dashes to the rear, the entire column rushing incoherently to retreat back up the hill and out of range of the incoming rockets and mortars. Some keep going all the way home to Benghazi, 135 miles away. The grav-est danger of the day is that of traffic accidents as they careen away, many still firing their machine guns as they swerve up the road.

In forty years of war reporting, I have never seen so disgraceful a performance under arms. Granted, just a few weeks ago most of these rebels were students and clerks and gas-station attendants, lawyers, teachers, and thugs released from prisons. Still, didn't anyone think to look up a basic training manual before they set out to make war?

The lack of discipline also manifests itself in behavior that is sometimes larcenous, as weapons and vehicles are snatched and stolen from fellow fighters, presumably because the snatcher believes he can do a better job than the snatchee. Besides, who wouldn't want their own AK-47?

When Greg Hart and my calm, hard-as-steel former British SAS commando bodyguard, Scott Board, and I were walking up that road toward the campus, not expecting to be met by the fusillade that came, we took cover off the road, beginning the running commentary that formed the basis for our special report, *The Firefight at Brega University*. As we did, several Gaddafi rockets and mortar rounds landed right where we had been standing minutes before.

My second cameraman, Greg Khananayev, who along with Mohammed Ali, our local stringer, had literally just physically fought off a larcenous rebel trying to steal our vehicle, watched in horror as the rounds landed right where we had been standing. Terrified that we had been killed, Khananayev drove our Toyota down the hill toward the firing to retrieve us. He thought we had been killed, but was determined not to leave us behind, dead or alive. His courage allowed us to avoid the walk back up that long hill through the cluster of fire coming from both sides. He probably saved our lives, and I will never forget that.

At one point, the vivid video shows me visibly limping as the crew vehicle mistakenly drives off without me in it. They came back for me, but the incident was so unimpeachably harrowing that Jon Stewart on Comedy Central did a mash-up that fell between mild ridicule and unmistakable compliment.

Sarcastically comparing me to the title character in *Lawrence of Arabia*, he superimposed my face on some of the iconic scenes from my favorite movie starring the great Peter O'Toole in his film debut. Then Stewart intercut sound and video from the movie with our real-life battle footage, calling it *Geraldo of Arabia*.

Stewart tagged the piece saying, "Whatever you think of Geraldo Rivera, dude's got major sack," indicating his genitals, as in big balls. Geraldo of Arabia considered "major sack" such high praise that I took Stewart's joke as homage, and thought hard before rejecting *Major Sack* as the title of this book.

Chapter 10

TRUMP, BIN LADEN, AND

DANCING WITH THE STARS

Nine years, seven months, and nineteen days after the 9/11 attacks that changed all of our lives for the worse, Erica and I attended the White House Correspondents' dinner in grand style. We sailed up the Potomac River to Washington, DC, in *Voyager.*

We had previously attended several of these glitzy occasions, amused by how star-starved Washington-based journalists react to famous guests, who are usually gracious. As a semi-celebrity, I usually got a warm welcome from the younger staffers, had fun sitting next to prominent guests such as the late Supreme Court Justice Antonin Scalia and astronaut Buzz Aldrin, the second man on the moon, and enjoyed some belly laughs at jokes from the president and the comedy host, who this year was an unusually acerbic Seth Meyers.

The target of the ruthlessly barbed jokes by Meyers and the president was my old friend Donald J. Trump, who had it coming after joining maliciously xenophobic Sheriff Joe Arpaio in resurrecting the long-simmering "birther" movement that sought to prove President Obama, who was seeking reelection in 2012, was really born in Kenya and was thus disqualified from occupying the Oval Office. However twisted, a straight line can be drawn from Trump's involvement in the birther crap and his election to the presidency. No one else running knew how potent the bogus issue would prove to be.

The dinner came just a week after President Obama released his long-form birth certificate, substantively putting the silly issue to rest. That night, with Trump in attendance, Obama enjoyed twisting the comic knife. He queried whether Trump's next probe might be whether the moon landing actually happened. Obama also showed a video of his own birth, which turned out to be the iconic clip of Simba being born in the cartoon movie *The Lion King*.

Trump would have better luck using the birther issue later against Ted Cruz in the Republican primaries. Since the Texas senator really was born abroad, in Canada, the argument could be made with a semi-straight face that Senator Cruz technically was not the "natural-born citizen" the Constitution requires of presidents.

The billionaire businessman-who-would-be-king was also in the bull's-eye at the correspondents' dinner because for several weeks he had been talking up another wacky idea: He was running to succeed Barack Obama in the White House. The forty-fourth president launched a string of stinging jokes about how Donald as the forty-fifth president, clearly a laughable idea to most of those smarty pants gathered in the cavernous Grand Ballroom, would convert the White House into a casino with a jacuzzi on the South Lawn.

The president mercilessly mocked Trump's inexperience for high office, pointing out that on that week's installment of *Celebrity Apprentice* Trump had just fired Gary Busey rather than Meat Loaf. The president deadpanned, "These are the types of decisions that would keep me up at night. Well handled, sir."

The man who would improbably become president was fuming. I am certain the mockery that night helped persuade Trump, after years of pondering, finally to make the run for the White House.

President Obama was in fine form, relaxed and funny. He and First Lady Michelle Obama gave Erica and me a warm greeting, waving and smiling broadly from their seats on the dais. Twenty-four hours later, when Erica and I realized what must have been going on in the president's head at the time of his wisecracking, we decided he was the world's best actor. If the weather had been better that same day in Afghanistan, he never would have made it to this Saturday party. He would have been concerned with the far-weightier matters that he dealt with on Sunday night.

THE GREATEST NIGHT OF MY CAREER, MAY 1, 2011

That Sunday night, May Day 2011, the White House announced that the president of the United States would be addressing the nation at around 10 PM. The prevailing wisdom was that he was going to tell the American people that the fugitive Gaddafi had been caught.

But even that dramatic premise caused major head-scratching. Gaddafi dead or alive, captured or free, did not warrant a presidential prime-time address to the nation. So as our live 10 PM show approached, we pondered what the hell was up.

At the Fox News Washington Bureau, Craig, Greg Hart, and a team of the bureau's young staffers were frantically calling sources and checking social media and the AP wires knowing that it was probably something connected with the military. On the other hand, it was not a major act of war like an atomic explosion because we would have heard about it by now. I was on the air speaking via remote with Fox News's White House correspondent, Mike Emanuel, when it hit me.

"Wait a minute—hold it. Ladies and gentlemen, something I just thought of," I interrupted Mike. "What if . . . what if it's Osama bin Laden?" When I said it, the words just out of my mouth, I knew that it was true. I sensed a gasp, then a wave of affirmation sweeping the nation.

I doubled down, cautioning the audience that I was not reporting the death of Osama bin Laden as fact, but saying, "This is a reporter relying on his experience telling you what my surmise is." Then I asked viewers and specifically my studio guest, retired Air Force Lieutenant General Thomas McInerney, "Is it possible that the terror mastermind who killed so many Americans, that striking from bases in Afghanistan, something may have happened to him?"

Was it too good to be true? Bin Laden, captured or dead? I promised high fives and cheers all around if that were the case.

At 10:40 PM ET, five minutes before CNN, my voice cracking with emotion and joy, I reported the confirmation from senior Capitol Hill producer Chad Pergram. I read a note from Chad out loud, saying over and over, "Osama bin Laden is dead. Osama bin Laden is dead. Can it be? Can it be, ladies and gentlemen? The man who caused so much misery and pain? Osama bin Laden is dead!"

Then, as I read the AP wire from my desktop computer, my voice filled with rising excitement, I said, "Hold it. Hold it. Hold it. Hold it. Hold it. Bin Laden is dead! Urgent confirmed! Bin Laden is dead. Multiple sources. Happy days. Happy days, everyone. This is the greatest night of my career. The bum is dead. The savage who hurt us so grievously, and I am so blessed, I am so privileged to be at this desk at this moment."

Beginning with a typically snotty headline, here is how the important website Mediaite described what happened:

GERALDO RIVERA'S FINEST MOMENT: HOW THE MUCH-MALIGNED ANCHOR BROKE THE BIN LADEN NEWS BEST

In breaking the news, no one could top Geraldo Rivera's pure euphoria. Rivera, who was on deck to anchor his regular program *At Large*, appeared as confused as all of Twitter around 10 PM, when the White House announced the news that the President would speak about an unknown topic within the hour. After about a half hour of errant speculation on the life and health of Muammar Gaddafi, a light bulb went off in Rivera's head.

It was true. Bin Laden was dead, and I was never more alive. When Fox News anchor Brett Baier and his impressive team of staff and experts took over the channel at midnight, at the urging of Darla Shine, wife of FNC's then-senior vice president and later co-president, Bill Shine, I hurried to join Craig and a live camera crew outside the White House, where a huge and boisterous crowd of college students had spontaneously gathered. They were cheering and high-fiving, and I was with them, "dancing on bin Laden's grave."

A funny story that I have never told . . . When I first got to the White House, I could not find Craig and the crew. In a panic, I asked to be admitted to the White House on the assumption that he and the rest of the media were somehow inside. The Secret Service guys at the heavily fortified gate reluctantly let me into the president's residence. They were as euphoric as I was, and they understood that I needed to find my crew. To make a long, silly story short, Craig and crew were not in the building. So after running through its historic halls I came out the other side, asked breathlessly to be allowed to exit, was permitted out, where I finally found them, and immediately went live, ebulliently reporting the news and the jubilant crowd reaction.

Amidst the raucous celebration, I somehow noticed that I had a text message from Afghanistan. My dear friend, then-two-star Major General John F. Campbell, was watching our coverage with a large contingent of his soldiers of the 101st Airborne Division (Air Assault). His command was having a very tough time on this deployment, having just lost six soldiers in a vicious firefight with the Taliban. The division would lose 245 soldiers killed in action by the end of the year's deployment when I joined them in Afghanistan in 2012.

But this night, they were cheering and celebrating along with the rest of the Free World. The monster was dead, and I was honored to bring the nation the news for which we had waited for so long.

It was as Mediaite further described, "The most significant and joyous national security announcement of the past several decades," and here is how I described the significance of the moment the next day in a column for Fox News Latino:

> He haunted my life since that crisp, clear September day almost ten years ago, when Osama bin Laden sent four hijacked airliners to inflict mass murder on innocent men, women, and children.
>
> When the twin towers fell on 9/11, among the business people, visitors, and first responders who died were several dads from my girls' former elementary school in Rumson, New Jersey.
>
> The loss of those fathers sent a tsunami of grief and disquiet through all of our children. The horrors and grief of war had come to the shore of America.
>
> At the time anchor of CNBC's highest rated show, I begged to be allowed to go into the field to chronicle the hunt for the mass murderers who killed those fathers. Refused permission, I quit my plum job and signed on as a war correspondent with Fox News, the spunky new network created by old friend Roger Ailes.

I started at Fox on a November Friday. By the following Tuesday, I was in Pakistan en route to the Khyber Pass and Afghanistan, reporting on the burgeoning effort to catch or kill bin Laden, and to punish the Afghan Taliban who had given al Qaeda sanctuary.

Ten difficult assignments in that war-torn region since brought little advance to the story. We marched, we searched, and we watched our soldiers, sailors, airmen, and Marines fight, kill, and be killed. Still bin Laden eluded us.

My secret fear was that he would outlive me, or that he would simply stay vanished and invisible, sending an occasional taunting or threatening video, mocking us: "Catch me if you can!"

Now Osama bin Laden is dead, killed in a hail of gunfire from an elite team of Navy SEALs raiding the terror mastermind's absurdly lavish compound in Pakistan.

We were there when he escaped our clutches in Tora Bora in December 2001. And we were on the air Sunday night when the news was confirmed that he was dead. In between those monumental events, life has gone on for my family, my country, and me. But the long shadow of the world's most wanted man darkened the sky and chilled the air. Now he is gone. Sure there are more storms ahead. But today the sky is again crisp and clear.

Mediaite's Frances Martel, whom I don't know, wrote the piece grudgingly praising my performance that fateful night, admitting,

It's difficult to give props to Geraldo Rivera. Building a legal career out of militant Puerto Rican separatism only to hop on TV and spend decades highlighting the absolute worst in America—from local news reports on crack houses to his *Jerry Springer*-esque talk show to the Milli Vanilli of journalism, *The Mystery Of Al Capone's Vault*—few can challenge his reign as America's most prominent media punch line.

That's not to be overly harsh on Rivera or to undermine the role he played to Americans last night, but only to emphasize how much more unexpected it was to see him rise so strikingly to the occasion. He is the last person one expects to accurately speak for all America on a serious issue, but he was the only journalist on the air that night with his heart sufficiently placed on his sleeve to stop being an anchor for a little bit of time and just react like a human, specifically, a New York.

Sure, many will refute that a journalist getting emotional is the proper decorum for someone privileged with such a responsibility . . . But last night was unquestionably the best broadcast of Rivera's life; he said so himself. No one better captured the breathless, unadulterated relief of knowing a man who had caused so much suffering had finally reached his end after a life that will go down as one of the most repulsive in human history, and for that, at least part of the debt of good reporting Rivera owes to his viewers has been paid.

"FOR GOD AND COUNTRY, GERONIMO, GERONIMO, GERONIMO," MAY 2011

Rob O'Neill, the member of SEAL Team 6 who killed the terror mastermind, has described how the corpse of bin Laden was first brought to Jalalabad Airport for tentative identification. The team was also waiting for a second aircraft ferrying the remaining members of the team, whose helicopter had been left behind and destroyed after crashing as it attempted to land in the bin Laden compound in Abbottabad, Pakistan. I interviewed Rob about it one day at Fox.

Rob O'Neill: It was neat because we were with the entire team. We are all obviously elated for a number of reasons: One, we just killed bin Laden; two, we lived. We are gonna live. We are gonna be best friends for the rest of our lives. This is so cool. We were part of this team that will be legendary. We didn't expect them to say SEAL Team 6, but the more we heard it, we were like, this is a bigger deal than even we thought. And then you were on the air and then I remember you started speculating the first time we heard bin Laden and then you confirmed, "bin Laden is dead, bin Laden is dead!"

And I was eating a sandwich as the president came out. And finally, 'cause what was happening before that was we were watching you on television and most people I am assuming were wondering why it was taking so long, but behind us, my boss is on the phone with probably the White House or the CIA and they are just trying to get a head count on what happened in the house; how many are dead; how many were wounded; how many women and children; what is the total head count; 'cause we always want that after a mission.

So they are just trying to straighten that out before they tell the president. Then the president comes out and I remember watching him and he said, "Tonight I can report to the American people and to the world, the United States conducted an operation that killed Osama bin Laden, the leader of al Qaeda." And I remember that so vividly because I hear him say bin Laden, Osama bin Laden, and I look at Osama bin Laden, like he is right there and just everything kinda flashes through all the missions, that "We are never gonna find him." "The guy is a ghost." "I will never be on that mission"; and realize, Oh my God, how in the world did I get here from [his hometown] Butte, Montana? [Laughs] And I killed him.

The melancholy side of the triumph is that the death of bin Laden did not end the War on Terror. In a pessimistic appraisal that was widely reported in February 2016, the director of national intelligence, James Clapper, told a Senate hearing, "There are now more Sunni violent extremist groups, members, and safe havens than at any time in history." Matthew Henman, head of the Terrorism and Insurgency Center, which analyzes international security risks, told reporters, "Five years after the killing of Osama bin Laden, it is not wrong to be fairly pessimistic in our outlook on the world."

It did not take long for Henman's pessimism to be realized. In June 2017, Tora Bora was back in the news for the worst of reasons. It had fallen back into the clutches of radical Islamists. Only this time it wasn't the Taliban or al Qaeda, it was ISIS. After gaining and then losing territory in Iraq, Syria, and Libya, this malignancy spread to Afghanistan. Smaller than the other extremist groups, ISIS in Afghanistan had been more or less contained in a network of tunnel hideouts in the Achin District, near the Pakistan border.

Our air forces found them there and attacked their refuge in April 2017, dropping the so-called Mother of All Bombs, a 20,000-pound giant said to be the most powerful nonnuclear weapon in our arsenal. By all accounts, the gigantic explosion inflicted scores of casualties and led to rejoicing among our military leaders. We had landed what seemed a killing blow. Rather than being wiped out, however, the terror organization simply regrouped and moved, choosing a sanctuary less vulnerable to our air strikes. According to my old friend Hazrat Ali, who is still in the area, a thousand surviving ISIS fighters attacked Tora Bora. As of this writing, ISIS occupies the infamous cave and tunnel complex that bin Laden built, and our side spent so much time, money, energy, and reputation trying to destroy.

I am almost tempted to let ISIS alone to discover the same sorry fate as every other would-be occupier of Afghanistan. Let them exhaust their blood and treasure trying to outmaneuver the Pashtun tribesmen and alter their brutal society. ISIS will not find the fertile ground they found in the Sunni heartland of Mesopotamia. However they fare in Tora Bora, there is no end in sight to their brand of terror. The peril posed by Sunni Muslim extremists will be just as bad or worse on the tenth anniversary of bin Laden's death as it was on the fifth, but at least he is dead. The United States did what we pledge to do to those who attack us. We tracked him down and took our revenge on the perpetrator for his terrible crime. I was not in New York when the planes hit the towers, but I was on the air almost a decade later when we learned justice had been done. And SEAL Team 6 and the world were watching.

LAST DANCE, DECEMBER 2011

Bin Laden's death did not end the War on Terror. Like President George W. Bush's preposterous "Mission Accomplished" banner eight years earlier, 2011 turned out to be President Barack Obama's year of cockeyed optimism. Six months after we celebrated bin Laden's death in Afghanistan, Obama told us our war in Iraq was also ending.

America was eager to move on, and bring our troops home. I had the privilege of being on what we all thought was the last US combat convoy out of Iraq in December 2011. As we left, bound for Kuwait, there was an omen of bad times ahead in the rearview mirror. It was a mob scene happening at the base behind us. Instead of the valuable assets we left behind being handed over to proper authorities, as we pulled out of the base, a mob of civilians poured over the fence, grabbing and stealing every piece of equipment they could get their hands on. Among the loot was row upon row of brand-new Ford F-150 pickups, symbolic of all the billions of American taxpayer dollars wasted on that sorry excuse for a country. I left apologizing for not opposing the Iraq War in the first place.

As I reported at the time, "For someone who considers himself a patriot, as I do, it is extremely difficult not to rally behind a president when he beats the drums of war. So it has always been. We can disagree about domestic policy, but when the nation's leader says we are threatened from abroad, the majority of Americans suspend misgivings or even gnawing disbelief and give the man in the Oval Office the benefit of the doubt.

Our war against Saddam Hussein's Iraq was the classic example. It was funky from the get-go, and I should have known better. Instead, I concentrated on chronicling the heroic efforts of our stressed Armed Forces as they followed goals that vacillated from attempted conquest, to force protection, to nation building, to finding a respectable way out.

We didn't go for the oil. We didn't go to establish a strong base in a dangerous, strategically important part of the world. We went as an act of national self-defense. But was it really?

Invading Iraq to find weapons of mass destruction that we had only flimsy evidence ever really existed required an act of willful blindness. That lame dog-and-pony show that Secretary of State Colin Powell put on in the United Nations in 2003 to prove our case that the Iraqi dictator was really attempting to build a nuclear weapon and then to rally international support for the invasion, showed how pathetically thin our proof was. For good reason, Secretary Powell's longtime military adviser and chief of staff, Colonel Lawrence Wilkerson, later called his own involvement in that UN presentation "the lowest point of his life."

Our proof then was a thousand times less convincing than the evidence today that neighboring Iran is heading down the road to nuclear weapons. And yet in 2003 we all nodded sagely when Powell, the hero of Gulf War I, spoke, and I dusted off my body armor and packed my bags, eager to follow our troops into action in the sands of Mesopotamia.

I had plenty of company in the pro-war camp in February and March 2003 during the inexorable run-up to the war, including Bill and Hillary Clinton. But that doesn't take me off the hook for enthusiastically backing a bloody conflict that turned out to be as unnecessary and costly as its critics predicted.

I don't for a second want to imply that what I experienced was even a fraction of the trauma endured by our deployed warfighters, but my experiences still rattled and deeply unsettled my soul.

The only salve to my conscience is that I always put my own ass as far out on the line as the GIs who fought and died in this God-forsaken place. After our vehicle got shot up outside Mosul in northern Iraq in 2004, I was convinced I was going to die there. On some trips I would come home and sit on my porch overlooking the Hudson River, staring in a kind of dark trance, drool leaking from the edge of my mouth, thinking about all the death and destruction we were seeing.

Two images haunt me to this day; both involve pickup trucks. The bed of one Toyota truck outside Baghdad in 2005 held the torn-up body of a woman killed because she wanted to vote. The bed of another pickup outside Fallujah in 2004 held a pile of dead insurgents piled one on top of the other like they were bloody lumber headed to the mill.

During the war's darkest days before the surge, between 2004 and 2007, we were losing two, three, or four GIs every single day. The line from the Sting song, "every step you take . . . " played in my brain every time we went out on foot patrol, because every step contained the possibility that the ground would explode in our faces.

All those images crowded my mind this past Saturday as our C-130 military transport aircraft landed at Camp Adder, our last Iraqi base. I was there at the beginning of the conflict. This was my eleventh and final trip into Iraq.

At the height of the war, this sprawling base in southern Iraq held 12,000 of our troops and airmen. It is a vast, dusty place, far larger than, say, JFK or LAX. Now it was almost deserted, save for the visiting brass and journalists gathered to mark the occasion of the withdrawal of the last US military unit in Iraq, 480 officers and enlisted personnel from the Third Brigade of the First Cavalry.

After speeches and interviews, the brass left on the aircraft, and I was privileged to be among five reporters given the high honor of making the four-hour drive out of Iraq and into neighboring Kuwait. And so the long war that claimed the lives of 4,487 GIs, spread so much pain and suffering, and cost a trillion US taxpayer dollars, ended not in victory, but with a profound sense of relief. It was over, and I survived.

Some of the friendships made with members of our fighting forces will endure forever. Having seen so much tumult and death together, we are friends for life. My heart aches for those who fell or were wounded or otherwise scarred by the grim experience. But the next time the president calls, they and I will be there again, however heavy it weighs on our hearts and minds.

HOORAY FOR HOLLYWOOD, 1990–2017

My final combat assignment was Afghanistan in 2012, where General John F. Campbell was by then the four-star commander of all our forces. As I arrived at the US Embassy for an interview with our brave and highly skilled ambassador Ryan Crocker, the compound came under Taliban mortar attack. The fortified building was immediately locked down, and to my dismay, I was trapped inside as the action raged outside.

Refused my urgent requests to be allowed to leave, I was comforted by the fact my brother, Craig, was outside the compound with a second camera crew. I knew that because the embassy had the TV on a live, local news broadcast reporting the action, and there was Craig doing his thing.

As the attack in Kabul and around the nation fizzled with minimal casualties, I had a life-affirming moment during a live broadcast of my own show the next morning. Akbar set up a phone interview with the spokesman for the Taliban, and I asked him, "How does it feel to get your ass kicked? All those dead Taliban and no US casualties?"

My most vivid recollection of that eleventh and final assignment in Afghanistan was a lot less macho. I was accompanying our forces on a pre-dawn helicopter raid on a suspected Taliban compound. The choppers landed in a tilled field about a quarter mile from the compound, and the troopers charged ahead. By then a limping gimp, I was humiliated when the sergeant in charge had to come back to ask me to hurry it up, because I was falling too far behind.

I twice tried to get back to war reporting in 2014, after ISIS invaded Syria and Iraq. But after initially being approved, the trips got canceled. The first time was when ISIS, the scourge that replaced al Qaeda, captured Iraq's Mosul Dam. Fox canceled that trip because it said there was no money in the budget.

As for the second cancellation, during the siege of the Syrian city of Kobani by ISIS, I was told it was the unavailability of appropriate insurance. By then James Foley and several other journalists had been beheaded by ISIS and all the networks were becoming reasonably very concerned about reporters' getting caught, tortured, and killed.

To stay busy during that long dry spell, I did mostly Hollywood true-life post mortems like *Elvis at 80*, *The Sad Life and Death of Anna Nicole Smith*, and *The Mysterious Death of Joan Rivers*. On the tenth anniversary of Scott Peterson's being sentenced to death for the murder of his eight-months-pregnant wife, Laci, and their unborn child, I did a special one-hour report on the surprisingly privileged life Scott was enjoying on death row in San Quentin prison.

There was also Hollywood. Many reporters have done cameos in films and television series over the years. I have done more than most. Most proudly, I appeared as myself in the finale of *Seinfeld*, directed personally by mad genius Larry David, and in the last season of *The Sopranos*, where I heaped a faux investigative reporter's scorn on James Gandolfini's fabulous Tony Soprano. Speaking of great mobsters, I joined Robert De Niro and Harvey Keitel in Sylvester Stallone's *Cop Land*, which was shot in and around my home in Bergen County, New Jersey, home to many NYPD officers. A couple of times, I related to Jerry Orbach's Lennie Briscoe in *Law and Order*, and got literally knocked out by Jane Lynch's wonderful Sue Sylvester in the finale of *Glee*.

Storm-tossed sharks ate me limb by limb in Ian Ziering's *Sharknado V, Silver Shamrock*, in a gory bit reminiscent of the bridge scene in *Monty Python's Monty Python and the Holy Grail*; remember, "It's just a flesh wound," the Black Knight says as he loses body parts. Creator and producer Greg Garcia put me in several episodes of his long-running hit comedy, *My Name is Earl*, starring funny, cool Jason Lee. I take an artiste's pride in having guest-starred as Alfred the Nerd in the highest-rated episode ever of *Baywatch*, bulking up opposite perennially hunky David Hasselhoff. I appeared, again as myself, in the Jody Foster film *Contact*; the John Travolta-as-Bill Clinton mash-up movie *Primary Colors*; and with Bruce Willis and Tom Hanks in the 1990 bomb *Bonfire of the Vanities*, directed by the otherwise great Brian De Palma.

One of my movies, *All About Steve*, a widely panned road romp starring Sandra Bullock and Bradley Cooper, was honored with two Golden Raspberry Awards, given to films the critics feel are the year's worst.

I hit the soaps back in 1991 with a smoldering performance in *The Young and the Restless*, which had a kissing scene. Speaking of passion, I was also murdered that year in the title role in the Perry Mason movie *The Death of the Tattletale Romeo*, starring Raymond Burr. *Tattletale Romeo* was a not-too-subtle play on what should have happened to me after I published my unfortunate tell-all autobiography earlier that year. The fun part of the film mystery was discovering which of the many infuriated women whom I "exposed" was the real perpetrator.

The assorted cameos keep my Screen Actors Guild card active, and while my acting resume is not exactly Hollywood Walk of Fame material, it has certainly been colorful. If only I could do *Game of Thrones* or *Star Wars* or maybe a remake of *Up in Smoke*, my acting career would be complete.

PRESIDENT TRUMP AND ME, 1976–2017

I have known him for decades, through various phases of life in the big city, including more than a dozen interviews, clubbing, and prominent attendance at pro fights at Madison Square Garden, and in Atlantic City. We met around 1976 when I was engaged to marry Francine LeFrak, the elegant daughter of another powerful real estate mogul, Sam LeFrak, a friendly rival of Donald's father, Fred. Both magnates hailed from the borough of Queens and came up at roughly the same time. The families remain close. Francine's billionaire brother, Richard, is one of President Trump's close friends.

We were class flirts during high school, and, while always working hard, were also fixtures on the New York scene. He kept zig-zagging to success, accumulating power and money, while I went from local reporter to network correspondent to talk show host and back again.

Beginning around 2000, we often discussed on camera and off the possibility of Trump's running for president. He brought up the topic so often I finally lost patience with the question. When he asked Sean Hannity and me after the *Celebrity Apprentice* finale in February 2015, whether he should "go for it?" I told him, essentially, put up or shut up. Still, I was shocked when he did, more for the platform he choose than the decision to do it. I thought he would run as a pro-choice, pro-immigration, pro-business, independent, Reform Party, fiscally pragmatic, social liberal, not unlike Hillary Clinton. Instead, I watched along with the rest of the world as he evolved from the flamboyant billionaire showman I knew, into a wildly unconventional, deeply conservative Republican candidate. I hold out hope that he will remember his core New York values on issues like the social safety net, choice, and health care, although his ideological transformation seems deep and permanent.

By steering hard right, he won the election, but not the affection of most women. My wife and her friends hate him. The scope of their alienation became apparent on the day after his January 2017 inauguration, when hundreds of thousands marched on Washington and in scores of other cities, here and abroad. The biggest day of protest in American history was specifically motivated by the fear that President Trump will stack the Supreme Court with pro-life justices, who will abolish a woman's right to choose. Their fears are exacerbated by the president's late-in-life conversion to the anti-abortion side of our divided society. He managed, by the day after his presidency began, to frighten, alienate, and motivate an entire gender.

The college-educated, more female and minority half of the country professes disgust and alarm that a chauvinist is our president. Yet, among the whiter, more male, less-educated half, he is beloved. Despite the hubris and chaos of his early presidency, many of his supporters are healthy traditionalists, old-fashioned, and politically incorrect. I am none of those things, yet I cling to the promise that Trump has it in him to be a great, or at least a good, president. As I will shortly argue in closing this book, I believe he is a good man, and I lament that saying that infuriates the Hillary Clinton/Erica Rivera half of the American electorate.

Whatever your feelings about the man, there is no denying that his election has jolted awake the economy. He is a cheerleader for capitalism and so far, it is paying off for everyone with a 401-k.

SEVENTY IS THE NEW FIFTY, JULY 2013

Aside from the physical battering of my life rigorously lived, now three-score and fourteen years, there has undoubtedly been an emotional toll. I have a form of post-traumatic stress, the most dramatic symptom of which is sitting more or less comatose for long stretches, immobile. As I mentioned, there were times after particularly grueling combat assignments, the ten or so during the really bad pre-Surge, Iraq War years, 2004–2008, when I would come home, sit on my porch, and simply stare.

After years devoted to staying fit, plus the blessings of good genes from long-lived ancestors, veneers on my teeth, the knee replacement and medicines, sprays and ointments focusing on but not limited to hair loss, high blood pressure, cholesterol, and wrinkles, I am holding my own. My workout regimen is not rigorous, but it is regular and frequent. I love old-fashioned newspapers, but refrain from reading them until I'm on the stationary bike. It is a reward that makes the pedaling easier. Then I do some medium weights and lots of abs. I do it four or five times a week, unless I am on assignment, when I just do the best I can in the hotel room.

When I'm in New York, I routinely take my real bicycle everywhere. From the Upper East Side of Manhattan to Fox News in midtown is twenty minutes tops, usually through Central Park, which is mostly closed to vehicles other than pedaled or horse-driven. During daytime traffic, on the always-jammed streets and avenues, a cab, Lyft, or Uber could take twice that long. The only impediment is weather; I do not ride in the rain, snow, or when it is below forty degrees. Biking is risky enough; there is a near-death experience almost every time out, and it may eventually kill me.

Despite the risk, the alternative to staying fit is too grim to bear. Dying slowly is bad enough. Do not go gentle; go kicking and screaming. Plus, I enjoy working out. Being physical sometimes leads to drunken self-confidence, as on the late night I sent a nude selfie out to the world to mark my seventieth birthday. As I said at the time, "70 is the new 50."

It became a big deal, going viral and hitting every entertainment news show. It later topped *Rolling Stone* magazine's list of "2013's Most Mind-Blowing Selfies." Happily, nobody got hurt and I didn't get fired. Roger was snide but not riled whenever it came up. Erica de-escalated the crisis by joking, "This is exactly the kind of thing that happens when I fall

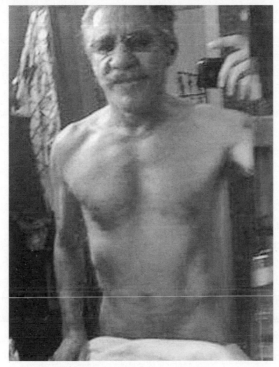

"70 is the new 50." July 2013.

asleep first. Thank God we have towels in the bathroom. (One was placed strategically.) But I'm proud my husband looks so hot."

I later tweeted, "Note to self: no tweeting after 1 AM." Having been initially critical of my impetuosity, several friends and business advisers later told me that the buffed nude shot was great promotion, especially for the Millennial viewers who do not usually watch cable news, certainly not Fox, and instead caught the septuagenarian strongman on the internet.

The only negative selfie feedback was the cancellation by Duquesne University of a July 2013 speech and panel discussion I was going to lead to mark the fiftieth anniversary of the assassination of JFK. As the first reporter in the United States to broadcast the Zapruder home movie of one of history's most significant murders, I had an undeniable connection to the story. That did not matter in the end. In announcing the cancellation of my appearance, the college called my selfie "inappropriate and not in line with the school's values as a Catholic University."

I launched a Twitter storm in response:

Duquesne's cancellation of my JFK panel appearance is pretentious censorship. Do students agree with administration? Am I banned for life? Are all prospective speakers similarly scrutinized, or is my sin receiving special attention? Does the selfie outweigh my Peabody, Emmys, RFKs, and other professional achievements on Duquesne's scale of morality? Are the students of Duquesne so sensitive and pro-tected that they will be unable to concentrate on the topic being dis-cussed because they cannot un-see the image?

Most of the internet agreed, criticizing the school's rigid policies regarding social media etiquette. Columbia University professor Marc Lamont Hill tweeted, "They did the same to me last year."

I posted another nude selfie a year later, but the picture was neither as salacious nor as widely disseminated. By then, around the time of my ominous and cautionary meeting with Roger about getting old, my tight bod began deteriorating. Running my hands over wrinkling alligator skin and atrophying muscles, I see an old man in the making, in slow motion. The camera may not blink or lie, but makeup and good lighting help cre-ate an illusion that I am more or less the same swashbuckler you grew up with. No longer cute like during the rock 'n' roll newsman days, I cling to being marginally appealing in a reminiscent way, still recognizable, at least to women over forty. Looks are only skin deep, but most days it feels like an old man lives inside.

Sitting on a bar stool, cigar-smoking and boozy, I maintain the illu-sion of toughness, relatively big shoulders and biceps; but that illusion only lasts as long as you don't ask me to take it outside. Too gimpy now for real street fights, I would limp into the alley as my opponent laughed. Adjusting to this new reality, I am in the late stages of making the televi-sion transition from roving bare-knuckled reporter to wise/faded/Ancient Mariner/Veteran Correspondent/Stoner Uncle.

As I mentioned in the prologue, my operating philosophy is pragmatic idealism, the need to deal realistically with the moral imperative to be good, do well, and be happy. Essentially it is "love the dream," but always remember that dreams do not put food on the table or pay college tuitions, charitable contributions, or make good on your wife's or kids' shopping and doctor bills.

FIGHTING FATHER TIME, 2014–2017

My hair color is probably fading brown over spreading white, but I cannot say for sure because it has been color-corrected ever since Roger Ailes went on a rant to our mutual old friend Woody Frazier, then Fox News coordinating producer. Woody has been around so long, he was my producer at *Good Morning America* in the mid-1970s. In the early 1990s he was my older son Gabriel's Little League coach in Brentwood, California.

One morning out of the blue, Woody asked why I was letting my hair go gray. "No wonder the younger demo [ratings demographic] sucks," etc. Since Bill Shine, then Roger's executive sidekick, asked me the same question that same morning, I knew it was Roger doing the asking and reached immediately for the Just for Men. When I failed to get the color right, at times looking cartoonish-dark brown or shoeshine black, I hooked up with Kirsten, a clever stylist at Truman's Hair Salon for Men on Madison Avenue, just happy I had hair left to color.

It may not have much to do with "fighting Father Time," but my generation was the first to embrace recreational drug use as a lifestyle. I smoked my first joint as a junior at the University of Arizona in 1964. The only semi-gringo playing in the intensely competitive Tucson intramural soccer league, composed mostly of Mexican and other Latin American university students and workers, I was introduced to *Reefer Madness* and have probably averaged a modest joint a week since. My pro-pot position has been consistent for the half-century since college. In the 1970s I was on the board of the National Organization for the Reform of Marijuana Laws (NORML).

With some notable exceptions (Bill O'Reilly and Donald Trump), virtually everybody I have ever known has at least tried pot. If you are reading this, the odds are that you have tried marijuana, which is why surveys consistently show that a majority of Americans, across a broad ideological spectrum, favors medical marijuana, broad decriminalization, or even total legalization, as in Colorado, Washington, Massachusetts, California, and a half dozen other states and counting.

Several stubborn holdouts, like Alabama, still treat pot possession as a felony, which is dumb. One of my deep fears is that in appealing to his right-wing base, President Trump will become a throwback to the bad old days of Prohibition. His pick of old-line, conservative, former

Alabama senator Jeff Sessions as attorney general is worrisome in this regard, although with Russiagate, a revolt by so-called Sanctuary Cities, and a fight over the border wall on his hands, the new AG may not have the energy to go after potheads.

As grass spreads, it needs personal regulation. As with booze, the rule is never to get high when you are trying to do anything except making love or chilling out. I agree with former president Obama that pot is less destructive than alcohol, but when you get high on your supply before you have fulfilled your duties as a responsible student, teacher, or parent, you are destined to be a lethargic dope-smoking dope. People who start smoking as young teenagers, and then try to go to school or work stoned, are the generation that makes up the slacker class of underachievers.

Pot isn't the only drug of choice among my age group. Baby Boomers now use an array of pharmaceutical weapons in the losing war against Father Time: Rogaine, Propecia, statins, Lyrica, medical marijuana, chin lifts, liposuction, eyebrow lifts, and other life-enhancing, penis-enlarging, artery-expanding, mental-health-extending therapies that have changed the social pecking order to an extent that is not yet fully appreciated.

FIRST (SENIOR) CITIZEN TRUMP, JUNE 2015 TO NOVEMBER 2016

Sexual capacity and a firm body are just two measures of vivacity. Internal health is still the ultimate arbiter. Seventy may be the new fifty, but a seventy-year-old neck still aches. Billy Crystal's classic *SNL* character Fernando says, "It is better to look good than feel good," and I do look better than I feel. Which brings me back to President Trump, and the extraordinary stamina he displayed during the grueling campaign.

A large man at six-foot-three inches tall and weighing anywhere from 230 to 250 pounds, he refuses to show any signs of wear and tear over the year and a half of nonstop campaigning, and now a year as the nation's chief executive. Despite a diet that was often composed of fast food, and a less-than-stressful exercise regimen that consists primarily of playing golf at Mar-a-Lago (sixteen times in the first hundred days) or at another of his fabulous resorts, he physically dominated the long campaign, behaving like a prime-of-life Energizer Bunny. At every stop along the way, he bounded onto the stage, enthusiastically greeting his swelling crowds of devoted followers, throwing kisses, waving his arms in triumph, and pumping his fists.

Then already seventy, fully five years past the traditional, sanctioned retirement age, Trump was more vibrant and energetic than his "low-energy" rivals for the nomination. In a funky appearance on *The Dr. Oz Show* two months before the election, he was hailed as "the healthiest person ever to run for president" by his colorful personal physician, Dr. Bornstein. When I asked the president in a conversation on board Air Force One in October 2017 to what he credited his extraordinary stamina, he said it was his parents and their "good genes."

Whatever his secret, there is no doubt Trump ran circles around Hillary Clinton, out-campaigning her every step of the way. When she faltered, wilting in the heat at the World Trade Center memorial service on September 11, 2016, stumbling as she entered her limousine, Trump pounced, ridiculing her frailty and saying bluntly that she lacked the stamina and energy to be president. She later disclosed that she had been secretly diagnosed as suffering from pneumonia. It was a plausible explanation, but that she kept it from the public just added fuel to the notion that she was a sneaky secret-keeper.

Love him or hate him, First Senior Citizen Trump on the campaign trail displayed amazing physical prowess. It could be a function of the fact that, unlike me, smoke-free President Trump never drank, either, reserving his body for his crusade to accumulate enormous wealth and then capture the White House.

CELEBRITY APPRENTICE, FEBRUARY 2015

In the months before the official beginning of the 2016 presidential campaign, I was shocked that Roger allowed me to do *Celebrity Apprentice*, my first reality show. In retrospect, my loving ex-boss, who was not yet laid low by scandal, probably wanted to give his aging, unpredictable, still explosive and ideologically suspect fading star reporter something to do as far away from Fox News as possible. I have a way of sometimes offending the conservative sensibilities of our audience, as I did, for example, asserting confidently during the campaign that there was zero chance Hillary Clinton was going to be indicted for the phony-baloney email controversy.

Celebrity Apprentice turned out to be a blast. I did well and spent quality time with soon-to-be president Trump and his family, whom I hold in high regard. I have spent time before and since with his older children, who were deeply involved in the show. Their dad and mother, businesswoman Ivana Marie Trump, did a great job raising them. As the campaign made clear, daughter Ivanka is enormously poised and impressive, and could well be our first female president. I lament the fact that hatred for her father has rebounded so negatively on Ivanka and her businesses, which should have nothing to do with politics. Her brothers, Eric and Donald Jr., are also solid citizens, and have theoretically taken full control of his far-flung business empire.

Until his father's run for the White House, Don Jr. and I shared the added connection of being dads with daughters in the same school. I ran into his wife, Vanessa, in the school elevator and told her a couple of months before the election that her father-in-law still had a shot. Stately, in a tall, blonde, stylish way, she joked, "He'd better, after all this work." Thirty-four-year-old Eric is nothing like the doofus portrayed on *Saturday Night Live*. A tall, good-looking, thoughtful young man, he and his wife, Lara, raised a ton of money, north of $15 million, for St. Jude Children's Hospital, an effort I was delighted to support.

On *Celebrity Apprentice*, the Trump kids were tough judges, but they gave me every benefit of the doubt. My journalism background and legal chops also helped immeasurably in outmaneuvering rivals like *Sharknado* star Ian Ziering, rocker Kevin Jonas, and helicopter-pilot-to-the-stars, *Falcon Crest*'s Lorenzo Lamas, who all conspired to get me fired. Despite his machinations with the other two plotters, I had a soft spot for Lorenzo. His dad, Fernando Lamas, was my dad Cruz Rivera's favorite actor. Pop loved the way Fernando represented the ideal Latin man—suave, sharp, and sexy.

SHE'S HIRED, FEBRUARY 2015

My stint on his *Celebrity Apprentice* required six weeks of taping, eight months of waiting for NBC to schedule the series, and a month and a half of highly rated, nail-biting, two-hour taped broadcasts, followed by a two-show live finale in February 2015. Beginning with an eclectic collection of sixteen strong personalities, the show went through incidents of backstabbing, phone looting, clothes shedding, shouting, and buckets of crying, finger-pointing drama.

The idea is that the two teams are assigned business-related tasks that are taped one day, and presented to boss Donald in the boardroom the next day.

One task was fairly typical, to compose and present a jingle for Budweiser's new wine coolers. My "Team Vortex" triumphed even as rival "Team Infinity" collapsed, and we easily won the competition, which featured our rapping to my memorable catchphrase for the wine-cooler commercial *Nice over Ice*.

To set up the final showdown between longtime television host and producer Leeza Gibbons and me, Trump fired everybody except Vivica A. Fox, the feisty and impressively talented actress. At that point, the lovely star of *Empire* and *Independence Day* graciously conceded that she could not match either Leeza's skills as a producer or mine as a fundraiser. It was a humbling moment for both Leeza and me, and we both love Vivica for bowing out with such grace.

The task for the finale began when Leeza and I were flown down to Universal Orlando Resort onboard one of the private jets in Donald Trump's aerial armada. Our task was to produce and shoot a new commercial for the theme park. At the same time, we were told there would be a finale fundraising gala for which we would be responsible not only to raise as much money as possible, but also to provide entertainment for the event.

The show began with the introduction of the teams brought together to help Leeza and me complete the complex task. It was like a class reunion. Her "Team Leeza" was buttressed by previously "fired" celebrities Brandi Glanville, the fiery and underrated *Housewife of Beverly Hills*; baseball great and man of deep integrity and soul Johnny Damon; and my arch-nemesis, former boy-band guitarist Kevin Jonas.

My squad consisted of Vivica and the two actors who had unsuccessfully conspired with Kevin to get me fired earlier on, Lorenzo Lamas, who starred in the soap operas *Falcon Crest* and *The Bold and the Beautiful*, and Ian Ziering of *Sharknado* and *Chippendale's* fame, whom I really did not like at the time. I have subsequently changed my mind, and now admire

Ian's work ethic and resolve. When he was conspiring with Lorenzo and Kevin Jonas to sabotage me, I called them out in the boardroom in a dramatic confrontation. Faced with firing either Ian, Kevin, or me, Trump gave the young rocker the heave-ho. President Trump later told me how NBC executives lobbied him to fire me instead of Kevin because he was a bigger draw for the younger demo coveted by television advertisers. The boss declined because, as he said, "It was the right thing to do."

In the final task, after Universal executives briefed both teams about the parameters of the commercial they were looking for, we set out to plan. As presented on the program, Leeza's team had a rocky start when Brandi and Johnny wandered off to have hot dogs and beer, as Leeza and Kevin strove to get the commercial scripted and cast.

Distracted by the need to raise even more money than the almost $600,000 I had already brought in, I reached the day of the commercial shoot with many loose ends still unresolved, as usual. I was the front man for our spot, which emphasized the adventurous aspects of Universal and the need for kids to have courage to experience it fully. I decided to focus on the new Harry Potter theme park, dressing as a caped wizard, wand and all.

When the time to shoot the spot came, we discovered that no one had taken responsibility to get our child actors gathered where we needed them, when we needed them. The episode ended with me charging off to find our crew, even as I muttered that from this point on I was taking full control of our production. As we faded to black and teased the next week's huge live finale, the odds seemed to favor my rival, Leeza, who despite her crew's partial desertion announced that she had landed Olivia Newton John to perform at the finale's big gala.

At that point, I had secured neither a performer nor enough donations to secure a victory. It was a nerve-wracking week, struggling to pull off a long-shot, come-from-behind win. Anyway, I tried mightily but fell short in fundraising because my generous donors were by that point tapped out. I did put on a great show, though, landing live performances at the celebrity-studded gala from Jose Feliciano and Tony Orlando, both friends of more than forty years.

The challenging competition culminated in a rousing, highly rated live finale, in which I lost to the formidable talk-show host and philanthropist Leeza Gibbons. When Trump declared Leeza his latest Apprentice, despite the fact that I raised more money, most of the cast members reacted favorably.

Leeza was much more popular than I during the taping. She was a soothing presence who kept her head below the line of fire. I was more sharp elbows and bare knuckles, earning the loyalty of just six of the sixteen contestants, including Kate "Plus 8" Gosselin. I have a soft spot for Kate because of all she was forced to cope with in her life before television, and was protective of her during the competition. Most responsible adults would be respectful of any woman who could successfully nurture that many kids, including surprise sextuplets, with such a lame husband.

After another task, which was to sell wedding dresses, Kate and I dressed as a newly wedded couple. She wore one of our dresses. I was in black tie and tails. In the boardroom scene that followed, Kate told the world that her ambition was to "be Geraldo's next ex-wife," a funny line that my straight-shooting, plain-talking, gorgeous wife, Erica, did not particularly appreciate.

What I appreciated beyond Erica's unvarnished and loving support was her donating $25,000 of her own money to my cause. My Fox News crowd also came through impressively. Because the show rules say no checks, and given the short notice that a particular task was a fundraiser, nobody had the chance to get cashier's checks.

Sean Hannity, who really has become one of my best friends, showed up with $10,000 in hundred-dollar bills. He still talks about how I planted a big kiss on his cheek during the network TV broadcast. In October 2017, Sean donated another $25,000 to the charity I designated for Puerto Rico's hurricane relief. He really has a heart of gold. Another generous conservative not given credit for his philanthropy (he could give away his fortune and liberals would say it was ill-gained anyway), Bill O'Reilly came through during *Celebrity Apprentice* with $15,000. Morning show cohosts Steve Doocy and Brian Kilmeade, both stand-up guys and terrific pals, came by with $5,000 each. Joseph Abboud, the famed suit maker, just happened to be walking by. He emptied his pockets, donating the $800 he had on him. Supermarket billionaire businessman and perennial mayoral candidate John Catsimatidis and his wife, Margo, brought more than $20,000 cash. They are among New York's most generous philanthropists, and I really like them.

Best of all was party-boy billionaire Stewart Rahr, better known as Stewie Rah Rah, who actually has an office in Trump Tower. In one of my earlier fundraising drives, Stewie had donated $50,000 through my radio show to help rebuild the Rockaways on Long Island after the devastation wrought by Hurricane Sandy. For *Celebrity Apprentice*, Stewie gave me another huge donation, a whopping grand total of $150,000. This man is a treasure and so much fun to be around. Short and stylish, a caricature of a Jewish entrepreneurial perpetual-motion machine, he made hundreds of millions when he sold his family's generic drug business. Now he's party central from the Hamptons to St. Tropez. When he and the other high rollers gave me all that money, Trump complained that my fundraising consisted of taking money from all our mutual friends.

At the announcement that Leeza had won the competition, my daughter Sol, sitting with Erica in the studio audience, began sobbing. She was bereft. Trump did something then that made him a friend for life. He was compassionate and grandfatherly to my then-ten-year-old, comforting her and even allowing her to sit in his big red chair to see what it felt like to be boss.

Also at the Leeza announcement, what was noteworthy to me was that Trump did not say that I was "fired," his signature line. Instead, on the last *Celebrity Apprentice* of his life, he said that Leeza was "hired." The distinction is important. He told me later that he informed network executives that despite their desire for him to "fire" me, he wanted to make it clear that Leeza and I were both winners.

After the dust settled and we were off the air, I confessed to the future president of the United States that I was relieved that he picked Leeza. Given the strong women on the show, and their majority preference for Leeza, I told him that he and I would have been reamed if he had picked me over her. "Those dames would have kicked our butts," I whispered.

He agreed, giving me a knowing glance and saying quietly as he looked around, "You're telling me." He said it shaking his head as only a man who understands contemporary gender politics would shake his head. When Hillary Clinton later played the "woman card" against him, I was relieved that she did not have a *Celebrity Apprentice* arrow in her quiver.

Reacting to being fired on *Celebrity Apprentice*, February 2015.

When I lost *Celebrity Apprentice*, Donald Trump "was compassionate and grandfatherly to my then-ten-year-old, comforting her and even allowing her to sit in his Big Red Chair." February 2015.

BIG MONEY FOR A GREAT CAUSE, MARCH 2015

Even though I lost in the end, doing *Celebrity Apprentice* was a terrific, posi-tive experience. I outran and outlasted fifteen of the sixteen younger com-petitors and thus became the first Peabody Award winner to be a finalist on *Celebrity Apprentice*. That was almost as cool as when I was on the cov-ers of both *Newsweek* and *Playgirl* magazines in the same year, an earlier (1988) distinction. I also renewed my friendship with the charismatic host, the man who would soon become our forty-fifth president.

The show brought me back to the prime-time mainstream television audi-ence, which had followed the talk show but usually does not watch Fox News. Black and Latino young people seemed especially delighted to see me again after such a long absence, given their reaction on the street or in airports.

I also made a new friend in fellow cast member Sig Hansen, the star of Discovery Channel's *Deadliest Catch*. A chain-smoking, hard-drinking free spirit, Sig is my kind of guy. He is bold, brave, and exists on a diet of coffee, cigarettes, and chocolate.

After the competition, I repaid his efforts on my behalf during the show by traveling to Alaska to attend a benefit for his charity, the US Coast Guard Foundation. At a gala in Anchorage attended by Coast Guard Commandant Admiral Paul Zukunft, since retired, and Senators Lisa Murkowski and Mark Begich, Erica, Sol, and I were pleased to be able to present a $40,000 gift to the foundation in honor of Sig.

Putting aside the usual ebb-and-flow melodrama of reality television, I was responsible for one discordant note. It began when former NFL great Terrell Owens, one of the best receivers in the history of football, a six-time Pro Bowler and future Hall of Famer for the Dallas Cowboys, was fired when his *Apprentice* team failed to generate any meaningful money during one of the fundraising challenges.

During the taped post-task analysis, after Terrell was fired and had left Trump Tower, I said casually to no one in particular that since Terrell was famously broke at the time, he should never have appeared on a program that was basically a fundraiser for charity. Just the week before, my daugh-ter had shown me a tape of Terrell on an episode of *Dr. Phil* in which mothers of his children were demanding unpaid support.

Unbeknownst to me at the time, Kenya Moore, the devious star of *Real Housewives of Atlanta*, took it upon herself to snitch to Terrell, who later that night called me demanding to know how I could do something so unnecessary. I begged forgiveness and lobbied the NBC producers to keep the obnoxious sequence off the air, which to their credit they did. Terrell was right. It was low, and the telling of it embarrasses me.

By the way, speaking of low, this was the season the treacherous yet charming *Real Housewife* Kenya Moore got thrown off *Apprentice* for stealing Vivica A. Fox's cell phone and posting bizarre, obnoxious tweets in sweet, religious Vivica's name. I would pay top price for an MMA bout between Kenya and her idol Omarosa, who, after terrorizing several seasons of *The Apprentice*, similarly rode roughshod for a year in the White House as an aide to President Trump.

Reunited with the entire cast at the show's live finale, Terrell could not have been nicer or more friendly and forgiving. I also lament that this fine fellow, indisputably one of the best NFL pass-catchers ever, has not yet made the Pro Football Hall of Fame. Hopefully, he'll join the class of 2018.

That sad story aside, *Apprentice* had a positive impact for me professionally, regenerating some of my old-school cool and leading to roles in shows such as the *Glee* finale and *Law and Order*, not to mention *Dancing with the Stars*, another reality show adventure in 2016. All my on-camera *Apprentice* feuds ended amicably. In 2017, my best frenemy, Ian Ziering, called personally to encourage me to do the hilarious *Sharknado* movie.

Celebrity Apprentice helped me raise $725,000 for Life's WORC, a charity founded in 1971 by parents of disabled children living in the squalor and filth of Willowbrook. Leeza raised just $464,000, but then won the $250,000 bonus from the show for a grand total of $714,000. Raising money is harder than earning it. I hate asking people for money even for a good cause, but these are great causes. Leeza's money went to a center dealing with Alzheimer's disease. Mine was used to open the Family Center for Autism, a service for stressed families dealing with autistic children in Nassau County outside of New York.

BEAUTY AND THE BEAST, FALL 2015

The funniest coincidence in my entire, modest show-business career came when I played myself in a Puerto Rican–themed version of the classic

Christmas tale *Miracle on 34th Street*. The film was called, perhaps unsur-prisingly, *Miracle in Spanish Harlem*. In limited theatrical release in 2013, it did better on video.

Since the lead actress was not in any of my scenes, what I did not real-ize until recently when I finally watched the entire film is that it costarred Kate del Castillo, a notorious Mexican-American actress. Her notoriety is not based on her celebrity. It is based on the fact that the biggest fan of her biggest hit show was a real-life Mexican drug lord, Joaquin Archivaldo Guzman Loera, otherwise known as El Chapo.

Three years after *Miracle in Spanish Harlem*, in spring 2016, I wrote and reported a Fox News special called *Beauty and the Beast: When Kate Met Chapo*. It documented how El Chapo, the savage head of the Sinaloa, Mexico, drug cartel, called by the DEA "the bin Laden of the drug trade," was undone by his need to see Kate del Castillo, at the time Mexico's hot-test actress, in the flesh, in the jungle.

I was drawn to the story, even identifying with the drug dealer. Not with his cancerous business, obviously, but with the absurd peril in which he put himself and his empire, just to be with the woman of his searing dreams. Remember in the movie *King Kong* when the giant gorilla is lying dead on Fifth Avenue? As the crowd gathers in wonder, a bystander speaks glowingly of the pilots of the military aircraft that have just knocked Kong from his perch atop the Empire State Building, congratulating them for killing the lovesick monster. Overhearing the conversation, the man who captured Kong, the promoter Carl Denham, played most recently by Jack Black, shakes his head and utters the movie's unforgettable line, saying it was not the pilots, "No, it was beauty killed the beast."

In my Fox News special on the drug lord's recapture, El Chapo is the beast. Kate del Castillo is the beauty. He was captured because of his burning need to see the sultry actress whose character Teresa Mendoza in the wildly popular Mexican prime-time soap opera *La Reina del Sur (Queen of the South)* became Chapo's destructive obsession.

The fictional Teresa was a ruthless, though charismatic, drug dealer. El Chapo identified with her and he was crazy about Kate. My in-depth spe-cial report chronicled how Chapo and Kate became pen pals, exchanging highly suggestive text messages both while he was in prison before his second escape, and later when he was on the lam.

With Kate del Castillo, the woman of El Chapo's searing dreams. May 2016.

So desperate was the world's most-wanted fugitive to see the object of his fascination that he risked everything to meet her face-to-face in a jungle rendezvous. Kate brought Oscar-winning actor Sean Penn with her for the high-stakes meeting.

Penn ended up screwing her businesswise, but that is another story. Mexican and American authorities agree that El Chapo's recapture was the direct result of the Beast's need to see his Beauty.

With reporting from Beverly Hills and from Altiplano Prison in Mexico, my Fox News special chronicled the obsession; the rendezvous; the semi-sleazy role actor Sean Penn played both during and after the steamy jungle meeting; the role of the Mexican government; the extradition of Guzman to the United States; his obsession with then-candidate Donald Trump, whom he threatened to kill; and finally, what impact (not much) Chapo's incarceration would have on the terrible drug scourge his Sinaloa cartel unleashed on the United States.

Before his recapture I was spry enough, barely, to climb down a dark, hundred-foot-long rickety ladder to gain access to the fugitive's remarkable mile-long tunnel, which should be the envy of civil engineers everywhere. I joked at the time of the escape in July 2015 that he should be hired to finish Manhattan's Second Avenue subway. It was approved in 1929 with a whopping budget of $86 million. Predicted to open between 1938 and 1941, the subway was finally inaugurated on New Year's Day 2017, seventy-six years late and about $4 billion over budget.

At Kate's request, before he was recaptured after four months on the run, the diminutive billionaire doper provided a tape to Sean Penn in lieu of the interview they never got around to doing in their October 2015 jungle rendezvous. In the tape Chapo deadpans that he is merely providing a service by distributing a desired product to a needy clientele and that if he did not, somebody else would. Then the lovestruck tough guy got caught in a shootout with Mexican Marines and extradited to the US, and now awaits trial in Brooklyn on several capital offenses.

THE *NEW YORK TIMES* LIES ABOUT ME (AGAIN), APRIL 2016

Roger had taken me off the bench to cover the rioting in Baltimore, which followed the death in police custody of a young man named Freddie Gray. Two days into the upheaval, the boss was unhappy with the network's coverage and ordered Bill Shine to order me down. Frustrated with being ignored by the Fox News producers, I welcomed the assignment. We got down there in a hurry and produced some important reports, including dramatic encounters with community members and rioters.

My team continued to monitor the situation in Baltimore until the riots simmered down with the indictment of six cops for the death of Freddie Gray, and a massive $6.4 million civil settlement to his family, which to me smacked more of a blackmail payout than reasonable compensation. The West Baltimore neighborhood remains in ruins.

My brother Craig produced a report that proposed a partial solution to what ails the racially fractured, half-wrecked city. He profiled a team of architects encouraging a massive rebuilding of West Baltimore by transferring ownership of its tens of thousands of derelict buildings to the residents in exchange for "sweat equity," their agreement to rehabilitate the ruined and abandoned structures with private and public help. If only the local and state politicians were interested in solving their problems rather than just complaining about them.

But for the rest of the year and beyond, the big news out of hapless Baltimore was the orgy of bloodshed in the wake of Freddie Gray's death in police custody. Most of the victims of the escalation of violence were young, black men shot to death by other young, black men at a rate that on a per-capita basis made 2015 the deadliest ever in the city, with 344 homicides. Although the city is one-thirteenth the size of New York, more were killed that year in Baltimore than in the Big Apple.

There have been no marches protesting the bloodshed in Baltimore. Instead, during the 2016 election campaign for a new mayor to replace Stephanie Rawlings-Blake, I was somehow made the issue. The *New York Times* blamed (credited?) me for providing the pivotal moment for the winning candidate for the Democratic nomination, which is tantamount to being elected in that overwhelmingly Democratic town.

Here is my blog protesting the wretchedly false characterization:

In a story appearing in the Thursday 28 April 2016 edition headlined *Victor in Mayoral Primary Is Ready to "Get Baltimore Working,"* reporter Sheryl Gay Stolberg writes that the apparent winner in the hotly contested Democratic primary for mayor, State Senate Majority Leader Catherine E. Pugh, "stared down Geraldo Rivera, the Fox News anchor, and berated him on national television for 'inciting people,'" during the devastating 2015 Baltimore riots.

Ms. Stolberg concludes that it was the defining moment for Senator (now Baltimore mayor) Pugh's successful primary campaign. It is a total fiction.

As the videotape Fox News has provided the *New York Times* makes clear, Senator Pugh and I were united in trying to report honestly and professionally about the chaos in West Baltimore a year ago, following the tragic death in police custody of Freddie Gray. We spent hours together during the urban turmoil and violence, the senator making several appearances on camera.

As the tape shows, Senator Pugh's disquiet was directed at the trouble-makers who were contributing to the mayhem, not at this reporter. Indeed it was my interview with Senator Pugh that the demonstrators, the most vocal of whom was later arrested, were attempting to disrupt.

In 2005 another *Times* reporter (Alessandra Stanley) wrote a similarly fictional account of my coverage of Hurricane Katrina. That discredited story alleged that I pushed rescue workers out of the way so that I would be seen on camera rescuing elderly victims of the storm.

There is a pattern. New Orleans was a fabrication the newspaper was forced to correct. So is Baltimore. Because the *NYT* wants it to be true doesn't make it true. Your hatred of Fox News and me clouds your judgment and distorts your reporting.

President Trump calls the *New York Times* "a failing newspaper," while still craving its acceptance. His ongoing complaint, particularly after the paper ran a front-page, two-page spread on his alleged exploitation of women, is that the self-proclaimed "Newspaper of Record" consistently exaggerates his failings.

During the presidential campaign, stories abounded in outlets like the *Times* and the *Washington Post* about the Trump University class-action lawsuit settlement, his bankrupt casinos, and his alleged mistreatment of women, most of which he still dismisses as "fake news." Yet nary any stories praised either Trump's civic accomplishments or his admirable family's accomplishments, except to criticize their potential for conflicts of interest. Still, it was a surprise the morning after my April 2015 confrontation with the bullies in the rubble-strewn, tear-gassed streets of West Baltimore to get a congratulatory telephone call from Trump, who tracked me down at a local radio station in that stricken town.

"I loved when you told that punk that he was making a fool of himself," the reality host about to turn formidable presidential candidate told me. Then he railed against urban anarchy and violent activists like Black Lives Matter and Occupy Wall Street and the gangbangers who just want to wreck and plunder.

Demonstrations, protests, and unrest initiated by those anti-police groups were polarizing the nation, fracturing it again along racial lines. When I criticized best-selling hip-hop artists like the highly talented Kendrick Lamar for exacerbating tensions with constant anti-police images in his videos, he retaliated by devoting an entire song on his top-selling album *DAMN.* to criticizing me. When President Obama told the country in his farewell address ten days before Trump's inauguration in January 2017 that race relations "have never been better," I wondered to which nation he referred. Each alleged act of police violence, like Freddie Gray's death in Baltimore Police custody, generated a furious and counterproductive response on the streets. All of it seemed to help Donald Trump's candidacy. Police unions and those sympathetic to law enforcement, and most of the white working class, rallied to him ever more vigorously as supporters of inner-city communities protested the divisive Republican candidate.

With typical moderation, President Obama tried to balance his response, condemning both cops who kill and cop killers, pleasing advocates of neither. Unseen or barely noticed was how street violence began ticking up in cities like Baltimore; Ferguson, Missouri; and Chicago as police began a subtle slowdown. In 2016 it was impossible not to notice that the Windy City had a bloody record 796 murders, more than New York and Los Angeles combined. I have neither doubt nor proof that the cop slowdown was intentional and perhaps even secretly coordinated among law enforcement agencies or constituent unions. "Blue flu" pulled cops back from the fray even as candidate Trump held boisterous rallies against rampant urban disorder in his often-inflammatory primary and general-election campaigns.

When he reached me at the radio station that day in Baltimore, he added that, before calling me, he had first called my boss, Roger Ailes, to praise my reporting in Baltimore. But mostly he wanted to praise the fact that I had not retreated during the confrontation on the street with the provocateur.

"You're a champion," he said, not for the last time. To great impact and mixed reviews, he draws harsh distinctions between champions and chokers.

CHAMPIONS, CHOKERS, CARICATURES, AND CONVENTIONAL THINKERS, 2015–2016

I thought Trump became a caricature to win the Republican nomination. You have to be a hard-right loco to win it. At least that was my conventional thinking. Trump, like any GOP presidential candidate, had to be a harshly conservative, hard-right-wing Attila the Hun to get nominated, and then a moderate-sounding Ronald Reagan or George H. W. Bush to get elected.

What the world and I did not expect was that, after securing the nomination, Trump never pivoted to the center. Instead, the harsh tone that won him the nomination later won him the White House. President Trump made a clear-eyed calculation that if he motivated both the frustrated and vaguely uneasy white working class, and the old, mostly but not exclusively southern, anti-civil rights, and yes, even semi-racist, whites who deeply resented political correctness, multiculturalism, undocumented immigration, and unmistakably, the eight-year tenure of our first black president—if he did all that, he had a shot.

Anyway, the person I thought I knew, my fantasy "real" Donald Trump, was visible when he spoke to the New York Republican Gala in April 2016, days before the Empire State's primary election. This was Trump the builder, speaking at the event in the Grand Hyatt Hotel, which he reminded everyone was once the crumbling, derelict Hotel Commodore until in 1978 he maneuvered to get control of it as a thirty-two-year-old novice developer from Queens.

A magnet for junkies, hookers, and derelicts, the hotel was redeveloped by him, saving the neighborhood and remaking East Forty-Second Street. He sold it twenty years later for a $143 million profit. He then went on to convert the West Side of Manhattan on the Hudson River waterfront from Fifty-Seventh Street to Seventy-Second Street. He overcame decades of neighborhood intransigence to remake a mangled rail yard, rusted tracks, and wrecked piers into a wonderful neighborhood, where Erica and I used to live.

After the city failed for a decade to get it done, in 1986 Trump made the Wollman Rink in Central Park an ice-skating asset for every kid in town, including mine. Twenty years later in 2016, he opened his terrific Trump Golf Links at Ferry Point in the Bronx, in an area that had been a garbage dump for decades as the city struggled to rehabilitate it.

As a mogul of uncertain reputation, he apparently made a habit of stiffing suppliers, some of whom I knew, which I duly reported beginning in 1991. But he also created jobs and made money from enterprise unlike any of his rivals for the nomination and certainly unlike Hillary Clinton. As candidate Trump brutally alleged during the campaign, she and husband Bill got rich, earning roughly a quarter-billion dollars, without ever having a real job in the private sector.

SUNDAY MORNING TRUMP, MAY 2016

Another small example of the president's unfailing friendship came during the campaign on a Sunday morning in May 2016. Trump had just appeared for a remote taping of *Fox News Sunday* with Chris Wallace from our studio on the twelfth floor of Fox News in New York. Chris, who would later receive deserved praise for his masterful moderating of the third and final presidential debate, was in the studio in Washington, DC.

I was downstairs in our first-floor *Fox and Friends* studio to commemorate the fifth anniversary of the killing of bin Laden, but first went upstairs to say hello to my controversial pal. He had not yet sealed the GOP nomination, but was getting close. When Trump finished taping, to prevent any competitive jealousy that I was stealing Chris's guest and scooping him by putting Trump on my show live before Chris's pre-taped show aired, I joked to Trump that I thought it was "Bring Your Friend to Work Day." Rather than ask the presumptive Republican nominee to come downstairs with me, I told him I was going on *Fox and Friends* and would be delighted if he stopped by.

He did, to my surprise, taking a seat on what we call the "curvy couch," for a long, live, newsworthy interview on the eve of a pivotal May 3 primary in Indiana. That friendly gesture is an example of why it is hard not to like him. He has always treated me with respect and affection. Of course, if he moves to deport innocent, undocumented immigrant youngsters or succeeds in banning Muslims or abortion, I will change my mind. But absent the implementation of some draconian policy, I am willing to give him the chance to surprise his critics and bring the country together. Indeed, there were some glimmers of hope. The compassionate way he handled the federal response to Hurricanes Harvey, Irma, and Maria was more like the president I hoped he would become.

To the extent that I can detect, Donald Trump does not have a racist bone in his body, although I certainly wish he had been quicker to condemn the KKK's David Duke during the campaign and the Charlottesville Neo-Nazi rioters after he was elected. Before becoming president, green was his most important color. Other than driving ambition and an irrepressible ego, the president is a down-to-earth, all-around good guy, a player in his younger years to be sure, but not now. What kept me from supporting him was his toxic immigration policy. As I discovered researching two books on the subject, *HisPanic* in 2007 and *The Great Progression* in 2008, we cannot deport our way out of this problem. These immigrant families contain adults who are undocumented, but most are otherwise law-abiding and have been here for decades. Many of their children are US-born citizens. Make all the undocumented get documented by registering, getting background checks, paying a fine, learning English, and getting in line. Don't muster a "deportation force" to round them up as if they are terrorists. They are the pizza deliverers, the babysitters, lawn mowers, poultry processors, and meatpackers. Some are computer whizzes and members of the military. They make America stronger, not weaker.

In that regard, I confess to being totally dismayed when Trump began spewing intemperate words against the federal judge hearing one of the class-action lawsuits pending against him, stemming from his now-defunct Trump University. In criticizing federal District Judge Gonzalo Curiel, Trump went out of his way to label the Indiana-born jurist a "Mexican"— not a Mexican-American, but a Mexican. Can you imagine the chaos if judges were disqualified because they happened to be Irish or Jewish or African-American?

At the time of the controversy involving Judge Curiel, it seemed inevitable that "The Donald" was going down to defeat. This is what I wrote for the now-defunct Fox News Latino website in the days before the nominating conventions. In retrospect it reflects uninspired conventional wisdom.

"Trump's obvious intemperance during this June 2016 controversy shrank the Republican Party, which needs to expand and be more inclusive. A Republican cannot win the presidency on white votes alone. There just are not enough to go around. He must moderate his rhetoric and reassess his apparently dim view of many in the Latino population and assure non-white, or non-Judeo-Christian Americans, that he does not consider us second class or some kind of enemy within. If he does not, then again, he knows that I could not vote for him. He may win anyway, but it is a long shot and he would take office in a nation divided."

Shows how little I know. Trump's long shot obviously paid off. The candidate ignited a movement grounded in white working-class men that uniquely captured the disquiet many Americans feel about our nation's being destabilized by unregulated immigration. The reality is not nearly as daunting as the hype from xenophobic nativists, whose real fear is that the country will lose its white majority. But that is not to suggest that there are not real problems with our southern border.

EL CHAPO'S REVENGE, FEBRUARY 2016

As candidate Trump pointed out in campaign stops from the postindustrial Midwest to stricken New Hampshire, Mexican drug cartels are flooding our towns and cities, particularly in the Northeast, with heroin and its lethal synthetic cousin fentanyl in amounts and potency unseen previously. The Sinaloa drug cartel, formerly run by the aforementioned billionaire drug kingpin and now inmate "El Chapo" Guzman, is responsible for the deaths of tens of thousands of Americans, ranging from the kid next door to the doomed entertainer formerly known as Prince. According to Drug Enforcement officials, the number of US heroin addicts has jumped 135 percent since 2002, about when the Mexican cartels expanded out of the ghetto and began targeting the American Heartland. Heroin deaths in the same period skyrocketed 533 percent.

In the February 2016 week leading up to the first-in-the-nation primary in New Hampshire, I filed a rare series of field reports investigating the impact of the drug scourge on folks in the Granite State. What I saw in New Hampshire was dire. This state of just 1.1 million mostly white, suburban, and rural people suffered four hundred overdose deaths in 2014 and another four hundred in 2015. Then 2016 and 2017 kept the pace with at least an O.D. death a day.

Reeling from that epidemic, authorities in New Hampshire and the Drug Enforcement Administration identified Chapo's Sinaloa drug cartel as the principal supplier of the poison responsible for so much misery in such an unlikely place. El Chapo is in federal prison, as I said awaiting the first of his many trials, but while the head has been taken off the snake, nobody in law enforcement expects the cartel to slither away. In fact, now that they have synthesized heroin with a substance called fentanyl, their body count is just getting higher.

Each of the candidates from both parties picked up on the heroin/fentanyl-abuse issue, but Trump tied it best to border security, and made the biggest impact, easily winning the New Hampshire primary and accelerating his bizarre and historic journey to the White House.

LET'S DANCE, MARCH 2016

From the physical demands alone, Trump's endurance during the campaign was a feat I could not have matched. I did not even get past the first elimination round on *Dancing with the Stars* in March 2016. By then my movements had lost fluidity, my legs were shot, my left knee creaky, having been replaced in 2009 with a titanium device that works well enough, the principal pain in the ass being at airports when the knee invariably sets off the metal detectors.

I no longer do my trademark strolling standups to camera because of the limp caused by the neuropathy in my right foot. Aside from swagger, the dead foot cost me a lost decade of senior tennis, skiing, and jogging. I have a perpetually sore back and wrists, ankles that crackle and pop, and a once-piercing stare that has become watery with age.

My main takeaway from *Dancing with the Stars*, Season 22 is that I probably should not have waited until I was a lame seventy-two-year-old to do the show. The physical challenges of the dance routines are rigorous, the training akin to the buildup to a boxing match. Actually, boxing has the advantage over dancing in that fighting is not as tough, at least not to me. A boxer for twenty-five years, getting punched in the face is nothing compared to the embarrassment of missing a dance step live in front of 12 or 13 million viewers, which I did routinely on *DWTS*.

My performance was lamentable, disastrous esthetically, but not lacking in good humor or charm. It was especially bad during the widely anticipated world-premiere event in March 2016. My partner, who deserved better, was Edyta Sliwinska. A glamorous, classically trained ballroom dancer who hails from Poland, Edyta was making her grand comeback to the program after an absence of five years.

Our dance that fateful premiere night was a Cha-Cha, a Latin number. Since dances on the show are actually thematic mini-musicals, ours needed a story. Returning to an old chestnut, *The Mystery of Al Capone's Vault*, our idea was that Edyta was the long-sought treasure that had eluded me when I opened the Prohibition-era gangster's vault in the

My Trump impression. In the backstage lot with Cheech
Marin at *Dancing with the Stars*, March 2016.

basement of Chicago's old Lexington Hotel in 1986. I blew the door
open onstage, and she slinked out in a cloud of smoke to dance. *DWTS*,
like *Capone's Vault*, is live television. (*Capone's* worldwide audience was
far larger, approaching 40 million in those days before cable and Netflix.)

Back in 1986, the Capone event was a gigantic embarrassment, but at
least I did not have to dance. Here, dancing is the whole point. Aside from
the theatrical aspects, the Cha-Cha demands considerable hip swiveling
and rhythm, which I never had. Infirm, disabled, and lacking rhythm, I
was a dance disaster.

Lack of rhythm aside, there was another reason I had turned down
several earlier requests to appear on *DWTS* when I was more physically
able: backstage romances were en vogue on the show in the early days.
One professional dancer became serially engaged to several of her celebrity dance partners. Clean and sober in regard to fidelity, I no longer stray.
I don't have the track record to judge anybody who does, but I am over it.

With Edyta Sliwinska, my professional partner in *Dancing with the Stars*. She deserved better. January 2016.

To ensure that everybody knew my *DWTS* partner and I were only in it for the dancing, Erica and I invited Edyta, husband Alec, and son Michael to dinner at our New York apartment the week ABC announced the cast and pairings.

Aside from checking it off my bucket list, another reason I wanted to do the show was to send the message to the big Boomer generation coming up behind me that they should get off the couch and shake their booty. Use it or lose it. Everybody our age has something that hurts. But move what you can, for as long as you can, since you will have plenty of time to be still after you die.

During rehearsals, the lame foot led to two body-slamming falls, but with the help of hidden braces on ankles, knees, and back, I got to the point where I felt I could make it through the routine without collapsing. My only beef was that the producers never communicated to the audience that I was an old man overcoming a physical impairment to compete.

Instead, I came off as just an old man who could not dance. The bigger problem was that I choked during the live show. Adding to my physical clumsiness, during the Cha-Cha I zigged when I should have zagged and as a result earned for poor Edyta and myself the lowest score of the twelve couples competing.

When crotchety *DWTS* judge Len Goodman heaped scorn on my inability to point my toes, I laughed since with my ankles immobilized by tape, toe pointing was impossible. In a way, even worse was the post-dance interview with cohost Erin Andrews. The brave and glamorous sportscaster had just won a $55 million jury verdict against parent companies of the Nashville, Tennessee, Marriott hotel, an award she deserved, the hotel having failed utterly to protect her against a stalker who videotaped her naked through the peephole in her room door. To add to her tough slog, she later announced she was battling cervical cancer.

Perhaps because of the enormous attention her case had attracted, she seemed uncomfortable with me, as if she thought I was paparazzo covering her case. In fairness, I may be reading more into that than existed, but when I used an old show-business adage to explain my clunky performance, she did not get it. I said of my performance, "It is not how well the bear dances, but that the bear dances at all." Her face was blank; then blinking as if snapping out of a mocking trance, she said she had no idea what I was talking about. My attempt at self-effacing humor dropped like a stone.

Anyway, it was ridiculous to think I could compete against the 2016 season's crew, which featured some great, young athletes including Superbowl MVP Von Miller of the Denver Broncos, and Antonio Brown, the Pittsburgh Steelers All-Star wide receiver. The deaf heartthrob Nyle DiMarco, winner of *America's Top Model*, performed impeccably, rousing the audience to cheers even as they wondered how he could keep the beat.

Wanja Morris, the charismatic heart of Boyz II Men, performed exuberantly with star dancer Lindsay Arnold, a gorgeous young blonde. Another budding star dancer who can also kick your eye out, UFC fighter Paige VanZant, was very impressive and a crowd favorite. Paige and Lindsay were both graceful and athletic.

Super-sweet Kim Fields, lately of *Real Housewives of Atlanta*, did a great job charming the crowd. So did the ABC Network hometown favorite Ginger Zee, who is the popular *Good Morning America* meteorologist. Ginger had a new baby, but she was trim, ferocious, and wowed the audience week after week.

The scrappy and wonderful Marla Maples, whom I have known since she was the second Mrs. Donald Trump, cartwheeled through the early weeks, easily handling with style the renewed and intense attention brought on by her ex's electoral success. It was impressive to see her keep her poise and balance on and off the dance floor, her daughter Tiffany frequently by her side. The often-forgotten child among her supercharged siblings, Tiffany is also underrated, impressive in her own right, thanks in part to her wonderful mother.

Mischa Barton seemed to have a bad time on the show. The actress who surged to fame on *The O.C.* danced just marginally better than I did and did not seem to enjoy being there. We had a heart-to-heart about how at barely thirty years old she had been aged out of her ingénue phase by the casting directors and was only being offered mother roles. She had a series of well-chronicled controversies later.

Meanwhile, *Full House* and *Fuller House* star Jodie Sweetin did a great job impressing both the audience and the judges. Like Mischa, Jodie had a difficult time dealing with life after youthful stardom, and both Mischa and Jodie saw the dance show as a way back to show-business success or at least heightened visibility. To tell you the truth, that is probably why I did it, even though I was lame and getting lamer.

Heisman Trophy winner and former pro quarterback Doug Flutie was the only other contestant over fifty, and he is almost twenty years younger than I am. Best remembered for throwing the monumental sixty-five-yard "Hail Mary" pass in the rain to bring his Boston College Eagles to victory in the 1984 Orange Bowl over a heavily favored Miami team, he is one of the nicest guys you would ever want to hang out with. I was reminded that among the host of NFL and CFL teams he played for professionally were the New Jersey Generals of the now defunct USFL, a team owned by Donald Trump, who paid $8 million for it before the league went belly-up after failing to merge with the NFL. The Generals were terrific but the league was awful.

Flutie tried hard on *DWTS*, practicing each evening with his daughter Alexa, a professional dancer and San Diego Chargers cheerleader. Calm and sincere, he is a real family man and deservedly lasted on the show far longer than I did. Comparing Doug and the rest of *DWTS* cast to my colleagues on Trump's *Celebrity Apprentice*, I'd say this was a much nicer bunch. They were loving and supportive instead of backstabbing and conspiratorial.

The pleasant vibe did not help my performance. After forgetting key steps during the first routine, I similarly botched an even more flamboyant second routine the next Monday night. That sketch began prophetically with President Donald Trump (me) being interrupted in the Oval Office on a phone call with Vladimir Putin by my drop-dead-gorgeous first lady Melania, played of course by Edyta, another equally gorgeous European import.

For the routine, two other sexy dancers in the troupe rip off my conservative presidential suit, and Edyta and I break out in dance, doing a hot salsa to "Mi Amigo," an upbeat classic by the late, great Tito Puente, who was *mi amigo* in real life. The idea was to stress the comic irony of Donald, the alleged anti-Latino who is hell-bent on building a great wall on our southern border after calling Mexicans rapists and drug dealers, dancing the Latin Night Salsa. We also aimed to ride the wave of attention that the candidates' wives were receiving at the time, March 2016, in the tacky, "Whose Wife Is Hotter" debate mudslinging between Trump and Senator Ted Cruz.

To make a long story short, my dance did not suck as badly as it did on premiere night but was still pretty bad. The score was the same as the first night, a meager 13 out of 30, but it did not matter since, unbeknownst to us, we had already been voted off. They should give scores based on a handicap, like in golf. I joked when Edyta and I were eliminated that if we had *not* been, "I would have demanded a recount."

My supporters in the studio audience included Erica, all five of my children, and Cheech and his beautiful Russian-born wife and brilliant concert pianist, Natasha. Everyone took the defeat fairly well, except then-ten-year-old Sol Liliana, who again, just like when I lost *Apprentice* the year before, started sobbing inconsolably. She loves her daddy and hates to see him hurt.

Since the only star she wanted to meet was Von Miller, I brought the strapping six-foot-three-inch, 250-pound Super Bowl MVP linebacker over to give her a hug, which went far to relieve her disappointment. He and the others, including the production team, were super-considerate, nice people.

At *Dancing with the Stars* with all five kids and Gabriel's wife, Deb. March 2016.

Nyle won the *DWTS* competition. Not only did he dance superbly, he did it without the benefit of being able to hear the music. It was an amazing and deeply impressive achievement. The runner-up was Paige VanZant, who I thought was equally impressive, going from using her feet to kick people in the face as an ultimate fighter to elegant, sensual dancing. She could easily have been the winner of the show's coveted "Mirror Ball Trophy."

Looking back on the experience, I only regret not doing more to keep Edyta on the show's center stage. That aside, having the far-flung kids all in one spot for those several days was wonderful. The girls giggled and shared "GLAMSQUAD On-Demand Beauty" makeup artists (the ones who come to your apartment or hotel room rather than you going to their salon) and tried on different dresses with Erica; the big boys hung with their daddy and I got to play with Desmond, aka Desi, my second grandson. The girls got to see me on a show their girlfriends actually watch. Trump got a kick out of my impression of him. Jon Peters and I hung out, endlessly talking about the good old days and the challenges of getting creaky; I lost five pounds and had a lot of laughs. All things considered, the whole *DWTS* experience was a life-affirming blast.

Chapter 11

FUROR AT FOX

S peaking of explosions, several months after I completed the first draft of this manuscript, in the summer of 2016, all hell broke loose at Fox News, when my boss, Roger Ailes, became embroiled in a catastrophic sexual-harassment scandal. One of my former colleagues, Gretchen Carlson, alleged that he had tormented her throughout her decade at Fox News. I responded to Gretchen's original allegations with extreme skepticism.

Along with all but a handful of my Fox colleagues, I figured Gretchen was motivated by sour grapes. At the time she got fired by Roger, she had the lowest-rated show on the network. She also withheld her allegations that Roger harassed her until she was fired at the end of June 2016, her contract not renewed. In ordinary times, before the #MeToo movement, there was ample reason to be skeptical, if not cynical. It is self-evident that those days are gone.

I am now beyond sorry that I doubted her, but at the time, her case was not a slam-dunk. Nobody knew that Gretchen had secretly recorded Roger being an obnoxiously macho deviant. At that initial point it was a he said/she said, based solely on her shocking allegations, which the monarch of Fox News, through his spokeswoman and ace attorney Susan Estrich, vehemently denied..

Aside from the accuser's motive to exaggerate, there was also the fact that the accused did not fit the stereotype. Roger did not seem the type.

While the man I knew was a lot of arguably bad things—brawler, bully, ideological zealot, to name a few—he did not seem a sex predator. For instance, I never heard him say anything sexually suggestive or inappropriate about a female colleague. Don't get me wrong. He was as harsh and insulting to women as he was to men. Remember the scene with Laurie Dhue and the necklace, but he was brutal rather than sexist. "Well, she's as dumb as a bag of rocks." "What in hell does she call that outfit?" Man, woman, straight, gay, he was an equal-opportunity insulter.

I never took his jibes personally, but maybe that was a function of our being roughly the same age, both products of the world before feminism, gender equality, equal rights, and sensitivity training. Now I feel like a sap, a sucker who did not know the score. I always pictured Roger as a hail-fellow-well-met, another backslapping scrapper, more likely to tear your throat out than engage in sweet talk, as my first tweet on the Gretchen scandal indicated:

Geraldo Rivera @GeraldoRivera
I've known him 40 years. He's about as flirty as the grizzly in #TheRevenant. I stand with Roger Ailes

Remembering how Roger always had my back through thick or thin, even as his scandal deepened during the Republican National Convention, and as many editorial writers were writing him off, I fired off this tweet:

Geraldo Rivera @GeraldoRivera
Don't believe the crap about #RogerAiles. Only ones talking dirt are those who hate #FoxNews & want to hurt network that's kicking their ass

Roger resigned two days later when it became apparent that Gretchen was not alone in alleging abhorrent behavior behind his closed doors. Disbelieving the charges against him, I almost walked out alongside him, enthusiastically joining a budding revolt by many of my colleagues. If Roger was forced unfairly to leave, we vowed to follow him.

Like many of Roger's big talent, I had a "key man" clause in my contract that allowed me to leave the network if for any reason Roger was ousted or left voluntarily. Roger encouraged the clause to be inserted in his talent deals to enhance his own invulnerability. If you messed with Roger, you risked having the whole enterprise crumble as the talent loyal to him left with him.

Many of us were fixing to follow him out the door. Under the leadership of an enraged Sean Hannity, with hearty cheerleading from hyper-conservative websites, we decided to join forces and demand that our company stand behind our embattled chief executive. To us Know Nothings, it seemed obvious that Roger was being hoisted on a petard of political correctness. Sure he was grizzled, gruff, and tough, but that was his charm. Like Donald Trump and millions of other old machos, including me, Roger was a 1950s relic of *The Front Page*.

We hail from an era when virtually every executive smoked and drank too much, while often behaving inappropriately with secretaries, female executives, or other men's wives. Necessarily, times, attitudes, and laws have changed, but my sympathy for Roger is based on the feeling that creaky old relics like him should be allowed to die off. He should have known better, but he was too arrogant and entitled to notice that the world had changed. Please note that I do not think that "dinosaur" excuse applies to the disgusting alleged rapist Harvey Weinstein or to pompous pervert *House of Cards* actor Kevin Spacey, the single most unpleasant person I have ever met in show business. Those twenty-first-century predators weren't even around in the 1960s.

When the Roger/Gretchen story broke, I remember vividly being at the Republican National Convention in the makeshift Fox News green room at Cleveland's Quicken Loans Arena, clenching my fists along with Sean and angrily condemning what felt like the railroading of our founder and leader.

Producer/brother Craig stopped me from destroying my own career and reputation. He prevented me from sending a third, even more outrageous tweet, blaming the victims and their co-conspirators in management while celebrating the perpetrator.

During that period of high drama and profound flux, I was especially impatient with Fox News anchor Megyn Kelly for refusing to back the man who had made her a star, thinking that the elegant, ambitious anchor was selfish and in it only for herself. A "Boycott Megyn" movement started within our ranks, with various on-air personalities muttering about how it was all part of Megyn's ongoing and ultimately very successful contract negotiations, albeit at another network, NBC. Many Fox talent loyal to Roger were vowing never to go on her *Kelly File* show again, and I was among them, not that I was often asked.

Without naming names, let me say that the older women at Fox were particularly vicious in their attacks on the soaring celebrity. Thank God that boycott nonsense never went anywhere beyond a few soon-deleted references on *Breitbart* and *Drudge*. The next day Sean pulled me aside to say the revolt was over because the allegations against Roger were true. "How bad is it?" I asked. "It's bad," Sean replied, shaking his head in melancholy and disbelief.

The most explosive allegation of Roger's several purported victims of unwanted advances came from Megyn Kelly herself. When word spread that he had allegedly sexually bullied and come on to her at the start of her Fox career, her reluctance to back Roger vs. Gretchen's lawsuit suddenly transformed from bitchy to heroic.

At that moment, to Roger's malignant misfortune, Megyn was the most important person at Fox News, maybe in the entire television news industry. For one thing, her contract was expiring the next summer, in 2017, and the network was desperate to keep her. She had become more

At the Democratic National Convention with *Fox and Friends* friends, Tucker Carlson, Heather Nauert, Steve Doocy, Ainsley Earhardt, Brian Kilmeade, me, Major Pete Hegseth, and Clayton Morris. Philadelphia, July 2016.

important than Roger. Her ratings success made her valuable from a commercial standpoint, but that was just the beginning of her appeal. Megyn had crossed over into mainstream recognition and respect. She had become a sought-after celebrity in her own right, separate and apart from Fox.

MEGYN ASCENDANT, AUGUST 2015

Megyn put the nail in Roger's professional coffin with her charges that he had harassed her back in the day. But it was her interaction with Donald Trump fifteen months earlier that almost changed the course of history. By taking on the candidate's past chauvinistic and coarse treatment of women during the first Republican presidential debate in August 2015, also in Cleveland, she both distinguished and distanced herself from others at Fox News.

Led by the unflinching Hannity, the slightly subtler O'Reilly, up-and-comer Eric Bolling (a talented broadcaster who gravely damaged his

Megyn Kelly and her husband, author Doug Brunt, at
Erica's fortieth birthday party, January 2015.

career with a dopey prank allegedly involving intimate pictures of himself to three female staffers), earnest Steve Doocy on *Fox and Friends*, and me, our network was already behaving deferentially to our hometown hero, the flamboyant Mr. Trump. I began trumpeting his certain nomination from the first day of his campaign in June 2015.

During that first debate in August 2015, Megyn embarrassed and infuriated Trump by brutally recalling previous public comments he had made about women generally and the actress-comedienne Rosie O'Donnell specifically. Megyn stuck a knife in Trump's ribs when she famously asked how a man who refers to women as "fat pigs," "slobs," and "animals" could ever be president of the United States.

The question was prescient, a harbinger of scandals to come for the forty-fifth president in his long-shot quest for the White House. Flushing with anger, he sputtered. His stunned response was to criticize Megyn for daring to ask so impolite a question. It was a sin for which he would never forgive her. Trump lamely suggested in response that he did not disrespect women generally, but only one woman, Rosie, who suffered his specific wrath for something she had said while hosting *The View*.

With Eric Bolling, Colonel Oliver North, and Sean Hannity.
Inauguration festivities, January 2017.

ROSIE VS. DONALD, DECEMBER 2006

The friction between Trump and the then-almost-as-large-as-life Rosie O'Donnell had its roots in a controversy ten years earlier. Rosie had the temerity in 2006 to tear into Trump, who was at the time the owner of the Miss USA contest.

It happened after he had held a news conference announcing grandly that he would overlook allegations of past drug and alcohol abuse by his current Miss USA, Tara Connor, and allow her to keep the title. "I've always been a believer in second chances," he told reporters, his tone dripping magnanimity.

As we later learned in the campaign, Tara Connor was not the first pageant winner to incur Trump's wrath for her alleged shortcomings. Hillary Clinton later uncovered another, Alicia Machado, his 1996 Miss Universe, whom he condemned for being overweight, calling her "Miss Piggy." Hillary used Alicia's story to flog her campaign theme that Trump and the Republicans were waging war on women.

The day after he gave Tara Connor a reprieve, Rosie ripped his throat out on *The View*. She ridiculed his hair, his business acumen, and his casino bankruptcies, while asking rhetorically how dare he, a deeply flawed man, pass judgment on anyone.

"He's the moral authority? Left the first wife, had an affair, left the second wife, had an affair, had kids both times, but he's the moral compass for twenty-year-olds in America? Donald, sit and spin, my friend," Rosie fumed. When one of her cohosts brought up that Trump was an extremely successful businessman, Rosie pounced, "He's been bankrupt so many times! The people that he owed money to got shorted out, but he got to try again and again," and so on.

Trump went ballistic in his rage, summoning a few of his longtime friends in the media, including me, to his side at his ornate office in Trump Tower to hear him excoriate Rosie, who is also a friend of mine. He was brutal: "She's a loser. She's always been a loser," and downhill from there. I was tempted to replay my damning 2006 Rosie tape when candidate Trump was on the ropes, embroiled in a devastating scandal involving outtakes from the *Access Hollywood* segment he shot the year before, in 2005, with another mutual friend, Billy Bush.

Three days before inauguration in Trump Tower with the president-elect, January 2017.

As I'll describe, the *Access* scandal almost sank him, and continues to haunt him among many women as the worldwide epidemic of sexual harassment allegations that started when Gretchen took down Roger continues to sweep through politics, media, Hollywood, and beyond. Despite the fact that Trump uttered his grossly inappropriate, politically incorrect remarks a generation ago, they continue to dog him. Almost a year after his caught-on-tape remarks were published, and six months into his presidency, in a widely read July 2017 piece in the *New York Times Sunday Review*, Michelle Goldberg called the president "an erotically incontinent libertine." Coming, though, as the *Access* scandal did, in the heat of the campaign, in October, a full month before the 2016 election, with two debates remaining, and before the FBI's James Comey and the Kremlin's Vladimir Putin/Wikileaks dropped their bombs on Hillary, Trump had just enough time to recover and pull off the greatest upset in recorded political history, bar none. His wife saved him. When Melania characterized the *Access* exchange as "locker-room banter," many men in her husband's and my generation knew what she was talking about.

As the *Access* scandal and the war with Megyn Kelly played havoc with the Trump candidacy, he lashed out at Megyn, condemning and berating her at every opportunity. Roger stared him down, deeply critical of the candidate's obsession with the correspondent. Isn't it ironic that in the same year Roger Ailes rode to Megyn's defense against the wrath of Donald Trump, her allegations of Roger's long-ago sexual harassment ended his career?

The scorn and ridicule from the media industry could not help but contribute to Roger's steep physical decline and death less than a year later. Megyn's damning allegations, as described in her bestselling memoir, *Settle for More*, joined the flood of condemnation from other accusers that swept away what remained of Roger's legacy so totally that these days scarcely a trace remains. Now, it is almost as if Roger never existed, despite the fact that he was one of the most important figures in the history of television news.

Despite the pity and guilt I feel over the circumstances of Roger's death, I am filled with regret for stubbornly discounting the accusations of his various accusers, and apologize for my skepticism. Like victims of sexual assault, those alleging harassment deserve the rebuttable presumption of credibility. Even Gabriel Sherman, Ailes's obsessive pursuer, the reporter who disclosed every sin Roger had ever committed and then some, Roger's personal Inspector Javert, the *New York Magazine* writer I called a "nerd with a grudge," deserves my apology. He was on the right side of history. Roger allegedly used his position to talk dirty to terrified women who worked for him. Might does not mean right. Roger was wrong, and in sticking up for him before I knew the score, I was part of the problem.

Various *New York Times* reporters, including Emily Steel, worked tirelessly for months to prove that the Ailes scandal was the tip of a Fox News iceberg. In a gigantic April 2017 exposé carried on her newspaper's front page for several days running, Steel's thesis was that Fox was Animal House, where horny executives routinely preyed upon vulnerable women. One of her eventual prizes was my old friend, Roger's aide-de-camp, Bill Shine. After being named one of Ailes's successors as co-president, Bill was forced to resign amidst the storm of controversy and swirl of lawsuits spawned by the sexual-harassment hurricane. He was essentially accused of aiding and abetting Ailes, although I believe, as our mutual friend Sean

"The *New York Times*'s real prize, though, was taking down the giant, Bill O'Reilly." At a Mets game, May 2017.

Hannity does, that Shine never did anything bad to anybody. He is a great guy, a terrific producer, and is sorely missed at Fox News.

The *New York Times*'s real prize, though, was taking down the giant, Bill O'Reilly, who was shamed into resigning about three weeks after the paper's initial exposé. Not the nicest or certainly not the smoothest guy, impatient and as volatile as an IED, O'Reilly was given to outbursts of rage. He could be scary and socially awkward, but as far as I knew, not evil.

O'Reilly fell off the cliff when the *Times* revealed that he had settled several sexual-harassment lawsuits, including one claim dating back fifteen years, for a total of around $13 million. He said it was all in an ultimately vain attempt to keep the cases quiet and protect his family and career from scandal. That news was shocking enough. Six months later, it got worse, when news leaked that he had bestowed an additional $32 million fortune on former Fox News legal analyst Lis Wiehl. I can't imagine that kind of money being paid out unless the underlying secret was undeniably grisly.

Our friend Lis's $32 million settlement almost equals the $33.5 million O.J. Simpson was ordered to pay to the families of Nicole Brown Simpson and her friend Ronald Goldman after being found liable for their brutal murders. Just for context, the $20 million Gretchen got from Fox is more than three times the typical settlement from cities to black families, like Freddie Gray's, whose beloved sons were killed by cops.

I can't say it often enough: sexual harassment is low down and dirty. If you are a senior staffer using your power and position to prey sexually on a subordinate, you should and will get your balls cut off. Which brings me back to the president.

The news that Donald Trump was caught on a hot *Access Hollywood* mic sounding like a filthy old Hollywood pervert hit the race for the White House like an exploding bomb. His unguarded remarks to Billy Bush about how he could physically molest any woman he wanted because of his celebrity nearly destroyed his chance to be president. The remarks were raw, arrogant, and ugly.

Donald Trump: I just kiss. I don't even wait. And when you're a star, they let you do it. You can do anything.

Billy Bush: Whatever you want.

Donald Trump: Grab them by the pussy. You can do anything.

Although the remarks were made in private eleven years earlier, most women cut him no slack. Even some die-hard Trump supporters who had been forced by loathing for Hillary Clinton to stick with him through thick and thin found this latest revelation beyond the pale. Certainly many folks not tuned in to the campaign spectacle found the remarks unsavory. How can we elect someone president when we could not let our children hear his profane remarks?

Prominent GOP senators and governors jammed the doors, jumping off the Trump train in the wake of the revelations. From former Secretary of State Condoleezza Rice to former California governor Arnold Schwarzenegger (who had his own series of similar scandals), some of the biggest stars in the GOP firmament announced they had turned off their already tepid support for Trump.

Speaker of the House Paul Ryan held his nose, indicating he would never appear with Trump again, despite the obvious threat a landslide defeat for the Republican at the top of the ticket posed to Ryan's majority in the House of Representatives.

Gross even in the old days, in today's hypersensitivity to the issue, that 2005 conversation sounds grotesque. I thought mistakenly that the arrogance he displayed talking then about his sexual prerogatives made it impossible for any but his most hard-core supporters to stick by candidate Trump. Remember, in October 2016, with the election just a month away, he was still running well behind Hillary Clinton in most polls.

Going into the second debate, Trump needed a miracle performance to salvage his crippled campaign. He did not quite get it, but did better than expected under the circumstances. His stunt, dragging Paula Jones and the other purported victims of Bill Clinton's predatory sexual behavior to the front row of the audience, was outrageous, ill-mannered, and out of line, but it was just barely plausible and worked to cheer Trump's deflated supporters.

Even though Bill was not running for president, Trump made Hillary the chump. Her husband, President Clinton, was punished for his transgressions with Impeachment by the House of Representatives, only the second in the history of the land to be so humiliated, but Bill beat that rap, winning an acquittal in the Senate. He was not forced from office. Eighteen years later, Hillary paid his old tab.

Trump's obnoxious stunt with Bill's ladies and his implacable attacks on Hillary's essential character and honesty wounded her candidacy. Although most liberal women had forgiven or refused to believe the ring-wing allegations against the progressive 42nd president in 1998, by 2016 his reckless, often low-brow adultery was no longer forgivable. Hillary was Bill's enabler, guilty by association of his sins. It is another reason so many women are angry that Trump is their president. Add to his many transgressions that he made a wife pay for the sins of her husband.

Trump narrowly won that second debate by attacking relentlessly in a way unseen in modern American history. His savage assault, including his pledge to put Secretary Clinton in jail ("Lock her up!"), got gasps from the audience in St. Louis and the millions watching on television, breathing new energy into his deflated followers. Thanks to his swaggering and extraordinarily aggressive performance, he dodged the *Access Hollywood* bullet and rallied his base. I did not think it would be enough to upend the race. I mistakenly believed that no candidate for the highest office in the land could prevail with just the support of high school–educated, low-to-middle-income white folks, many of whom are deeply religious, and presumably offended by his coarse language and stated sexual prerogatives. I was obviously wrong. That base was solid for Trump, of course, but he also did surprisingly well with suburban dwellers and people over forty who quietly cast their ballots for Mr. Us vs. Them Clintons. Trump even attracted 42 percent of the female vote, but not my wife or her friends.

BOYCOTTING THE IOWA GOP DEBATE, JANUARY 2016

His shocking victory was a long way off when Megyn Kelly lobbed her atomic question at candidate Trump ("You've called women you don't like 'fat pigs,' 'dogs,' 'slobs,' and 'disgusting animals' . . .") at the first Republican presidential debate, setting in motion their extraordinary feud. In one fell swoop, Megyn managed to do what no other journalist or candidate did all campaign long. She cut Trump down to size, infuriating him and many of her own viewers of Fox News.

Megyn catapulted herself into the first tier of political journalists. Among the liberal media and mainstream audience, she became that rare phenomenon, a hero, the Rosa Parks, Susan B. Anthony, or Malala of broadcast news, especially among the educated women who despised candidate Trump. She showed strength and courage in the face of bluster and fury, and as she would throughout the campaign, she refused to back down or lose her elegant composure.

He attacked her relentlessly with barrages of negative tweets, which put me in an awkward position. He was being a bully. She was standing against Goliath, reporting fairly on the candidate's various foibles and woes. As he has shown even in his presidency, Donald Trump is not the kind of guy who forgives and forgets. As he typically tweeted:

Donald J. Trump @realDonaldTrump
Everybody should boycott the @megynkelly show. Never worth watching. Always a hit on Trump! She is sick, & the most overrated person on tv.

My less-than-bold response:

Geraldo Rivera @GeraldoRivera
@realDonaldTrump @megynkelly I love you man but basta. This obsession w @megynkelly is weird & unhelpful. She's doing her job, you do yours.

Megyn later thanked me, although unlike her, I was not a profile in courage, but in compromise. Contrast my muted remarks to what Roger said about Trump, whom he had known nearly as long as I have: "Donald Trump's vitriolic attacks against Megyn Kelly and his extreme, sick obsession with her is beneath the dignity of a presidential candidate who wants to occupy the highest office in the land."

That is how you put down someone messing with your colleague. Whatever his personal feelings about the candidate or his star journalist, Roger bathed himself and the network in the glory of principle, not that it helped him when his own shit hit the fan.

I was conflicted throughout. My dilemma was that Trump is a closer friend than Megyn. In person she is smart and funny, with a terrific husband and wonderful family, but she rarely booked me on her show. In contrast, aside from my knowing the guy forever, Trump and I had just done *Celebrity Apprentice*. Together constantly for six weeks, just a couple of months before he began his run for the White House, he gave me the benefit of every doubt on the show.

"Trump puts me on television a lot more than Megyn Kelly does," I told friends to explain my initial ambivalence and relatively tepid support of what later became clear was an incredibly brave stance by Megyn. Trump was already a monstrously popular, super-connected candidate whose past alleged misogynist treatment of women was certainly fair game at the time she asked her seminal question. In some ways, the divide it revealed between the old ways and the new are at the heart of our current split nation and of the culture of scandal that is devouring macho icons on both sides of the divide.

THE WRATH OF ROGER, JANUARY 2016

The morning after the Trump-boycotted Iowa debate, I incurred Roger's wrath for what turned out to be the last time. He had nobly sacrificed an enormous ratings bonanza by refusing to capitulate to Trump's demand to remove Megyn as debate moderator, saying that it would "violate all journalistic standards" to remove her from the panel.

On *Fox and Friends* that next morning, asked who "won" the Trump-less debate, I answered that in my opinion both Megyn and Trump emerged as winners. She won because of her courage in the face of the Trump steamroller, but he won, too, I said, because his boycott and simultaneous telethon to benefit veterans attracted enough attention to overshadow his rivals. Looking back, I was wrong substantively. Trump's absence from the Iowa debate probably cost him that state's primary, which he ended up losing to Ted Cruz, and he barely beat Marco Rubio, who came in a close third.

That night my scheduled appearance on what was then our most important program, *The O'Reilly Factor*, was suddenly canceled, as were scheduled appearances over the next several days on other high-profile Fox News shows. I was on ice. When I confronted O'Reilly's longtime producer David Tabacoff as to why my appearance was canceled, he admitted that the order to take me off, and keep me off, had come from Roger Ailes himself. After an absence that lasted until the next week, I apologized on the air for equivocating and not more vigorously backing the home team.

THE RAT PACK ERA IS DEAD, JANUARY 2017

On the issues of workplace morality and sexual harassment, having worked at all the networks over the last forty-seven years, I can say definitively that the social culture is industry-wide. For lots of reasons, TV news is a flirty business. There is a constant and usually harmless sexual banter that goes on. Men tell women they look good, and vice versa, or at least we did before it became fraught with profound consequence.

When grown-ups of equal status are involved, it is usually the kind of lighthearted fun you might hear on a family-hour sitcom. There has to be room for consensual adults to do their thing without the threat of black-mail if relationships don't work out, which is what I think happened with my Fox News colleague Charles Payne. With its pressure-cooker environment and long hours, the newsroom is sometimes the only place young professionals and old can meet. How do you think MSNBC co-anchors Joe Scarborough and Mika Brzezinski and scores of other happy couples hooked up? After work? Add up all the newsroom romances that have resulted in marriage over the years, including three of my own. Where are busy professional supposed to meet, Match.com or Tinder?

Management's role is to keep the playing field level, professional, and fair. As society evolved from the *Mad Men* era, giant steps have been taken to protect subordinate employees from harassment and unwelcome advances, particularly by superiors. Human resources departments have been enormously beefed up and empowered. Roger got drummed out of the business, and he was king of the world. Bill O'Reilly was also banished from Fox News despite having the highest-rated cable news history for twenty years running. Eric Bolling, Charlie Rose, Matt Lauer, and many other powerful men lost their jobs even though they were hugely popular and had ironclad contracts. At the time of his Armageddon, Tavis Smiley was the most important African American personality on PBS.

Sure, there is far to go, but as the seismic response to Gretchen, Megyn, and the other purported victims of real harassment makes clear, the news business will no longer tolerate loutish conduct by anyone, however powerful. The danger is that in the national reckoning, some few are using the current climate to even old scores with bad boyfriends or despised ex-bosses. Harassers are most often schmucky lowlifes anyway. There is nothing cool about it, and there is no place for them. Perpetrators harass at tremendous peril to their careers and families. Strict policies are in place. Everyone gets mandatory sensitivity training. I had a mandatory session on a Tuesday, which happened to be Valentine's Day, 2017.

I wrote in a widely circulated Facebook post, "To all the victims of sexual harassment, direct and indirect, I am sorry for what happened to you. As the father of three daughters, including one in the news business, I urge all who have been offended to reach out. Similarly, if you see harassment, say harassment, even if the alleged offender is an old friend."

The stern point was made in spades. Rico Suave is dead. No man or woman, however exalted or powerful, has the right to impose him- or herself on a subordinate. As one of the aged poster boys of the era, Roger was shamed, shunned, and stripped of all honors, his legacy despoiled, his legend ruined. He has been erased from television history, his name stripped from schools and civic institutions he endowed, even as several of his alleged and lavishly compensated victims have gone on to celebrity and societal acclaim. When I look back on how severely Roger was punished, I regret helping write his professional obituary with my Facebook post. Maybe he had it coming, but given the harsh justice already imposed, the last thing his family needed was a disillusioned old friend piling on.

As I wrote that line, I paused to call him to tell him of my regret, but he did not pick up the phone. Three months later, on May 18, 2017, I did get a call—not from Roger, but about him. The old lion was dead. A hemophiliac, living in the vast Florida oceanfront estate he purchased with his $40 million settlement from Fox, he died after stumbling in his bathroom and hitting his head. Roger left behind his wife, Beth, and teenage son, Zack, and I feel awful whenever I think of the circumstances of his decline and fall.

EPILOGUE

JANUARY–OCTOBER 2017

Erica, our three daughters, and I went to South Africa on safari at the Mala Mala Game Reserve over the Christmas holidays, December 2016. We hooked up with Kevin and Julietta, our old *Voyager* crewmates. After sailing around the world with us, and up the Amazon River, they live now in Kevin's native Cape Town. It was Sol's first safari; it brought up memories of past African adventures, and a wonderful time was had by all. After stopping in Amsterdam, Holland, on the way back for a visit with my firstborn son, Gabriel, and his wife, Deb, and their firstborn child, Desmond, we got home to an uneasy America about to give a decidedly mixed welcome to President-elect Donald Trump, the longest of long-shot chief executives.

It was a tumultuous transition amidst sharp charges that Trump's presidency was illegitimate. Aside from the fact that he lost the popular vote to Hillary Clinton, who garnered almost 2.9 million more than he did, my friend Donald was being tarred by serial scandals. One included alleged Russian-sponsored hacking of Democratic Party operatives, and the inference that Russian president Vladimir Putin poisoned the minds of American voters with damaging leaks. The hard left was having a field day alluding to the *Manchurian Candidate*–elect who was a stooge for the wily Kremlin boss.

Adding to the toxic atmosphere surrounding Trump's ascendency to the White House were the actions of FBI Director James Comey, who destroyed Hillary's momentum in the last week and a half of the campaign

With Erica, Isabella, Simone, and Sol boarding the Blue
Train in Pretoria, South Africa, December 2016.

With Erica, Sol, and Isabella near the Cape of Good Hope, South Africa, December 2016.

with a bogus story of ultimately nonexistent illegal emails. There were also salacious and almost surely false and slanderous allegations of shenanigans leveled at Trump and/or his staffers during the 2013 Miss Universe Pageant in a Moscow hotel room with prostitutes, golden showers, and so forth. True or false, it all conspired to make him the most unpopular president-elect in the history of polling. By midsummer 2017, he was the most unpopular president in the seventy-year history of polling.

As he carried on with his lurching transition, he did something shortly after our arrival home to New York that, despite everything, stirred optimism in my heart. On the night of January 2, 2017, with Congress officially out of session, GOP leaders had voted virtually in secret to disembowel the Office of Congressional Ethics. Some of those voting to eviscerate the office had themselves been investigated and punished for ethical lapses. President-elect Trump would not hear of it, letting Republican congressional leaders know that he opposed the underhanded move. The next morning I tweeted twice:

Geraldo Rivera @GeraldoRivera
Nice move by #PEOTUS Trump putting Republican lawmakers in their place for attempting to weaken #Ethics laws. Strong, significant signal.

Geraldo Rivera @GeraldoRivera
#GOP is about to find out who is in charge. Hint: it ain't them & it won't be business as usual. It is #POTUS45 #draintheswamp

On January 12, eight days before his inauguration, I got an email from Trump assistant Meredith McIver that copied both tweets. Scrawled across it was a handwritten note from Trump: "Geraldo-Miss You-Thanks! Donald"

Worried that my opposition to his policies on everything from Mexican immigration to Muslims to former POW senator John McCain's service had soured our friendship, I was delighted to hear from him. I emailed Meredith immediately, telling her I was honored, and asking if I could stop by to say hello before he left for Washington and the inauguration. She wrote back, "He asks if you are here now? Can you come up? Let us know your schedule. He's here Tues/Weds next week as well . . ."

Glad that I had shaved my scrawny vacation beard, at four o'clock that afternoon I was escorted up the gilded elevator at Trump Tower to his transition office. After waiting a few minutes as he and the first lady–elect met with Missouri senator Roy Blunt and his wife, who were helping organize the inaugural festivities, I was escorted in. As he was leaving, Senator Blunt was helpful, pointing out that I had been among the first to predict that Trump would be the eventual GOP nominee. I was grateful no one asked whom I voted for in the general election; it would have been awkward. As the Missourians left, Melania lingered to ask by name how Erica and Sol were doing. She told me how excited she was about her husband's extraordinary success.

Trump was relaxed and confident, sharing his sincere excitement at the prospect of living in the White House, belying the notion that he would consider it slumming after the luxury of his Trump Tower digs and his winter palace, Mar a Lago in Palm Beach, Florida.

The next day I posted a picture of us, and said on Facebook:

Great spending time with the President-elect yesterday afternoon. He started by joking that I look better without the beard. But then he went right into a serious discussion about how he is getting the American taxpayer a break on the F-35 fighter jet. The first lady-elect, Melania,

With Bret Michaels, Ainsley, Sean, and friends during the inauguration. January 2017.

was there. She could not have been more gracious. She remembered Erica's name and invited us to the White House. The President-elect joked about *Celebrity Apprentice* and about how Arnold Schwarzenegger is not doing nearly as well as he did.

It wasn't the last time he brought up the subject of ratings with me. He returned to the topic when we spoke on the phone, months into his presidency. He loved talking about how badly his reality-show successor had performed, bizarrely bringing up Arnold's tanking ratings, and comparing them to his own, even during his address at the traditionally dignified National Prayer Breakfast on the day after he was inaugurated. Trump slammed Schwarzenegger again after the former governor was fired from *Apprentice* for low ratings at the end of his first season. What made it bizarre was that it came in the middle of a major controversy that had President Trump accusing President Obama of wiretapping his Trump Tower offices during the campaign and the transition.

That was all ahead for the forty-fifth president, like the endless debate over repealing and replacing Obamacare, building a border wall and banning Muslims, and cancerous Russiagate. At our Trump Tower meeting, he was in a good mood, looking forward to his inauguration, and decidedly annoyed by those calling his election as president illegitimate. I wrote, "That is of course bogus. He is our president, our one and only president, and on January 20th after his inauguration, he will be the 45th person in the history of the republic to have that honor. We wish him well."

At the time of the Trump Tower meeting, still–Fox News executive Bill Shine had asked me to get the president-elect's signature on a printout of an internal Fox News Election Day memo. The document was published around 5 PM on that historic Tuesday, November 8, and spoke of how the polls were forecasting a certain Hillary Clinton victory, which our Fox News experts predicted we would be able to call for the Democrat at 11 PM Eastern Time.

Sitting behind his desk in the transition office, President-elect Trump autographed it with his customary black marker, writing, "It didn't turn out that way. Love, Donald."

During the transition, I commented on how disappointing attempts to delegitimize President Trump's election were, and reacted with humility upon discovering I was one of forty-one people he follows on Twitter, which, for better and worse, is still his go-to method of communicating with the American people. We spoke too on the night of his controversial inaugural address, which I thought was way too militant. At the Freedom Ball in Washington, DC, with Sean Hannity and *Fox and Friends* cohost Ainsley Earhardt, a lovely person inside and out, we were waiting for showtime backstage, hiding from the euphoric crowd gathered at the Convention Center, one of the three official celebrations. Sean was covering the ball with a live two-hour Fox News Special Report, and Ainsley and I were there to give color commentary on the show about the festivities and our take on the day's historic events.

Through his unfailing support and vigorous advocacy during the campaign, Hannity had become the nation's most important commentator, surpassing even Rush Limbaugh and Bill O'Reilly in his prime. By inaugural night, Sean was one of the president's closest unofficial advisers, and he had the president's old cell phone number, which to our surprise still worked. It would be shut down permanently at midnight.

It was so noisy in the cavernous hall, I could not hear what either Sean or Ainsley was saying to newly elected POTUS 45. When it was my turn, I congratulated him warmly, alternating between calling him Mr. President and "Boss," the nickname I used during *Celebrity Apprentice*. At that moment, he was en route to the various balls with the first lady and his ecstatic children and their spouses, in the elaborate presidential convoy.

Surprisingly, he was not merely accepting of my warm wishes, he was combative, angrily criticizing the media for underestimating the size of the crowd that attended his address on the National Mall, ranting about the "dishonest media." It was the beginning of his crusade against fake news. I tried to soothe him as best I could and promised to watch his back. A couple of hours later, he and the family showed up at the Freedom Ball. They danced to Paul Anka's "My Way," which became Frank Sinatra's anthem in 1969, but which was seldom more appropriately used than on that inaugural night 2017.

The next day, the gigantic gender revolt, larger by far than his inaugural crowd, manifested itself on the boulevards of the capital and around the country. The vast sea of mostly women and girls hit the streets to demonstrate against Trump's ascendency to the highest office in the land. It was perhaps the biggest day of protest in American history and an inauspicious way to begin a presidency.

Sean Hannity was covering the presidential ball for a live two-hour *Fox News Special Report*, and Ainsley Earhardt and I were there to give color commentary. January 2017.

The demonstrators used the color pink to symbolize their profound disquiet that the reins of power had been handed to a chief executive who in their minds, among all the other things, views women as sex objects, and their reproductive rights as revocable. Rather than being off-put by the obvious schism in American society, I am heartened that the progressive half of the country, for months before and after the election lethargic and unfocused, that day found its voice. As the massive post-Inaugural protests and another on the president's first anniversary in office made clear, there is now energetic opposition to President Trump, much of it fair-minded and fact-based, though some of it "fake," to use the president's characterization. Erica at one point asked me to stop supporting him with tweets because I was embarrassing her with her girlfriends.

"Why the implacable hatred directed at Trump?" I asked my loving, but steadfastly feminist wife during one of our kitchen debates that are reflected in millions of politically divided American households. She replied with anguished sincerity, "I feel like, what is it going to take to stop you defending him?!" She paused before firing another volley, "Him not speaking out about hate crimes or white supremacists? Him wrecking Obamacare and not replacing it? Him doing away with the global warming accord?" And so on. Her brother Josh Levy, a well-regarded Washington lawyer and former Democratic staffer whose firm represents GPS Fusion, the group that sponsored the infamous Trump Russia Dossier, has apparently stopped speaking to me because of my tireless effort to find silver linings in the president's actions.

As in my family, the divisions within the country are bad and getting worse. The danger is that the two sides are so scornful of each other, that rather than checking and balancing, we are now at each other's throats, fighting an ideological civil war. Amidst flashes of economic competence and riding a strong stock market and booming economy toward optimism, President Trump doesn't help quell the discord. He still gives ammunition to his enemies, while making life difficult for his friends, careening from Twitter storm to Twitter storm of his own making.

Bottom line, I am dismayed by both his hard head and the unrelenting hatred directed his way. He may not think as you do, but that doesn't make

"Why the implacable hatred directed at Trump?" I asked my lovely, loving wife during one of our debates. December 2016.

him bad. Although his policy choices are sometimes hard for me personally to tolerate, and as he and his administration deal sometimes haphaz-
ardly with crises like the Iran nuclear deal or issues like climate change, I
am still determined to be the man in the middle. Roger Ailes once warned
me that the only thing in the middle of the road was roadkill. Still, I want
to be a small voice in the president's ear and the country's that says, "Cool
down. Let us work this out. We are in this together." Sometimes the president listens.

And sometimes the president makes it difficult. As we went to press,
and just a few days after Mr. Trump had called to tell me he appreciated
my defending him and his family against some of author Michael Wolff's
more scurrilous attacks in his bombshell book *Fire and Fury*, the president
got in hot water again when he reportedly asked, "Why do we want people from Haiti here?" and demanded to know, in reference to Africa, why
he should accept immigrants from "shithole countries." It's impossible to
excuse this sort of statement, and it's hard to understand why the president makes it so easy for his opponents to paint him as a racist.

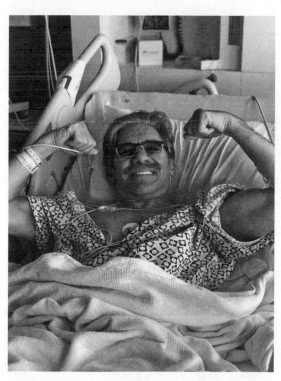

I tweeted him from my bed in the Cleveland Clinic.

Geraldo Rivera @GeraldoRivera
@realDonaldTrump last week I told you on phone that I love you
like a brother. In that spirit I ask you to apologize for your unfortunate remarks. I'm in hospital getting back surgery My skilled compassionate nurse is from #Kenya She told me how you'd hurt her
family's feelings.

But there are times when President Trump gets it right. When histor-
ically vicious Hurricane Maria slammed into Puerto Rico in September
2017 with winds in excess of 150 mph, it laid waste to the countryside.
Civil society on my adored but battered Isla del Encanto teetered on the
brink of breakdown.

Assigned by *Fox and Friends* to cover the disaster because of my lifelong ties to the island, limping into action, I spent almost two painful
weeks in rough conditions bouncing between coverage of the general population's suffering and helping my own family members in distress. My
eighty-four-year-old Aunt Eli, youngest of my father's sixteen siblings, and
one of just three surviving, was living in the dark with a tree through her
roof. It was my abuelos' old house in Bayamón, where I lived and learned
Spanish during the summer of 1958, when I turned sixteen years old.

Craig and I got Eli a generator and other supplies, but big picture, I
was frightened by the extent of the destruction islandwide. In terms of the
number of people negatively affected, Maria is the worst natural disaster
in modern U.S. history, and I wrote the following open letter to President
Trump a couple of days before he was scheduled to visit:

Dear Mr. President,

As a concerned citizen with deep personal ties to the Puerto Rican
people, I am heartened by your coming visit to this storm-ravaged
island, home to 3.4 million of our fellow citizens, including members
of my own family. This is a community in dire need of outside assistance after two devastating hurricane strikes in two weeks. As you
know, Mr. President, the entire agricultural crop has been wiped out.
The whole island is still without electrical power. Half the people

I turned sixteen in the Rivera family home, Bayamón, Puerto Rico, 1958.

My eighty-four-year-old Aunt Eli, youngest of my late father's sixteen siblings,
in the Hurricane Maria aftermath. Puerto Rico, October 2017.

have no running water, and the communications network has also been destroyed. Cell phone towers are down everywhere, and numerous streets remain clogged by downed trees and debris from the storm. Hospitals and other vital institutions are also severely damaged and vital staff struggles to get to their jobs because of fuel shortages that require waits of six hours or more at stations lucky enough to have gas. I am concerned that the relief effort up to this point does not seem to reach the scale necessary to alleviate the misery inflicted by the storms. Relief flights have finally started after a distressing delay, but what this beleaguered island needs are giant ships bearing cargoes of fuel, telephone poles, generators, heavy equipment and the like.

My tour of the port of San Juan does not show anything like the effort required to turn this awful thing around. Suspend the Jones Act, at least temporarily, so foreign flag vessels can join an armada of US ships bearing critically needed assets to rebuild and replace the wreck that exists now.

He delivered. The next day, President Trump temporarily suspended the Jones Act, opening San Juan Harbor to foreign flag vessels, and escalating the pace of the relief effort. He selected Lt. General Jeffrey Buchanan, an excellent soldier I met in Baghdad in 2011, to coordinate. Then the president called me. Luckily the operator on Air Force One got through on my cell phone in a rare area along the highway where cell service existed. We pulled over so as not to lose the signal as the operator put through his familiar voice.

He restated our friendship, promised to do all he could to help, and asked me to accompany him and First Lady Melania as they toured storm-ravaged areas. He gave me an exclusive interview when he arrived, the only one he did during this visit, and made news saying that the bankrupt island's crushing $73 billion debt would have to be wiped out at the expense of bondholders like Goldman Sachs and "my friends on Wall Street." Unfortunately, that idea never made it past the drawing board.

When the visit was over, he gave Craig, cameraman Benjamin West, and me a ride home on AF-1. The president and I talked about old times in several conversations on board the gigantic, plush aircraft, and I promised again to "watch his back," as I did when I criticized two reports that

With the Coast Guard during a relief mission. Aguadilla, Puerto Rico, October 2017.

"He gave me an exclusive interview when he arrived, the only one he did during
this visit" to the Hurricane Maria aftermath. Puerto Rico, October 2017.

were falsely alleging Trump fiddled when Puerto Rico burned. One of them blamed his alleged neglect for a nonexistent cholera epidemic on the island. Another sought to make him responsible for Puerto Rico's notoriously corrupt, inept, and bankrupt power authority.

We parted at Joint Base Andrews near Washington, DC, he and the first lady to head to the scene of the horrific Las Vegas massacre early the next morning, me to get home to Cleveland to recover from twelve days of nonstop reporting.

Despite the contempt in which half the country holds him, I do still consider him a friend. Erica thinks I have stopped being objective. In her opinion, the dark side has seduced me, my moral compass overcome. I disagree, and argue that while there is plenty to criticize, the reality is more nuanced. Never, or at least not since Nixon, has any president had a worse relationship with the press. Not the slickest ad-libber, everything President Trump says or does is construed in the most evil, negative way possible. Blessed as I am that many folks still trust what I have to say, I insist that POTUS 45 is not wicked. He has thin skin, but a big heart. He is not his stereotype. Neither am I. Otherwise, how could either of us have defied conventional wisdom for so long?

Everything Trump does or says is construed as evil. San Juan, Puerto Rico, October 2017.

ACKNOWLEDGMENTS

Hopefully I've made clear in this book how much Erica has changed my life and made me a better person. There is perhaps no greater evidence of how important she is than the fact that this native New Yorker to the bone agreed to relocate to her suburban Cleveland, Ohio, hometown. I also want to acknowledge her parents, Nancy and the late Howard A. Levy, for trusting this ancient mariner to marry their daughter, and my kids, Gabriel, Cruz, Isabella, Simone, and Sol, who despite my eccentricities love their dad and are a Modern Family unit despite their varied ethnic, religious, and geographic backgrounds.

I treasure also the friendship of Bernard Carabello, the former resident of Willowbrook, whose life has been an inspiration; Leo Kayser III, my cranky lawyer and former roommate down on Avenue C; Marty Berman who has been there from the first days of *Eyewitness News*, and who, with publisher Glenn Yeffeth, had the grit to bring this book back from the dead; and Jon Peters, who still calls me every week to share memories of the old days. My kid brother, Craig, and our partner in peril, producer/cameraman Greg Hart, are very special to me. Neither man ever said no when I asked them to follow me off the cliff.

General John F. Campbell, retired, was a noble and near-constant presence in my life as a Fox News war correspondent in Afghanistan and Iraq from 2003 to 2012. Tracking the meteoric rise of this hero soldier I dubbed "America's Spartan" as he earned his way up through the ranks from colonel to four-star general was deeply impressive. I hope he runs for high office because he would make a terrific senator. Even more inspiring has been spending long days and nights with our war fighters, young men and women far from home who serve our country with honor and distinction. I cannot walk through an airport in America without one coming up to me and saying we met and maybe took a picture in this or that forward operating base or other deployment.

I want to acknowledge also my boss Rupert Murdoch, who kept me on when so many others bit the dust; the forty-fifth president, who treasures friendship above politics or ideology; my steadfastly loyal Fox News colleagues, especially Sean Hannity, Kimberly Guilfoyle, Ainsley Earhardt, Brian Kilmeade, Liz Claman, Charles Payne, Shepard Smith, Juan Williams, Rick Leventhal, Mike Tobin, Steve Harrigan, Steve Doocy, Bill Hemmer, Dana Perino, Janice Dean, and Arthel Neville; and, finally, the folks who still like to watch what I do, if only to shout their disagreement at the screen. You have kept me on the air for almost half a century.

"Even more inspiring has been spending long days and nights with our war fighters, young men and women far from home who serve our country." Afghanistan, 2008.

ABOUT THE AUTHOR

One of America's most enduring broadcasters, Emmy and Peabody Award–winning journalist Geraldo Rivera is a Fox News correspondent-at-large and host of breaking news specials, the *Geraldo Rivera Reports*. He also provides weekly reporting and commentary for FNC's *Fox and Friends* and *Hannity*. A native New Yorker outraged by the terror attacks of 9/11, he left CNBC's *Rivera Live* to become an FNC senior war correspondent, reporting live from Afghanistan beginning with the initial siege on Osama bin Laden's Tora Bora hideout, and broke the news ten years later that the terror mastermind had finally been killed by SEAL Team 6. He has reported extensively on the Arab–Israeli conflict and other armed conflicts around the globe, including the 2003 invasion of Iraq, one of eleven extended assignments there.

Rivera began his forty-eight-year television career at WABC-TV in New York where he presented a series exposing the deplorable conditions at the Willowbrook State School for residents then described as mentally retarded. These historic reports are credited with helping end the nation's policy of warehousing the developmentally disabled.

Before becoming a member of the original cast of ABC's *Good Morning America*, Rivera presented the first television broadcast of the Zapruder film of the assassination of President John Kennedy as host of ABC's *Goodnight America*. He then began an eight-year association with ABC's *20/20* as senior correspondent. One of his hour-long reports, "The Elvis Cover-Up," was for more than two decades *20/20*'s highest rated. Between 1987 and 1998, he produced and hosted *Geraldo!*, later called *The Geraldo*

Rivera Show, for daytime TV. The winner of the 2000 Robert F. Kennedy journalism award (his third) for his NBC News documentary on "Women in Prison," and the Scripps Howard Foundation national journalism award for another NBC special report, "Back to Bedlam," Rivera has received hundreds of honors for journalism and community service, including the prestigious George Foster Peabody, the Columbia duPont, and three national and seven local Emmys.

An avid sailor who circumnavigated the globe, skippered four Marion to Bermuda yacht races, and took his vessel *Voyager* hundreds of miles up the Amazon River, Rivera is a graduate of the University of Arizona and Brooklyn Law School, and is the author of seven previous books. A philanthropist whose causes include the care and treatment of the disabled, he is married to the former Erica Michelle Levy and has five children, four of them adults. Geraldo and Erica live happily ever after with their twelve-year-old daughter, Sol, in Cleveland, Ohio. Go Cavs.